D0857654

Disputed Temple

Disputed Temple

A Rhetorical Analysis of the Book of Haggai

John Robert Barker, OFM

Fortress Press
Minneapolis

DISPUTED TEMPLE

A Rhetorical Analysis of the Book of Haggai

Copyright © 2017 Fortress Press. All rights reserved. Except for brief quotations in critical articles or reviews, no part of this book may be reproduced in any manner without prior written permission from the publisher. Email copyright@1517.media or write to Permissions, Fortress Press, PO Box 1209, Minneapolis, MN 55440-1209.

Print ISBN: 978-1-5064-3314-1

eBook ISBN: 978-1-5064-3842-9

The paper used in this publication meets the minimum requirements of American National Standard for Information Sciences — Permanence of Paper for Printed Library Materials, ANSI Z329.48-1984.

Manufactured in the U.S.A.

Contents

Abbreviations   vii

Acknowledgments   xiii

The Haggai Narrative   xv

1. Introduction to the Rhetorical Analysis of Haggai   1

2. Text-Critical Analysis, Composition of Narrative, and Notes on Translation   21

3. Objections and Obstacles to Reconstruction of the Temple   69

4. Rhetorical Analysis of Haggai 1   139

5. Rhetorical Analysis of Haggai 2   203

6. Summary of Findings   251

Bibliography   261

Index of Scriptures   289

Index of Name and Subjects   293

Abbreviations

AB	Anchor Bible
ABD	*The Anchor Bible Dictionary*. Edited by D. N. Freedman. 6 vols. New York, NY: Doubleday, 1992
ABR	Australian Biblical Review
ABRL	Anchor Bible Reference Library
ABS	Archaeology and Biblical Studies
AGJU	Arbeiten zur Geschichte des antiken Judentums und des Urchristentums
AIL	Ancient Israel and Its Literature
AJBI	*Annual of the Japanese Biblical Institute*
AJSL	*American Journal of Semitic Languages and Literature*
AnBib	Analecta Biblica
AOAT	Alter Orient und Altes Testament
ATD	Das Alte Testament Deutsch
AUMSR	Andrews University Monographs: Studies in Religion
BASOR	*Bulletin of the American Schools of Oriental Research*
BDB	Brown, Francis, S. R. Driver, and Charles A. Briggs. *A Hebrew and English Lexicon of the Old Testament*
BEATAJ	Beiträge zur Erforschung des Alten Testaments und das antiken Judentum
BHQ	*Biblia Hebraica Quinta*. Edited by Adrian Schenker et al. Stuttgart: Deutsche Bibelgesellschaft, 2004–
BHS	*Biblia Hebraica Stuttgartensia*. Edited by Karl Elliger and Wilhelm Rudolph. Stuttgart: Deutsche Bibelgesellschaft, 1983
Bib	*Biblica*

BibAlex	La Bible d'Alexandrie
BibInt	*Biblical Interpretation*
BibInt	Biblical Interpretation Series
BibOr	Biblica et Orientalia
Bijdr	*Bijdragen: Tijdschrift voor filosofie en theologie*
BJSUCSD	Biblical and Judaic Studies from the University of California, San Diego
BKAT	Biblischer Kommentar, Altes Testament
BN	*Biblische Notizen*
BTSt	Biblisch-Theologische Studien
BUS	Brown University Studies
BWANT	Beiträge zur Wissenschaft vom Alten und Neuen Testament
BZAW	Beihefte zur Zeitschrift für altorientalische und biblische Rechtsgeschichte
CAT	Commentaire de l'Ancien Testament
CBQ	*Catholic Biblical Quarterly*
CC	Continental Commentaries
CCC	*College Composition and Communication*
CHANE	Culture and History of the Ancient Near East
CHJ	*Cambridge History of Judaism.* Edited by William D. Davies and Louis Finkelstein. 4 vols. Cambridge: Cambridge University Press, 1984–2006.
CommQ	*Communication Quarterly*
ConBOT	Coniectanea Biblica: Old Testament Series
COS	*The Context of Scripture.* Edited by William W. Hallo. 3 vols. Leiden: Brill, 1997–2002
CritInq	*Critical Inquiry*
CTAT	*Critique textuelle de l'Ancien Testament*
CurBR	*Currents in Biblical Research*
DCH	*Dictionary of Classical Hebrew.* Edited by David J. A. Clines. 9 vols. Sheffield: Sheffield Phoenix, 1993–2014
DJD	Discoveries in the Judaean Desert
ECC	Eerdmans Critical Commentary
EHLL	*Encyclopedia of Hebrew Language and Linguistics.* Edited by Geoffrey Khan. Brill Online, 2016.

EHPR	Etudes d'histoire et de philosophie religieuses
ExpTim	*Expository Times*
FAT	Forschungen zum Alten Testament
FOTL	Forms of the Old Testament Literature
GKC	*Gesenius' Hebrew Grammar*. Edited by Emil Kautzsch. Translated by A. E. Cowley. 2nd ed. Oxford: Clarendon, 1910
GTA	Göttinger theologischer Arbeiten
HALOT	*The Hebrew and Aramaic Lexicon of the Old Testament*. Ludwig Koehler, Walter Baumgartner, and Johann J. Stamm. Translated and edited under the supervision of Mervyn E. J. Richardson. 2 vols. Leiden: Brill, 2001
HAR	*Hebrew Annual Review*
HAT	Handbuch zum Alten Testament
HCOT	Historical Commentary on the Old Testament
HSAT	*Die Heilige Schrift des Alten Testaments*. Edited by Emil Kautzsch and Alfred Bertholet. 4th ed. Tübingen: Mohr Siebeck, 1922–1923
HSM	Harvard Semitic Monographs
HThKAT	Herders Theologischer Kommentar zum Alten Testament
HUCA	*Hebrew Union College Annual*
HUCM	Monographs of the Hebrew Union College
IBHS	*An Introduction to Biblical Hebrew Syntax*. Bruce K. Waltke and Michael O'Connor. Winona Lake, IN: Eisenbrauns, 1990
ICC	International Critical Commentary
IEJ	*Israel Exploration Journal*
JANESCU	*Journal of the Ancient Near Eastern Society of Columbia University*
JAOS	*Journal of the American Oriental Society*
JBL	*Journal of Biblical Literature*
JBS	Jerusalem Biblical Studies
JETS	*Journal of the Evangelical Theological Society*
JHebS	*Journal of Hebrew Scriptures*
JJS	*Journal of Jewish Studies*
JLSP	*Journal of Language and Social Psychology*
JNES	*Journal of Near Eastern Studies*
JNST	*Journal of New Testament Studies*

JOTT	*Journal of Translation and Textlinguistics*
Joüon	Joüon, Paul. *A Grammar of Biblical Hebrew.* Translated and revised by T. Muraoka. 2 vols. Rome: Pontifical Biblical Institute, 1991
JPragmat	*Journal of Pragmatics*
JPSP	*Journal of Personality and Social Psychology*
JR	*Journal of Religion*
JSJSup	Journal for the Study of Judaism in the Persian, Hellenistic, and Roman Periods Supplement Series
JSOT	*Journal for the Study of the Old Testament*
JSOTSup	Journal for the Study of the Old Testament Supplement Series
JSP	*Journal of Social Psychology*
JSS	*Journal of Semitic Studies*
JTS	*Journal of Theological Studies*
KAT	Kommentar zum Alten Testament
KHC	Kurzer Hand-Commentar zum Alten Testament
LAI	Library of Ancient Israel
LHBOTS	Library of Hebrew Bible/Old Testament Studies
LD	Lectio Divina
LSTS	The Library of Second Temple Studies
MSU	Mitteilungen des Septuaginta-Unternehmens
NCB	New Century Bible
NICOT	New International Commentary on the Old Testament
OBO	Orbis Biblicus et Orientalis
OLA	Orientalia Lovaniensia Analecta
Or	*Orientalia* (NS)
OTE	*Old Testament Essays*
OTG	Old Testament Guides
OTL	Old Testament Library
OTR	Old Testament Readings
OtSt	*Oudtestamentische Studiën*
PEQ	*Palestine Exploration Quarterly*

Ph&Rh	*Philosophy & Rhetoric*
QJS	*Quarterly Journal of Speech*
RB	*Revue biblique*
RBL	*Review of Biblical Literature*
RComm	*Review of Communication*
RhetR	*Rhetoric Review*
RSQ	*Rhetoric Society Quarterly*
RTR	*Reformed Theological Review*
SANT	Studien zum Alten und Neuen Testaments
SB	Sources bibliques
SBLDS	Society of Biblical Literature Dissertation Series
SBLSymS	Society of Biblical Literature Symposium Series
SCJ	*Southern Communication Journal*
SEÅ	*Svensk exegetisk årsbok*
SEJGBE	Studien zur Entstehungsgeschichte der jüdischen Gemeinde nach dem babylonischen Exil
SHANE	Studies in the History of the Ancient Near East
SJOT	*Scandinavian Journal of the Old Testament*
SSE	Stockholm Studies in English
STR	Studies in Theology and Religion
TAD	*Textbook of Aramaic Documents from Ancient Egypt*. Edited by Bezalel Porten and Ada Yardeni. Jerusalem: Hebrew University, 1986
TB	Theologische Bücherei: Neudrucke und Berichte aus dem 20. Jahrhundert
TDNT	*Theological Dictionary of the New Testament*. Edited by Gerhard Kittel and Gerhard Friedrich. Translated by G. W. Bromiley. 10 vols. Grand Rapids, MI: Eerdmans, 2000
TDOT	*Theological Dictionary of the Old Testament*. Edited by G. Johannes Botterweck and Helmer Ringgren. Translated by J. T. Willis et al. 15 vols. Grand Rapids, MI: Eerdmans, 1974–2006
TLZ	*Theologische Literaturzeitung*
Transeu	*Transeuphratène*
TSAJ	Texts and Studies in Ancient Judaism
TynBul	*Tyndale Bulletin*

TZ	*Theologische Zeitschrift*
UF	*Ugarit-Forschung*
USQR	*Union Seminary Quarterly Review*
VT	*Vetus Testamentum*
VTSup	Supplements to Vetus Testamentum
WBC	Word Biblical Commentary
WJSC	*Western Journal of Speech Communication*
WMANT	Wissenschaftliche Monographien zum Alten und Neuen Testament
WUNT	Wissenschaftliche Untersuchungen zum Neuen Testament
YNER	Yale Near Eastern Researches
ZAW	*Zeitschrift für die alttestamentliche Wissenschaft*
ZBK	Zürcher Bibelkommentare

Acknowledgments

This volume is the result of a PhD dissertation completed at Boston College. I am grateful to my mentors at Boston College: David Vander-hooft, Jeffrey Cooley, and Pheme Perkins. I am obliged to all three for the ways they have contributed to my development as a scholar. I also wish to acknowledge the support I have received from my colleagues and students at Catholic Theological Union in Chicago. I am indebted to all of them, but especially to the President of CTU, Mark Francis, CSV; Vice President and Academic Dean Barbara Reid, OP; and my colleagues in the Department of Biblical Languages and Literature: Dianne Bergant, CSA; Laurie Brink, OP; Leslie Hoppe, OFM; vănThanh Nguyễn, SVD; Sallie Latkovitch, CSJ; and Donald Senior, CP. Helping me make the transition from dissertation to published manuscript were many good people at Fortress Press, including Neil Elliott, Emily Holm, and Marissa Wold Uhrina. I am grateful to them and to all who have assisted me in this project.

The Haggai Narrative

^{1:1}¹ In the second year of Darius the king, in the sixth month, on the first day of the month, the word of YHWH came through Haggai the prophet to Zerubbabel son of Shealtiel, governor of Judah, and to Joshua son of Jehozadak, the high priest: ² "Thus says YHWH of hosts: This people has said, 'It is not the time for coming, the time for the house of YHWH to be rebuilt.'" ³ Then the word of YHWH came through Haggai the prophet:

⁴ "Is it time for you yourselves to dwell in your houses—finished! While this house—desolate!

⁵ Come now! Thus says YHWH of hosts: Consider carefully your experience.

⁶ You have sown much, but brought in little; eat, but there is no fullness; drink, but there is no inebriation; dress, but there is no warmth for anyone. And the wage earner earns wages for a bag with holes in it!

⁷ Thus says YHWH of hosts: Consider carefully your experience!

⁸ Go up to the mountains, bring back wood, and build the house so that I may take pleasure in it and that I may be glorified, says YHWH.

⁹ You expected much but it has turned out to be little, and when you brought that home, I blew it away! And why? Declaration of YHWH of hosts: Because it is my house that is desolate, while each of you runs off to his own house.

¹⁰ Therefore it is on your account that the skies have withheld their dew and the earth has withheld its produce.

¹¹ I have called forth a desolation upon the land, upon the mountains, upon the grain, upon the new wine, upon the oil—upon whatever the

---

1. An annotated translation explaining some of the translational choices is included at the end of chap. 2. Further explanation of other choices is developed in the rhetorical analysis of the text in chaps. 4 and 5.

ground brings forth—upon people and upon the beasts and upon all their labors."

12 Then Zerubbabel son of Shaltiel and Joshua son of Jehozadak, the high priest, and all the remnant of the people obeyed the voice of YHWH their God, that is to say, the words of Haggai the prophet, because YHWH their God had sent him. But the people were afraid of YHWH. 13 So Haggai, the messenger of YHWH, said in a message of YHWH for the people: "I am with you! Declaration of YHWH!" 14 Then YHWH aroused the spirit of Zerubbabel son of Shaltiel, governor of Judah, and the spirit of Joshua son of Jehozadak, the high priest, and the spirit of all the remnant of the people, and they came and worked on the house of YHWH of hosts their God 15 on the twenty-fourth day of the month—the sixth one.

In the second year of Darius the king, 2:1 in the seventh month, on the twenty-first day of the month, the word of YHWH came to Haggai the prophet: 2 "Say to Zerubbabel son of Shaltiel, governor of Judah, and to Joshua son of Jehozadak, the high priest, and to the remnant of the people:

> 3 "Who is left among you who saw this house in its former glory? And how are you seeing it now? Surely it's like nothing in your eyes!
> 4 Nevertheless, be strong Zerubbabel! Declaration of YHWH! And be strong Joshua son of Jehozadak, the high priest, and be strong all people of the land! Declaration of YHWH! Act, for I am with you! Declaration of YHWH of hosts! 5b And my spirit stands in your midst; do not be afraid.
> 6 For thus says YHWH of hosts: Once more—and soon—I am going to cause the heavens and the earth, the sea and the dry land to quake.
> 7 I will cause all the nations to quake, and the treasures of all the nations will come, and I will fill this house with glory, says YHWH of hosts.
> 8 Mine is the silver and mine is the gold! Declaration of YHWH of hosts!
> 9 Greater will be the glory of this latter house than the former, says YHWH of hosts, and in this place I will grant well-being. Declaration of YHWH of hosts!"

10 On the twenty-fourth day of the ninth month in the second year of Darius, the word of YHWH came to Haggai the prophet: 11 "Thus says YHWH of hosts: Request from the priests a ruling." 12 "If someone is carrying consecrated meat in the skirt of his garment and with his skirt he touches bread, stew, wine, oil, or any food, will it become conse-

crated?" The priests answered, "No." ¹³ Then Haggai asked, "If someone who has become unclean by touching a dead body touches any of these, does it become unclean?" The priests answered, "It does become unclean." ¹⁴ Then Haggai responded,

> "Thus it is with this people and this nation in my judgment. Declaration of YHWH! And thus it is with every work of their hands and whatever they offer there: it is (all) unclean.
> ¹⁵ Now, consider carefully from this day forward: Before setting stone upon stone in the temple of YHWH, ¹⁶ how were you?
> One came to a heap for twenty (measures), but there were (only) ten. One came to the wine vat to draw off fifty (measures) from the vat, but there were (only) twenty.
> ¹⁷ I struck you with blight and mold and hail—every work of your hands—and with you I was not! Declaration of YHWH!
> ¹⁸ Consider carefully from this day forward—from the twenty-fourth day of the ninth month, that is, from the day the temple of YHWH was founded—consider carefully!
> ¹⁹ Is there still seed in the grain pit, while the vine, the fig, the pomegranate, and the olive tree have not produced?
> From this day I will bless!"

²⁰ Then the word of YHWH came a second time to Haggai on the twenty-fourth day of the month: ²¹ Say to Zerubbabel, governor of Judah:

> "I am about to cause the heavens and the earth to quake.
> ²² I will overturn the thrones of kingdoms, destroy the strength of the kingdoms of the nations. I will overturn chariots and their riders, and horses and their riders will fall, each by the sword of his fellow.
> ²³ On that day—Declaration of YHWH of hosts!—I will take you, Zerubbabel son of Shealtiel, my servant—Declaration of YHWH!—and I will make you as a signet ring, for it is you I have chosen. Declaration of YHWH of hosts!"

1

Introduction to the Rhetorical Analysis
of Haggai

Introduction

Until recently, the book of Haggai suffered from general neglect or disdain by many scholars.[1] The content of the prophet's message as well as the literary quality of the words attributed to him failed to meet the high standards set by earlier prophets such as Isaiah and Jeremiah. On the basis of a long-held but now generally discarded interpretation of the "priestly torah" section of the book (2:10–14), the prophet was sometimes accused of provincialism and "Jewish exclusivism" for rejecting the offer of the "Samarians" to help rebuild the temple.[2] Hag-

---

1. Many scholars have made this observation. See, for example, Hinckley G. Mitchell et al., *A Critical and Exegetical Commentary on Haggai, Zechariah, Malachi and Jonah*, ICC (New York, NY: Scribner, 1912), 36–39; Brevard S. Childs, *Introduction to the Old Testament as Scripture* (Philadelphia, PA: Fortress Press, 1979), 466; Carol L. Meyers and Eric M. Meyers, *Haggai, Zechariah 1-8*, AB 25B (Garden City, NY: Doubleday, 1987), xli; Henning G. Reventlow, *Die Propheten Haggai, Sacharja und Maleachi* (Göttingen: Vandenhoeck & Ruprecht, 1993), 7; John Kessler, *The Book of Haggai: Prophecy and Society in Early Persian Yehud*, VTSup 91 (Leiden: Brill, 2002), 2–12; Richard J. Coggins, "Haggai," in *Six Minor Prophets through the Centuries*, ed. Richard Coggins and Jin H. Han, Blackwell Bible Commentaries (Malden, MA: Wiley-Blackwell, 2011), 135–36. Kessler (*Haggai*, 11) notes that several earlier scholars, however, defended the prophet and the book, including S. R. Driver, Mitchell, Bennett, and Davidson.

gai's emphasis on the reconstruction of the temple and his promise that agricultural abundance and economic recovery would accompany its completion led to charges that he initiated a "grossly materialistic" vision of the period of restoration (or salvation) that was unworthy of his predecessors, who were true prophets concerned with more authentically spiritual matters.[3] Even the language used to express Haggai's message was displeasing in its lack of style and clearly derivative character. For these reasons Haggai was seen as a prime example of the "decline of prophecy" thought to mark the Persian period.[4] Kessler neatly captures the general attitude of scholars in the nineteenth and early twentieth centuries, for whom the book of Haggai was "something of an embarrassment within the prophetic corpus of the Hebrew Bible."[5]

This earlier tendency to dismiss Haggai and his eponymous book is most evident in general introductions to the Old Testament, which did not have the luxury of presenting a sustained, careful examination of the second shortest text in the Hebrew Bible (thirty-eight verses).[6] Oesterley and Robinson offer a particularly frank example of such critical assessments:

> Haggai is called a prophet, but compared with the pre-exilic prophets he is hardly deserving of the title. The chief activity of the prophets had been the teaching of the ethical righteousness of Yahweh and His demand that

2. As noted by Childs, *Introduction*, 466; Ralph L. Smith, *Micah-Malachi*, WBC 32 (Waco, TX: Word, 1984), 149; Meyers and Meyers, *Haggai*, xli; Kessler, *Haggai*, 2.

3. "Der krasse Materialismus in der Ausmalung der Heilszeit . . . hat mit Hag 2, 7 begonnen." Ernst Sellin, *Das Zwölfprophetenbuch*, KAT 12 (Leipzig: Erlangen, 1922), 398.

4. The idea that the Persian period saw such a decline is widespread. We find it already in the Babylonian Talmud (Yoma 9b): "After the later prophets Haggai, Zechariah, and Malachi had died, the Holy Spirit [of prophecy] departed from Israel" (*Babylonian Talmud*, trans. Isidore Epstein [London: Soncino, 1938]). Although the rabbis appear not to have included these prophets in the actual decline, Emil G. Hirsch suggested as much when he remarked that "Haggai's style certainly justifies the rabbinical observation that he marks the period of decline in prophecy (Yoma 9b). He scarcely rises above the level of good prose" ("Book of Haggai," in *The Jewish Encyclopedia* [New York, NY: Funk & Wagnalls, 1916], 6:148). Julius Wellhausen did not even acknowledge post-exilic prophecy, stating that "[w]e may call Jeremiah the last of the prophets: those who came after him were prophets only in name" (*Prolegomena to the History of Israel*, trans. J. Sutherland Black and Allan Menzies [New York, NY: Meridian Books, 1957], 403). Even without making such dogmatic judgments, many scholars have since echoed Wellhausen's understanding of the degeneration of prophecy after the monarchic period, while others have argued against it. For a discussion of the scholarly debate, see Benjamin D. Sommer, "Did Prophecy Cease? Evaluating a Reevaluation," *JBL* 115 (1996): 31–47.

5. Kessler, *Haggai*, 2.

6. The book of Obadiah comprises a single oracle of twenty-one verses.

His chosen people should show faithfulness to Him by moral living and spiritual worship; stern denunciation of sin, whether in the social, political, or religious life of the people; the certainty of divine judgment on the wicked, and the promise of a restored people when purified. Of all this there is scarcely a trace to be found in the teaching of Haggai. . . . His designation of Zerubbabel as the Messiah shows that his mind was concentrated only on earthly things; of higher religious thought or the reign of righteousness in the Messiah's kingdom there is not a word. His whole mental outlook and utilitarian religious point of view . . . is sufficient to show that he can have no place among the prophets in the real sense of the word.[7]

This derogation of the message of Haggai as discordant with proper prophetic concerns is found elsewhere. Robinson, for example, claimed that in Haggai "[t]here is no longer a really spiritual message" because "the Prophet seems to have included stone and timber amongst the essentials of his spiritual and religious ideal."[8] Thus one source of earlier criticism was the content and focus of Haggai's message, which "concentrated only on earthly things" and on "stone and timber." One might say that for these commentators, Haggai's concern was with matters too immediate, material, and mundane to qualify them or him as authentically "spiritual" or prophetic.

The low quality of the prophet's thought was matched by his prose, which was often characterized as unoriginal. Marti, for example, downgraded Haggai to a prophet only "to whom light flows from the words of the earlier prophets."[9] Reuss likewise found the prose of the book "most colorless," failing as it did to "flow from fresh sources."[10] Haggai's derivative and generally "clumsy and heavy style" was seen, along with the "banal" content of his message, as symptomatic of the supposed decline in prophecy in the post-exilic period.[11] Such evaluations

---

7. W. O. E. Oesterley and Theodore H. Robinson, *An Introduction to the Books of the Old Testament* (London: SPCK, 1961), 408–9.
8. Theodore H. Robinson, *Prophecy and the Prophets in Ancient Israel* (London: Duckworth, 1923), 177.
9. ". . . denen das Licht aus den Worten der früheren Propheten zuströmt." Karl Marti, *Das Dodekapropheton*, KHC 13 (Tübingen: Mohr Siebeck, 1904), 380.
10. "Sonst wäre zu sagen, daß er sich im allgemeinen in der farblosesten Prosa ergeht; und wenn er ein paarmal, am Ende des zweiten Stückes und im vierten, einen anderen Ton anschlägt und sich zur dichterisch blumenreichen Beredsamkeit erhebt, so sieht man leicht, daß dies nicht aus frischer Quelle fließt. Die schönen Zeiten des Prophetismus waren eben vorüber." Eduard Reuss, *Die Propheten*, vol. 2 of *Das Alte Testament: Übersetzt, eingeleitet und erläutert* (Braunschweig: Schwetschke, 1892), 544. (Both Marti and Reuss cited by Mitchell, *Haggai*, 36.)
11. Such are the words and judgment of J. Alberto Soggin, *Introduction to the Old Testament: From Its Ori-*

are summarized in Fohrer's much-quoted comment that "Haggai ist nicht mehr als ein prophetischer Epigone...."[12] This is a telling and useful word—epigone—because it highlights not just Haggai's supposed inferiority as a prophet, but also the imitative nature of his language.[13] Haggai's unoriginal and derivative language, according to these critics, diminished his claim to be a true prophet.[14]

My purpose here is not to assess these critiques of earlier commentators, but to note the areas in which these scholars often found fault with the prophet, which are relevant to the present study. The focus of criticism tended to be on the materiality of the message (build the temple to attain economic prosperity) and the ponderous, imitative language. In other words, for these earlier critics, Haggai was simply too concerned with the earthly problems of his people to be a true prophet, one who presumably would have been directing the people to look beyond the temporary and mundane to the eternal. The putative inauthenticity of Haggai as prophet showed also through his language, which appeared to be merely cribbed from earlier prophets. Regardless of what one thinks of their evaluations of Haggai as prophet, these earlier critics were correct: Haggai's message does focus on the immediate and material concerns of the Yehudites—his audience—and he does use language that is reminiscent enough of earlier prophets to qualify as "derivative."[15] Both of these observations, as we will see, are directly related to Haggai's role as rhetor and to the nature of his message as rhetoric. That is, Haggai's message reflects argumentative strategies

---

gins to the *Closing of the Alexandrian Canon*, 3rd ed., trans. John Bowden, OTL (Louisville, KY: Westminster John Knox, 1989), 384.

12. In Ernst Sellin, *Einleitung in das Alte Testament*, rev. and rewritten by Georg Fohrer (Heidelberg: Quelle & Meyer, 1969), 506.

13. Kessler (*Haggai*, 2) notes that Artur Weiser found Haggai be nothing more than "an imitator of the prophets" (*The Old Testament: Its Formation and Development*, trans. Dorothea M. Barton [New York, NY: Association Press, 1961]).

14. Scholars have long noted that the prophetic literature is marked by a high degree of intertextuality and inner-biblical exegesis, in which one text appears to be citing, alluding to, or commenting on other texts. Thus Haggai is not exceptional in his use of language reminiscent or even borrowed from earlier texts. Perhaps it was not Haggai's use of earlier material *per se* that was so off-putting to earlier critics as much as it was the resulting "clumsy and heavy style" and "materialistic" message.

15. More recent scholarship has tended to confirm earlier observations about Haggai and his language, yet without passing overt judgment on their quality. Meyers and Meyers, for example, also note that Haggai's style is similar to earlier prophets, but rather than interpret this as evidence of Haggai's inauthenticity or lesser status as "epigone," they decide it places him "in the prophetic tradition in language, idiom, and point of view" (*Haggai*, xli).

chosen to persuade a particular audience in unique sociohistorical circumstances to adopt a specific course of action.[16]

Whereas much earlier scholarship fixed its eye on the theological quality and value of the Haggai's message and language—that is, on his prophetic role—recently more attention has been paid to his historical role. Increased interest in the early Persian period has produced numerous studies on the socioeconomic conditions and religious transformations of the time. Biblical texts related to the period are being examined with fresh eyes and interrogated with new questions. The book of Haggai is now regularly mined for what evidence it may provide for historical reconstruction, and with this development has come a tendency to think of Haggai in terms of his historical and social influence. In contrast to the earlier criticisms of the prophet and his prose, recent commentators have been inclined to laud Haggai (and Zechariah) for their leadership. Meyers and Meyers state that Haggai "must be credited with steering Israel over the most delicate stage in this critical transition period," and they find the value of book of Haggai less in its "words" than in what it tells us of its main character, who "foster[ed] the transition of a people from national autonomy to an existence which transcended political definition and which centered upon a view of God and his moral demands."[17] Verhoef commends the prophet for giving the people of Israel in the temple "a new spiritual center, without which they would have perished as the people of God in the vortex of history."[18] Others who have avoided such evaluative language have nevertheless noted the significant social role of the prophet. Of all the summations of this role, Childs offered perhaps the most insightful when he referred to Haggai as a "political activist."[19]

Indeed, the book of Haggai portrays the intention of the prophet as explicitly political. His claim that YHWH was displeased with the people, his exhortation to rebuild YHWH's house, and his promises that YHWH would bless the people and even (perhaps) restore the Davidic monarchy are classically prophetic. Yet these were all offered as part

---

16. I am using "rhetoric" here as it has been traditionally understood, namely as spoken or written discourse designed to persuade or motivate an audience to adopt the speaker's perspective or to undertake a particular action.

17. Meyers and Meyers, *Haggai*, xlii, xliii.

18. Pieter A. Verhoef, *The Books of Haggai and Malachi*, NICOT (Grand Rapids, MI: Eerdmans, 1987), 33.

19. Childs, *Introduction*, 470.

of an extended argument designed to influence the outcome of a specific, timely question related to the public affairs of the Yehudite community. The decision whether to rebuild the temple "in the second year of Darius the king" was not merely "theological," nor did it affect only a small subpopulation of Yehud. Temple reconstruction required the allocation of scarce community resources (time, money, materials, labor), which could have been used in other ways. Once completed, the temple, along with its personnel, would undoubtedly exert social and economic influence, as they had in the past. This situation would not necessarily have been welcomed by all Yehudites. These considerations as well as others made the question of temple reconstruction not only theological, but also public, social, economic, and controversial—in other words, political. By urging his fellow Yehudites to rebuild the temple, Haggai was engaging, in effect, in a political campaign or policy debate to influence the outcome of a public decision.

Policy disputes are carried out through rhetorical argumentation. Unable to *force* the Yehudites to rebuild the temple, Haggai was required to *persuade* them of the necessity of reconstruction and of its ultimate public benefit, an explicitly rhetorical act.[20] Because Haggai was engaging in political rhetoric, as opposed to offering only a theological vision, it is understandable why his focus is so narrow, his message so "crudely material," and his religious outlook so "utilitarian." It also explains why his words are recognizably "prophetic" and imitatively "derivative" in their clear allusions to images and concepts of previous, acknowledged prophets. This is what we would expect of persuasive discourse designed to affect the outcome of a timely policy question by appealing to (rather than contributing to) theological tradition as part of its argumentation.

Insofar as the book of Haggai purports to record the prophet's attempt to persuade his fellow Yehudites to adopt a particular policy regarding the temple, as well as the outcome (to some extent) of that attempt, it is an "artifact" of Haggai's rhetorical act.[21] At the same time,

20. Roderick P. Hart and Suzanne Daughton note three features that make a message rhetorical: it delineates the good, has meaning for a particular audience, and makes or has clearly implied policy recommendations (*Modern Rhetorical Criticism*, 3rd ed. [Boston, MA: Pearson, 2005], 12).

21. Rhetorical artifacts may be distinguished from rhetorical acts. Acts are "executed in the presence of a rhetor's intended audience," whereas an artifact is "the text, trace, or tangible evidence of the act" (Sonja K. Foss, *Rhetorical Criticism: Exploration and Practice*, 4th ed. [Long Grove, IL: Waveland,

the book itself does more than merely record the suasory attempts of the prophet. Its composer manipulated them by placing them into a narrative framework with dates and narrative comments, presumably for his own persuasive purposes. This makes the composition of the book itself a rhetorical act. Thus the book the modern critic examines is both an artifact of the original rhetorical act of the prophet and an artifact of the rhetorical act of composition for an original reading or listening audience. Both as a record of the prophet's contribution to a specific policy dispute and as itself a contribution to that debate, the book of Haggai is inherently a rhetorical document and thus a good candidate for rhetorical analysis.

Previous Rhetorical Criticism of the Book of Haggai

Despite the recognizably rhetorical character of the book of Haggai, it has been subjected to only limited rhetorical analysis. To some extent this is because rhetorical criticism is a relative newcomer to modern biblical scholarship. In his 1968 Presidential Address to the Society of Biblical Literature, James Muilenburg called biblical scholars to engage in what he called "rhetorical criticism," by which he meant

> understanding the nature of Hebrew literary composition, in exhibiting the structural patterns that are employed for the fashioning of a literary unit ... and in discerning the many and various devices by which the predications are formulated and ordered into a unified whole.[22]

On the basis of formal structure, "rhetorical devices," and other literary elements, the critic could more adequately make judgments about the writer's intentions for the work. The years that followed Muilenburg's call to "move beyond form criticism" saw tremendous growth in biblical rhetorical criticism.[23] Yet when Watson and Hauser completed their 1994 comprehensive bibliography of contributions to the new

---

2009], 6). Hart and Daughton describe artifacts as "the leftovers of rhetorical acts: the records that remain and can be re-examined after the speech, letter, debate, editorial, or performance has been created and in some cases, ended" (*Modern Rhetorical Criticism*, 2).

22. James Muilenburg, "Form Criticism and Beyond," *JBL* 88 (1969): 9.

23. For summaries of the development of rhetorical criticism of the Hebrew Bible, see Matthew R. Schlimm, "Biblical Studies and Rhetorical Criticism: Bridging the Divide between the Hebrew Bible and Communication," *RComm* 7 (2007): 244–75; Phyllis Trible, *Rhetorical Criticism: Context, Method, and the Book of Jonah*, OTG (Minneapolis, MN: Fortress Press, 1994), 5–87.

field, Haggai was the only book in the entire Christian canon not represented at all.[24] In his 2003 bibliography of Haggai and Zechariah, Boda referred in the section titled "Rhetorical and Canonical Criticism" to works of only two scholars, Clark and Bauer.[25] Clark wrote a number of short studies of "discourse structure analysis," only one of which concerns Haggai directly.[26] Another article, by Holbrook, that also provides a discourse structure analysis of Haggai was not included in Boda's list.[27] Boda noted that Bauer's monograph is a "literary analysis" carried out in service of Bauer's "presentation of the socio-economic themes" of the Haggai-Zechariah-Malachi corpus.[28] Boda himself wrote an article in 2000 entitled, "Haggai: Mastor Rhetorician."[29] In it, he also engaged in rhetorical analysis to argue for the original unity of the "oral material" of the book, yet limited his analysis to structure, style, and technique. All these studies are text-immanent, which means they offer only literary analysis, attending solely to the internal dynamics of the text and not taking into consideration the historical and social circumstances that gave rise to the text in the first place. This, as we will see, is a primary element of rhetorical analysis of persuasive texts.

In the years since Boda compiled his bibliography, a handful of rhetorical analyses of Haggai have appeared. In 2007 Assis, who has written several articles on Haggai, looked at the "composition, rhetoric, and theology" of a short passage in Haggai to gain a better understanding of the prophet's argument, ultimately making claims on the basis of his analysis for the compositional unity of the book.[30] As in the earlier studies, Assis' study was limited to text-immanent structural analysis. Similarly, Swinburnson's 2008 rhetorical examination of

24. Duane F. Watson and Alan J. Hauser, eds., *Rhetorical Criticism of the Bible: A Comprehensive Bibliography with Notes on History and Method*, BibInt 4 (Leiden: Brill, 1994).

25. Mark J. Boda, "Majoring on the Minors: Recent Research on Haggai and Zechariah," *CurBR* 2 (2003): 33–68; *Haggai and Zechariah Research: A Bibliographic Study*, Tools for Biblical Study 5 (Leiden: Deo, 2003).

26. David J. Clark, "Discourse Structure in Haggai," *JOTT* 5.1 (1992): 13–24.

27. David J. Holbrook, "Narrowing Down Haggai: Examining Style in Light of Discourse and Content," *JOTT* 7.2 (1995): 1–12.

28. See Lutz Bauer, *Zeit des zweiten Tempels-Zeit der Gerechtigkeit: Zur sozio-ökonomischen Konzeption im Haggai-Sacharja-Maleachi Korpus*, BEATAJ 31 (Frankfurt: Lang, 1992).

29. Mark J. Boda, "Haggai: Master Rhetorician," *TynBul* 51 (2000): 295–304.

30. Elie Assis, "Composition, Rhetoric and Theology in Haggai 1:1–11," *JHebS* 7 (2007): article 11, available at http://purl.org/JHS and at http://www.JHSonline.org.

Haggai did not go beyond the "literary and rhetorical structure" of the book.[31]

Such works, worthwhile as they may be, demonstrate only a restricted appropriation of particular approaches to rhetorical criticism, one in line with Muilenburg's earliest articulation of the method, which focused on "structural patterns" and "devices." Thus they reflect an approach to rhetorical criticism that is purely literary, which Trible has referred to as the study of "the art of composition."[32] While it is true that some attend to the suasory nature of portions of the book, their analyses are nevertheless not intended to examine in depth a key element of criticism of rhetorical documents, namely how precisely they relate to the historical and social circumstances that prompted the original rhetorical act of either the prophet or the composer of the text.

Other studies have offered such an approach. In a two-part article on Haggai (2005 and 2006), Wendland moved beyond purely structural or discourse analysis to examine the "rhetorical situation" that prompted the prophetic preaching and devoted several pages to the relationship of the argument and argumentative strategies of the text to the specific historical circumstances of the prophet.[33] (I will define this term "rhetorical situation" below.) The study is recognizably "rhetorical," but is limited in size and scope.

In a more extensive, earlier monograph on Haggai (2002), Kessler aimed "to examine the specific vision of prophecy and society portrayed in the book of Haggai set against the social context in which the book was produced."[34] Kessler's book analyzes the biblical text and investigates what it can reveal about the social environment in which it was produced. As such, it represents a rhetorical approach that takes into account both the literary features of a text and the "situation" that gave rise to and influenced the rhetorical act. Kessler's work is

---

31. Benjamin W. Swinburnson, "The Glory of the Latter Temple: A Structural and Biblical-Theological Analysis of Haggai 2:1–9," *Kerux* 23 (2008): 28–46.

32. Trible, *Rhetorical Criticism*, 32–40. Trible refers also to later developments in biblical rhetorical criticism that focus on rhetoric as "the art of persuasion." The present study is an example of this latter category.

33. Ernst R. Wendland, "The Structure, Style, Sense, and Significance of Haggai's Prophecy Concerning the 'House of the LORD': With Special Reference to Bible Interpretation and Translation in Africa," *OTE* 18 (2005): 907–26; 19 (2006): 281–306.

34. Kessler, *Haggai*, 1.

a detailed and comprehensive analysis of Haggai, which offers many insights into the persuasive elements and nature of the text, but he confines his explicit rhetorical analysis of Haggai to a section he calls "Rhetorical and Hermeneutical Use of Religious Traditions," which is attached to his exegesis of each section of the book. He argues that Haggai makes use of religious traditions as "rhetorical and hermeneutical strategies to deal with the tension created by the radically changed circumstances of the Persian period vis-à-vis earlier periods in which many of these traditions are current."[35] Kessler's elucidation of how the book of Haggai shows the appropriation of earlier traditions, what has been done with them, and how they are used, is clearly rhetorical criticism. This criticism, however, is largely limited in both the scope and the depth of its analysis of the persuasive nature of the text. For example, Kessler explicitly addresses only the rhetorical use of traditions, and only occasionally dwells on other rhetorical strategies or forms of argumentation. Kessler's analysis illuminates important rhetorical elements of the book of Haggai, but he does not intend to offer a complete rhetorical analysis of the text.

Before and since Kessler's monograph, shorter studies of the literary features or historical circumstances surrounding the book of Haggai have appeared, but only occasionally has a detailed analysis of the relationship between the two been offered, and then only to a limited extent, often in passing or as part of a different aim. Thus a full-length exploration of the book of Haggai specifically as a persuasive text is still needed.

Such a study will bring a different set of questions to, and thus offer different insights into, the text and historical context than other studies, the majority of which have focused on the theological content of the book. Generally speaking, commentators have tended to see the book of Haggai primarily and essentially as a theological document, rather than as a persuasive text. This lens presupposes that the main purpose of the prophet's original speeches and of the composition that records and interprets them was to articulate a theological message, first for the original audience and then, presumably, for the ages. Such an approach to a biblical text is perhaps to be expected, especially

---

35. Ibid., 153.

in commentaries or other works written for Jewish or Christian audiences, but it places the emphasis on the content of the theological formulations and gives less attention to their persuasive functions. What has been important for the critic is to deduce and articulate the theological vision of the prophet; examination of rhetorical strategies or "devices" in the theological text is either in service of this main purpose or offered as a side note of relatively little theological importance.

If, on the other hand, one recognizes that Haggai's primary concern was not to articulate a theological vision but to persuade his audience to adopt a particular policy, then one's understanding of the primary character of the book changes from a theological document with some "rhetorical" features to a rhetorical artifact that uses theology to makes its argument. Even if, as we might presume, the prophet's desire to see the temple rebuilt right away had a theological basis, his motivation for actually exhorting the Yehudites to build it was to persuade them to adopt his perspective and proposed course of action. His speeches were thus primarily rhetorical acts. In addition, the book that records and interprets those speeches was composed, I will argue, to further the persuasive aim of supporting the reconstruction of the temple by arguing that Haggai was a true prophet who accurately reflected YHWH's desire to have his house rebuilt. The book of Haggai ought to be read with its essentially—not incidentally—persuasive character in mind. That is, it ought to be read as a rhetorical artifact through a careful, detailed rhetorical analysis.

Such an analysis, which looks at the book from a different perspective and asks new questions, illuminates the circumstances that impelled its composition. Haggai, along with contemporaneous texts, has been used to reconstruct the historical, religious, and socioeconomic realities and events of the early Persian period. Such reconstructions have generally depended on readings that have paid insufficient attention to the argumentative character of the *entire* book of Haggai. Consequently, the substantial grounds for and especially the persistence of objections to reconstructing the temple in the second year of Darius have been underappreciated. One regularly finds, for example, scholars repeating the idea that the reason the Yehudites had failed to rebuild the temple was because they were preoccupied with their own homes, that is, because they were selfishly negligent. It is true that Haggai implies as much in his first oracle, but he does so for strategic purposes as part of an argumentative scheme. The assumption that Haggai's implication of selfishness may be taken as an accurate reflection of the Yehudites' actual attitudes and motivation for "neglecting" the temple leaves unexplored other, more substantial objections to reconstruction rooted in theological traditions as well as the socioeconomic circumstances of the time.[36] A main argument of this study is that all of the prophet's speeches, not just the first one, were intended to urge the Yehudites to work on the temple, despite growing or persistent doubts about Haggai's claim that YHWH not only supported but commanded the reconstruction of his house. The entire book, in other words, constitutes evidence that the question of reconstruction was not settled once the prophet made his first policy pitch. Rhetorical analysis attends to the argumentative nature of the entire book and to strategies employed to gain insight into the nature and persistence of objections. This in turn contributes to our understanding of circumstances in Yehud at the time.

Rhetorical analysis also offers the possibility of resolving long-standing exegetical problems, ranging from text-critical questions to interpretation of specific passages.[37] For example, the "priestly torah" section (2:10–14) has proven difficult to understand because of its sudden and severe criticism of a group called העם הזה הגוי הזה.[38] This group is not further identified in the oracle, and attempts to do so, and to explain why the prophet calls them "unclean" (טמא), have failed to garner widespread support. Earlier suggestions that Haggai must be referring to the "enemies of Judah and Benjamin" who attempted to help with the temple but who were rejected (Ezra 4:15) had the advantage of explaining why the prophet would refer to them as גוי and טמא. But this explanation no longer enjoys much support, not only because it rests on problematic readings of Ezra but also because it fits poorly

---

36. Many commentators do, of course, recognize that the Yehudites may have had substantive reasons to oppose temple reconstruction (which will be discussed in chap. 3). Yet most ignore or downplay the possibility that Haggai's characterization of the Yehudites may not be completely accurate or fair, but rather deliberately chosen for its persuasive potential.

37. For text-critical problems and proposed solutions, see chap. 2, pp. 24–39, and throughout chaps. 4 and 5.

38. This passage and the problems of its interpretation are discussed in detail in chap. 5, pp. 220–31.

with the rest of Haggai. Most scholars have determined that the referent in question is the people of Yehud, all of whom, it is almost universally assumed, are busily working on or supporting the work of temple reconstruction. This raises the question of why the prophet would unexpectedly call them גוי and טמא. Moral and cultic explanations that find no support in the text have failed to persuade, although they have remained the best guesses. Rhetorical analysis of the strategies and argument of the book yields a solution to this problem by showing, first, that Haggai failed to persuade all the Yehudites to support the temple reconstruction and, second, that it is those who persist in their refusal and who threaten to cause others to abandon the project, that are both גוי and טמא.

Rhetorical analysis of Haggai that focuses on the persuasive character, intent, and strategies of the entire book thus yields greater information about the historical circumstances surrounding the reconstruction of the temple, contributing to a fuller, more accurate understanding of the early Persian period, and it offers solutions to difficult problems of interpretation, such as—but not limited to—the "priestly torah" section.

Rhetorical Analysis

The modern discipline of rhetorical criticism is not monolithic. There are a number of ways to approach any given artifact, and the discipline evinces constant discussion about the suppositions, methods, and aims of rhetorical criticism of cultural artifacts—verbal, written, or otherwise. Nevertheless, most rhetoricians would agree with Bryant that

> rhetorical criticism is systematically getting inside transactions of communication to discover and describe their elements, their form, and their dynamics and to explore the situations, past or present, which generate them and in which they are essential constituents to be comprehended.[39]

Bryant's statement highlights two aspects of rhetorical criticism that inform almost all modern studies (outside of biblical studies, at least): analysis of the text itself (individual elements and their relationship to

---

39. Donald C. Bryant, *Rhetorical Dimensions in Criticism* (Baton Rouge, LA: Louisiana State University Press, 1973), 35.

each other) and analysis of the milieu in which the text was formed and to which it contributes (the situation that generates it and of which it is a constituent).

The first, text-immanent aspect of criticism analyzes the elements and dynamics of the text—structure and form, syntax, lexical characteristics, imagery, style, and patterns of argument—to discern how they contribute to the persuasive force of a text. By careful, detailed, and comprehensive analysis of the text's features, the critic hopes to gain insight into how the original speaker or the creator of the text (the "rhetor") perceived and hoped to influence the situation that gave rise to the original rhetorical act, as well as the nature of the society in which the act emerged and which the rhetor sought to influence. As we have seen, this largely has been the extent of rhetorical criticism of Haggai, although the detail and comprehensiveness of the analysis have varied.

Such literary analysis, which itself can shed light on the expectations, values, and sources of authority within a society, is supplemented and combined with the particular "situation" that gave rise to the rhetorical act and that it sought to influence. What characterizes rhetorical criticism, and distinguishes it from purely literary analysis, is its concern for the "external reference of discourse, the context both immediate and antecedent, the suasory potential in the situation" that plays an "organic part" of the analysis.[40]

This dual aspect of rhetorical criticism arises from the basic recognition that all acts, textual or otherwise, that have a rhetorical character are "situated," that is, they arise within a unique historical time and place and are essentially tied to it (no matter how "universal" their message or aims may be). It is, I believe, the essentially situated nature of the book of Haggai that contributed to earlier dissatisfaction with its message and even its language. It is inextricably linked to the historical circumstances to which it was responding and has often been found to have relatively little meaning or resonance apart from those circumstances. This is why, in both Jewish and Christian traditions, the book has received much less attention than other prophetic texts: the text

---

40. Ibid., 35.

has a tendency to resist the often-strained efforts to extract from it a "deep spiritual meaning" beyond the most abstract and general.

A basic way of discussing the extra-textual aspects of a rhetorical act is to describe them in terms of the "rhetorical situation." Bitzer, in 1968, developed the concept of "situation," which has generated considerable scholarship in an effort to contest, redefine, or refine his original definition.[41] The dominant model for discussing the situation of a rhetorical act is to delineate four main elements of the situation: "rhetor" (the one performing the act), "exigence," "audience," and "constraints." The last three require a brief explanation.

Exigence refers to the reality that stimulates the rhetorical act, experienced by the rhetor as "an imperfection marked by urgency . . . a thing which is other than it should be."[42] Rhetorical critics have emphasized that this exigence is subjective, in the sense that it is the rhetor's interpretation of external reality, not the external reality itself, that constitutes the exigence. In the case of the book of Haggai, the exigence is the still-unreconstructed state of the temple, which is for Haggai "a thing which is other than it should be" that urgently needs to be addressed. What creates the need for persuasion is the fact that for others the unreconstructed temple is not "other than it should be," or at least not urgently so.

Audience is a central aspect of rhetorical studies, and has generally been considered the most influential element of a rhetorical situation.[43] Audience determines the content, delivery, and argumentative strategies of a rhetorical act. The rhetor will only adopt those elements

---

41. Lloyd F. Bitzer, "The Rhetorical Situation," *Ph&Rh* 1 (1968): 1–14; Richard L. Larson, "Lloyd Bitzer's 'Rhetorical Situation' and the Classification of Discourse: Problems and Implications," *Ph&Rh* 3 (1970): 165–68; Richard E. Vatz, "The Myth of the Rhetorical Situation," *Ph&Rh* 6 (1973): 154–61; Scott Consigny, "Rhetoric and Its Situations," *Ph&Rh* 7 (1974): 175–86; John H. Patton, "Causation and Creativity in Rhetorical Situations: Distinctions and Implications," *QJS* 65 (1979): 36–55; Lloyd F. Bitzer, "Functional Communication: A Situational Perspective," in *Rhetoric in Transition: Studies in the Nature and Uses of Rhetoric*, ed. Eugene E. White (University Park, PA: Pennsylvania State University Press, 1980), 21–38; Alan Brinton, "Situation in the Theory of Rhetoric," *Ph&Rh* 14 (1981): 234–48; Mary Garret and Xiaosui Xiao, "The Rhetorical Situation Revisited," *RSQ* 23 (1993): 30–40; William L. Benoit, "The Genesis of Rhetorical Action," *SCJ* 59 (1994): 342–55; Craig R. Smith and Scott Lybarger, "Bitzer's Model Reconsidered," *CommQ* 44 (1996): 197–213; Donna Gorrell, "The Rhetorical Situation Again: Linked Components in a Venn Diagram," *Ph&Rh* 30 (1997): 395–412; Keith Grant-Davie, "Rhetorical Situations and Their Constituents," *RhetR* 15 (1997): 264–79.
42. Bitzer, "Rhetorical Situation," 6.
43. Celeste Condit, "Rhetorical Criticism and Audiences: The Extremes of McGee and Leff," *WJSC* 64 (1990): 330.

that he has reason to believe will help persuade his audience to adopt his position or proposed course of action. It is what the audience will find compelling and will motivate them to act, not necessarily what the rhetor himself finds compelling or reason to act, that constitutes the main content and manner of a rhetorical act. Whatever Haggai's personal reasons for wanting the temple rebuilt may have been, his argumentive strategy throughout the book focuses on the material concerns—agricultural and economic—that were primary for the Yehudites. The reason the book of Haggai is so "crudely materialistic" is because Haggai's audience cared about such things and could not have been persuaded to build the temple unless doing so would have positively affected their material well-being.

Constraints in a rhetorical situation are those elements, apart from the exigence or audience, in a particular social milieu that are relevant to the performance or production of the rhetorical act.[44] Such elements may indeed "constrain" the rhetor's choices. For example, if one wanted the audience to adopt a course of action, it would be counterproductive to point out how well it has worked for another social group that the audience happened to consider an enemy or a lesser social group they had no desire to emulate. Even if this were, logically, the most compelling piece of evidence, rhetorically it would be disastrous if offered. But constraints can also include strongly persuasive elements that the audience would be "constrained" to accept. In the book of Haggai, the prophet is shown drawing on earlier prophetic tropes and divine promises because he has reason to believe that these will move the audience to accept him as an authentic prophet and his message as originating from YHWH. Thus the previous words and themes of Israelite prophecy serve as resources that, Haggai hopes, will constrain his audience to accept his call to rebuild.

The relationship among all four elements of a rhetorical situation—rhetor, exigence, audience, constraints—is complex and highly integrated, but each must be examined as carefully and thoroughly as possible to illuminate their mutual relationships. This makes for a complex analysis, but one that can yield insights into the rhetorical act and the social forces to which it was responding and of which, in turn,

---

44. Bitzer, "Rhetorical Situation," 8.

it became a part, and thus helps provide a fuller picture of Yehudite reality in the early Persian period. How one chooses to examine the complex relationship between act and elements of the rhetorical situation depends on the peculiarities of the study; there is no pre-exisiting "method" for discerning, articulating, and interpreting these relationships.

Like much modern rhetorical criticism, the present study is eclectic, drawing on terms, concepts, and insights from both classical and modern rhetoric. As I have already noted, the question of whether or not to rebuild the temple in 520 BCE was essentially a policy dispute, and this is a primary lens through which I will analyze the persuasive aims and argumentative strategies of the book of Haggai. To use terms from a period much later than Haggai's, policy dispute is a subgenre of deliberative speech, one of three kinds of rhetoric identified by Aristotle.[45] All policy disputes involve areas of potential disagreement that rhetoricians call "stock issues." Advocates for the adoption or change of policy must address these issues successfully before an audience will accept their proposals. Because all policy disputes—no matter what the specific circumstances—involve them, stock issues provide a "taxonomy, a system of classifying the kinds of questions that can be at issue in a controversy."[46] This makes them a useful tool for rhetorical analysis of a text that reflects or plays a role in a policy dispute.

The concept of stock issues was originally developed to aid in the formation of legal argumentation. Later it was adapted to deliberative disputes by Hultzén, whose work, though usually modified by other rhetoricians for greater analytical precision, remains the standard approach to stock issues. Hultzén referred to four frames of reference, or issues, in deliberative analysis: *ill* (or *harm*), *reformability* (now usually called *cause* or *blame*), *remedy*, and *cost* (or *consequences*). Within each of these frames of reference lies one or more potential point of

---

45. *Rhet.* 1.3.3, 1358a36–1358b9. By applying Aristotle's terms and categories to the book of Haggai, I am not assuming that they would have been known to Haggai. Aristotle was simply describing basic genres of rhetoric, which existed before he described them.

46. Jeanne R. Fahnestock and Marie J. Secor, "Grounds for Argument: Stasis Theory and Topoi," in *Argument in Transition: Proceedings of the Third Summer Conference on Argumentation*, ed. D. Zarefsky (Annandale, VA: Speech Communication Association, 1983), 137. (Cited in James Jasinski, *Sourcebook on Rhetoric: Key Concepts in Contemporary Rhetorical Studies*, Rhetoric and Society [Thousand Oaks, CA: SAGE, 2001], 528).

disagreement in a policy dispute. As will be explained in more detail in chapter 4, *ill* refers to the perceived problem that the policy is meant to eliminate or ameliorate, whereas *blame* and *remedy* refer respectively to the cause of the of the ill and what is needed to resolve it. *Cost* encompasses not just financial, but also any other repercussions or results of implementing the policy, some of which may be undesirable. To persuade their audience to accept a policy proposal, advocates must be prepared to address each of these frames of reference, overcoming any points of disagreement or resistance that may emerge during the course of controversy. If they fail to do so, it will be difficult if not impossible to persuade their audience to adopt the policy.[47]

The analysis of the book of Haggai as an artifact from a policy dispute may be developed according to these stock issues, providing "a systematic methodology for breaking the [debate] proposition down into its vital component parts."[48] This has the advantage of offering a thorough, relevant approach to the analysis while leaving room for further analysis of persuasive elements of the text that are not peculiar to policy disputes (such as appeals to *ethos* or figures and tropes).

Plan of This Study

In chapter 2, I establish through text and redaction criticism the rhetorical artifact to be analyzed. For the most part, this artifact is the MT of the book of Haggai. With the exception of 2:5a, which is probably a later addition to the text, the MT represents the original composition, created around 520 BCE. Text criticism suggests only a few emendations, some of which are nevertheless critical for understanding the text of Haggai.

In chapter 3, I examine the historical background relevant to the book. Reconstructing the circumstances surrounding the rebuilding of the temple is a difficult and complex task that must rely on biblical and extrabiblical evidence whose reliability and interpretation have been controversial. The chapter begins by examining the probable history of

---

47. Lee S. Hultzén, "Status in Deliberative Analysis," in *The Rhetorical Idiom: Essays in Rhetoric, Oratory, Language, and Drama*, ed. Donald C. Bryant (Ithaca, NY: Cornell University Press, 1958), 108–23.

48. George W. Ziegelmueller, Jack Kay, and Charles A. Dause, *Argumentation: Inquiry and Advocacy* (Englewood Cliffs, NJ: Prentice Hall, 1990), 39. (Cited in Jasinski, *Sourcebook*, 532.)

the temple reconstruction as well as the question of the role of the Persian authorities in commanding, sponsoring, or allowing it. The second part of the chapter looks at various theological, political, social, and economic factors that would have factored into any decision to build or not to build the temple.

All of this information is relevant for the rhetorical analysis of Haggai, in chapters 4 and 5. To anticipate a major argument of these chapters: historical probability as well as the text itself strongly suggest that Haggai's original call to rebuild the temple was heeded only by some members of the Yehudite community. Others remained dubious of Haggai's claim to speak for YHWH, who wanted his house rebuilt immediately. This position is contrary to most Haggai scholarship, which assumes (but generally does not argue) that all of Yehud immediately accepted the prophet's call to rebuild. Yet as I will argue throughout my analysis, a divided response to Haggai's call is not only more likely historically, but it also contributes to a better understanding of much of the rest of the text. For example, the priestly torah section of 2:10–14 appears to strongly criticize some group called "this people, this nation" (העם הזה והגוי הזה). This group is not explicitly identified. Earlier attempts to assign it to the "Samarians" have been set aside in recent decades. Assuming that the referent must be the people of Yehud, who (it is also assumed) have been diligently working on the temple, scholars have been at a loss to explain why the prophet criticizes them by calling them "unclean" (טמא). If we proceed not from the position that all of Yehud is working on the temple, but rather that some have resisted Haggai's claim to speak for YHWH, it becomes more likely that Haggai is criticizing that group of people, rather than those who accepted his call.

The study concludes in chapter 6 with a summary of findings and possibilities raised by the analysis for further inquiry into the early Persian period and the reconstruction of the temple.

2

Text-Critical Analysis, Composition of Narrative, and Notes on Translation

Introduction

The purpose of this chapter is to establish the text for rhetorical analysis. This text is not the final form of the book of Haggai, represented by the MT, but a hypothetical, intermediate stage in the literary development of the book. This stage, in which a composer placed pre-existing materials attributed to the prophet Haggai into a narrative framework, is the major compositional phase in the development of the book. The resulting text underwent only minor changes before reaching its final form as we find it in the MT.[1] By identifying and removing these post-compositional developments, we are able to reconstruct the major creative stage in the formation of the book of Haggai. Throughout this study I will refer to this stage as the Haggai Narrative (HN), to distinguish it from the final form of the text, properly called the book of Haggai. (When I refer to the "composer" in following pages, I mean the

---

1. The difference between them lies in the later addition of short gloss to the original work (2:5aα in the MT) and a handful of small (but sometimes important) consonantal and vocalic discrepancies.

person(s) responsible for the HN, unless I indicate otherwise.) The HN is the rhetorical text under analysis in this study.

The HN is a suitable candidate for rhetorical analysis for two reasons. First, the narrative structure and dating scheme imposed on (presumably) pre-existing prophetic oracles places those materials in a particular framework that recontextualizes them and creates a text from them. While the rhetorical aims and persuasive strategies of the oracles clearly inform the shape of the new composition, the HN nevertheless has aims and strategies of its own that may exceed or differ in some respects from those of the original prophetic oracles. The result is thus a rhetorical composition in its own right.[2] Any later changes to the HN would possibly alter—whether to a significant degree or not—the configuration of elements that comprise the persuasive strategies of the text as a whole. For this reason, those elements of the MT that I have determined represent changes to the HN are excluded from analysis. The second reason the HN is the appropriate text for analysis is because, as I will argue below, it represents the main compositional stage in the history of the book. Once composed, the HN underwent very little development before reaching its final form in the book of Haggai.

The Haggai Narrative is necessarily a reconstruction. There are no extant manuscripts of it. As it represents an earlier stage in the formation of the book of Haggai, the logical point from which to begin reconstructing the HN is this final form of the text. The MT is the best "base text" with which to begin. It is the only complete Hebrew text of the book, and the other witnesses to the Hebrew text—Murabbaʿat 88, 4Q77b, and 4Q80e—agree with the MT in almost all particulars. The OG of Haggai also provides important evidence for reconstructing the HN. In the redaction-critical analysis below, I will examine in more detail the insight the OG gives regarding the literary development of Haggai, and the possibility it raises of two text traditions for the book.

The reconstruction of the HN will begin with a text-critical analysis

---

2. In saying that the formation of the HN involved the recontextualizing of pre-existing materials in a narrative framework, I am not presuming that the work of the composer was limited to the narrative and dating elements of the text. He may also have contributed material to the prophetic speeches themselves. The assumption that the composer did not add material to the speeches is a peculiar feature of much Haggai scholarship, and one that has implications for models of the literary formation of the text. I will discuss this in more detail below.

of the MT. This short text—a mere thirty-eight verses—has a number of problematic points. In the notes that follow I consider those that have received the most attention and the most plausible suggestions for emendation, even when I have not accepted those proposals. When I have not been able to establish a strong case for any proposed alternate reading, I have retained the MT. In most if not all cases the differences between the MT and possible emendations are minor and do not affect analysis of the persuasive features of the text. In those instances where they have proved to be significant, I provide extended treatment of the variants.

After the text-critical analysis, I take up a consideration of the literary development of Haggai to determine the most likely shape and content of the HN. My approach here is conservative: only those elements that appear *likely* to be later additions will be removed. I have retained those that are only *possible* or *plausible* additions. A guiding principle in my considerations has been to avoid unnecessary multiplication of redactional layers or interventions, accepting only those for which there is strong evidence. If we can offer a reasonable accounting for a particular textual phenomenon without resorting to an additional redactional intervention, I have done so.

I conclude the chapter with an annotated English translation of the HN for the sake of completeness and also to present more clearly for the reader my understanding of the rhetorical dynamics of the text. For the most part, the notations concern only difficult matters of translation related largely to textual or lexical ambiguities. Here, as in the text-critical and redaction-critical sections, matters of interpretation of the text have been limited to what is necessary for the work at hand. Reasons for some of the more "stylistic" translation choices will become apparent in the rhetorical analysis of the text.

Text-Critical Analysis of the Haggai Narrative[3]

בִּשְׁנַת שְׁתַּיִם לְדָרְיָוֶשׁ הַמֶּלֶךְ בַּחֹדֶשׁ הַשִּׁשִּׁי בְּיוֹם אֶחָד לַחֹדֶשׁ הָיָה דְבַר יְהוָה בְּיַד 1:1
חַגַּי הַנָּבִיא אֶל זְרֻבָּבֶל בֶּן שְׁאַלְתִּיאֵל פַּחַת[a] יְהוּדָה וְאֶל יְהוֹשֻׁעַ בֶּן יְהוֹצָדָק הַכֹּהֵן
הַגָּדוֹל לֵאמֹר׃

2 כֹּה אָמַר יְהוָה צְבָאוֹת לֵאמֹר הָעָם הַזֶּה אָמְרוּ לֹא עֶת בֹּא עֶת בֵּית[a] יְהוָה לְהִבָּנוֹת׃

1:1a פַּחַת — OG: ἐκ φυλῆς; Mur, Vg, Syr, Tg, λ' = MT; the OG not considered a reflection of the HT. Mitchell suggested the translator of the OG may have mistaken the word for מִשְׁפָּחַת, while Rudolph thought it might be an abbreviation of that term.[4] Others, noting פחת is correctly translated in Mal 1:8, consider the Greek an "intentional mistranslation" of the original פחת.[5] The same translation occurs in the OG of 1:12, 14; 2:1, 2, 21.

1:2a עֶת בֹּא עֶת בֵּית — OG: ἥκει ὁ καιρὸς (= Syr); Vg: *nondum venit tempus* (= Tg). Because none of the versions reflects the first עת, Sebök suggests it results from dittography; others argue that the entire phrase עת בא is a dittograph of עת בית.[6] Numerous commentators, following Hitzig, would retain the consonantal text and revocalize to עַתָּ בָא.[7] Lack of

---

3. The following text represents the completed text critical and redaction critical work of the chapter. Rationales for departure from the MT will be addressed in the body of the chapter. The Hebrew text and notes are divided for ease of reference, not according to any particular understanding of the structure of the text.

4. Mitchell, *Haggai*, 51; Wilhelm Rudolph, *Haggai, Sacharja 1-8, Sacharja 9-14, Maleachi*, KAT 13/4 (Gütersloh: Gütersloher Verlagshaus, 1976), 29.

5. It is perhaps a messianic interpretation, according to Samuel Amsler (*Aggée-Zacharie 1-8, Zacharie 9-14, Malachi*, CAT 11c [Geneva: Labor et Fides, 1988], 21). Hans Wolff (*Haggai: A Commentary*, trans. M. Kohl, CC [Minneapolis, MN: Ausgburg Fortress, 1988], 29) suggests that Zerubbabel's Judahite origins were more important to the translator than his official position in the Persian Empire. The relevance of Mal 1:8 here derives from the commonly accepted notion that the OG of the Twelve is the work of a single translator or small group of translators, who presumably employed the same translation techniques. See below for further discussion of this.

6. Mark Sebök (Schönberger), *Die syrische Übersetzung der zwölf kleinen Propheten und ihr Verhältniss zu dem massoretischen Text und zu den älteren Übersetzungen namentlich den LXX und dem Targum* (Breslau: Preuss & Jünger, 1887), 67; Mitchell, *Haggai*, 51; Odil H. Steck, "Zu Haggai 1:2–11," ZAW 83 (1971): 361n21.

7. Julius Wellhausen, *Die kleinen Propheten übersetzt und erklärt* (Berlin: Reimer, 1898), 168; Paul F. Bloomhardt, "The Poems of Haggai," HUCA 5 (1928): 176; Friedrich Horst, *Die zwölf kleinen Propheten*, 2nd ed., HAT 1/14 (Tübingen: Mohr Siebeck, 1954), 204; Karl Elliger, *Das Buch der zwölf kleinen Propheten II: Die Propheten Nahum, Habakuk, Zephanja, Haggai, Sacharja, Maleachi*, ATD 25 (Göttingen: Vandenhoeck & Ruprecht, 1967), 85; Théophane Chary, *Aggée-Zacharie-Malachie*, SB (Paris: Gabalda, 1969), 20n2; Verhoef, *Haggai*, 54 (although he admits that the emendation "is probable but not absolutely necessary"); BHS.

textual support for this, and the presence of the *plene* form of עתה elsewhere (1:5; 2:3, 4, 15), do not support revocalizing the text. More importantly, it is not necessary: the MT makes sense, and consequently more recent commentators retain the MT reading as the *lectio difficilior*. Gelston suggests the repetition of עת caused confusion for the translators, which accounts for the different renditions.[8] On the basis of the parallelism with the conclusion of the verse ("the time for the house of YHWH to be built"), the translators of the versions, along with many commentators, appear to have decided that בא (either retained as an infinitive construct or revocalized to בָא) is acting as a finite verb with עת as the subject: "the time has not come." It is possible, though, that the infinitive is genitival ("the time of coming" or "the time to come"),[9] in which case the לא, which usually occurs immediately before the verb it negates,[10] is negating the entire phrase (the entire rest of the verse, in fact). Understood this way, the differences in the versions can be seen as interpretations of a syntactically ambiguous phrase, and not evidence that the text lacked this phrase or parts of it.[11]

³ וַיְהִי דְּבַר־יְהוָה בְּיַד־חַגַּי הַנָּבִיא לֵאמֹר:

⁴ הַעֵת לָכֶם אַתֶּם לָשֶׁבֶת בְּבָתֵּיכֶם ᵃ סְפוּנִים וְהַבַּיִת הַזֶּה חָרֵב:

⁵ וְעַתָּה כֹּה אָמַר יְהוָה צְבָאוֹת שִׂימוּ לְבַבְכֶם עַל דַּרְכֵיכֶם:

---

8. Anthony Gelston, *The Twelve Minor Prophets* (תרי עשר), BHQ 13 (Stuttgart: Deutsche Bibelgesellschaft, 2010), 130*–31*. The following agree: Willem A. M. Beuken, *Haggai-Sacharja 1-8: Studien zur Überlieferungsgeschichte der frühnachexilischen Prophetie* (Assen: Van Gorcum), 29n2; Peter R. Ackroyd, *Exile and Restoration: A Study of Hebrew Thought of the Sixth Century B.C.*, OTL (Philadelphia, PA: Westminster, 1968), 155n8; Amsler, *Aggée*, 21; Dominique Barthélemy, *CTAT*, OBO 50/3 (Fribourg: Éditions Universitairesl Göttingen: Vandenhoeck & Ruprecht, 1992), 3.923–24; Reventlow, *Haggai*, 12; John Kessler, "'T (le temps) en Aggée 1 2-4: Conflit théologique ou 'sagesse mondaine'?," VT 48 (1998): 558n4; idem, *Haggai*, 103n7, 244–45; Jakob Wöhrle, *Die frühen Sammlungen des Zwölfprophetenbuches: Entstehung und Komposition*, BZAW 360 (Berlin: de Gruyter, 2006), 295n27. James Nogalski suggests that, while the "strained syntax" of עת־בא may be a stylistic peculiarity, the verse is fine without the phrase. This indicates to him that it is likely to be an addition, probably added later as part of the larger redaction of the Twelve (*Literary Precursors to the Book of the Twelve*, BZAW 217 [Berlin: de Gruyter, 1993], 220–21). To my knowledge, no one has adopted this hypothesis.

9. GKC §114b.

10. GKC §152d notes that nominal clauses with a "substantival subject" (as here, with "time of coming" comprising the subject) are generally negated with לא. Gen 29:7 has an identical construction: לא עת האסף.

11. Gelston (*BHQ*, 112) characterizes them as interpretations of an ambiguous phrase, while suggesting in his notes (130*–31*) the possibility that they arose from translators' confusion. See the translation notes below for further discussion.

1:4a   בְּבָתֵּיכֶם — Some G mss.: ἐν οἴκοις (= Vg, Tg); OG and Syr agree with MT in including the second person suffix. Budde, along with several later scholars, accepted Dort's proposed emendation to בבתים.[12] The textual evidence for this proposal is provided by the lack of article for the following adjective, which one would expect if the noun were made definite by the suffix.[13] This is not always the case, however.[14] Wellhausen noted that ספונים is an adjective in the stative form, and can thus stand after the determined noun without an article.[15] More recent commentators have accepted the MT as well, arguing also that the suffix reinforces the clear emphasis on the 2mp audience addressed in the verse (לכם אתם).[16] Thus grammatical considerations as well as context support retaining the MT.

⁶ זְרַעְתֶּם הַרְבֵּה וְהָבֵא מְעָט אָכוֹל וְאֵין לְשָׂבְעָה שָׁתוֹ וְאֵין לְשָׁכְרָה לָבוֹשׁ וְאֵין לְחֹם לוֹ
וְהַמִּשְׂתַּכֵּר מִשְׂתַּכֵּרᵃ אֶל צְרוֹר נָקוּב:

⁷ כֹּה אָמַר יְהוָה צְבָאוֹת שִׂימוּ לְבַבְכֶם עַל דַּרְכֵיכֶם:ᵃ

⁸ עֲלוּ הָהָר וַהֲבֵאתֶם עֵץ וּבְנוּ הַבָּיִת וְאֶרְצֶה בּוֹ וְאֶכָּבֵדᵃ אָמַר יְהוָה:

1:6a   מִשְׂתַּכֵּר — OG has the aorist form συνήγαγεν (= Vg: congregavit); Tg and Syr = MT; Mur insufficient. BHS suggests emendation to ישתכר.[17] Meyers and Meyers argue that the occurrence of the participle twice in succession "does not fit well with the terse style of the previous bicola" and suggest omitting the second participle as a dittograph.[18] The past tense forms of OG and Vg do not argue for emendation, however, because both versions render all of the infinitives in the preceding clauses in the same way. There is thus no compelling reason for emendation.[19]

---

12. Karl Budde, "Zum Text der drei letzten kleinen Propheten," ZAW 26 (1906): 11; Mitchell, Haggai, 51; Horst, Zwölf kleinen Propheten, 204; Elliger, Zwölf kleinen Propheten, 85; BHS; Chary, Aggée, 20.

13. GKC §§125a; 127a; 126u.

14. See GKC §126y–aa.

15. Wellhausen, Kleinen Propheten, 168; GKC (§126z) and Joüon (§127a) cite this verse as an example of this form.

16. David L. Petersen, Haggai and Zechariah 1–8: A Commentary, OTL (Philadelphia, PA: Westminster, 1984), 48; Meyers and Meyers, Haggai, 23; Amsler, Aggée, 21; Wolff, Haggai, 30; Reventlow, Haggai, 8; Kessler, Haggai, 104n9; Gelston, BHQ, 131*.

17. Horst (Zwölf kleinen Propheten, 204) and Chary (Aggée, 20) accept this.

18. Meyers and Meyers, Haggai, 26. Their translation, however, appears to retain the word: "As for the hired hand, he works for a bag full of holes" (4).

19. See Mitchell, Haggai, 52; Verhoef, Haggai, 62; Amsler, Aggée, 21; Wolff, Haggai, 30; Kessler, Haggai, 105.

1:7a שִׂימוּ לְבַבְכֶם עַל דַּרְכֵיכֶם — Wellhausen argued that the repetition of this phrase from 1:5 interrupts the oracle, disturbing the connection between 1:7a and 1:8, and therefore should be removed as "falsch wiederholt."[20] Others who agree that the phrase disrupts the oracle have accepted Hoonacker's suggestion that it should be moved after 1:8.[21] There is no textual evidence for omitting or moving the phrase, however, and a majority of commentators accept the MT reading.[22] Analysis will show that the phrase has a rhetorical function in its present location.[23]

1:8a וְאֶכָּבֵד — MT: ואכבד (K). The Q renders this וְאֶכָּבְדָה (cohortative). The versions offer no reason to emend to the Q: Syr assimilates to context; Tg paraphrases; OG and Vg are indeterminate; Mur is insufficient.[24] The difference in sense between the cohortative of Q and the imperfect of K is minimal, in any case.[25] A number of scholars accordingly favor retaining the K and vocalizing as a *niphal*, which I have accepted here.[26]

[9] פְּנֹה אֶל הַרְבֵּה וְהִנֵּה לִמְעָט[a] וַהֲבֵאתֶם הַבַּיִת וְנָפַחְתִּי בוֹ יַעַן מֶה נְאֻם יְהוָה
צְבָאוֹת יַעַן בֵּיתִי אֲשֶׁר הוּא חָרֵב וְאַתֶּם רָצִים אִישׁ לְבֵיתוֹ:
[10] עַל כֵּן עֲלֵיכֶם[a] כָּלְאוּ שָׁמַיִם טָּל[b] וְהָאָרֶץ כָּלְאָה יְבוּלָהּ:

1:9a וְהִנֵּה לִמְעָט — MT: לִמְעָט הִנֵּה; OG: καὶ ἐγένετο ὀλίγα (= Syr and Tg); Vg supports MT (*et ecce factum est minus*); Mur = MT. Wellhausen argued that הנה must change to היה or the *lamed* of למעט be dropped, and accordingly, a number of commentators emend to הָיָה or הָיֹה to reflect the OG and to render the phrase less syntactically problematic.[27] Oth-

20. Wellhausen, *Kleinen Propheten*, 168. Accepting this were Marti, *Dodekapropheton*, 383; Elliger, *Zwölf kleinen Propheten*, 85–86; BHS.
21. Horst, *Zwölf kleinen Propheten*, 204; Chary, *Aggée*, 20; Amsler, *Aggée*, 21n6.
22. Budde, "Zum Text," 11; Mitchell, *Haggai*, 52; Beuken, *Haggai*, 20–21, 25–26; Rudolph, *Haggai*, 28; Petersen, *Haggai*, 41; Verhoef, *Haggai*, 63–64; Wolff, *Haggai*, 28, 45; Meyers and Meyers, *Haggai*, 3; Boda, "Haggai: Master Rhetorician," 300; Kessler, *Haggai*, 105n15. The question of how the phrase relates to the surrounding material will be addressed in the next chapter.
23. See chap. 4, p. 170.
24. Gelston, BHQ, 131*.
25. Rudolph, *Haggai*, 29; Reventlow, *Haggai*, 14n21; Gelston, BHQ, 131*.
26. Marti, *Dodekapropheton*, 383; Horst, *Zwölf kleinen Propheten*, 204; Chary, *Aggée*, 20; Meyers and Meyers, *Haggai*, 28; Amsler, *Aggée*, 22n1; Wolff, *Haggai*, 30; Kessler, *Haggai*, 105n8; Martin Hallaschka, *Haggai und Sacharja 1–8: Eine redaktionsgeschichtliche Untersuchung*, BZAW 411 (Berlin: de Gruyter, 2011), 27n89.

ers have suggested the *lamed* is emphatic,[28] and see no need for emendation.[29] Wolff states that the OG does not necessarily presuppose היה; it could also presuppose הנה.[30] This suggestion is unlikely, however, as the other instances of the Greek phrase in Haggai (1:3; 2:16, 20) translate a form of היה, and the same is true for the other thirteen occurrences in the OG of the Twelve as a whole.[31] Conversely, הנה, which occurs throughout the MT of the Twelve, is never translated ἐγένετο. Emendation to וְהָיָה, while retaining the *lamed*, results in the construction היה ל, a common idiom meaning "to become."[32] This accords well with the context ("you expected much but it turned into little").

1:10a עַל כֵּן עֲלֵיכֶם — OG: διὰ τοῦτο, lacking the second element; Syr lacks the first element; Mur and Vg = MT. While a number of commentators would omit, with OG, עליכם, many others accept the MT.[33] Barthélemy and Gelston note that the OG and Syr have each dropped an element through haplography, but they are *different* elements. This would seem to confirm that both elements were present in the *Vorlage*, which they shared.[34] Haplography would appear to explain the differences between the versions and the MT better than the alternative explanation that the MT resulted from dittography. As will be discussed in the translation notes below, the context also supports retaining the second element as part of the argument being put forth by the prophet (or composer of the text).

---

27. Wellhausen, *Kleinen Propheten*, 169; Marti, *Dodekapropheton*, 383; Budde, "Zum Text," 12; Horst, *Zwölf kleinen Propheten*, 204; Chary, *Aggée*, 20; BHS, Meyers and Meyers, *Haggai*, 29.

28. See *IBHS* 11.2.10i.

29. Mitchell, *Haggai*, 52; Steck, "Zu Haggai," 370n45; Rudolph, *Haggai*, 29; Verhoef, *Haggai*, 69–70; Wolff, *Haggai*, 30; Kessler, *Haggai*, 106n21; Gelston, *BHQ*, 131*. Rudolph (*Haggai*, 29), who accepts the MT, does not consider this reading of the *lamed* necessary.

30. Wolff, *Haggai*, 30.

31. Mic 1:1; Jonah 1:1, 4; 3:1; 4:8; Zech 4:8; 6:9; 7:1, 4, 8, 12; 8:1, 18.

32. "היה," *BDB* 226.

33. For omission: Wellhausen, *Kleinen Propheten*, 169; Marti, *Dodekapropheton*, 384; Mitchell, *Haggai*, 53 (it may be a dittograph or gloss); Chary, *Aggée*, 20; Beuken, *Haggai*, 188n1; Elliger, *Zwölf kleinen Propheten*, 85; BHS; Petersen, *Haggai*, 42 (perhaps). For accepting MT: Budde, "Zum Text," 12; Rudolph, *Haggai*, 30; Meyers and Meyers, *Haggai*, 30; Verhoef, *Haggai*, 72–73; Amsler, *Aggée*, 22n2; Barthélemy, *CTAT*, 925; Kessler, *Haggai*, 106n24; *BHQ*; Hallaschka, *Haggai*, 29n104. Wolff (*Haggai*, 30–31) suggests עליכם may have been added by a Dtr redactor. Kessler (*Haggai*, 106n24) accepts this as a possibility. There is no positive evidence to suggest it was not part of the HN.

34. Barthélemy, *CTAT*, 924–25; Gelston, *BHQ*, 131*.

1:10b טָלָם — MT: מִטָּל (= OG, Vg, Syr); Tg: מטרא. Although most of the versions appear to reflect the MT, many scholars have found the construction problematic enough to suggest emending to טלם or מטר. Others have suggested removing the *mem* altogether.[35] Those who would (re)move the *mem* argue that it serves no grammatical purpose in its present position. Meyers and Meyers, however, understand the *mem* as partitive, not only for טל, but also for יבולה (claiming the *mem* does "double duty").[36] Rudolph claims the *mem* cannot be partitive here and, further, emending to טלם renders the clause parallel with the following, which ends with יבולה.[37] Also in support of this emendation, Budde notes that there is a similar phrase in Zechariah 8:12: והארץ תתן את־יבולה והשמים יתנו טלם.[38] Although there is no textual support for emending to טלם, the suggestion is reasonable because the MT *is* grammatically problematic, as the construction seems to suggest that some unspecified thing is being withheld "from dew." The verb כלא appears in conjunction with מן in a number of places, and in none of them does the preposition govern the object or action being withheld, avoided, or prevented.[39] It is possible that the *mem*, which perhaps appeared in the MT as a dittograph of the final *mem* of שמים, should simply be dropped. I have instead accepted Rudolph's observation about parallel structure, such that each clause ends in a pronominal suffix. The minor emendation has the further advantage of being in conformity with the closely related text of Zechariah 8:12.

[11] וָאֶקְרָא חֹרֶב עַל־הָאָרֶץ וְעַל־הֶהָרִים וְעַל־הַדָּגָן וְעַל־הַתִּירוֹשׁ וְעַל־הַיִּצְהָר וְעַל[a] אֲשֶׁר תּוֹצִיא הָאֲדָמָה וְעַל־הָאָדָם וְעַל־הַבְּהֵמָה וְעַל כָּל־יְגִיעַ כַּפָּיִם:

---

35. טלם: Marti, *Dodekapropheton*, 384; Budde, "Zum Text," 12; Bloomhardt, "Poems," 179; Elliger, *Zwölf kleinen Propheten*, 85; Ackroyd, *Exile and Restoration*, 157n19; Rudolph, *Haggai*, 30 (perhaps); Amsler, *Aggée*, 22n3; Wolff, *Haggai*, 31; BHS (while accepting the possibility of מטר). מטר: Mitchell, *Haggai*, 53; Horst, *Zwölf kleinen Propheten*, 204; Chary, *Aggée*, 20; To strike *mem*: Wellhausen, *Kleinen Propheten*, 169. To retain the MT: Verhoef, *Haggai*, 73; Meyers and Meyers, *Haggai*, 30–31; Barthélemy, *CTAT*, 925; Kessler, *Haggai*, 106n25; Gelston, *BHQ*.

36. Meyers and Meyers, *Haggai*, 30–31. They explain that the partitive is used because the drought is not total; the heavens have only withheld their dew "in part." Kessler (*Haggai*, 106n26) accepts this argument. Both the explanation of the use of the partitive and the thesis of "double duty" seem forced.

37. Rudolph, *Haggai*, 30. Whether or not he is correct that the *mem* cannot be partitive here, his observation about the parallelism is apt.

38. Budde, "Zum Text," 12.

39. Gen 8:2; 23:6; Exod 36:6; 1 Sam 25:33; Pss 40:12; 119:101.

1:11a וְעַל — OG: καὶ ὅσα; Vg: *quaecumque*, which Gelston and others believe may presuppose כל rather than עַל; Syr and Tg appear to presuppose both.[40] Accordingly, many scholars suggest the כל has dropped out from haplography.[41] The OG and Vg, however, do not necessarily presuppose כל. The other occurrences of ὅσα in the Twelve, for example, are renderings of אשר only.[42] While it is true that in the Vg *quaecumque* often corresponds to כל אשר, it also frequently translates אשר only.[43] Conversely, the two other occurrences of כל אשר in the Twelve are rendered with πᾶς in the Greek and *omnia* in the Latin.[44] This, as well as the fact that כל at the end of this verse is rendered with πᾶς and *omnia* in OG and Vg, make it less likely that the *Vorlage(n)* of these translators had כל instead of עַל.[45]

[12] וַיִּשְׁמַע זְרֻבָּבֶל בֶּן שַׁלְתִּיאֵל וִיהוֹשֻׁעַ בֶּן יְהוֹצָדָק הַכֹּהֵן הַגָּדוֹל וְכֹל שְׁאֵרִית הָעָם בְּקוֹל יְהוָה אֱלֹהֵיהֶם וְעַל דִּבְרֵי חַגַּי הַנָּבִיא כַּאֲשֶׁר שְׁלָחוֹ יְהוָה אֱלֹהֵיהֶם[a] וַיִּירְאוּ הָעָם מִפְּנֵי יְהוָה:

[13] וַיֹּאמֶר חַגַּי מַלְאַךְ יְהוָה בְּמַלְאֲכוּת יְהוָה[a] לָעָם לֵאמֹר אֲנִי אִתְּכֶם נְאֻם יְהוָה:

[14] וַיָּעַר יְהוָה אֶת רוּחַ זְרֻבָּבֶל בֶּן שַׁלְתִּיאֵל פַּחַת יְהוּדָה וְאֶת רוּחַ יְהוֹשֻׁעַ בֶּן יְהוֹצָדָק הַכֹּהֵן הַגָּדוֹל וְאֶת רוּחַ כֹּל שְׁאֵרִית הָעָם וַיָּבֹאוּ וַיַּעֲשׂוּ מְלָאכָה בְּבֵית יְהוָה צְבָאוֹת אֱלֹהֵיהֶם:

[15] בְּיוֹם עֶשְׂרִים וְאַרְבָּעָה לַחֹדֶשׁ בַּשִּׁשִּׁי

1:12a אֱלֹהֵיהֶם — OG: πρὸς αὐτούς; some G mss.: ο θεος αυτων προς αυτους (= Vg, Syr, one ms. of Tg); Mur and Tg = MT. The versions may reflect a text that had אליהם אלהיהם, or may merely be giving the sense of the verse.[46] The translator of OG could have misread the text. All these

40. Gelston, BHQ, 131*.
41. Wellhausen, *Kleinen Propheten*, 37; Marti, *Dodekapropheton*, 384; Budde, "Zum Text," 12; Mitchell, *Haggai*, 53; Horst, *Zwölf kleinen Propheten*, 204; Chary, *Aggée*, 20; BHS; Rudolph, *Haggai*, 30; Meyers and Meyers, *Haggai*, 33; Amsler, *Aggée*, 22n4. Wolff (*Haggai*, 31), Barthélemy (*CTAT*, 926–27), Kessler (*Haggai*, 106n29), and Gelston (*BHQ*, 131*) retain MT.
42. Hos 2:14; Jonah 2:10; Zeph 3:7; Zech 1:6; 14:18, 19. Hosea 2:7 has πάντα ὅσα, which appears to be a translator's addition.
43. Gen 34:11; Exod 23:16; 1 Kgs 16:5; Jonah 2:10; 2 Chr 6:16 and others.
44. Joel 3:5: πας ος; omnia; Zeph 3:7: παντα οσα; omnia.
45. Why neither rendered the עַל remains, however, unexplained.
46. On the basis of the OG, the following change to אליהם: Wellhausen, *Kleinen Propheten*, 169; Marti, *Dodekapropheton*, 384; Elliger, *Zwölf kleinen Propheten*, 85; Horst, *Zwölf kleinen Propheten*, 204; Chary, *Aggée* 22; Petersen, *Haggai*, 55; Amsler, *Aggée*, 20n7; Wolff, *Haggai*, 31. Bloomhardt ("Poems," 181), Rudolph (*Haggai*, 30), and Meyers and Meyers (*Haggai*, 4) read with the other versions and add אליהם. Kessler (*Haggai*, 107n34) and Hallaschka (*Haggai*, 35) retain the MT.

options are plausible, but internal contextual evidence (slightly) favors retaining אלהיהם, as the term is found earlier in this verse and at the end of 1:14.

1:13a בְּמַלְאֲכוּת יְהוָה — Mur, Syr, and Tg = MT; θ': ἐν ἀγγέλοις κυρίου. The phrase missing in OG; Gelston suggests perhaps an instance of homoioteleuton. The word appears nowhere else in the HB, adding to the cause for skepticism. Yet its presence in all other versions, as well as its integral function within the verse (as I will show in chapter 4) suggests it is original to the HT.

2:1ᵃ בִּשְׁנַת שְׁתַּיִם לְדָרְיָוֶשׁ הַמֶּלֶךְ: בַּשְּׁבִיעִי בְּעֶשְׂרִים וְאֶחָד לַחֹדֶשׁ הָיָה דְּבַר יְהוָה בְּיַד־חַגַּיᵃ הַנָּבִיא לֵאמֹר: 2 אֱמָר נָא אֶל זְרֻבָּבֶל בֶּן שַׁלְתִּיאֵל פַּחַת יְהוּדָה וְאֶל יְהוֹשֻׁעַ בֶּן יְהוֹצָדָק הַכֹּהֵן הַגָּדוֹל וְאֶל שְׁאֵרִית הָעָם לֵאמֹר: 3 מִי בָכֶם הַנִּשְׁאָר אֲשֶׁר רָאָה אֶת הַבַּיִת הַזֶּה בִּכְבוֹדוֹ הָרִאשׁוֹן וּמָה אַתֶּם רֹאִים אֹתוֹ עַתָּה הֲלוֹא כָמֹהוּ כְּאַיִן בְּעֵינֵיכֶם: 4 וְעַתָּה חֲזַק זְרֻבָּבֶל נְאֻם יְהוָה וַחֲזַק יְהוֹשֻׁעַ בֶּן יְהוֹצָדָק הַכֹּהֵן הַגָּדוֹל וַחֲזַק כָּל עַם הָאָרֶץ נְאֻם יְהוָה וַעֲשׂוּ כִּי אֲנִי אִתְּכֶם נְאֻם יְהוָה צְבָאוֹת: 5 [*] וְרוּחִי עֹמֶדֶת בְּתוֹכְכֶם אַל תִּירָאוּ:

1:15a   See the redaction-critical discussion below for the division of this verse.

2:1a בְּיַד חַגַּי (= OG, Vg, Tg, Syr); Mur: אל חגי. The majority of scholars believe that Mur has likely assimilated to 2:10, 20, as well as improved the sense of the verse, as the prophet is the recipient, not the intermediary, of a message. The versions all support the MT reading. Thus most scholars would retain the MT as the *lectio difficilior*.[47]

2:5[*]   The first half of the verse has been removed as a later addition to the HN. See redaction critical discussion below.

47. Beuken, *Haggai*, 51; Petersen, *Haggai*, 60–61; Verhoef, *Haggai*, 94–95; Amsler, *Aggée*, 31n1; Wolff, *Haggai*, 70; Meyers and Meyers, *Haggai*, 47; Kessler, *Haggai*, 159n1; Wöhrle, *Frühen Sammlungen*, 286; Gelston, *BHQ*, 132*. Rudolph is one of the few who accepts the Mur reading as reflecting the "original" (*Haggai*, 40).

⁶ כִּי כֹה אָמַר יְהוָה צְבָאוֹת עוֹד אַחַת מְעַט הִיא^a וַאֲנִי מַרְעִישׁ אֶת הַשָּׁמַיִם וְאֶת הָאָרֶץ וְאֶת הַיָּם וְאֶת הֶחָרָבָה:

⁷ וְהִרְעַשְׁתִּי אֶת־כָּל־הַגּוֹיִם וּבָאוּ חֶמְדַּת^a כָּל הַגּוֹיִם וּמִלֵּאתִי אֶת הַבַּיִת הַזֶּה כָּבוֹד אָמַר יְהוָה צְבָאוֹת:

⁸ לִי הַכֶּסֶף וְלִי הַזָּהָב נְאֻם יְהוָה צְבָאוֹת:

⁹ גָּדוֹל יִהְיֶה כְּבוֹד הַבַּיִת הַזֶּה הָאַחֲרוֹן מִן הָרִאשׁוֹן אָמַר יְהוָה צְבָאוֹת וּבַמָּקוֹם הַזֶּה אֶתֵּן שָׁלוֹם נְאֻם יְהוָה צְבָאוֹת:^a

2:6a עוֹד אַחַת מְעַט הִיא — OG and Syr omit מעט היא; Vg, T, Mur = MT. Most commentators read with the MT.[48] A few read with the OG,[49] but Gelston suggests the translation either arises from a simpler rendering or from a lack of understanding of the Hebrew.[50] Rudolph accepts Sellin's suggestion that the translators dropped the last two words (which mean something like, "and it will be soon") because they had not come true.[51] Wellhausen opted to remove אחת and Mitchell removed both אחת and היא, but there is no textual evidence for either emendation.[52] Because there is no reason to suppose the MT's unusual phrase arises from scribal error, the evidence suggests the MT should be retained.

2:7a חֶמְדַּת — OG: τὰ ἐκλεκτὰ; Vg: desideratus; Syr and Tg = MT. A number of scholars advocate revocalizing as plural (חֲמֻדֹת) because of the OG and the plural verb of the MT.[53] Others note that חֶמְדַּת is a collective plural, which explains both the plural verb in MT and the plural noun in the OG.[54] Emendation of MT is unnecessary.

48. Ackroyd, *Exile and Restoration*, 153–54; Chary, *Aggée*, 26–27; *BHS*; Wolff, *Haggai*, 71; Barthélemy, *CTAT*, 928–29; Reventlow, *Haggai*, 21n35; Petersen, *Haggai*, 61–62; Meyers and Meyers, *Haggai*, 52; Verhoef, *Haggai*, 101–2; Amsler, *Aggée*, 32, 34; Kessler, *Haggai*, 160n11; Gelston, *BHQ*, 132*.

49. Horst, *Zwölf kleinen Propheten*, 206; Elliger, *Zwölf kleinen Propheten*, 91n5 (although he is ambivalent); Rudolph, *Haggai*, 40–41.

50. Gelston, *BHQ*, 132*.

51. Rudolph, *Haggai*, 41. Kessler also considers this possible (*Haggai*, 160n11).

52. Wellhausen, *Kleinen Propheten*, 170. Marti accepts this (*Dodekapropheton*, 386), as does Mitchell (*Haggai*, 65).

53. Wellhausen, *Kleinen Propheten*, 170; Marti, *Dodekapropheton*, 386; Bloomhardt, "Poems," 159, 170, 184; Mitchell, *Haggai*, 65; Horst, *Zwölf kleinen Propheten*, Chary, *Aggée*, 26; Ackroyd, *Exile and Restoration*, 161n38; Elliger, *Zwölf kleinen Propheten*, 91; *BHS*; Meyers and Meyers, *Haggai*, 53; Wolff, *Haggai*, 71.

54. Rudolph, *Haggai*, 41; Reventlow, *Haggai*, 18, 22; Kessler, *Haggai*, 161n14; Gelston, *BHQ*, 132*.

2:9a   OG adds: καὶ εἰρήνην ψυχῆς εἰς περιποίησιν παντὶ τῷ κτίζοντι τοῦ ἀναστῆσαι τὸν ναὸν τοῦτον; Vg, Tg, Syr = MT. As all versions agree with the MT, almost all scholars have regarded it as a gloss. Wellhausen, however, considered the OG to be a translation from *Vorlage*, a position Budde accepted as plausible, suggesting that the MT breaks off rather suddenly before the oracle formula.[55] Ackroyd thought that perhaps the OG reflected a Hebrew gloss (such as we see in 2:5aα), which either dropped out again or was transmitted in a different manuscript tradition that is no longer extant.[56] See further argument against accepting this, or the OG plus in 2:14, as original to the HN in the redaction-critical discussion of 2:5aα below.

10 בְּעֶשְׂרִים וְאַרְבָּעָה לַתְּשִׁיעִי בִּשְׁנַת שְׁתַּיִם לְדָרְיָוֶשׁ הָיָה דְבַר־יְהוָה אֶל־חַגַּי הַנָּבִיא לֵאמֹר: 11 כֹּה אָמַר יְהוָה צְבָאוֹת שְׁאַל־נָא אֶת־הַכֹּהֲנִים תּוֹרָה לֵאמֹר:

12 הֵן יִשָּׂא־אִישׁ בְּשַׂר־קֹדֶשׁ בִּכְנַף בִּגְדוֹ וְנָגַע בִּכְנָפוֹ אֶל־הַלֶּחֶם וְאֶל־הַנָּזִיד וְאֶל־הַיַּיִן וְאֶל־שֶׁמֶן וְאֶל־כָּל־מַאֲכָל הֲיִקְדָּשׁ וַיַּעֲנוּ הַכֹּהֲנִים וַיֹּאמְרוּ לֹא:

13 וַיֹּאמֶר חַגַּי אִם־יִגַּע טְמֵא־נֶפֶשׁ בְּכָל־אֵלֶּה הֲיִטְמָא וַיַּעֲנוּ הַכֹּהֲנִים וַיֹּאמְרוּ יִטְמָא:

14 וַיַּעַן חַגַּי וַיֹּאמֶר

כֵּן הָעָם־הַזֶּה וְכֵן־הַגּוֹי הַזֶּה לְפָנַי נְאֻם־יְהוָה

וְכֵן כָּל־מַעֲשֵׂה יְדֵיהֶם וַאֲשֶׁר יַקְרִיבוּ שָׁם טָמֵא הוּא:[a]

15 וְעַתָּה שִׂימוּ־נָא לְבַבְכֶם מִן־הַיּוֹם הַזֶּה וָמָעְלָה מִטֶּרֶם שׂוּם־אֶבֶן אֶל־אֶבֶן בְּהֵיכַל יְהוָה:

16 מָה הֱיִיתֶם[a] בָּא[b] אֶל־עֲרֵמַת עֶשְׂרִים וְהָיְתָה עֲשָׂרָה בָּא[b] אֶל־הַיֶּקֶב לַחְשֹׂף חֲמִשִּׁים פּוּרָה[c] וְהָיְתָה עֶשְׂרִים:

2:16a   מָה הֱיִיתֶם — MT: מְהִיוֹתָם; OG: τίνες ἦτε; Vg: *cum accederitis* (= Syr, Tg). The scholarly consensus is that the MT is incomprehensible and is probably corrupt. Two main suggestions for emendation are מִי הֱיִיתֶם and מָה הֱיִיתֶם.[57] It is perhaps slightly easier to understand how a scribe could render מָה הֱיִיתֶם as the present MT, and so I have chosen this

55. Wellhausen, *Kleinen Propheten*, 170; Budde, "Zum Text," 14.
56. Peter R. Ackroyd, "Some Interpretive Glosses in the Book of Haggai," *JJS* 7 (1956): 164–65.
57. Favoring מי: Budde, "Zum Text," 14–15; Bloomhardt, "Poems," 188; Horst, *Zwölf kleinen Propheten*, 206; Barthélemy, *CTAT*, 929–30; Kessler, *Haggai*, 198n11; Gelston, *BHQ*, 132*. Favoring מה: Marti, *Dodekapropheton*, 389; Ackroyd, *Exile and Restoration*, 128n4; Beuken, *Haggai*, 211; Chary, *Aggée*, 22; *BHS*; Petersen, *Haggai*, 86; Meyers and Meyers, *Haggai*, 48; Wöhrle, *Frühen Sammlungen*, 306n65. The OG presupposes one or the other.

option, recognizing that מִי הֱיִיתֶם is also possible.[58] Both options ask approximately the same rhetorical question.

2:16b בָּא — The use of infinitives in similar discourse in 1:6, 9 has led many commentators to suggest emending both instances of בָא to בֹא.[59] There is no textual basis for this emendation, however, and the MT makes good sense if the verb is understood as impersonal.[60]

2:16c פּוּרָה — OG: μετρητάς; Vg: lagoenas; Tg: גרבין דחמר The uncertain meaning of this rare word (occurring only here and in Isa 63:3) probably explains the versions.[61] Some have suggested emending to מְפוּרָה, the *mem* having fallen out from haplography (the previous word being חמשים).[62] This may be the case (although Budde[63] argues that, if that were true, the Hebrew would have been מִן־הַפּוּרָה), but there is no textual evidence to support this, and the MT can be understood as it is. See translation notes below for further discussion.

$$\text{הִכֵּיתִי אֶתְכֶם בַּשִּׁדָּפוֹן וּבַיֵּרָקוֹן וּבַבָּרָד אֵת כָּל מַעֲשֵׂה יְדֵיכֶם} \quad {}^{17}$$
$$\text{וְאֵין אֶתְכֶם אֲנִי}^{a} \text{ נְאֻם יְהוָה:}$$

2:17a וְאֵין אֶתְכֶם אֲנִי — MT: וְאֵין אֶתְכֶם אֵלַי; OG: καὶ οὐκ ἐπεστρέψατε πρός με (= Syr); Vg: *et non fuit in vobis qui reverteretur ad me*; Tg: וליתיכון תיבין לפלחני; Mur: [כם א]. Arguing that the MT is incomprehensible, some scholars have recommended emendations. The most common suggestion is to change אתכם to שבתם, for two related reasons.[64] The first four

58. Elliger, *Zwölf kleinen Propheten*, 89, Amsler, *Aggée*, 28n2; Wolff, *Haggai*, 58; Reventlow also acknowledge that both options are equally plausible (*Haggai*, 24).
59. Marti, *Dodekapropheton*, 389; Budde, "Zum Text," 15; Horst, *Zwölf kleinen Propheten*, 206; Ackroyd, *Exile and Restoration*, 158n25 (although he is ambivalent); Chary, *Aggée*; BHS; Petersen, *Haggai*, 86 (although he is ambivalent); Wolff, *Haggai*, 58; Kessler, *Book of Haggai*, 198n12.
60. Bloomhardt, "Poems," 189; Rudolph, *Haggai*, 45; Amsler, *Aggée*, 28n3; Gelston, BHQ, 133*; and Hallaschka, *Haggai*, 85n479 also accept the MT (although Hallaschka is ambivalent).
61. Gelston, BHQ, 133*. The following have suggested that the word is a gloss on יקב: Marti, *Dodekapropheton*, 389; Mitchell, *Haggai*, 74–75; Horst, *Zwölf kleinen Propheten*, 206; Elliger, *Zwölf kleinen Propheten*, 89; Chary, *Aggée*, 22; Reventlow, *Haggai*, 24. Wolff (*Haggai*, 58) Verhoef (*Haggai*, 111n9); and Barthélemy (*CTAT*, 929–30) suggest that a rare word (in the biblical texts) would hardly have been introduced as a gloss on a more common word.
62. Wellhausen, *Kleinen Propheten*, 171; Bloomhardt, "Poems," 189; Ackroyd, *Exile and Restoration*, 158n26; Amsler, *Aggée*, 28n5.
63. Budde, "Zum Text," 15.
64. Mitchell, *Haggai*, 75 (אין שבתם); Chary, *Aggée*, 22 (ולא שבתם); Marti, *Dodekapropheton*, 389 (either of the preceding options). Rudolph (*Haggai*, 46) also considers the MT clause incomprehensible, but opts for the more modest emendation of אלי to אני (see below).

words of 2:17 replicate Amos 4:9aα, a verse that ends with ולא שבתם
עדי נאם יהוה (4:9b). In addition, all of the ancient versions reflect in
some way the concept of "return," a reading reflected in many modern
translations as well.[65] Assuming that Haggai 2:17 is consciously quoting Amos 4:9, these commentators have suggested that the Haggai text
originally ended much the same way as the Amos verse, a conclusion
the versions would appear to confirm. While it is possible that Haggai 2:17 is drawing on Amos 4:9aα, this alone is not enough to suggest
emending the MT to reflect the end of the Amos verse.[66] In the first
place, Haggai 2:17 is not quoting Amos 4:9 in its entirety; Amos 4:9aβ
is not present. Haggai 2:17 also has additional material not found in
Amos. We cannot assume, then, that the end of Haggai 2:17 is meant to
echo Amos 4:9b. Second, it is difficult to see how ולא שבתם עדי could
have become corrupted into ואין אתכם אלי.[67] The usual causes of corruption, such as graphic or phonological similarity, ligatures, metathe-
sis, haplography, or dittography, would not explain the differences
between the two, even if we limit the putative change to שבתם for
אתכם.[68] An unusual or unaccountable change in one letter is possible,
but such changes in at least three consecutive letters is implausible.[69]

More recent commentators have maintained that, while unusual,
the MT is nevertheless comprehensible.[70] Gelston, for example, considers the clause a "nominal sentence" (i.e., a verbless clause), and points
to Jer 15:1 (אין נפשי אל העם הזה) as an example of a similar construction.[71] For this parallel to hold, however, אֶתְכֶם must function as the

65. See in English, for example, JPS, NRSV, NABR, NIV. The same is reflected in translations into French, German, Spanish, etc.

66. For a discussion of the possible use of Amos 4:9aα in Haggai 2:17 see below, pp. 44–46.

67. Assuming that the change was unintentional, which we must do if we accept the claim that the resulting text is incoherent.

68. The proposed change would probably require others, especially replacing ואין with ולא, since inde-pendent verbal clauses are negated with לא rather than אין, which is reserved for verbless clauses (which include those with participles). *IBHS* 39.3.3a–b; Joüon §160; GKC §152. It would also bring it into closer conformity with the Amos verse.

69. Tov notes, for example, no instances in early Hebrew script or square script of a *shin/sin* being mistaken for an *alef*, a *bet* for a *tav*, or a *tav* for a *kaf*. See Emanuel Tov, *Textual Criticism of the Hebrew Bible*, 3rd ed. (Minneapolis, MN: Fortress Press, 2012), 222–34. For this reason S. R. Driver calls emendation to ולא שבתם "violent" (*The Minor Prophets: Nahum, Habakkuk, Zephaniah, Haggai, Zechariah, Malachi*, Century Bible [New York, NY: Frowde, 1906], 167).

70. Beuken, *Haggai*, 210n4; Petersen, *Haggai*, 86–87; Meyers and Meyers, *Haggai*, 61; Verhoef, *Haggai*, 128; Amsler, *Aggée*, 28n7; Barthélemy, *CTAT*, 931–32; Gelston, *BHQ*, 133*; Hallaschka, *Haggai*, 85n485.

71. Gelston, *BHQ*, 133*. NRSV translates this phrase as "my heart would not turn toward this people"

subject of the clause (as נפשי does in Jer 15:1), since verbless clauses must have a subject and a predicate, and in this case אלי only makes sense as the predicate.[72] Is this grammatically possible? Waltke and O'Connor point to two examples (Josh 22:17 and 2 Kgs 10:15) in which את marks the subject of verbless clauses, and suggest that Haggai 2:17 is a third. Thus, while אֶתְכֶם normally signifies a 2mp object, here we are to read it as a 2mp subject.[73] But others have accounted for these examples in ways that do not support the proposed reading here, making this expedient grammatically doubtful.[74] Although many commentators have been willing to accept this reading, it is not particularly plausible.

A better solution is Sellin's suggestion that אֶתְכֶם אֵלַי is a corruption of an original אֶתְכֶם אֲנִי.[75] This reading has significant advantages. The resulting clause is comprehensible and grammatically unproblematic: וְאֵין אֶתְכֶם אֲנִי.[76] It requires the emendation of only one letter of the consonantal text (as opposed to at least three for the emendation proposals noted above). The phrase אתכם/אתך אנכי/אני is attested in several places.[77] In fact, apart from Haggai 1:13 and 2:4, the subject always fol-

---

and JPS renders it "I would not be won over to that people." The OG has ουκ εστιν η ψυχη μου προς αυτους εξαποστειλον τον λαον τουτον.

72. A predicate in a verbless clause can be a noun, an adjective or participle, a numeral, a pronoun, or an adverb, which can be formed with a preposition. Such an adverb specifies "time, place, quality, possessor, &c." (GKC §141b; see also Joüon §154). Driver took אל to mean here "with," "on the side of" or "for," translating the clause as, "yet were ye not towards me" (*Minor Prophets*, 167). Driver cites as examples of this usage 2 Kgs 6:11: מי משלנו אל מלך ישראל; and Ezek 36:9: הנני אליכם. Other scholars have accepted this reading. See, for example, Verhoef (*Haggai*, 128): "and yet you did not turn to me" and Kessler (*Haggai*, 200n20): "but you did not return to me."

73. *IBHS* 10.3.2b–c. All the commentators who accept the MT likewise take אֶתְכֶם to be the subject of the clause.

74. For Josh 22:17, Joüon (§125j) takes the את to be a *nota accusativa* marking an accusative of limitation. GKC (§117aa) does the same, construing המעט לנו as equivalent to a verb of deficiency (*verbum inopiae*), which takes עון as an object. T. Muraoka accepts this reading also (*Emphatic Words and Structures in Biblical Hebrew* [Jerusalem: Magnes; Leiden: Brill, 1985], 156). Not being able to find any other explanation for the use of the את in 2 Kgs 10:15, Muraoka suggests there is no alternative but to emend and, following the lead of the OG, corrects it to את הלבבב ישר לבבי (*Emphatic Words*, 157). The point here is not that these solutions are correct, but that the use of את in these verses is not straightforward enough to take it as evidence to support the MT reading.

75. Sellin, *Zwölfprophetenbuch*, 407. This reading is accepted by Rudolph, who translates the clause, ". . . und ich war nicht mit euch . . ." (*Haggai*, 44, 46).

76. One would normally expect the pronoun to occur as a suffix of the negative particle (אתכם אינני) rather than independently, as here (see GKC §152n). The placement of the particle alone at the beginning of the clause before אתכם allows for emphasis on the negation of presence. See further discussion of this verse in chap. 5.

77. The clause כי אתכם/אתך אנכי/אני occurs at Gen 26:24; Isa 43:5; Jer 1:8, 19; 15:20; 30:11; 42:11; 46:28. In Isa 41:10, the clause likewise follows P-S order, although here the preposition is different: כי

lows the predicate, as here. Finally, the larger context supports this reading. As Rudolph notes, it serves as a counterpoint to the divine claim in 1:13 and 2:4 that אני אתכם. This is an important observation, the full force of which I will develop in the rhetorical analysis (chap. 5).

19 שִׂימוּ נָא לְבַבְכֶם מִן הַיּוֹם הַזֶּה וָמָעְלָה מִיּוֹם עֶשְׂרִים וְאַרְבָּעָה לַתְּשִׁיעִי לְמִן הַיּוֹם
אֲשֶׁר יֻסַּד הֵיכַל יְהוָה שִׂימוּ לְבַבְכֶם:

20 הַעוֹד הַזֶּרַע בַּמְּגוּרָה וְעַד הַגֶּפֶן[a] וְהַתְּאֵנָה וְהָרִמּוֹן וְעֵץ הַזַּיִת לֹא נָשָׂא מִן הַיּוֹם
הַזֶּה אֲבָרֵךְ:

2:19a וְעַד — OG: καὶ εἰ ἔτι (= Vg, Tg); Syr retains copula only; the OG, Vg, and Tg appear to have read the Hebrew as וְעֹד. Assuming that this is the "correct" reading of the consonantal text, a number of commentators have emended accordingly.[78] A smaller number have argued that the versions are assimilating to the עוֹד at the beginning of the verse.[79] As it stands, the MT makes sense (they argue), and means "not even" (citing 2 Sam 17:22; Job 25:5; Gen 6:7 as similar constructions).[80] Other options have been offered. Citing Jonah 4:2; Job 1:18; and Nehemiah 7:3, Rendsburg argues that עַד here reflects LBH under the influence of Aramaic, and means the same as עוֹד, namely "still, while."[81] As the unvocalized text can be read either way, there are a number of approaches to the problem. The translators may have "misread" the text (reading עוֹד when they "should" have read עַד); they may have "read" עַד but understood it to mean "yet" and translated accordingly; the Masoretes may have vocalized the text "correctly" (that is, according to the inten-

---

עמָךְ אני. Only in Gen 28:15, which features עם instead of את, do we find a case of S-P when the subject is the deity: אנכי עמָך.

78. Marti, *Dodekapropheton*, 390; Budde, "Zum Text," 16; Mitchell, *Haggai*, 76; Bloomhardt, "Poems," 190; Horst, *Zwölf kleinen Propheten*, 206; Ackroyd, *Exile and Restoration*, 158; Chary, *Aggée*, 24; Rudolph, *Haggai*, 44, 46; Petersen, *Haggai*, 86–87; Meyers and Meyers, *Haggai*, 48; Verhoef, *Haggai*, 111n12; Wolff, *Haggai*, 59.

79. Amsler, *Aggée*, 29n1; Barthélemy, *CTAT*, 932–33; Gelston, *BHQ*, 133*; Kessler, *Haggai*, 200n27. Amsler states that emendation to עוֹד would result in a syntactical structure not usual for that adverb, although he does not elaborate on this.

80. Gelston, *BHQ*, 133*; Amsler, *Aggée*, 29n1. Similarly, *HALOT* cites this construction (along with Job 25:5) as an example of an expression of measure or degree, translating עד . . . לא as "not once" (III.4).

81. Gary Rendsburg notes that this use of עַד occurs also in BH in 2 Kgs 9:22; Ps 141:10; Judg 3:26; 1 Sam 14:19 and other places as a northern or Benjaminite dialectical variation. The use of this form immediately after the use of עוֹד—seen also in Job 1:16, 17 and 1:18—is, according to Rendsburg, an example of morphological variation or possibly "neologistic usage" ("Late Biblical Hebrew in the Book of Haggai" [forthcoming], 6 and n. 9).

tion of the composer of the text); or, the Masoretes may have vocalized it "incorrectly." Kessler argues that, given the *plene* spelling of עוד elsewhere (2:6; 2:19a), it is unlikely that עוד would have been spelled defectively here.[82] While orthography is not always consistent even within the same context,[83] the text of Haggai displays almost complete consistency in this regard, and thus this may be taken as internal evidence against emending to עד, on the assumption that if the composer had meant עוד, he would have written it *plene*. On the other hand, Tov has argued that the *Vorlage* of the OG was generally more "defective" than the MT.[84] This suggests the possibility that all of the forms of this word were originally "defective," and only later were the forms in the proto-MT text tradition made *plene*. The present form would then reflect an exegetical tradition that, for whatever reason, understood the word as עד rather than עוד. Rendsburg's observation that עד means "while" (as in "during the same time as") in several instances is relevant here.[85] Accepting that meaning here, we arrive at: "Is there still seed in the grain pit, while the vine, the fig, the pomegranate and the olive tree have not produced?" The meaning of the question itself will be explored in the course of the rhetorical analysis.

20 וַיְהִי דְבַר־יְהוָה שֵׁנִית אֶל־חַגַּי בְּעֶשְׂרִים וְאַרְבָּעָה לַחֹדֶשׁ לֵאמֹר:

21 אֱמֹר אֶל־זְרֻבָּבֶל פַּחַת־יְהוּדָה לֵאמֹר אֲנִי מַרְעִישׁ אֶת־הַשָּׁמַיִם וְאֶת־הָאָרֶץ:

22 וְהָפַכְתִּי כִּסֵּא מַמְלָכוֹת וְהִשְׁמַדְתִּי חֹזֶק מַמְלְכוֹתᵃ הַגּוֹיִם וְהָפַכְתִּי מֶרְכָּבָה וְרֹכְבֶיהָ וְיָרְדוּ סוּסִים וְרֹכְבֵיהֶם אִישׁ בְּחֶרֶב אָחִיו:

23 בַּיּוֹם הַהוּא נְאֻם־יְהוָה צְבָאוֹת אֶקָּחֲךָ זְרֻבָּבֶל בֶּן־שְׁאַלְתִּיאֵל עַבְדִּי נְאֻם־יְהוָה וְשַׂמְתִּיךָ כַּחוֹתָם כִּי־בְךָ בָחַרְתִּי נְאֻם יְהוָה צְבָאוֹת:

2:22a מַמְלָכוֹת = OG, Tg, Vg, Syr, Mur. Several scholars would remove this as intrusive, preferring חזק הגוים.[86] Yet all of the versions agree

82. Kessler, *Haggai*, 200n27.
83. Tov, *Textual Criticism*, 213–16.
84. Emanuel Tov, *The Text-Critical Use of the Septuagint in Biblical Research*, 2nd ed. (JBS 8; Jerusalem: Simor, 1997), 144–45.
85. See Judg 3:26; 1 Sam 14:19; 2 Kgs 9:22; Jonah 4:2; Ps 141:10; Job 1:18; Neh 7:3.
86. See *BHS*; Horst, *Haggai*, 208; Chary, *Aggée*, 34; Mitchell, *Haggai*, 78–79; Amsler, *Aggée*, 40n3; Wolff, *Haggai*, 98; Elliger, *Zwölf kleinen Propheten*, 96. Petersen (*Haggai*, 96–97) thinks it was an early dittographic expansion, which is why it is reflected in all the versions and in Mur.

with the MT, and the phrase makes sense as it stands. There is no reason to emend.[87]

Composition of the Haggai Narrative

The present scholarly consensus is that the book of Haggai is the result of a "fundamental and systematic redaction"[88] in which pre-existing materials, widely understood to stem from the prophet himself, were placed within a narrative framework by a composer to form the HN.[89] That consensus does not extend to the content of the pre-HN materials or of later redactional interventions. In this section we will examine current models of the formation of the book of Haggai, particularly proposals concerning post-HN additions to the text. The models fall into two basic categories. The "traditional" model holds that a single redaction produced the HN, which subsequently received only minor additions to its content. One significant variation of this model maintains that part of this content was rearranged at some point. Some recent models are more complex, positing a much attenuated HN that later underwent two or more large expansions.

Traditional Model(s)

Most scholars hold that the *content* of the present book of Haggai goes back to its original composition as the HN, with only minor subsequent additions.[90] The text is typically divided into the pre-redactional

---

87. Kessler, *Haggai*, 219n5; Meyers and Meyers, *Haggai*, 67; Barthélemy, *CTAT*, 933–34.

88. Petersen, *Haggai*, 38.

89. Otto Eissfeldt argued that it was likely that the prophet himself composed the entire text, choosing to refer to himself in the third person to "enhance the impression of the complete objectivity of his report" (*The Old Testament: An Introduction*, trans. Peter R. Ackroyd [New York, NY: Harper & Row, 1965], 428). Meyers and Meyers (*Haggai*, xlvii) suggest that "it is not inconceivable" that Haggai (and Zechariah) compiled their respective works and introduced their work with third person references: "Nothing that we have discovered in the two prophets has proved definitive in arguing against the assumption that Haggai and Zechariah were the authors of virtually all that is attributed to them." This remains the minority opinion.

90. Marti, *Dodekapropheton*, 378–79; Budde, "Zum Text," 7; Mitchell, *Haggai*, 27–31; Bloomhardt, "Poems," 156–57; Peter R. Ackroyd, "Studies in the Book of Haggai," *JJS* 2 (1951): 164, 173–74; Horst, *Zwölf kleinen Propheten*, 203; Beuken, *Haggai*; Elliger, *Zwölf kleinen Propheten*, 84; Chary, *Aggée*, 12–13; Rudolph, *Haggai*, 23, 39; Rex Mason, "The Purpose of the 'Editorial Framework' of the Book of Haggai," *VT* 27 (1977): 421; Verhoef, *Haggai*, 10–13; Amsler, *Aggée*, 13–14; Reventlow, *Haggai*, 5–6; Rainer Albertz, *A History of Israelite Religion in the Old Testament Period*, trans. J. Bowden, OTL (Louisville, KY: Westminster John Knox, 1994), 2.455; Petersen, *Haggai*, 36–38; Wolff, *Haggai*,

prophetic material (1: [2], 4–11, 13b; 2:3–4, 5b, 6–9; 11–19; 21b–23) and the redactional narrative framework (1:1, [2], 3, 12–13a, 14–15; 2:1–2, 10, 20–21a).[91] As my purpose in this chapter is only to establish the text of the HN, it is not necessary to examine here the various suggestions concerning the the pre-HN materials, except when they are relevant to the main task. For now, we need only consider suggestions concerning modifications of the HN after its composition. Within the traditional model of composition, 2:5aα, which has no counterpart in the OG, is almost universally regarded as a later addition. Beyond this, a number of scholars have suggested that 1:13, 2:17(aα), and 2:18b(α) ought to be considered later additions to the oracles, although they differ as to whether they should be ascribed to the composer of the HN or to a later hand. Finally, a number of scholars in the past have argued that the oracle in what is currently 2:15–19 was originally attached to 1:15a and later moved to its present location. We will investigate each of these suggestions in turn.[92]

Haggai 2:5aα

את הדבר אשר כרתי אתכם בצאתכם ממצרים

The OG does not reflect this first portion of 2:5, although it is found in later versions (V, T, S, and some later G mss.[93]) and is represented in Murabbaʿat 88 by צאתכם. Its absence in OG has led most commentators to argue or assume that it is a post-HN interpretive gloss, albeit an early one, intended to ground the prophetic assurance of YHWH's presence with the community in the ongoing validity of the Sinai covenant.[94] Additional suggested grounds for its secondary nature are

---

18–19; Meyers and Meyers, *Haggai*, xliv–xlvii; Kessler, *Haggai*, 31–39; Nogalski, *Literary Precursors*, 216, 235–36.

91. Various scholars differ in some of the details regarding what is pre-redactional and what is part of the HN redaction. For example, some ascribe 1:2 or parts of it to the HN redaction, while others consider it pre-redactional. They nevertheless ascribe all of these verses to one or the other rather than to a later, post-HN redaction.

92. These are the redactional suggestions that have received the most discussion in the literature. Other, less widely discussed suggestions will be noted and briefly evaluated along with text critical notes accompanying the translation.

93. Gelston, *BHQ*, 115; Joseph Ziegler, *Duodecim prophetae*, Septuaginta 13 (Göttingen: Vandenhoeck & Ruprecht, 1984), 287.

94. Wellhausen, *Kleinen Propheten*, 170; Marti, *Dodekapropheton*, 385; Bloomhardt, "Poems," 171; Petersen, *Haggai*, 61; Wolff, *Haggai*, 71; Amsler, *Aggée*, 32 and n. 1, 34; Reventlow, *Haggai*, 21; Ack-

that it interrupts the parallelism between כי אני אתכם (4:bα) and ורוחי
עמדת בתוככם (5aβ)[95] and that mention of the Sinai tradition seems
incongruous here.[96]

Kessler, on the other hand, has argued that the phrase was introduced by the composer of the HN, suggesting that an omission in OG is
easier to explain than its late introduction into the proto-MT tradition
(although he does not give a reason for this judgment). The phrase was
likely added by the composer as "an elaboration of the implicit connotations of Haggai's words," which is "consistent with the nature of
the whole book as an interpretation of the significance of the prophet's
words and their effect."[97] He argues further that the appeal to the
covenant is not incongruous: 2:21–22 reflects language found in the
Sea of Reeds tradition, and both 1:4–11 and 1:12–14 are lexically and
conceptually rooted in Deuteronomistic covenantal concerns.[98] Kessler
may be correct that mention of the Exodus tradition is not out of place
in the HN, but his assertion that its omission by OG is easier to explain
than its later addition to the proto-MT is not compelling. If the phrase
could have been added by the composer of HN, it could also have been
added by a later scribe, either as a marginal gloss or as an intentional
expansion.[99]

In fact, the possibility of an *intentional* omission by the OG is difficult
to explain.[100] Barthélemy has suggested that the phrase may have been
omitted by the translator because it was difficult to understand.[101] This
is improbable in light of what appears to be the general translational
technique of the OG of Haggai and of the Twelve as a whole. It seems

royd, *Exile and Restoration*, 161; Horst, *Zwölf kleinen Propheten*, 206; Verhoef, *Haggai*, 99; Chary, *Aggée*,
26; Mitchell, *Haggai*, 64; Rudolph, *Haggai*, 40; Elliger, *Zwölf kleinen Propheten*, 9; Wöhrle, *Frühen
Sammlungen*, 300, 321; Beuken, *Haggai*, 46nn2, 57; Hallaschka, *Haggai*, 56; Gelston, BHQ; BHS. Albertz
includes it in a secondary level of redaction, along with minor portions of Zechariah 1–8 (*History
of Israelite Religion*, 2.455).

95. Ackroyd, "Interpretive Glosses," 163; Wolff, *Haggai*, 71; Reventlow, *Haggai*, 21; Mitchell, *Haggai*, 64;
   Smith, *Micah-Malachi*, 156.
96. Petersen, *Haggai*, 61; Amsler, *Aggée*, 34; Wöhrle, *Frühen Sammlungen*, 300, 321.
97. Kessler, *Haggai*, 170 and n. 66.
98. Ibid., 170–71.
99. Barthélemy claims that it is difficult to admit that a phrase that so many consider to be out of
   place here should have been added by a glossator (*CTAT*, 927–28). But the phrase was added by
   someone who did not consider it out of place, and theoretically this could have been a glossator.
100. An unintentional omission is, of course, possible, but the suggestion is entirely speculative and to
   my knowledge no one has made it.
101. Barthélemy, *CTAT*, 927.

41

very likely that the Twelve were translated into OG by a single translator or a small circle of collaborators. Thackeray argued this point in 1903 on the basis of the recurrence of rare words and usages throughout the OG of the Twelve. He further noted that the translation as a whole was marked by a desire to be literal, with clear attempts to provide an equivalent for every Hebrew word: "deliberate deviation from the original is quite foreign."[102] The case for a single translator or small group of translators, as well as for their literal translational technique, was later strengthened by the observations of Zeigler, Tov, and Muraoka.[103] Unless we speculate that Haggai was translated apart from the rest of the Twelve, an intentional omission of this or any phrase found in the translator's *Vorlage* is unlikely. Barthélemy's suggestion that the phrase was omitted because of difficulty is implausible.

Rather than a deliberate omission by the translator or a late addition to the proto-MT, the absence of the phrase in the OG may be evidence of two text traditions for Haggai. In addition to the "minus" at 2:5aα, the OG of Haggai possesses in relation to the MT two significant "pluses" (2:9, 14).[104] Large pluses and minuses are very rare in this translation noted for fidelity to its *Vorlage*.[105] The presence of three substantial deviations between the OG and the MT is so incongruent with the translation technique that they are unlikely to be the work of the translator(s). Jones and Dogniez have argued that the most reasonable explanation is that the *Vorlage* of the OG represents a different text tradition from that of the proto-MT.[106] Given the well-established evi-

---

102. Henry Thackeray, "The Greek Translators of the Prophetical Books," *JTS* 4 (1903): 583.

103. Joseph Ziegler, "Die Einheit der Septuaginta zum Zwölfprophetenbuch," in *Sylloge: Gesammelte Aufsätze zur Septuaginta*, MSU 10 (Göttingen: Vandenhoeck & Ruprecht, 1971), 29–42; Emanuel Tov, *The Septuagint Translation of Jeremiah and Baruch: A Discussion of an Early Revision of the LXX of Jeremiah 29–52 and Baruch 1:1–3:8*, HSM 8 (Missoula, MT: Scholars Press, 1976), 135–51; Takamitsu Muraoka, "In Defence of the Unity of the Septuagint Minor Prophets," *AJBI* 15 (1989): 25–36; Takamitsu Muraoka, "Introduction aux douze petits prophètes," in *Les douze prophètes: Osée*, ed. Eberhard Bons, Jan Joosten, and Stephen Kessler, BibAlex 23/1 (Paris: Cerf, 2002), i–xxiii.

104. Two miniscule manuscripts of the Alexandrine text tradition, A-106 and A-26, also contain a significant plus at 2:22. This is otherwise unattested in the OG of Haggai. See Ziegler, *Duodecim prophetae*, 290.

105. The only comparably sized plus is at Hos 13:4. A much smaller plus (five words) is at Hos 8:12. The other notable plus is at Mal 1:1, which appears to be drawing on Hag 1:5, 7; 2:15, 18: αγγελου αυτου θεσθε δη επι τας καρδιας υμων.

106. Barry A. Jones, *The Formation of the Book of the Twelve: A Study in Text and Canon*, SBLDS 149 (Atlanta, GA: Scholars Press, 1995), 113–18, 125; Cécile Dogniez, "Aggée et ses supplements (TM et LXX) ou le développement littéraire d'un livre biblique," in *L'apport de la Septante aux études sur l'Antiquité*, ed. Philippe Le Moigne and Jan Joosten (Paris: Cerf, 2005), 208–9. Ackroyd ("Interpretive Glosses,"

dence that other texts of the prophetic corpus existed in different text traditions, it is possible that the text of Haggai did as well.[107] The evidence of the OG and the MT suggest that the pluses in 2:9 and 2:14 were already present in the *Vorlage* of the OG, whereas MT 2:5aα was not. Conversely, unless we assume that such large pluses were in the proto-MT and then later removed (accidentally or not), the proto-MT text does not appear to have contained them, whereas at some point it did acquire 2:5aα. We lack any evidence that such omissions did occur, and it is difficult to imagine that the tradents of the proto-MT would have removed large elements from their text on purpose. A logical inference from the evidence of the MT and the OG, then, is that they represent two text traditions stemming from a base text—which cannot have been earlier than the HN—that contained neither the pluses in 2:9 and 2:14, nor the minus in 2:5aα. All three elements can therefore be excluded from the HN as later additions.

Haggai 1:13

ויאמר חגי מלאך יהוה במלאכות יהוה לעם לאמר אני אתכם נאם יהוה

The language in verse 1:13 differs in a number of ways from the rest of the text. The prophet is referred to as מלאך, rather than the usual נביא.[108] Rather than the divine message being delivered ביד, it is במלאכות יהוה.[109] This sudden, unrepeated, and apparently inexplicable change in language led Böhme to conclude that the verse was a late

---

164–65) also considered it possible that both pluses, while certainly later interpretive additions to the HN, were present in the *Vorlage* of the translator(s). If this is the case, the question remains how it is that of the Twelve, only the OG of Haggai seems to represent a non-proto-MT text tradition. Although well beyond the scope of this study, further inquiry into the literary history of the OG of Haggai remains to be done.

107. Why Haggai should exhibit such a high degree of textual variation relative to most of the other books of the Twelve (according to present evidence) is an intriguing question that cannot be addressed here, but one that would be worth further consideration.

108. The term is used to refer to Haggai five times (1:1, 3, 13; 2:1, 10). As a term for a prophet, it is only used elsewhere in Isa 44:26 and 2 Chr 36:15, 16. We might also include the eponym of the book of Malachi.

109. This term, which occurs only here, has been understood in various ways: "l'envoi" (Amsler, *Aggée*, 22); "with the LORD's message" (Janet E. Tollington, *Tradition and Innovation in Haggai and Zechariah 1–8*, JSOTSup 150 [Sheffield: JSOT Press, 1993], 62); "im Auftrag Jahwes" (Hans W. Wolff, *Dodekapropheton 6: Haggai*, BKAT 14/6 [Neukirchen-Vluyn: Neukirchener Verlag, 1986], 13); "through Yahweh's mandate" (Kessler, *Haggai*, 107); "Yahweh's message" (Petersen, *Haggai*, 55). It is missing in the OG, perhaps through homoioteleuton (Gelston, BHQ, 114).

addition, possibly a marginal gloss that was eventually incorporated into the text.[110] Mitchell also notes that the phrase לעם only occurs here, whereas throughout the rest of the text the preposition אל is used to indicate the recipients of messages (1:1; 2:2, 10, 20, 21).[111] A number of commentators accepted Böhme's assessment, some supporting this with the claim that the verse seemed "unnecessary."[112] The judgment regarding the necessity of the verse is, of course, subjective and in itself cannot be accepted as evidence for or against an interpolation.[113] As I will argue in chapter 4, this verse plays an important role in this section and for that reason should be taken as integral to it. The vocabulary choices do not reflect the language of another scribe, nor are they merely stylistic variations. The language has been chosen intentionally.

Haggai 2:17

הכיתי אתכם בשדפון ובירקון ובברד את כל מעשה ידיכם ואין אתכם אלי נאם יהוה

This verse, or at least the first part of it, is widely considered a gloss or secondary addition. The first four words of the verse match the beginning of Amos 4:9, and it is generally assumed that they, and much of the rest of the verse also, are therefore directly or indirectly derived from it.[114] Consequently many have concluded that the verse could not stem from the prophet himself, or have been part of the HN. Elliger, for example, suggests that it is probably a marginal gloss that

110. Walter Böhme, "Zu Maleachi und Haggai," *ZAW* 7 (1887): 215–16. He also thought that the language itself was just ugly, which only confirmed his conviction that the verse could not be anything other than a gloss: "Welches übrigens in unmittelbarer Nähe des Substantivs, von dem es gebildet ist, einen üblen Eindruck macht."

111. Mitchell, *Haggai*, 56–57.

112. Wellhausen, *Kleinen Propheten*, 169; Mitchell, *Haggai*, 55, 56–57; Marti, *Dodekapropheton*, 384; Budde, "Zum Text," 13; Elliger, *Zwölf kleinen Propheten*, 85n3; Horst, *Zwölf kleinen Propheten*, 206; Amsler, *Aggée*, 27; Bloomhardt, "Poems," 180. Of more recent exegetes, only Hallaschka agrees with this assessment (*Haggai*, 45, 54).

113. Only a few commentators, such as Verhoef (*Haggai*, 83–84), have argued that the verse is "necessary." Most others accept the verse without comment. As I will demonstrate in chap. 4, this verse is integral to the context and has a clear rhetorical function.

114. *BHS*; Elliger, *Zwölf kleinen Propheten*, 89–90; Wellhausen, *Kleinen Propheten*, 38; Budde, "Zum Text," 15; Nogalski, *Literary Precursors*, 226–28; Ackroyd, "Interpretive Glosses," 166; Hallaschka, *Haggai*, 85n485; Beuken, *Haggai*, 210–11; Reventlow, *Haggai*, 27; Wolff, *Haggai*, 58; Chary, *Aggée*, 22; Horst, *Zwölf kleinen Propheten*, 206; Marti, *Dodekapropheton*, 389; Petersen, *Haggai*, 86–87; Wöhrle, *Frühen Sammlungen*, 305–6.

was later incorporated.[115] The apparent incongruity of the text with the surrounding material has been offered as corroborating evidence. The claim that YHWH has struck the people בשדפון ובירקון ובברד —the first being a scorching wind and the latter two being the result of too much moisture—has seemed to many to have nothing to do with the main agricultural problem mentioned earlier in the text, which is described as drought (1:10–11; 2:16).[116] Finally, in this verse the voice appears to switch suddenly from the prophet's to YHWH's and then back to the prophet's. This switch has suggested to some that the verse is not original to the HN.[117]

None of these observations compels us to see this verse as an interpolation into the HN. Even if this verse does draw on the language of Amos 4:9, that language could stem from Haggai, any pre-HN forms of the oracles, or the composer of HN. Intertextuality is a common and complex phenomenon in the prophetic literature. Consequently, its presence here need not be the work of a later redactor.[118] The apparent incongruity is also not an argument for interpolation. Ackroyd rightly characterizes as unduly literalistic those who suggest that phenomena related to too much moisture do not belong.[119] In any case, the agricultural problems averted to in 1:10–11 and 2:16 are probably not limited to lack of water. The term חֹרֶב in 1:11 is often understood to mean simply "drought," but it can also mean more generally "desolation," a sense that is more appropriate here.[120] While "drought" is part of what is being described (1:10), the focus is on the failure of the people to raise crops and the animals to produce anything. When the prophet says that YHWH is calling down חֹרֶב on the people and the beasts and the "works of their hands," he implies much more than "drought."

---

115. Elliger, *Zwölf kleinen Propheten*, 90.

116. Bloomhardt, "Poems," 175; Marti, *Dodekapropheton*, 389; Nogalski, *Literary Precursors*, 226; Wöhrle, *Frühen Sammlungen*, 305–6.

117. Wöhrle, *Frühen Sammlungen*, 305–6; Hallaschka, *Haggai*, 95.

118. It is also not necessarily the case that whoever is responsible for this phrase in Hag 2:17 was drawing explicitly on Amos 4:9. The terms שדפון and ירקון appear together also in Deut 28:22; 1 Kgs 8:37 // 2 Chr 6:28, and may reflect a standard word pair found, for example, in treaty curses. The relationship of Amos 4:9 to Hag 2:17 will be discussed more fully in chap. 5.

119. Peter R. Ackroyd, "Studies in the Book of Haggai," *JJS* 3 (1952): 7.

120. The related term חָרֵב (1:4, 9), which refers to the "desolation" of the temple, is linguistically and rhetorically related to חֹרֶב. This is, as well, a more comprehensive term that captures the sense of the verse, namely, that more than just a "drought" has been summoned—*all* of the labors of people and beasts are for nought. For חֹרֶב as "desolation," see Isa 61:4; Jer 49:13; Ezek 29:10.

Therefore, the content of the first part of 2:17 is consistent with the rest of the text.

Finally, there is not necessarily a sudden change of voice from the prophet to YHWH and back again. Verse 2:14 begins with "Then Haggai said," but the short clause that immediately follows ends with "oracle of YHWH," as does v. 17. The oracle ends at 2:19 with first person divine speech (אברך). This indicates that the entire oracle, vv. 14–19, is divine speech. There is no sudden turn to this speech in 2:17. Even if there were a change of voice, the role of the prophet as spokesperson for YHWH often results in speech in the prophetic literature that is ambiguous in this regard, sometimes appearing to be the words of the prophet, and at other times as the word of YHWH. It is not always possible to maintain a distinction between the two.

Arguments that all or part of 2:17 is secondary to the HN are not convincing. Most importantly for my purposes, while it may be true that the verse does not stem from the prophet himself, it could have been incorporated by the composer of the HN (or possibly at an earlier stage). We cannot assume that the work of the composer was limited to imposing the narrative framework.

Haggai 1:15; 2:1, 15–19; 2:18b(α)

In the Leningrad and Cairo Codices, as well as Murabbaʿat 88, a *petuḥa* separates 1:15 from 1:14. This suggests that the narrative ends with v. 14 and that the date formula in v. 15 introduces the next section.[121] This verse gives what appears to be a complete date, albeit in a sequence that differs from 1:1: ביום עשרים וארבעה לחדש בששי בשנת שתים לדריוש המלך.[122] This is immediately followed by another date in 2:1: בשביעי בעשרים ואחד לחדש. Virtually all commentators agree that 1:15b belongs with 2:1 to form an integral date similar to that of 1:1. The question then becomes what to do with 1:15a, to what activity should it be attached? A number of scholars suggest that it properly concludes the previous section and should be associated with 1:14. Others have argued that 1:15a is the remnant of a date formula that originally intro-

---

121. Gelston, *BHQ*, 12*–15*. The *petuḥa* is not present in the Aleppo Codex.
122. Verse 1:1 reads: בשנת שתים לדריוש המלך בחדש הששי ביום אחד לחדש.

duced another section of text. At some point in the history of the text this section was later dropped or moved, leaving 1:15a "orphaned."

Rothstein's version of this latter thesis is the one most often accepted by subsequent commentators. Modifying Sellin's suggestion that the material originally introduced by 1:15a had simply fallen out of the text, Rothstein argued instead that the "missing" text is what is now 2:15–19.[123] He offered two observations to support his proposal. First, the content of 2:15–19 fits poorly in its present context. It is thematically closer to the material in the first chapter of the text, which also addresses agricultural problems, and was probably originally associated with it. Second, the dates of the present text do not make sense. Sellin had earlier accepted Hoonacker's suggestion that the founding could not have occurred in the ninth month (2:10, 18) because it falls during the rainy season.[124] The content of the oracle itself, which speaks of מטרם שום אבן אל אבן (2:15b), implied for Sellin that this laying of stone upon stone—the foundation of the temple—happened earlier, probably in the sixth month with the resumption of the work indicated in 1:14.[125] Rothstein developed this line of thought, arguing that 2:15–19 was originally uttered at the resumption of the work and that in the original form of the HN, it occurred at this earlier place in the text.[126] Thus the oracle was originally dated to the twenty-fourth of the sixth month (of the second year of Darius). At some point in the history of the text, these verses got displaced, leaving their original date at 1:15a and gaining a new, "incorrect" date in the ninth month. Rothstein suggested that 2:15–19 should therefore be "returned" to its proper place between 1:15a and 1:15b. This textual revision has been so persuasive that several commentaries have presented and commented on the text in this reconstructed form.[127]

123. Johann W. Rothstein, *Juden und Samaritaner: Die grundlegende Scheidung von Judentum und Heidentum: Eine kritische Studie zum Buche Haggai und zur jüdischen Geschichte im ersten nachexilischen Jahrhundert*, BWAT 3 (Leipzig: Hinrichs, 1908), 53–54.
124. Ernst Sellin, *Die Restauration der jüdischen Gemeinde in der Jahren 538–516: Das Schicksal Serubbabels*, SEJGBE 2 (Leipzig: Deichert, 1905), 50. This calculation assumes that the months in Haggai are counted according to the Babylonian system in which the first month of the year is Nisan, in the spring. The ninth month, which is Kislev, would then fall in November/December, which is indeed the rainy season in Israel. This understanding of the dating system is accepted by all scholars who have commented on Haggai. I discuss the dating system in Haggai more fully in chap. 4.
125. Sellin, *Restauration*, 50.
126. Rothstein, *Juden und Samaritaner*, 53–56.

However, the thesis has two main weaknesses. First, there is no textual evidence to support it; all versions reflect the MT arrangement. Second, no one has convincingly explained how and when 2:15–19 reached its present location. Amsler suggested that the redactor, or a redactor, moved the text to "fill out" the story of the consultation of the priests in 2:10–14, whose final declaration may have been seen as "too brief."[128] Others have accepted Rothstein's larger thesis that the "unclean people" of 2:10–14 refers to the Samaritans and have accordingly seen the transposition as possibly the work of a (later) redactor who wanted to show with this speech the significance of the separation of the unclean people from the גולה.[129] The date of the blessing indicated in 2:19 would then be the day the decision was made about who would be allowed to build the temple, rather than the date the work began (as it was originally intended).[130] Others who accept the transposition but do not agree with Rothstein's thesis about the Samaritans are not able to offer any reason for the textual manipulation. Some see it as accidental, others as the work of a redactor after the formation of the HN, and others as the work of the HN composer. Without textual evidence or a compelling reason to explain why the text was moved, it is very difficult to accept Rothstein's thesis.[131]

The second option, which allows for the present arrangement of the text, presents fewer problems. Those who accept the present Masoretic consonantal text suggest that the date in 1:15a concludes the narrative of the resumption of work on the temple (1:12–15a) and that the petuḥa between 1:14 and 1:15 is misplaced.[132] Verse 1:15b should then be con-

---

127. For example, Wolff, *Haggai*; Amsler, *Aggée*; Chary, *Aggée*; Horst, *Zwölf kleinen Propheten*; Elliger, *Zwölf kleinen Propheten*.
128. Amsler, *Aggée*, 29.
129. Beuken, *Haggai*, 74; Elliger, *Zwölf kleinen Propheten*, 89–90. Rothstein's conclusions regarding 2:10–14 will be addressed in chap. 5.
130. Wolff, *Haggai*, 60–61.
131. Some commentators who reject this thesis also point to Klaus Koch's argument for the literary unity of 2:10–19 as positive evidence for the originality of the present location of 2:15–19 ("Haggais unreines Volk," *ZAW* 79 [1967]: 52–66).
132. Mitchell, *Haggai*, 57–58; Rudolph, *Haggai*, 38–39; Verhoef, *Haggai*, 88–89; Hallaschka, *Haggai*, 47, 54, 315; Kessler, *Haggai*, 108 and n. 4, 153 (he also believes the date does "double duty"); Petersen, *Haggai*, 55, 60; Meyers and Meyers (*Haggai*, 4, 36–37; they believe the date does "double duty" and relates to both what precedes it and what follows it), Rüdiger Lux, "Das Zweiprophetenbuch: Beobachtungen zu Aufbau und Struktur von Haggai und Sacharja 1–8," in *"Word JHWHs, das Geschah . . ." (Hos 1,1): Studien zum Zwölfprophetenbuch*, ed. Erich Zenger, Herders Biblische Studien 35 (Freiburg: Herder, 2002), 192n10; Reventlow, *Haggai*, 9, 17.

sidered the beginning of a new date and attached to 2:1, which concludes the date. The resulting text would then read:

ויבאו ויעשו מלאכה בבית יהוה צבאות אלהיהם ביום עשרים וארבעה לחדש בששי
בשנת שתים לדריוש המלך בשביעי בעשרים ואחד לחדש היה דבר יהוה אל חגי

The advantage of this suggestion is that it leaves the MT intact, while the resulting dating scheme in 1:15b–2:1 is similar to that of 1:1 and can therefore easily be seen as the work of the same composer.

Some scholars object that it is implausible that 1:15a would conclude the previous section. Wolff, for example, argues that it is stylistically unlikely that the composer of the HN would conclude a section with a date, as he always puts the dates at the beginning of oracles.[133] Chary goes so far as to state that a date can introduce an oracle but it *cannot* terminate one.[134] Such an objection constrains the composer unnecessarily. While it is true that all of the oracles begin with a date, there is no reason to conclude from this that he *could not* have concluded this narrative portion of the text with a date.[135] One can also find reasons for his having done so, such as a desire to indicate the importance of the day that the people began to work on the temple.[136]

Given all of the above, it is better to accept—along with most recent scholars—the MT arrangement as the HN, while noting that the *petuḥah* is more appropriately placed after 1:15a, indicating that 1:15b-2:1 begins the next section.

Related to the question of the original form of the text is the frequent proposal that the date in 2:18b (מיום עשרים וארבעה לתשיעי) is secondary, having been added to the text when it was moved to its present

---

133. Wolff, *Haggai*, 58.

134. Chary, *Aggée*, 24.

135. Modern Bible translations are divided on this question, even when they agree that the date formula concludes the narrative portion. For example, among the English translations, JPS, NRSV, and NIV separate v. 15a from v. 15b: ". . . on the twenty-fourth day of the sixth month. In the second year. . . ." NABR, on the other hand, follows the current chapter division, but not accepting the MT division between 1:14 and 1:15. Thus it renders v. 15 as a single, "full" date formula (". . . on the twenty-fourth day of the sixth month in the second year of Darius the king.") and begins Haggai 2 with the "truncated" date formula.

136. Meyers and Meyers, *Haggai*, 36. In Ezra 6:15 we find the date of the completion of the temple, and in Neh 6:15 a date is given at the completion of Jerusalem's walls. Both of these events were significant in their respective books. The resumption of work on the temple was a similarly momentous occasion in the book of Haggai and was dated accordingly. This will be discussed in more detail in chap. 4.

location.[137] The date matches that of 2:10, and is presumably meant to emphasize, or clarify, that this is the day referred to in the immediately preceding phrase מן־היום הזה ומעלה. The phrase, being a date, is almost certainly secondary to the oracle; it was probably not uttered by the prophet. It seems likely that it has been added to emphasize or clarify the date, and this was probably added by the individual who arranged the material in its present form. As I have just argued above, there was no post-compositional rearrangement, so this date is not secondary to the HN. It is the work of the composer.[138]

Recent Redactional Models—Wöhrle, Hallaschka, Leuenberger

Recently a few scholars have challenged the traditional compositional model of Haggai, in which pre-existing prophetic materials were transformed through one comprehensive redaction into a text that has undergone relatively little further development. In particular, Wöhrle, Hallaschka, and Leuenberger have argued that the "shaking of the nations" verses (2:6–9, 20–23) were added some time after the creation of the basic text. Wöhrle and Hallaschka have suggested also that the priestly torah narrative (2:10–14) is a late addition.[139]

---

137. Hans W. Wolff, "Haggai literarhistorisch untersucht," in *Studien zur Prophetie—Probleme und Erträge*, TB 76 (Munich: Kaiser, 1987), 138–41; Wolff, *Haggai*, 65–66; Reventlow, *Haggai*, 27; Marti, *Dodekapropheton*, 389; Mitchell, *Haggai*, 75; Ackroyd, "Studies in the Book of Haggai," 7; Ackroyd, *Exile and Restoration*, 159; Amsler, *Aggée*, 28n7; Chary, *Aggée*, 24; Wöhrle, *Frühen Sammlungen*, 292; Hallaschka, *Haggai*, 95, 138; Elliger, *Zwölf kleinen Propheten*, 89–90.

138. Wolff agrees with this, although he believes the material in question was originally located after 1:15a, and was moved when the narrative framework was added (*Haggai*, 60–61). He nevertheless places 2:15–19 back in its "original" place in his commentary. Kessler (*Haggai*, 200 and n. 21) and Meyers and Meyers (*Haggai*, 63) also argue that the date in 2:18 is part of the composition and not a later addition. Both suggest its presence is meant to emphasize the importance of the day. The nature and function of the dates as part of the persuasive strategies of the composer will be discussed in chs. 4 and 5.

139. Leuenberger's article is only concerned with 2:6–9, 20–23. Wöhrle's model ascribes four main stages of growth to the book: an original *Grundschicht* (1:2, 4–11, 12b, 13; 2:3, 4*, 5aβb, 9, 15–16, 18abβ, 19, 23); the formation of a Haggai Chronicle (which added 1:1, 3, 12a, 14–15; 2:1–2, 4*, 10, 20–21a); a redaction that added 2:11–14; and the final redaction that added 2:6–8, 21b–22. Verses 2:5aα, 17, 18bα—already considered above—were added individually at other times. Hallaschka's model is more complex, involving six stages of growth: the *Grundbestand* (1:1abα, 4, 8, 1:15b–2:1, 3, 9a), which was later supplemented through a *Fluch-und-Segen* redaction (adding 1:5–7; 2:15–16, 18a, 19) before being incorporated into a narrative framework (1:1–3, 12a, 14–15a, 15b–2:2). Subsequently, 2:10–14 was added, then 2:4–5*, 6–7, 8, 9b, 17, 18b, and finally 2:20–23. As the purpose of this chapter is to determine what additions were made to the HN, if any, after its main composition, the proposals of Wöhrle and Hallaschka concerning the pre-HN stage(s) of the text will not be considered here.

Haggai 2:6–9, 20–23

These two passages are thematically and lexically connected and it is suggested therefore that either they are part of the same redaction (Wöhrle, Leuenberger) or the latter is dependent on the former (Hallaschka). Both sections constitute oracles announcing in identical language that YHWH is or will soon cause the heavens and earth to quake: מרעיש את השמים ואת הארץ: (2:6a, 21b). In the first oracle (2:6–9) YHWH will also shake את הים ואת החרבה and כל הגוים.[140] The riches of the latter will then fill the temple, which will be made glorious once again and שלום established במקום הזה. In the second oracle (2:20–23), after causing the heavens and the earth to quake, YHWH will overthrow the thrones of kings and destroy the kingdoms (ממלכות) of the nations—and their chariots, horses, and riders—before establishing Zerubbabel as his "signet ring" (חותם).

The arguments of Wöhrle, Hallaschka, and Leuenberger for the late inclusion of 2:6–9 and 2:20–23 (or portions of them) can be summarized under three main headings: (1) thematic coherence, either with the book as a whole or with the immediate context; (2) formal differences between the verses in question and the surrounding material; (3) the relationship of the material to global events, which is used to date the material. We will examine the work of each scholar in turn.

Wöhrle argues that 2:6–8 and 2:21b–22 were added at the same time as part of a buchübergreifend redaction of the Twelve, although he presents his case independently of any consideration of that larger redactional intervention.[141] The similar language and theme of both sections suggests they are the work of the same author. But, as a pair, the sec-

---

140. The first phrase is lacking in the MT of 2:21, although the OG includes it. This may be either the harmonizing work of the translator(s) or, as Jones suggests, an earlier harmonization present in the text tradition represented by the *Vorlage* of the OG. In either case, it would not have been part of the HN.

141. Wöhrle's stated approach in his two-volume work on the formation of the Book of the Twelve is to determine the redactional history of each book individually, and then bring those findings together to develop a model for the redactional history of the Twelve as a whole (*Frühen Sammlungen*, 24–27). Thus he claims to have arrived at his conclusions regarding the formation of the book of Haggai apart from any considerations of its literary relationship with the larger corpus. This permits evaluation of his findings without consideration of his findings regarding the *buchübergreifend* redaction of the Twelve.

tions represent a departure from the rest of the book both in content and language, and should therefore be considered secondary additions.

In the first place, the passages have to do with cosmic upheaval and judgment of the peoples. This represents for Wöhrle a foreign element in a text that is concerned only with the current agrarian problems plaguing the people and the relation of these problems to the building of the temple. According to Wöhrle the motif of cosmic upheaval has nothing to do with this concern and therefore cannot have been part of the original prophetic oracle or of the original HN.[142]

Wöhrle also sees the material in 2:6–8 as intrusive in its immediate context, which further indicates its secondary nature. The notion of the shaking of the nations is not prepared for by the question that introduces the oracle in 2:3 because it does not, for example, mention any conflict with other peoples.[143] Instead, the question of the appearance of the temple is not addressed directly until 2:9, in which the description of the more glorious temple of the (near) future can be understood as both the motivation for the work urged in 2:4–5 and a response to the concern posed in 2:3. For Wöhrle, 2:6–8 thus introduces an "unnecessary" element that does not pertain to the question raised by the prophet.[144] Although the inclusion of these verses leads the text to suggest that the shaking of the nations will contribute to the glory of the new temple, this implied causal connection is not developed in the text; the riches of the people are not referred to in 2:9.[145] Further, although the שלום of 2:9 might seem to be related to the (implied) warfare of the previous verses, in fact it does not refer to the absence or cessation of warfare, but to agrarian success, and so is not related to the preceding verses.[146] The content of the verses, then, does not appear to be integral to its immediate context.

According to Wöhrle, certain formal characteristics also mark 2:6–8 as distinct from the HN. The text as a whole is characterized by direct speech to the people, whereas these verses present an extended speech

---

142. "Denn die Darstellung des Gerichts an den Völkern und die Ankündigung, daß deren Reichtümer nach Jerusalem kommen, geht über den Horizont dieses Wortes, wie ohnehin über den Horizont des sonstigen Haggaibuches, hinaus" (Wöhrle, *Frühen Sammlungen*, 300).
143. Wöhrle, *Frühen Sammlungen*, 300; Hallaschka also cites this as evidence (*Haggai*, 66–67).
144. Wöhrle, *Frühen Sammlungen*, 300.
145. Ibid., 300–301.
146. Ibid., 302.

that, Wöhrle claims, is not directed to the people.[147] Finally, only at 2:6 and 2:21b do we find the future action of YHWH described using a participle (מרעיש) rather than the prefix-conjugation.[148]

Verses 2:21b–22 share with 2:6–8 the theme and language of shaking the nations, and Wöhrle offers the same arguments for their secondary nature: they also have a *völkerfeindlich* orientation—which does not accord with the interests of Haggai or the composer of the HN—and they use the participial construction. It is clear they belong together with 2:6–8 as part of the same redaction.[149] Wöhrle suggests that 2:21b–22 were placed before 2:23 to connect the promise to Zerubbabel with the "judgment of the peoples."[150] He proposes as the date for the inclusion of both sections around 400 BCE, the shaking of the nations alluding to the numerous revolts in the Persian Empire at that time.[151]

Hallaschka concurs with Wöhrle's assessment that 2:6–8 is secondary. In addition to the observation that 2:3 is not really addressed until 2:9, he notes that the language of 2:3 (הבית הזה and כבוד) is also found in 2:7. This indicates that 2:7 (and the accompanying verses) are *dependent* on 2:3 but not from the same source, because they are part of what Hallaschka considers intrusive material.[152] Furthermore, Hallaschka sees 2:6–7 as a unit on which 2:8 is dependent (and therefore inserted later). Verses 2:4–5* are an even later addition because they interrupt the movement from the question of 2:3 to the (now expanded) answer begun in 2:6.[153] The result is a series of dependent redactional insertions: 2:3, 9 is the original text; this was supplemented by 2:6–7 which was then later supplemented by 2:8; to all of this was added at another stage 2:4–5*.

Hallaschka notes (with Wöhrle) that 2:6–8 may be dealing with judgment or it may refer to pilgrimage of the nations to Jerusalem, or a

147. Ibid., 301.
148. Ibid. The use of the prefix-conjugation to indicate what YHWH intends to do, or is doing, occurs at 1:8b, 11a; 2:19b.
149. Ibid., 292, 310–13.
150. Ibid., 310–13.
151. Jakob Wöhrle, *Der Abschluss des Zwölfprophetenbuches: Buchübergreifende Redaktionsprozesse in den späten Sammlungen*, BZAW 389 (Berlin: de Gruyter, 2008), 161–63.
152. Hallaschka, *Haggai*, 66. Here he is drawing on earlier observations by Reinhard Kratz (*Das Judentum im Zeitalter des Zweiten Tempels*, FAT 42 [Tübingen: Mohr Siebeck, 2004], 88).
153. Hallaschka, *Haggai*, 67. He does not rule out the possibility, however, that the sequence of verses has been disrupted.

combination of the two. If the theme is understood as pilgrimage, then the verses display the same concern as Isaiah 60–61, and according to Hallaschka, likely stem from the same period. Steck dates this Isaianic material to the middle of the fifth century. Hallaschka accepts this date and accordingly places 2:6–8 as a pilgrimage oracle in the same period. If, on the other hand, the theme is universal judgment of the peoples, the date of the addition should be pushed forward to the Hellenistic period.[154]

Unlike Wöhrle, Hallaschka considers 2:20–23 an integral literary unit, which was introduced into the text as a whole as a final addition to the book.[155] He dates this addition to the Hellenistic period; the theme of the destruction of the nations accords well with the disintegration of the *pax persica* and the accompanying power struggles.[156] This late date raises an obvious question about the relevance of an oracle concerning Zerubbabel, who departed the historical stage centuries before the rise of Alexander.[157] Hallaschka acknowledges this problem, and notes that hopes for the continuation of the Davidic line were alive in this period, as Schmid has argued in his effort to date Jeremiah 33:14–26 to the first half of the third century.[158] Even at this late date Zerubbabel remained a viable symbolic representative of these hopes, having been the last Davidide to hold any political power. He could therefore stand as a cipher for the future ruler.[159] In introducing 2:20–23 to the text, the later redactor took the (already present) shaking of the nations in 2:6–7 and represented it as a universal judgment of the peoples, the goal of which was the promised restoration of the Davidic line. This restoration was now tied to Zerubbabel as a legitimate temple builder and therefore appropriate successor to David. According to Hallaschka, the most likely period for this inclu-

---

154. Ibid., 68. The passages in question are Isa 60:1–9, 13–16; 61.

155. Ibid., 108–20.

156. Ibid., 117–18.

157. The oracle to Zerubbabel is one of the main reasons most modern scholars date that oracle, and the composition of the HN as a whole, to the late sixth century. This is also why Wöhrle and Leuenberger consider only 2:21b–22 to be additions to the text. Hallaschka is, to my knowledge, the only modern scholar who argues for a late date for the promise to Zerubbabel.

158. Hallaschka, *Haggai*, 117–18.

159. Ibid., 119–20. Zerubbabel's high profile throughout Haggai is one of the main reasons that most commentators have argued for an early date for the composition of the book. Once he passed from history, there would have been no real reason to feature him so prominently in a text that concluded, moreover, with a promise to him that manifestly was not fulfilled.

sion would have been the Hellenistic period during which the rise of Alexander led to the overthrow of "thrones of kingdoms" (2:22) and, presumably, the rejuvenation of hopes for the restoration of a Davidic monarchy.[160]

Finally, Leuenberger also has argued that 2:6–9 and 2:21b–22 together represent a single *Fortschreibung* that adds the theme of cosmic upheaval and the resolution of problems with "the peoples" to the original theme of Zerubbabel and the temple.[161] This textual development shifts the time perspective from the present of the original oracle to the imminent yet indeterminate future. This temporal shift itself indicates redactional intervention. In particular, adding 2:21b–22 makes the oracle concerning Zerubbabel already present at the end of the text an analog for other "messianic" texts in the OT, and giving the entire book a new, messianic perspective. Regarding formal elements, Leuenberger also notes the unusual participial construction, and as well as the fact that 2:6 begins with a new messenger formula.[162]

Leuenberger dates the additions of 2:6–9 and 2:21b–22 to the late Persian period. He rejects—on (unspecified) content and redactional grounds—earlier attempts to connect these passages concerning upheaval among the "nations" with Darius's troubles and the unrest in the early Persian period.[163] Neither do they fit the early Hellenistic "apocalyptic" world judgment texts.[164] Rather, Leuenberger dates the additions to between the late fifth and middle fourth centuries, when the Persian Empire was again experiencing convulsions. The additions, he notes, may have been part of the growth of the Twelve, although he does not develop this thought further.[165]

The arguments of Wöhrle, Hallaschka, and Leuenberger for the late inclusion of 2:6–9 and 2:20–23 (or portions of them) have three heads,

---

160. Ibid., 138.
161. Martin Leuenberger, "Gegenwart und Zukunft im Haggaibuch: Das dynamische Zeit- und Geschichtsverständnis von Hag 2,6–9.20–23," in *Gott in Bewegung: Religions- und theologiegeschichtliche Beiträge zu Gottesvorstellungen im alten Israel*, FAT 76 (Tübingen: Mohr Siebeck, 2011), 242.
162. Leuenberger, "Gegenwart," 242–43.
163. Ibid., 244. He cites as examples Meyers and Meyers, *Haggai*, 53, and Rainer Albertz, "The Thwarted Restoration," in *Yahwism after the Exile: Perspectives on Israelite Religion in the Persian Era*, ed. Rainer Albertz and Bob Becking, Studies in Theology and Religion 5 (Assen: Van Gorcum, 2003), 7.
164. Leuenberger, "Gegenwart," 244. Here (n. 26) he cites Konrad Schmid, *Literaturgeschichte des Alten Testaments: Eine Einführung* (Darmstadt: Wissenschaftliche Buchgesellschaft, 2008), 192–94.
165. Leuenberger, "Gegenwart," 244.

each of which I will consider in turn: (1) these verses do not fit thematically with their immediate contexts or the HN as a whole and are therefore "intrusive"; (2) formal differences between the verses in question and the surrounding material indicate that they are not from the same hand as the HN; (3) the relationship of the material to later global events suggests they arose during those periods.

Two assumptions appear to underlie the argument that the material in question introduces "foreign" thematic elements into the original material, or otherwise fits only poorly with its context. The first is that the original material must have addressed a single theme (agrarian problems and their relation to the temple), and developed that theme following a linear logic. Thus Wöhrle states that the motif of cosmic upheaval goes beyond the "horizon" of not only the oracle in 2:3–9, but the HN as a whole. Yet the only way to determine the thematic horizon of a text is by examining its contents. To identify material not immediately related to agrarian concerns as secondary on this basis is to make an unwarranted *a priori* judgment about the text. Here the problem is compounded by the fact that Wöhrle is making this judgment about a hypothetically reconstructed text that has been reconstructed, at least in part, according to his understanding of what it must have originally been about.

Even at the level of the oracle itself, the concern for thematic coherence is problematic. Some of Wöhrle's observations, while correct, do not lead inevitably to his conclusions. For example, while it is true that 2:3 does not mention "the peoples," this does not mean that any material that does mention "the peoples" could only have been introduced by a later redactor. Similarly, the observation that 2:9 does not mention the riches of the peoples does not mean that the material immediately preceding it, which does mention the riches of the peoples, must therefore be secondary. Why, for example, should 2:9 mention the riches of the peoples when they have just been mentioned?

Prophetic oracles do not always follow linear guidelines of argumentation or conceptual development. Therefore, we cannot assume that the original oracle lacked elements later commentators would consider "unnecessary" merely because they are not perceived to address *immediately* and *directly* the question posed in 2:3 concerning the appearance of the temple. In fact, vv. 4–8 do address the concern posed in 2:3, namely the condition of the temple. As I will show more fully in chapter 5, the command to be strong and continue the work is intended to address the people's concern about their ability to successfully complete the temple (and therefore whether YHWH has indeed commanded its reconstruction). This is followed by an oracle that explains why, when they have done their part, the people can expect a glorious temple after all: YHWH will do his part by bringing the wealth of the nations to Jerusalem.

Here we can also note an option that Wöhrle and Hallaschka do not consider, namely that the material they view as intrusive may have been added at an earlier rather than a later stage in the formation of the text. It is at least possible that an "original" oracle (2:3, 9) was expanded before it reached the composer of the HN. As a final option, we must consider the possibility that some of this material could stem from the composer himself. I have already questioned the apparent assumption that this individual did not add material to the oracles, but only arranged them in a narrative framework.

Thus, even if we agree that some of the material at 2:6–9 (or, for Hallaschka, 2:4–5*, 6–8) appears to "intrude" or fail to cohere with its immediate literary context—a thesis I do not accept—we need to consider the possibility that it stems from a prophet, a later compiler, or the composer of the HN. There is nothing about the fact that the text appears to have intrusions or thematically divergent materials that compels us to believe that they were introduced after the composition of the HN.

Observations about formal differences between the material in question and the surrounding texts are equally subject to challenge. The use of the participle in 2:6 and 2:21, rather than the prefix conjugations used in other verses, need not indicate different authorship. As examples of the participial *futurum instans* they give a sense of imminence to what is being announced, rooting the promised future result in the present action of YHWH.[166] There is no reason to assume that the prophet or the composer of the text would refrain from exercising the

---

166. GKC §116p. See in the prophetic literature, for example, this use of the participle in Isa 65:7; Jer 30:30; Zech 2:13; 3:8.

various expressive options, always maintaining a consistent grammatical profile, especially if the "variations" can be shown to serve a rhetorical function. As both sections are thematically and lexically linked, it is unsurprising that we would find in them the same grammatical structures, having the same effect, and that this would be somewhat different than the other material. Again, these distinctive features may be due to a different source from the surrounding material, but there is nothing to prevent it from being the work of the HN composer or an earlier tradent.[167]

All three scholars ultimately base their claims for the late date of these verses on what they consider to be the thematic parallels between the material and events in the later Persian or Hellenistic periods, or, in the case of Hallaschka, parallels with other texts dated to a particular period. Wöhrle and Leuenberger suggest both sections are related to the upheavals of the Persian empire in the late fifth century. Hallaschka dates 2:20–23 to the Hellenistic period and 2:6–8 either to the mid-fifth century or to the Hellenistic period.

The methodological problem of dating texts by matching their contents with a particular time period continues to plague biblical scholarship generally. Sommer has recently re-argued that it "holds no validity whatsoever."[168] Although Sommer is referring specifically to the dating of Pentateuchal texts, the problems he discusses are the same for dating prophetic texts, and "mistakes" to which he points are relevant here. The first is the common assumption that a particular idea—for example, cosmic judgment—is associated with one particular period. Ideas that originated in one period can, if they are fruitful, be relevant when they are appropriated and reinterpreted for new circumstances in later periods.[169] If 2:6–9 and 2:20–23 are referring to global political disturbance and judgment, such images need not have

---

167. The use of participles at 1:6 and 2:5aβ also indicates that they are not foreign to the text.

168. Benjamin Sommer, "Dating Pentateuchal Texts and the Perils of Pseudo-Historicism," in *The Pentateuch: International Perspectives on Current Research*, ed. Thomas B. Dozeman, Konrad Schmid, and Baruch J. Schwartz, FAT 78 (Tübingen: Mohr Siebeck, 2011), 85.

169. Sommer, "Dating," 85–94. John Kessler ("The Shaking of the Nations: An Eschatological View," *JETS* 30 [1987]: 159–66) argued that the background for these two texts was not the upheavals of any particular period, during which they were created. Instead, the texts reflect traditional eschatological motifs. Hallaschka himself notes that 2:6b is drawing on classic theophany imagery (*Haggai*, 59). This will be discussed in more detail in the following chapters. Here I only note that it seems more likely that the text is drawing on traditional materials than that it is referring to any particular world event.

originated in the late Persian or Hellenistic periods simply because those periods experienced geopolitical upheavals and therefore seemed to offer the possibility of a "judgment of the nations" and the reestablishment of a Davidic dynasty, represented symbolically by Zerubbabel.

The second mistake is related to the first: failing to recognize that if a text seems appropriate for a particular point in history, it may be equally important at another time as well.[170] Thus, as Leuenberger points out, several scholars argued that the oracles at 2:6–9 and 2:21b–22 have in mind the upheavals attendant on the troubled accession of Darius, or to a period before this, or after it.[171] Even if, for the sake of argument, the oracles have as their background a particular global situation, deciding which situation gave rise to the oracle remains a problem. It is certainly a question whether the oracles, at least at the time of their composition (or utterance) had a particular set of historical events in mind at all. (This will be explored in more detail in chapter 5.)

Hallaschka also tries to date 2:6–7 by relating it to Isaiah 60–61, which has a similar theme, and which Steck dates to the middle of the fifth century. As we saw above, a theme shared by two texts is not sufficient evidence that they stem from the same era. In addition, Steck's date for the Isaiah material is controversial.[172] Hallaschka's dating of 2:6–7 rests, then, on an already unstable base.

For these reasons the late dates of 2:6–9 and 2:20–23 cannot be accepted solely because they appear thematically relevant for global events in the Persian or Hellenistic periods. They may be additions to the original oracles, but there is nothing that compels acceptance of this position. Even if they are later additions, the possibility remains that they were added by a follower of the prophet or the composer of the HN himself.

---

170. Sommer, "Dating," 94–95. Sommer uses Isa 2:1–4 and Mic 4:1–3 to illustrate the problem with this approach.

171. Leuenberger, "Gegenwart," 244.

172. Lena-Sofia Tiemeyer, review of *Haggai und Sacharja 1–8*, by Martin Hallaschka, *RBL* (2012): 2–3. She notes that if one does not accept Steck's dating, "there are no compelling reasons for dating Hag 2:6–7 to that same period." For current theses regarding the date of these texts, see, for example, the discussion in Joseph Blenkinsopp, *Isaiah 56–66*, AB 19B (New Haven: Yale University Press, 2003), 207–10. He notes that Steck's position is currently outside the consensus.

One linguistic feature of 2:22 even provides positive evidence for its early date, and therefore an early date for the whole complex of texts. The verse contains two plural forms of מַמְלָכָה, namely, מַמְלְכוֹת and מַמְלְכוֹת. Late BH, however, shows an overwhelming preference for מַלְכוּת, which appears throughout Chronicles, as well as in Esther, Daniel, Ezra, and Nehemiah.[173] Given the widely attested preference for מַלְכוּת versus מַמְלָכָה in later literature, one could reasonably expect that if this text in Haggai arose in the late Persian or Hellenistic period it would have employed מַלְכוּת. This linguistic evidence suggests that 2:22, and therefore the other verses in question, were composed earlier rather than later.

In sum, the arguments that 2:6–9 and 2:20–23, or parts therein, are post-HN additions are not compelling enough to remove them from the text under analysis, and there is at least sufficient reason to believe that they stem from an earlier period.

Haggai 2:10–14

Wöhrle and Hallaschka argue that this section concerning consultation of the priests is secondary to the HN. Wöhrle gives three reasons: (1) 2:11–14 constitutes a *Prophetenbiographie*, a genre that does not fit with the rest of the book; (2) the absence of a date for the oracle at 2:15–19 indicates this oracle was originally attached to and introduced by the date in 2:10;[174] 2:11–14 is thus an intrusive insertion; (3) the concern of the surrounding material is motivation for working on the temple, whereas this section (as Wöhrle interprets it) has nothing to do with the temple, which is not even mentioned except perhaps elliptically as שׁם in 2:14. The section is therefore completely foreign to its present context.[175] Wöhrle acknowledges that it is difficult to know the reason for the addition; he only suggests that the text might be a remnant

---

173. Eduard Y. Kutscher, *A History of the Hebrew Language* (Jerusalem: Magnes, 1982), 84. Jean Margain notes that מַלְכוּת appears six times in the literature usually dated to the exilic period or earlier, whereas it occurs approximately 85 times in the post-exilic literature ("Observations sur *I Chroniques*, XXII à propos des anachronisms linguistiques dans la Bible," *Semitica* 24 [1974]: 39).

174. Wöhrle notes that 1:9–11 does not have a date. But, he argues, 1:2–8 and 1:9–11 are thematically more closely related than are 2:11–14 and 2:15–19, so the former do not require a date to link them (*Frühen Sammlungen*, 305).

175. Wöhrle, *Frühen Sammlungen*, 304–5.

from a later discussion of the significance of the book of Haggai. He does not propose a date for the addition.[176]

Hallaschka also notes that 2:10–14 introduces into the text a new theme, with new addressees (the priests, rather than the people). For this reason it should be considered secondary. Hallaschka dates this new material to the middle of the Persian period, for two reasons. First, the priestly torah assumes the purity writings of the *Priesterschrift*, which Hallaschka dates to the period after the rebuilding of the temple.[177] As evidence that the Haggai text is dependent on the priestly writings, Hallaschka cites Meyers and Meyers: "the pentateuchal texts seem to provide straightforward answers" to the questions posed by Haggai: "The authoritative status of pentateuchal law can hence be presupposed."[178] Second, the theme of impurity of the people and of their offerings is similar to that of Malachi 1:6–2:9; 3:6–12. The position of the section before the promise of blessing in 2:15–19 indicates that the impurity of the people was a hindrance to their salvation and grounds for their agrarian and economic woes, a theme similar to that of Malachi 2:1–4; 3:6–12. Therefore, on the basis of similar theme and historical situation, 2:10–14 probably arose out of the same historical and theological context as Malachi 1:2–2:9 and 3:6–12 (although the Haggai text may be somewhat older).

The same responses may be given to the arguments of Wöhrle and Hallaschka here as with those for 2:6–9 and 2:20–23. Neither Wöhrle's observation that the apparent genre of the text does not "fit" the rest of the book, nor his claim that it has nothing really to do with the temple—the main concern of the whole book—can be taken as arguments that the text could not have been part of the HN. Aside from the question of the "horizon" of the book, addressed above, even if we accept for the sake of argument that the text originally had nothing to do with temple, it now does in its present context. As Wöhrle notes, the reference to שׁם, as elliptical as it may be, appears to tie the consultation of the priests with the question of the temple, even if the exact relationship is unclear.[179] If the story does not stem from prophet himself, it

---

176. Ibid., 320–21.
177. Hallaschka, *Haggai*, 92. He cites as relevant texts Lev 7:11–21; Leviticus 11–15; 21–22; and Numbers 19.
178. Ibid., 92; citing Meyers and Meyers, *Haggai*, 56–57.

may still have been a source available to the HN, who chose to incorporate it for his own purposes.[180] It is irrelevant that the text is a different genre. Prophetic texts frequently mix genres and generic variation alone cannot be taken as evidence of expansion.

Wöhrle's observation that 2:15–19 is not introduced by a date formula suggests, not that the text is an intrusion into the more integral 2:10, 15–19*, but that the entire complex was a single oracle, as it is presented in the current text. He also notes that not every *Wort* has a date.[181] Wöhrle's understandable difficulty assigning a purpose, date, or source for the insertion of this text suggests that its status as a post-HN addition is not secure.

Hallaschka's argument that this section is a later addition rests on its supposed dependence on the *Priesterscrhift* and its congruence with the texts from Malachi dealing with similar material. For reasons discussed above, the similarities between texts in Malachi and Haggai cannot be taken as evidence for the dating of the latter.[182] The supposition that this text presumes the priestly *writings* is an equally tenuous claim. The text does appear to be familiar with laws, or at least teachings, concerning purity found also in the Pentateuch. But setting aside the controverted question of the date of those writings, we need not assume that the teaching in Haggai is based on written texts of any sort, much less those of the Pentateuch. Presumably the laws or teachings of the Pentateuch concerning corpse contamination existed before the composition of, for example, Numbers 19.[183] There is no reason to assume that the priestly torah in this text is dependent the priestly writings of the Pentateuch.

I do not consider the arguments that this text is a later addition to the HN to be compelling, both because secondary materials may have been incorporated by the HN composer, and because the late date arguments of Hallaschka are not particularly strong. As with those for the

179. Wöhrle, *Frühen Sammlungen*, 304.
180. What that may have been will be discussed in some detail in the following chapters.
181. Ibid., 304.
182. Tiemeyer also makes this critique ("Review," 2).
183. Jacob Milgrom, for example, has argued that the ritual using the lustral ashes of the red cow contains vestiges of a pre-Israelite rite of exorcism for corpse-contaminated persons and that, in fact, the priestly legislation here can be seen as a development that has reduced the degree of contamination incurred by touching a corpse (*Leviticus 1–16*, AB 3 [New York: Doubleday, 1991], 275–77).

secondary status of 2:6–9 and 2:20–23, these arguments are at most only *plausible*. I have therefore retained 2:10–14 in the HN as well.

In sum, the foregoing examination of the models for the redactional history of the book of Haggai has supported the traditional model of a single, comprehensive redaction that produced the HN out of preexisting materials. Subsequently, this text received only one minor addition, 2:5aα. This element has been removed from the text that will be analyzed in the chapters 4 and 5.

Translation with Notes of the Haggai Narrative

[1:1] In the second year of Darius the king, in the sixth month, on the first day of the month, the word of YHWH came through Haggai the prophet to Zerubbabel son of Shealtiel, governor of Judah, and to Joshua son of Jehozadak, the high priest: [2] "Thus says YHWH of hosts: This people has said, 'It is not the time for coming,[184] the time for the house of YHWH to be rebuilt.'" [3] Then the word of YHWH came through Haggai the prophet:

[4] "Is it time for you yourselves to dwell in your houses—finished![185] While this house—desolate!

[5] Come now! Thus says YHWH of hosts: Consider fully your experience.[186]

---

184. The subject of the phrase עת בא לא עת can be construed as either עת, thus "the time has not come" (Elliger, *Zwölf kleinen Propheten*, 85; Petersen, *Haggai*, 41, 47–48; Meyers and Meyers, *Haggai*, 3, 19–20; Wolff, *Haggai*, 27, 29; Reventlow, *Haggai*, 12), or an implicit "the people," thus "it is not the time [for us] to come" (Ackroyd, *Exile and Restoration*, 155 and n. 8; Amsler, *Aggée*, 21; Barthélemy, *CTAT*, 924; Kessler, "Le temps," 558n4; Kessler, *Haggai*, 103 and n. 7). Barthélemy notes that "toute la tradition exégétique occidentale," beginning with the versions, has understood the second, not the first עת, as the subject of בא, which then led to the perceived necessity of emending the MT (see text-critical notes above). If, however, the builders are seen as the subject, the perceived need for emendation disappears. In either case, the problem is that the people have not been rebuilding the temple, for whatever reason. The subject in the following clause is not "the time," but the house of YHWH, which is to be rebuilt. This suggests—without demanding—that the subject of the clause in question is likewise not "time" but rather, "the people."

185. See text-critical notes regarding the stative use of this adjective. The word ספונים can be translated as "paneled," "covered," or "roofed" (see, for example, Rudolph, *Haggai*, 29). The function of the word is to highlight the contrast between the condition of the peoples' houses and that of the house of YHWH (as Meyers and Meyers [*Haggai*, 3, 23] also note). His is desolate and in disrepair, whereas theirs are completed. I have chosen to render the word, then, as "finished," to convey the point Haggai is making. For further discussion of the translation of this verse, see the rhetorical analysis in chap. 4.

186. Kessler, who translates the term as "your conduct and its results," suggests that the meaning of דרכיכם here is comprehensive, referring to "the choices the people have made and the outcome of those choices" (*Haggai*, 105n10). This accords with a common translation of the term, namely

[6] You have sown much, but brought in little; eat, but there is no fullness[187]; drink, but there is no inebriation; dress, but there is no warmth for anyone.[188] And the wage earner earns wages for a bag with holes in it!

[7] Thus says YHWH of hosts: Consider carefully your experience!

[8] Go up to the mountains, bring back wood, and build the house so that I may take pleasure in it and that I may be glorified[189], says YHWH.

[9] You expected much but it has turned out to be little, and when you brought that home,[190] I blew it away! And why? Declaration of YHWH of hosts: Because it is my house that is desolate, while each of you runs off to his own house.

[10] Therefore it is on your account[191] that the skies have withheld their dew and the earth has withheld its produce.

[11] I have called forth a desolation[192] upon the land, upon the mountains,

---

"your ways." While it is true that failure to rebuild the temple is being critiqued in the larger context, in the *immediate* context, their choices or ways are not what the people are being asked to consider, as if they should have chosen other than to sow seed or clothe themselves. Rather, they are being asked to consider the fact that there is not a satisfactory relationship between their (perfectly acceptable) actions and the results. For similar meanings of דרך, see Isa 40:27 and Jer 10:23. See the more detailed discussion in chap. 4.

187. The construction אין ל noun is unusual (that is, when the construction isn't indicating possession or lack of it on the part of the "noun"). I find it only in Neh 5:5, where it occurs in an idiom: ואין לאל ידנו. Joseph Blenkinsopp (*Ezra-Nehemiah*, OTL [Philadelphia, PA: Westminster, 1988], 254) and others translate the Nehemiah phrase as "not within the power of our hands." The same idiom occurs with אין in Deut 28:32, and with יש in Gen 31:29 and Mic 2:1. It is difficult to understand the syntactical function of the *lamed* in Hag 1:6. It seems unnecessary, but is perhaps meant to convey the sense that as much as one eats, one never reaches the point of satiety, or as much as one drinks, one never reaches the point of inebriation, but this seems to go against the sense of the verse, which is stressing that there is not enough food or drink. This construction, which is not addressed in the standard grammars, is therefore puzzling.

188. Taking לו as an "individualizing singular" in an impersonal construction. Rudolph, *Haggai*, 28, 29; Meyers and Meyers, *Haggai*, 3; Verhoef, *Haggai*, 61; Wolff, *Haggai*, 28, 30. See Joüon §152d; *IBHS* 22.7b; GKC §144b.

189. The *niphal* form here can be taken as passive: "I will be glorified" (Horst, *Zwölf kleinen Propheten*, 204; Chary, *Aggée*, 20, Meyers and Meyers, *Haggai*, 3, 28), or reflexive: "I will glorify myself" or "I will show my glory" (Bloomhardt, "Poems," 157, 163; Verhoef, *Haggai*, 67–68; Amsler, *Aggée*, 22, 25; Wolff, *Haggai*, 28; Hallaschka, *Haggai*, 27n89). Kessler has "I will receive the glory it brings me" (*Haggai*, 105), and Ackroyd, finding "I will honour myself" "too restrictive," prefers "I will let myself be honoured" (*Exile and Restoration*, 160n32). Very likely the verb is meant to be understood in both ways. See further discussion in chap. 4.

190. Although a few scholars have accepted the thesis of Friedrich Peter ("Zu Haggai 1, 9," *TZ* 7 [1951]: 150–51) that הבית here refers to the temple and that נפחתי therefore means "I despised [your offering]" (Ackroyd, *Exile and Restoration*, 158; Steck, "Zu Haggai," 370n46; Meyers and Meyers, *Haggai*, 29), most have seen it as a reference to the homes of the people; what little they managed to bring home was then blown away (Beuken, *Haggai*, 187–88; Elliger, *Zwölf kleinen Propheten*, 85, 87; Rudolph, *Haggai*, 29–30; Petersen, *Haggai*, 52–53; Wolff, *Haggai*, 46–47; Reventlow, *Haggai*, 14; Kessler, *Haggai*, 106, 137; Wöhrle, *Frühen Sammlungen*, 296n32; Hallaschka, *Haggai*, 28 and n. 95).

191. Some understand עליכם spatially: "the skies above you" (for example: Vg; Budde, "Zum Text," 12; Amsler, *Aggée*, 22; Kessler, *Haggai*, 106). The emphatic placement before the verb and the clear purpose of that emphasis in the argumentation suggest it should be translated "because of you" (for example: Rudolph, *Haggai*, 30; Meyers and Meyers, *Haggai*, 4, 30; Verhoef, *Haggai*, 72–73; Hallaschka, *Haggai*, 29 and n. 104). Others omit the word on text critical grounds (as discussed above).

192. The usual translation here of חֹרֶב is "drought." In order to signal its rhetorical as well as linguistic

upon the grain, upon the new wine, upon the oil—upon whatever the ground brings forth—upon people and upon the beasts and upon all their labors."

[12] Then Zerubbabel son of Shaltiel[193] and Joshua son of Jehozadak, the high priest, and all the remnant of the people obeyed the voice of YHWH their God, that is to say, the words[194] of Haggai the prophet, because[195] YHWH their God had sent him. But the people were afraid of YHWH.[196] [13] So Haggai, the messenger of YHWH, said in a message[197] of YHWH for the people:[198] "I am with you! Declaration of YHWH!" [14] Then YHWH aroused the spirit of Zerubbabel son of Shaltiel, governor of Judah, and the spirit of Joshua son of Jehozadak, the high priest, and the spirit of all the remnant of the people, and they came and worked

relationship with the significant term חֹרֶב (1:4, 9), I have translated the word as "desolation." This is, as well, a more comprehensive term that captures the sense of the verse, namely, that more than just a "drought" has been summoned—all of the labors of people and beasts are for nought. For חֹרֶב as "desolation," see Isa 61:4; Jer 49:13; Ezek 29:10.

193. The apocopated form of the name: שאלתיאל. See also 1:14, 2:2.

194. Thus Wolff, *Haggai*, 31; Reventlow, *Haggai*, 9; Kessler, *Haggai*, 106 with n. 32. Wolff identifies the *waw* in ועל as a *waw-explicativum* (GKC §14n1b). This translation emphasizes the close relationship between deity and prophet. Rudolph (*Haggai*, 28), Petersen (*Haggai*, 55), and Amsler (*Aggée*, 22) see the relationship as causal: "because of the word of Haggai." Kessler suggests that the *waw* makes this unlikely (Kessler, *Haggai*, 106n32), but it could be a *waw-explicativum* in this sense as well: "that is, [they obeyed] because of the words of the prophet." The relationship between deity and prophet would not be quite as intimate in this case. Following Wellhausen (*Kleinen Propheten*, 169), who emended the text to read ואל, a number of others have simply rendered it as "and to the words . . ." (Horst, *Zwölf kleinen Propheten*, 204; Elliger, *Zwölf kleinen Propheten*, 85; Chary, *Aggée*, 22; Verhoef, *Haggai*, 79 [although without emendation]). Not only is there no textual warrant for emendation, but the resulting sense would be an emphasis on the distinction between the "voice of YHWH" and the words of the prophet, which hardly seems likely. See following note.

195. Here I follow Kessler (*Haggai*, 107n38) in translating this conjunction in relation to the preceding claim of the text that the voice of YHWH and the words of the prophet are, in a sense, identical. This subsequent clause explains why this is the case. For כאשר as causal, see Joüon §170n; BDB 455b; Gen 16:29; Num 27:14; Judg 6:27; 1 Sam 28:18; 2 Kgs 17:26; Mic 3:4. Petersen (*Haggai*, 55) renders the phrase as "whom Yahweh had sent"; Meyers and Meyers (*Haggai*, 4) as "when"; and Verhoef (*Haggai*, 82–83) and Amsler (*Aggée*, 20), respectively, as "according to that which" and "selon que YHWH l'avait envoyé."

196. The verb ירא מפני generally means "to be afraid of," not "to fear" in the reverential sense. See chap. 4 for discussion.

197. במלאכות יהוה. The noun is a *hapax legomenon* generally taken to mean something like "a commissioned message" ("מלאכות," *HALOT* 1:586).

198. The *lamed* is taken here in the sense of a *dativus commodi* or possession. The phrase לעם modifies מלאכות יהוה ("a message of YHWH for/to the people") rather than being governed by the verb, as is generally thought (the prophet spoke "to" the people through a message of YHWH). Numerous commentators have suggested that this verse is a later addition, pointing to the use of ל rather than אל to indicate the recipient of the speech (as in, for example, 2:2) as evidence that it is not by the same hand. The assumption is that the *lamed* is intended to function in the same way as an אל normally would. Rather, the ל indicates that this is a message specifically intended *for* "the people," the significance of which will be discussed in chap. 4.

on the house of YHWH of hosts their God [15] on the twenty-fourth day of the month—the sixth one.[199]

In the second year of Darius the king, [2:1] in the seventh month, on the first day of the month, the word of YHWH came to Haggai the prophet: [2] "Say to Zerubbabel son of Shaltiel, governor of Judah, and to Joshua son of Jehozadak, the high priest, and to the remnant of the people:

[3] Who is left among you who saw this house in its former glory? And how are you seeing it now? Surely it's like nothing in your eyes![200]

[4] Nevertheless,[201] be strong Zerubbabel! Declaration of YHWH! And be strong Joshua son of Jehozadak, the high priest, and be strong all people of the land! Declaration of YHWH! Act, for I am with you! Declaration of YHWH of hosts! [5b] And my spirit stands in your midst; do not be afraid.

[6] For thus says YHWH of hosts: Once more—and soon—[202] I am going to cause[203] the heavens and the earth, the sea and the dry land to quake.

[7] I will cause all the nations to quake, and the treasures of all the nations will come, and I will fill this house with glory, says YHWH of hosts.

[8] Mine is the silver and mine is the gold! Declaration of YHWH of hosts!

199. An awkward translation of an awkward phrase in the MT (לחדש בששי). For discussion of this phrase, as well as the relationship of 1:15a to 1:14, see the redaction critical section above.

200. Hebrew במהו כאין. See Joüon §174i for the use of כ . . . כ in comparisons. In this construction, the two items being compared are identical. The use of the negative interrogative הלוא often signals that the speaker expects and wants an affirmative answer. The sentence can be rendered as a question ("It's as nothing in your eyes, isn't it?") or as a statement. See Robert Gordis, "A Rhetorical Use of Interrogative Sentences in Biblical Hebrew," *AJSL* 49 (1933): 212; Hendrik A. Brongers, "Some Remarks on the Biblical Particle *halō*,'" in *Remembering All the Way . . .: A Collection of Old Testament Studies Published on the Occasion of the Fortieth Anniversary of the Oudtestamentisch Werkgezelschap in Nederland*, OtSt 21 (Leiden: Brill, 1981), 178–85; Michael L. Brown, "'Is It Not?' or 'Indeed!': HL' in Northwest Semitic," *Maarav* 4 (1987): 201–19; Godfrey R. Driver, "Affirmation by Exclamatory Negation," *JANESCU* 5 (1973): 107–8.

201. The particle ועתה can function in a number of ways. Here the context suggests it expresses encouragement (Hendrik A. Brongers, "Bemerkungen zum Gebrauch des adverbialen *we'attāh* im Alten Testament," *VT* 15 [1965]: 295).

202. As noted above, the Hebrew (עוד אחת מעט היא) is a difficult phrase. Ackroyd notes that it literally reads "yet one, and it is only a little one" (*Exile and Restoration*, 153–54). Some have taken it to mean simply "very soon," but this interpretation does not appear to account for all the elements of the phrase (see, for example, Petersen, *Haggai*, 61, who has "in just a little while"). The course taken by those commentators who see the last two words as parenthetical and explicative seems, however, to honor this unusual phrase better. Thus Rudolph renders it "Einmal noch—in Bälde!" (*Haggai*, 40–41); Wolff, "nur noch eine kurze Frist ist es" (*Dodekapropheton*, 50); Amsler, "encore un temps, sous peu" (*Aggée*, 32); and Kessler, "one more time, and it will happen soon" (*Haggai*, 160). The important difference between the two interpretations is the concept of "once more," which implies previous "quaking," a rhetorically significant element, the discussion of which will be taken up in detail in later chapters.

203. The indication of time given by the preceding phrase suggests מרעיש is a participle of *futurum instans*, indicating an imminent, not presently occurring, event (GKC §116p). This reading is strengthened by the succeeding series of *weqataltí* verbs, which typically continue the future meaning of the participle (Joüon §119n).

[9] Greater will be the glory of this latter house than the former,[204] says YHWH of hosts, and in this place I will grant well-being.[205] Declaration of YHWH of hosts!"

[10] On the twenty-fourth day of the ninth month in the second year of Darius, the word of YHWH came to Haggai the prophet: [11] "Thus says YHWH of hosts: Request from the priests a ruling." [12] "If someone is carrying consecrated meat in the skirt of his garment and with his skirt he touches bread, stew, wine, oil, or any food, will it become consecrated?" The priests answered, "No." [13] Then Haggai asked, "If someone who has become unclean by touching a dead body[206] touches any of these, does it become unclean?" The priests answered, "It does become unclean." [14] Then Haggai responded,

"Thus it is with this people and this nation in my judgment. Declaration of YHWH! And thus it is with every work of their hands and whatever they offer there: it is (all) unclean.[207]

[15] Now, consider carefully from this day forward: Before[208] setting stone upon stone in the temple of YHWH, [16] how were you?[209]

One came to a grain-heap for twenty (measures), but there were (only) ten. One came to the winepress to draw off fifty (measures) from the vat,[210] but there were (only) twenty.

[17] I struck you with blight and mold and hail—every work of your hands—and with you I was not![211] Declaration of YHWH!

[18] Consider carefully from this day forward—from the twenty-fourth day of the ninth month, that is, from the day the temple of YHWH was founded—consider carefully!

---

204. "Former" and "latter" may refer to the "house" or to the "glory." The difference in meaning is minimal.

205. Hebrew שלום.

206. Hebrew טמא נפש. For this phrase, or a variation of it, see Lev 22:4; Num 5:2; 9:6, 7, 10.

207. It is not clear from the syntax to what "it" (הוא) is meant to refer. But as my analysis will show, the point of the declaration is that everything—"there," the offerings, the work of their hands, and "this people"—is unclean. Probably the place referred to as "there" (שם) is considered the source of the defilement, but this defilement spreads to everything else.

208. With Petersen (Haggai, 59), Meyers and Meyers (Haggai, 58), Wolff (Haggai, 57, 64), Amsler (Aggée, 26), and Kessler (Haggai, 198), I take the מן before טרם to be pleonastic and so not to be translated.

209. Hebrew מה הייתם (see text critical notes above).

210. Hebrew פורה. The meaning of the word, which only occurs here and in Isa 63:3, is disputed. The versions took it to be a measure of some sort (see text-critical discussion above). Modern commentators suggest it is another word for vat, although not a gloss on יקב (Rudolph, Haggai, 44; Wolff, Haggai, 57; Kessler, Haggai, 199), or perhaps the wine-press (Petersen, Haggai, 86; Verhoef, Haggai, 126).

211. See text-critical notes above for the emendation from ואין אתכם אלי to ואין אתכם אני. This translation will be discussed further in chap. 5.

[19] Is there still grain in the grain pit,[212] while the vine, the fig, the pomegranate, and the olive tree have not produced?[213] From this day I will bless!"

[20] Then the word of YHWH came a second time to Haggai on the twenty-fourth day of the month: [21] Say to Zerubbabel, governor of Judah:

"I am about to cause the heavens and the earth to quake.
[22] I will overturn the thrones of kingdoms, destroy the strength of the kingdoms of the nations. I will overturn chariots and their riders, and horses and   their riders will fall, each by the sword of his fellow.
[23] On that day—Declaration of YHWH of hosts!—I will take you, Zerubbabel son of Shealtiel, my servant—Declaration of YHWH!—and I will make you as a signet ring, for it is you I have chosen. Declaration of YHWH of hosts!"

---

212. Hebrew מְגוּרָה is a *hapax legomenon*. It is generally taken to be the storage space of the grain after it was harvested. Some of the grain from the previous year's harvest would be saved and sown the following year after the rain had prepared the ground. The suggestion here, as I will argue in more detail in chap. 5, is that the rain has not come and thus the grain reserved as "seed" remains in the storage area.

213. While most take the -ה at the beginning of the verse to be an interrogative, some interpret it as an emphatic and translate it as "certainly" (Beuken, *Haggai*, 211–13; Wolff, *Haggai*, 58–59; Joüon §161b). Kessler notes that the second clause may be considered either a statement or a second question (*Haggai*, 200n25). Given the prominent function of questions in this text, I have taken the verse to be a question, which is continued in the second clause.

3

Objections and Obstacles to Reconstruction
of the Temple

Introduction

The rhetorical aim of the prophet Haggai was to persuade the Yehudites to rebuild the Jerusalem temple in the second year of Darius I.[1] Persuasion was necessary because the political and economic realities at the time did not suggest that restitution of the former national shrine was approved by YHWH, a necessary condition for reconstruction. The poor agricultural and economic conditions, as well as the lack of a Davidic ruler or any political autonomy, could be taken as signs that YHWH had not yet decided to restore his people and return to

---

1. This approximate date for the reconstruction of the temple is accepted by nearly all scholars, despite the attempts of Dequeker and Edelman to argue that it was not built until, respectively, the reigns of Darius II or Artaxerxes I. See Luc Dequeker, "Darius the Persian and the Reconstruction of the Jewish Temple in Jerusalem (Ezra 4,24)," in *Ritual and Sacrifice in the Ancient Near East: Proceedings of the International Conference Organized by the Katholieke Universiteit Leuven from the 17th to the 20th of April 1991*, ed. J. Quaegebeur, OLA 55 (Leuven: Peeters, 1993), 69–72; Diana V. Edelman, *The Origins of the "Second" Temple: Persian Imperial Policy and the Rebuilding of Jerusalem*, Bible World (London: Equinox, 2005). One of the main supports of Edelman's argument is her contention that Zerubbabel and Nehemiah were near contemporaries. For a refutation of this position, see Ralph W. Klein "Were Joshua, Zerubbabel, and Nehemiah Contemporaries? A Response to Diana Edelman's Proposed Late Date for the Second Temple," *JBL* 127 (2008): 697–701.

Jerusalem to reside in his temple. Instead, these realities could be read to indicate that the time of judgment begun with the Babylonian conquest and destruction was still in effect. Until conditions suggested that YHWH's anger had passed, it was inconceivable to rebuild his house in Jerusalem. Furthermore, the agricultural and economic problems would have led to scarce labor and resources to devote to reconstruction. These objections and obstacles were significant and would not have been easily or quickly overcome.

The rhetorical strategies employed by the prophet, as well as by the composer of the narrative portions of the HN, were designed to counter opposition to reconstruction by refuting material and theological objections and by offering an alternative interpretation of conditions in Yehud. Analysis of these strategies must therefore begin with a preliminary examination of the reasons Yehudites would have had to resist rebuilding in 520 BCE. The second part of the chapter is devoted to these objections and obstacles.

The first part of the chapter examines what role, if any, the Persian Empire played in the reconstruction. Answering this question informs our understanding of when and under what circumstances it became possible to rebuild the temple, which in turn illumines the extent and depth of Yehudite opposition. If, for example, it was not politically *possible* to rebuild the temple until the reign of Darius, Yehudite resistance to the project cannot be invoked to explain the fact that work did not begin until then. If, on the other hand, it had been possible, as far as Persian policy was concerned, to rebuild as early as the reign of Cyrus, the fact that work did not begin until much later suggests that Yehudite opposition was long-standing and probably well-entrenched.

To anticipate the conclusions of this chapter: although it was politically possible to begin rebuilding the temple already in the reign of Cyrus, work did not begin until the reign of Darius I. There were no Persian constraints preventing reconstruction, and therefore all reasons for a "delay" must be found in Yehudite reluctance or inability to rebuild in the early Persian period. Objections and obstacles to reconstruction did indeed exist, and they were both theological and material. Isaiah 66 and Zechariah 1–8 provide evidence of theological objections to the temple and of doubts about the authenticity of prophetic calls to rebuild. Agricultural disasters and economic depression, as well as a lack of a Davidic royal builder, would have been interpreted as evidence that the expected restoration and period of divine favor had not yet arrived. Until signs appeared that YHWH's anger had passed and that he was once again prepared to dwell among his people in Jerusalem, reconstruction of the house he had commanded to be destroyed was out of the question. The agricultural disasters and poor economic conditions would have made it difficult to muster labor and fiscal support for reconstruction of a large national temple, especially if existing cultic sites offered viable alternatives for Yahwistic worship. For all of these reasons, Haggai's call to rebuild the temple would have encountered principled, sustained resistance.

The Persian Empire and the Jerusalem Temple

Consideration of the circumstances surrounding the reconstruction of the Jerusalem temple in the early Persian period must take account of the role, if any, of the Achaemenid administration. With Cyrus's defeat of Babylon, that empire's former provinces came under the control of the Persians and were thus subject in principle to oversight of their cultic institutions.[2] In practice the Persians were often content to leave local cultic matters alone, particularly when a locality was not considered politically or economically significant.[3] Yehud was a small, poor outpost that would not have qualified as significant in most respects. It is therefore not surprising that apart from the account of the reconstruction of the temple in Ezra 1–6 there is little evidence that the Persians took much interest in the Jerusalem temple. The question of Persian involvement, however, is relevant and so must be briefly examined.

There are four possible scenarios regarding Persian attitudes toward the Jerusalem temple. One: permission was not required to rebuild the

2. Roland de Vaux examines several examples in which the early Achaemenids did intervene in local cultic affairs ("The Decrees of Cyrus and Darius on the Rebuilding of the Temple," in *The Bible and the Ancient Near East*, trans. Damian McHugh [Garden City, NY: Doubleday, 1971]). See also Peter R. Bedford, *Temple Restoration in Early Achaemenid Judah*, JSJSup 65 (Leiden: Brill, 2001), 137–47.
3. Bedford, *Temple Restoration*, 140–47. Amélie Kuhrt also notes that it was not always the case that even smaller cults could simply carry on as they wished. Temples could be destroyed just as tax exemptions and other privileges could be extended to small as well as large temples. It all depended on the situation (*The Ancient Near East c. 3000–330 BC* [London: Routledge, 1995], 2.699).

temple, leaving the decision entirely in the hands of Yahwists in Yehud and elsewhere. Two: Persian permission was required and was given by Cyrus (much as recounted in Ezra 1–6), yet the Persians had no particular interest in whether or not the Jerusalem temple was built. Three: permission was required but for whatever reason was not given until the reign of Darius I, again with no further Persian interest in the temple. Four: the Persians perceived an imperial interest in having the temple built and commanded its reconstruction, making the temple at least to a degree a "Persian project" that the Yehudites would hardly have been able to effectively resist.

Was Permission Required?

Scholarly attention to the question of permission has tended to focus on whether authorization was given under Cyrus or under Darius, but rarely considers whether it was in fact needed or given at all. Questions about the historicity of the Ezra account have occupied commentators for decades. While many have doubted the authenticity of the "Hebrew edict" (1:2–4), and a few have also rejected the "Aramaic memorandum" (6:3–5), most scholars have accepted the historical claim of these texts that permission to rebuild the temple was given by Cyrus. These commentators, regardless of when they think work actually began, assume that reconstruction of the temple in Jerusalem could only have commenced with the approval of the Persian administration. Someone had to grant permission; the only real question is who. But is this the case?

Building on Kuhrt's analysis of the Cyrus Cylinder, Bedford has argued that when it came to cultic matters Achaemenid rulers did not treat all localities alike, but differentiated between major and minor entities. Whereas in politically and culturally significant areas, such as Egypt or Babylon, the Persian rulers would take responsibility for the cults in the manner of indigenous monarchs, in less important areas they showed little interest in such things. Beneficence toward local cults was largely a matter of political expedience. In those areas where the political payoff would be minimal, the Achaemenids appear for the most part to have ignored the local cults. As Bedford notes, there is little reason to suppose that Cyrus or the other Persian kings made an effort to address the cultic needs of subject peoples unless it was useful to do so.[4] It seems more likely that they simply let smaller local cults operate according to their own lights and, if the locals could afford it, to build or rebuild their sanctuaries as they saw fit.[5] The province of Yehud was small, poor, and peripheral, and so, according to the logic of political expediency, it is unlikely that the Persians would have made the reconstruction of its temple a priority.

On the other hand, the temple was a national sanctuary destroyed as part of punishment for rebellion. For this reason, Bedford suggests, the status of the temple would have been of interest to the Persians, who would have had to give special permission for it to be rebuilt. Bedford finds evidence for this primarily in the example of the Jewish temple at Elephantine, destroyed by local Egyptian priests of the god Khnum in 410 BCE. Although this temple was not destroyed as a result of rebellion, the Elephantine Jews clearly thought they needed permission to rebuild and requested it through the Persian governor of Yehud, Bagavahya.[6] Bedford concludes from this that permission probably would have been necessary to rebuild a destroyed temple in general and therefore the Jerusalem temple in particular.[7]

The situation in Elephantine, however, differs from that of the Jerusalem temple. The petition from Jedaniah and the Jews of Elephantine indicates that permission to rebuild had first been sought not from the Persians but from the high priest in Jerusalem, Jehohanan, and other Jewish nobles.[8] Having received no response, the petitioners were now turning to the Persian governor. One wonders whether permission from the Persians would have been sought if a positive response from the Jerusalem authorities had been forthcoming. The petition specifically asks Bagavahya to "take thought of that Temple to (re)build (it) since they do not let us (re)build it" (למבניה לן שבקן לא בזי (למבנה זך אגורא על אתעשת).[9] Who "they" are is not specified; it could be

4. Peter R. Bedford, "Early Achaemenid Monarchs and Indigenous Cults: Toward a Definition of Imperial Policy," in *Religion in the Ancient World: New Themes and Approaches*, ed. Matthew Dillon (Amsterdam: Hakkert, 1996), 17–39; *Temple Restoration*, 141–42.
5. Bedford, *Temple Restoration*, 143n125.
6. The relevant Aramaic documents recovered from Elephantine are *TAD* A4.7 and A4.8.
7. Bedford, *Temple Restoration*, 149–51.
8. *TAD* A4.7.
9. *TAD* 4.7.23.

the Egyptians, the Persians, or even perhaps the Jerusalemites, whose silence had been taken as a rejection. In any case, it appears that Bagavahya was asked to intercede only after permission had been denied by someone else, and we cannot assume "they" were Persians. The question is complicated by indications in the petition that the destruction of the temple at Elephantine was not the work of Egyptian priests acting on their own, but took place with the help of the local Persian governor, Vidranga, and his son, the troop commander at Elephantine. If permission *was* required of the Persians to rebuild this temple, it may be primarily because a Persian gave permission for it to be destroyed in the first place. These significant differences between Elephantine and Jerusalem (not to mention the difference of a century, during which policies likely change) suggest that this example is not sufficient to establish that permission would have been necessary to rebuild the temple in Jerusalem in the late sixth century.

Fried has offered another possible indication that the decision to build did not rest with the Yehudites. When Cyrus came into possession of the temple vessels stored in Babylon, "he came into possession of the decision to rebuild the Temple in Jerusalem. The decision was his . . . because he controlled the vessels."[10] In the aniconic Yahwistic tradition, the vessels became the ideological equivalent of a divine image and, in the biblical literature at least, the symbol of YHWH's presence.[11] Thus Fried concludes that once Cyrus came into possession of the vessels, he controlled the "tangible proof of YHWH's presence," and thus possessed the only authority to rebuild. As far as the Yehudites were concerned, it would not have been possible to rebuild the temple as long as the vessels remained in Babylon, and they could only be returned to Yehud with the permission of Cyrus.[12]

It is true that the vessels play a key role in the biblical literature concerning the end of the exile and the rebuilding of Jerusalem and the temple.[13] Fried assumes, however, that the vessels did in fact exist

---

10. Lisbeth S. Fried, "The Land Lay Desolate: Conquest and Restoration in the Ancient Near East," in *Judah and the Judeans in the Neo-Babylonian Period*, ed. Oded Lipschits and Joseph Blenkinsopp (Winona Lake, IN: Eisenbrauns, 2003), 51.

11. Fried, "Land Lay Desolate," 51 (citing Peter R. Ackroyd, "The Temple Vessels: A Continuity Theme," in *Studies in the Religion of Ancient Israel*, VTSup 23 [Leiden: Brill, 1972], 166–81).

12. Fried, "Land Lay Desolate," 51–52.

13. See, for example, Ezra 1:8–11; 5:14, 15; 6:5; Isa 52:11.

at this time. Ackroyd has shown the ideological role that the vessels played in the literature, but in doing so he also raises the possibility that by the late sixth century they only really existed in the literary and theological imagination of the writers.[14] The biblical evidence about the fate of the vessels is ambiguous: some texts indicate they were completely destroyed by the Babylonians while others suggest they were merely carried away.[15] The actual fate of the vessels is not known and we cannot assume that when Cyrus conquered Babylon he came into possession of vessels that would have represented for Yahwists "tangible proof of YHWH's presence."

While neither Bedford nor Fried offers indisputable evidence that Persian permission would have been necessary to rebuild the Jerusalem temple, there is a logic to Bedford's suggestion that the Yehudites could not simply decide to rebuild a national shrine destroyed as punishment for rebellion. Ezra 1–6 makes much not only of the permission given by Cyrus but also of the confirmation of that permission in the face of questions by the governor Tattenai (Ezra 5:3–6:12). Even without assuming the historicity of that scene, one can appreciate the historical plausibility of an authority questioning whether the reconstruction of the temple has been authorized.

It is possible, but not certain, that permission from the Persian administration was necessary for the rebuilding of a national sanctuary destroyed by the Babylonians. If, for the sake of argument, we assume such a requirement, we then have to ask when such permission was given—during the reign of Cyrus or not until later under Darius?

Was the Temple Permitted or Commanded by Cyrus?

The book of Ezra reports that Cyrus gave permission to rebuild the temple in Jerusalem in the first year of his reign (1:1–4).[16] With the exception of 2 Chronicles 36:22–23, a parallel passage, no other texts

---

14. Ackroyd, "Temple Vessels," 168, 181.

15. 2 Kgs 24:13; 25:13–17; Jer 52:17 indicate significant if not complete destruction. Ackroyd comments that the "final effect" of the 2 Kings passages is "to stress that temple and vessels were brought to an end. There is no room for restoration" ("Temple Vessels," 174). Jer 27:16–22; 28:3; Ezra 1:7–11; 5:14, 15; 6:5; 2 Chr 36:7, 10 all refer to the vessels going off to Babylon or being returned from there.

16. In fact the text has him stating that the God of Israel has "appointed" (פקד) him to build the temple (1:2).

refer to such permission.[17] Any historical reconstruction that claims or depends upon such early permission must rely almost entirely on the evidentiary strength of the Ezra account and the materials within it. Some scholars have also turned to extrabiblical evidence such as the Cyrus Cylinder to suggest that in the time of Cyrus there was a general Persian policy of permitting and even actively supporting the reestablishment of national cults. This has been offered as corroboration of the basic claim of Ezra that permission was granted in the reign of Cyrus, in other words, that such an assertion is at least plausible given what we "know" about Cyrus's attitude toward local cults. Yet Ezra's claim that Cyrus gave permission to rebuild the temple in Jerusalem and the notion that there was an empire-wide Persian policy have been subjected to considerable critique.

The book of Ezra presents two documents in support of its claim that Cyrus ordered or permitted the reconstruction of the temple. The first is the Hebrew-language proclamation purported to be from Cyrus (1:2–4), and the second is the Aramaic-language memorandum apparently from the same time, discovered in the reign of Darius in Ecbatana (6:1–5). The Ezra account of initial work on the temple under Cyrus, its cessation shortly afterward, and resumption in the reign of Darius depends on these two documents. So also does the historical reliability of the broad outlines of this narrative, even if we accept that particular aspects of it are not historically credible. If one or both of these documents can be considered reliable in its general content, we have evidence that Cyrus gave permission to rebuild the temple. The authenticity of these documents has been disputed, however. Because the two documents differ in substantive ways, each has been subjected to its own critique and can be considered separately.

The Hebrew edict of 1:2–4 is widely considered spurious, its authenticity being defended by only a handful of scholars in the last decades.[18]

---

17. Possible exceptions to this are 1 Esdras and Josephus, *Ant.* 11:1, neither of which can be considered an independent source. The account in Josephus is derivative and although there is some scholarly debate concerning the direction of dependence between Ezra and 1 Esdras, all agree that the works are not independent of each other. For a discussion of the relationship between 1 Esdras and Ezra see, for example, Charles C. Torrey, *Ezra Studies* (Chicago, IL: University of Chicago Press, 1910; repr., New York, NY: Ktav, 1970), 11–36, and more recently, *Was 1 Esdras First? An Investigation into the Priority and Nature of 1 Esdras*, ed. Lisbeth S. Fried, Ancient Israel and Its Literature 7 (Atlanta, GA: Society of Biblical Literature, 2011).

18. Elias J. Bickerman, "The Edict of Cyrus in Ezra 1," *JBL* 65 (1946): 249–75; updated and expanded

The majority has accepted the argument of Galling, who took it to be a "free composition" by the composer of Ezra, possibly based on the Aramaic document but certainly not a product of the Persian court.[19] I accept the majority judgment that the Hebrew edict cannot be considered evidence for authorization from Cyrus to rebuild the Jerusalem temple.[20]

in *Studies in Jewish and Christian History, Part One*, AGJU 9 (Leiden: Brill, 1976), 72–108; David J. A. Clines, *Ezra, Nehemiah, Esther*, NCB (Grand Rapids, MI: Eerdmans, 1984), 34; H. G. M. Williamson, *Ezra, Nehemiah*, WBC 16 (Waco, TX: Word Books, 1985), 6–7, 41; "The Composition of Ezra i–vi," *JTS* (n.s.) 34 (1983): 8–9; F. Charles Fensham, *The Books of Ezra and Nehemiah*, NICOT (Grand Rapids, MI: Eerdmans, 1982), 44; Loring W. Batten, *Critical and Exegetical Commentary on the Books of Ezra and Nehemiah*, ICC (Edinburgh: T&T Clark, 1946), 60–61. Some acknowledge the plausibility of its authenticity, but remain agnostic: Frank Michaeli, *Les Livres des Chroniques, d'Esdras, et de Néhémie*, CAT 16 (Neuchâtel: Delachaux & Niestle, 1967), 254; Wilhelm Rudolph, *Esra und Nehemia samt 3. Esra*, KAT 20 (Tübingen: Mohr Siebeck, 1949), 6–7.

19. Kurt Galling, *Studien zur Geschichte Israels in persichen Zeitalter* (Tübingen: Mohr Siebeck, 1964), 61–77; Blenkinsopp, *Ezra - Nehemiah*, 74; Torrey, *Ezra Studies*, 301–3; Norman H. Baynes, "Zerubbabel's Rebuilding of the Temple," *JTS* 25 (1924): 154–60; Lester L. Grabbe, *Ezra - Nehemiah*, OTR (London: Routledge, 1998), 126–8; "The 'Persian Documents' in the Book of Ezra: Are They Authentic?" in *Judah and the Judeans in the Persian Period*, ed. Oded Lipschitz and Manfred Oeming (Winona Lake, IN: Eisenbrauns, 2006), 541–44; Sara Japhet, "The Temple in the Restoration Period: Reality and Ideology," *USQR* 44 (1991): 210–14; Antonius H. J. Gunneweg, *Esra*, KAT 19/1 (Gütersloh: Gütersloher Verlagshaus, 1985), 105–6; Bedford, *Temple Restoration*, 128; Jacques Briend, "L'édit de Cyrus et sa valeur historique," *Transeu* 11 (1996): 33–44; Rainer Albertz, *Israel in Exile: The History and Literature of the Sixth Century B.C.E.*, trans. D. Green, Studies in Biblical Literature 3 (Atlanta, GA: Society of Biblical Literature, 2003), 121; Ackroyd, *Exile and Restoration*, 142–44; Baruch Halpern, "A Historiographic Commentary on Ezra 1–6: A Chronological Narrative and Dual Chronology in Israelite Historiography," in *The Hebrew Bible and Its Interpreters*, ed. William Henry Propp, Baruch Halpern, and David Noel Freedman, BJSUCSD 1 (Winona Lake, IN: Eisenbrauns, 1990), 88–93.

20. In addition to the use of the Tetragrammaton, Galling found several features of the text that he considered unlikely to be present in a Persian document of the period, but which could easily be explained as originating from a Jewish scribe. For example, the phrase כה אמר כרש (1:2) lacks parallels in Achaemenid inscriptions, whereas its Yahwistic equivalent is pervasive in biblical literature. The phrase מלך פרס (1:2) is not found in any of the Aramaic documents of Ezra (which Galling considered authentic), nor does it occur by itself in any titles used by Cyrus in attested Persian documents. This title was first used, according to Galling, by Darius I, suggesting that the composer of Ezra was drawing on examples from his own time. The mention of אשר ירושלם ביהודה (1:2, 3) suggested to Galling that the writer understood Judah to be a province, which was not the case until the time of Darius I. Finally, he argued that the concept of the "people of YHWH" in the phrase מי בכם מכל עמו יהי אלהיו עמו (1:3) has a distinctly theological cast to it that would be more at home in Jewish scribal circles than in the Persian chancery. All of these elements, Galling claimed, make it very unlikely that this document came from the Persians. Instead, it is a theological creation of the composer of Ezra designed to join the idea of the return of the exiles as a new exodus with the restoration of the temple.

Galling's argument on the basis of the literary features of the edict itself has been countered on a number of fronts. Williamson's objections ("Composition of Ezra," 11–13) may stand as representative. He has suggested, for example, that some of the apparently incongruous elements may be editorial addenda to a basically authentic text. Thus the apparently inappropriate "of Persia" may be an "unconscious" scribal addition. He also suggests, as have others, that the edict very likely was a response to a Jewish request to rebuild the temple, not a spontaneous decision of the Persian court. Such a request may have contained distinctly Jewish language and concepts, such as the Tetragrammaton or the idea of the people of YHWH, that found its way into the resulting proclamation. To Galling's suggestion that the document's reference to "Judah" was anachronistic

Unlike the Hebrew edict, the Aramaic memorandum (6:3–5) continues to be regarded as basically authentic by most commentators, although some recent scholarship has dissented from the accepted position.[21] Arguments for or against the authenticity of the memorandum generally have been made as part of a larger argument about the authenticity of the Aramaic documents in Ezra as a whole; it has been widely assumed that either all of the Aramaic documents are more or less genuine, or none of them are.[22] Arguments against their authenticity were developed at length several decades ago by Torrey, but failed to have much influence on scholarship, although they continue to be noted throughout the literature.[23] Recently his position has been reargued and extended by Gunneweg and others, leading to a concomitant restatement of arguments in favor of authenticity.

The arguments over the authenticity of the Aramaic documents as a whole fall into two general categories: literary or compositional, and linguistic. Doubts about the historical plausibility of the contents of the memorandum of 6:3–5 have added to charges that it is inauthentic. All of these arguments against authenticity have been rebutted.

Torrey observed that speeches or documents widely recognized as free compositions are a common feature of biblical and non-biblical texts from various periods. He suggested, for example, that no one can really take seriously the possibility that the "letters" of 2 Kings 5:6; 10:2–3; or 2 Chronicles 2:2–15 reflect actual documents.[24] According to

---

for its presupposition of provincial status, Williamson counters that the text does not require this reading; "Judah" could just as easily denote a general geographic area or be a continuation of use of the earlier name. He also adds that there is no positive evidence that Judah was not a province already in the time of Cyrus.

   Despite the efforts of Williamson and others the general sense among scholars is that the text is so consistent in language and aim with Ezra, and reflects such a clear knowledge and acceptance of a Jewish theological perspective in general, that it is not persuasive as a Persian document. I am inclined to agree with this assessment, while acknowledging that to some degree it is subjective. I also note that Williamson's comment that any permission to rebuild would likely have been the response to a Jewish petition has merit, although to what extent the language of the petition would be reflected in an official document is difficult to say. But the objections to authenticity are plausible and need not reflect an inordinate suspicion of the text as a source of historical information. This is not to argue that there was no permission given by Cyrus to return and rebuild the temple, only that Ezra 1:2–4 constitutes at best problematic evidence for this.

21. For example, Grabbe, "Persian Documents," 549–51; Gunneweg, *Esra*, 105–11. These are picking up and developing the arguments of Torrey, *Ezra Studies*, 301–3.
22. With the exception of Grabbe, who tends to consider each document on its own merits ("Persian Documents," 541–60).
23. Torrey, *Ezra Studies*, 140–207.
24. Nor do scholars typically insist on the authenticity of the decrees of, for example, Daniel 3:31–4:34

Torrey, if the "fictional" nature of these examples along with countless other speeches, prayers, letters, decrees, treaties, etc., is so widely acknowledged, there is no reason *not* to assume that the Aramaic documents of Ezra are of the same character.[25] Torrey also argued that everything in the Aramaic documents of Ezra could have been derived from earlier biblical texts such as Haggai, Zechariah 1–8, or 2 Kings 25, as well as from information about the Persian administration, all of which would have been available to any scribe.[26] In other words, these documents easily could have been created by a Jewish author on the basis of existing sources, rather than produced by the Persian chancery. Therefore, Torrey concluded, they were.

Torrey's first point concerning the prevalence of putative decrees and other "reported speech" through the biblical and extra-biblical corpus of Jewish texts is incontestable. Of course it is possible that the Aramaic documents could have been fabricated during the composition of the larger text. The question is whether there is good reason to *assume* that they are inventions. In his evaluation of these materials, Torrey made a presumption of fabrication that leaves all burden of proof to those who would argue for authenticity, or who would even wish to accept them at face value barring evidence to the contrary. There should be no objection to determining that any putative document is a fabrication if there is reason to do so, but it seems too much to make the sweeping judgment that because many such documents in the Bible are very likely compositions of the authors, they all must be. Just as there is no reason to assume *a priori* that the documents are real, there is no reason to assume *a priori* that they are not.

Torrey's second point was that the documents could have been composed on the basis of earlier Jewish texts and available information about Persian matters. This argument presumes that they are "occasional compositions," created specifically for the purposes of the narrative. This possibility has been countered by Williamson, who sug-

---

[MT] and 6:26–28 or those reported in Esther, 1 Maccabees, or 3 Macc 3:12–29 and 7:1–9. And, as have we seen, almost no one accepts the authenticity of the Hebrew edict in Ezra 1.

25. Torrey, *Ezra Studies,* 145–48. Note that he did not argue that there is no reason to assume they are authentic; he specifically said there is no good reason not to think they are fictional. In other words, the presumption is of fictionality, and therefore the burden of proof falls on those who claim authenticity for them.

26. Ibid., 155.

gests that, on the contrary, the Aramaic narrative of Ezra 4:7–6:18 as a whole appears to have been derived entirely *from* the documents.[27] Williamson's argument rests on the observation that the composer of the account appears to have limited it to that for which he had documentation. He notes that there is nowhere an actual record of the rebuilding of the temple, which one would have expected in a narrative about that very topic if the author had composed freely. Instead, all we have are the letters sent between Tattenai and Darius.[28] Williamson readily acknowledges that this is an argument from silence, but offers as more positive evidence the observation that the wording of the narrative portions seems to be derived from the letters, or from other documents. For example, 5:1–2 could have been derived from Haggai and Zechariah 1–8, and 5:3–5 is a nearly verbatim rendition of 5:9–10. The date for the conclusion of the work (6:15), if authentic, could have come from a building inscription or other official record.[29]

Two things may be said about this argument. The first is that it is really the reverse of Torrey's. The latter argued that the documents could have been derived from other sources, whereas Williamson insists that the narrative has been derived from the documents or other sources. Williamson at least presents some evidence for his position, although it is hardly dispositive. Torrey merely raises the possibility of composition from other sources, and then assumes that because such composition is possible, and had been done before with other texts, it must have been done here as well. The second thing to be said for Williamson's argument is that its truth does not necessarily imply that the documents are genuine. They could have been composed freely and still have been used as a source by the composer of the Aramaic narrative.[30] Williamson's reply to this objection is that it is difficult to imagine what reason there would have been to fabricate such documents, what function they could have served apart from this narrative if they were not genuine.[31] This is a fair point, although not one that alone supports authenticity.

27. H. G. M. Williamson, "The Aramaic Documents in Ezra Revisited," *JTS* NS 59 (2008): 47.
28. Ibid., 47.
29. Ibid., 47–48.
30. Antonius H. J. Gunneweg, "Die aramäische und die hebräische Erzählung über die nachexilische Restauration - ein Vergleich," *ZAW* 94 (1982): 300.
31. Williamson, "Aramaic Documents," 48.

These compositional arguments are not much help in assessing the authenticity of the Aramaic documents. Torrey's position rests on too many assumptions and Williamson's argument, while based on some evidence, is inconclusive at best. Arguments regarding authenticity are grounded better on more objective arguments based on analysis of linguistic or formal features.

In a monograph on the subject, Schwiderski has argued from epistolary features that the Aramaic documents are spurious. Rather than finding expected elements characteristic of the Persian period, he discerns epistolary features typical of the Hellenistic period.[32] For example, whereas in the Persian period the addressee of an Aramaic letter was introduced by על (as in Ezra 4:11, 17) or אל, in Ezra 5:7 the addressee is introduced by ל, a usage of the Hellenistic period.[33] In addition, while the greetings of the Persian period tend to be elaborate, in the Hellenistic period we see, under the influence of χαίρειν, the use of a simple שלם, such as we find in Ezra 4:17.[34] Schwiderski also notes various aspects of the way senders or addressees are introduced in most of the letters that do not correspond to what one would expect of Achaemenid period letters.[35] On the basis of this evidence, Schwiderski concludes that the letters of the Aramaic narrative cannot have been written in the Achaemenid period, but have been composed according to Hellenistic epistolary conventions.[36]

In assessing the work of Schwiderski, scholars have acknowledged that the letters as they are presently found in Ezra "fall short of proper Imperial Aramaic epistolary usage" in several important ways, and also have certain exclusively Hellenistic elements.[37] They have nevertheless challenged some of Schwiderski's conclusions. Conklin, for example,

32. Dirk Schwiderski, *Handbuch des nordwestsemitischen Briefformulars: Ein Beitrag zur Echtheitsfrage der aramäischen Briefe des Esrabuches*, BZAW 295 (Berlin: de Gruyter, 2000).
33. Ibid., 355–60.
34. Ibid., 364–68.
35. Ibid., 361–64; 368–75.
36. Ibid., 375–80.
37. The phrase is from Blane W. Conklin, review of *Handbuch des nordwestsemitischen Briefformulars: Ein Beitrag zur Echtheitsfrage der aramäischen Briefe des Esrabuches*, by Dirk Schwiderski, *JSS* 48 (2003): 139. For other critiques of Schwiderski, see Jerome A. Lund, "Aramaic Language," in *Dictionary of the Old Testament: Historical Books*, ed. Bill T. Arnold and H. G. M. Williamson (Downers Grove, IL: InterVarsity Press, 2005), 51; Frank H. Polak, "Sociolinguistics and the Judean Speech Community in the Achaemenid Empire," in *Judah and the Judeans in the Persian Period*, ed. Oded Lipschitz and Manfred Oeming (Winona Lake, IN: Eisenbrauns, 2006), 596n32; Williamson, "Aramaic Documents," 57–61; Andrew E. Steinmann, "Letters of Kings about Votive Offerings, the God of

notes that some of the "omissions and infelicities" Schwiderski cites as evidence against Persian-period composition would also be a problem for Hellenistic usage.[38] In other words, the letters in their present state are no more clearly Hellenistic than they are Achaemenid. Others have argued that some of the deviations from Achaemenid style are possibly due to judicious editing on the part of a Hellenistic editor or composer. Polak, for example, suggests that the absence of the expected addressees or introductory greetings is likely the work of the composer who incorporated them into the larger narrative.[39]

With regard to the shorter greeting, שלם, the form used as greeting is also found in several fifth-century ostraca, suggesting it would have been intelligible in an earlier period.[40] This proposal is problematic because the evidence is from a later period than the putative date of these documents. In addition, one would hardly expect such a foreshortened greeting in official correspondence. Williamson anticipated this objection, positing that the present form is the work of editor, who removed elements of a longer form.[41]

The use of ל to introduce addressees, a Hellenistic feature, has been explained in two ways. The first is to note that this usage is not consistent; the older, expected forms of על and אל also appear in some of the Ezra letters. Schwiderski argues that this is an attempt at archaizing to give the documents an air of authenticity. This expedient is hardly persuasive, considering how haphazard—and therefore incompetent—such an attempt, if it were real, would be. Williamson is surely correct to suggest that earlier forms should be seen as remnants from earlier texts rather than as half-hearted, sporadic attempts at archaizing.[42] A second explanation is that, as with the greeting שלם, it is possible that the usage was already present before the Hellenistic period. Lund cites several fifth-century examples of ל introducing an

---

Israel, and the Aramaic Document in Ezra 4:8–6:18," *JHS* 8 (2008): article 23, available at http://www.JHSonline.org, 5–6.

38. Conklin, "Review," 139.

39. Polak, "Sociolinguistics," 596n32. See also Williamson, "Aramaic Documents," 59–61.

40. Williamson, "Aramaic Documents," 60. The references to which Williamson refers can be found in Lund, "Aramaic Language," 51.

41. Williamson, "Aramaic Documents," 59. See also Steinman, "Letters," 5.

42. Williamson, "Aramaic Documents," 59. We will also see below that one of the hallmarks of these texts is the presence of both later and earlier forms of Aramaic, making it difficult to argue that archaizing accounts for any earlier forms.

addressee.[43] Here we have the same possible problem as with שלם, namely that the evidence comes from a later period than that ascribed to the documents in question.

Those who are critical of Schwiderski's interpretation have also noted that he does not sufficiently consider a key epistolary feature characteristic of the Achaemenid period, namely the markers used to transition from the greeting to the contents of a letter: בעת, כען, כענת.[44] Schwiderski discusses these markers in some detail, and even notes that in the Hellenistic period these are replaced by די in Aramaic.[45] Yet he does not account for their consistent appearance in the Aramaic letters of Ezra, except to posit again an attempt to give an air of antiquity to the letters, an explanation that has failed to persuade his critics.

The epistolary evidence examined is not conclusive, but it does suggest that the Aramaic documents did not originate in the Hellenistic period. Schwiderski's evidence is vitiated by the presence of earlier elements that cannot be explained away simply by hypothesizing archaisms. At the same time, evidence for a pre-Hellenistic origin does not demonstrate that the documents are the product of the early Persian period or that they are authentic documents of the Achaemenid administration of any period. This rather limited conclusion is also supported by an examination of certain linguistic and lexical features of the Aramaic documents. Here also we have a mixture of earlier and later forms.

One of the cornerstones of "anti-authenticity" arguments is that the Aramaic of the documents is a form of the language that emerged or became common much later than the early Persian period. Torrey noted that it had been widely agreed for some time that Daniel 2–7 and Ezra reflected the same stage of Aramaic, which he dated to the third or second century.[46] Bedford has subsequently claimed that this judgment can be set aside, "since Aramaicists agree that the Aramaic of the book of Ezra does indeed predate that of Daniel, although both are categorized as being Imperial Aramaic."[47] Whether the Aramaic of Ezra is

---

43. Lund, "Aramaic Language," 51; Williamson, "Aramaic Documents," 59.
44. Williamson, "Aramaic Documents," 58; Richard C. Steiner, "Bishlam's Archival Search Report in Nehemiah's Archive: Multiple Introductions and Reverse Chronological Order as Clues to the Origin of the Aramaic Letters in Ezra 4–6," *JBL* 125 (2006): 680; Steinmann, "Letters," 5–6.
45. Schwiderski, *Handbuch*, 155–64; 250–52.
46. Torrey, *Ezra Studies*, 161–66.

earlier than that of Daniel is irrelevant, however, if it is still later than the early Persian period (and this is especially true of the memorandum, as this document is reported to date from the first year of Cyrus).

Torrey's argument that the sibilants and dentals of the Aramaic of Ezra reflect those seen in the Targums and classical Syriac, rather than in Imperial Aramaic, is stronger, and has been taken up as the most prominent bit of evidence for late dating of the texts. Whereas Ezra has throughout the relative pronoun or genitive marker די,[48] this form is found with some exceptions only in texts from the fourth century and later. Earlier texts, such as the fifth-century finds from Egypt, generally employ the older form, זי, which does not appear anywhere in Ezra.[49] This strongly suggests the documents are from a later period. However, Folmer, who has produced a detailed study of the variability of Aramaic in the Achaemenid period, presents three examples of די from Elephantine as early as the late fifth century.[50] Given the *exclusive* use of the later form in Ezra it is possible that Williamson and others are correct that this later form can be attributed to scribal updating of orthography, a practice attested in other places, and so not impossible here.[51]

Additional evidence for an earlier dating may be found in the use and distribution of earlier and later forms of the second and third person pronominal suffixes. The earlier forms, -כם and -הם, are found throughout the Aramaic portions of Ezra, as is the later form, -הון. This is relatively unhelpful for dating, except when we take into account the distribution of the forms. Folmer notes that eight of the eleven instances of the earlier form -הם are found in the documents, while eleven of the fifteen instances of the later form -הון are found in the narrative portions of the text.[52] This difference in the distribution is hardly dispositive, but the fact that the older forms are predominantly

---

47. Bedford, *Temple Restoration*, 130. It is unclear how well Bedford supports this statement, as he does not cite anyone who maintains this position. He only points to F. Rosenthal (*Die aramaistische Forschung seit Th. Nöldekes Veröffentlichungen* [Leiden: Brill, 1939], 48–71) for a summary of the main issues (130n101). In the same footnote he mentions a few scholars who do date the Aramaic of the two works to the same period, only much earlier than Torrey (Kitchen, Hasel, Beyer).

48. The form occurs 67 times in Ezra 4–6.

49. Torrey, *Ezra Studies*, 162–24. See also Grabbe, "Persian Documents," 533.

50. Williamson, "Aramaic Documents," 55 (citing Margaretha L. Folmer, *The Aramaic Language in the Achaemenid Period: A Study in Linguistic Variation*, OLA 68 [Leuven: Peeters, 1995], 50–51).

51. Williamson, "Aramaic Documents," 51–52; see Grabbe, "Persian Documents," 533; Folmer, *Aramaic Language*, 754.

52. Folmer, *Aramaic Language*, 150; Williamson, "Aramaic Documents," 55.

in the documents is at least consistent with the idea that they are older than the surrounding narrative material. If this is the case, we are still left with the notion of a scribe or scribes who inconsistently or haphazardly updated the orthography. This might be acceptable, if we were not at the same time left with the seemingly incoherent notion that these same scribes inconsistently or haphazardly archaized the orthography of the narrative portions, occasionally using older forms for no apparent reason. It seems more likely that older forms were used throughout both the documents and the narrative portion and that these were (inconsistently) updated at a later stage or stages of redaction or copying. This is essentially the same explanation Williamson offered for the exclusive use of די throughout the text, and it may be the best explanation we have. At this point, those who argue for earlier provenience of the documents have a slight advantage, although it must be stressed that this is not an argument *for* authenticity, but a counter-argument to those who argue that the documents *cannot be* authentic because they display late features.

The Aramaic documents in Ezra contain certain lexical elements that have not, so far, been found in later documents, and this too has been taken as evidence in favor of earlier dating. Two elements observed by Steiner and cited by Williamson are the idiomatic use of שמה following a proper name and the use of the phrase בעל טעם. The first phrase (ששבצר שמה), found in Ezra 5:14, is used to "de-definitize" a proper name: "a certain Sheshbazzar," and has so far not been found in later Aramaic documents. The same is true for the phrase בעל טעם ("commander" or "commissioner"), which occurs at Ezra 4:8–9.[53] Finally, Grabbe has identified three loan words for which he finds no evidence of post-Achaemenid use: אספרנו בלו, and אדרזדא.[54] Of course this evidence is far from conclusive.

To these observations in favor of Persian-period dating, Porten has added a list of ten parallels between the Aramaic documents and epigraphic material from the Achaemenid period: (1) numerous Akkadian and Persian loan words; (2) the presence of the transitional markers; (3) an opening statement that portends a negative situation; (4) verbs

53. Williamson, "Aramaic Documents," 56 (citing Steiner, "Archival Search Report," 643–46).
54. Grabbe, "Persian Documents," 558.

of motion; (5) regular use of the anaphoric demonstrative; (6) a summary formula explaining the dispatch of the letter; (7) fixed formulas for issuing an order; (8) a formula for warning or threat; (9) titles; and (10) repetition of key words in successive paragraphs. None of these elements taken alone is proof of anything, but taken as a whole, and in conjunction with the ambiguous or positive linguistic evidence, they support dating the Aramaic documents to the Achaemenid period.[55]

All of this evidence supports early dating for the Aramaic documents in Ezra, albeit ambiguously and inconclusively. Yet it brings us no closer to the question of authenticity. If we accept that the documents arise out of the early Achaemenid period, we are still unsure whether or not they were created by the composer of Ezra or another non-Persian source.

The recent work of Polak on the syntactic structure of the Aramaic documents offers some substantive and objective support for authenticity. Polak observes that the letters that purport to come from the Achaemenid chancery are indeed marked by a syntax that is characteristic of eastern Aramaic (object preceding verbal predicate). This suggests that its use in these documents "fits the eastern center of gravity of the Achaemenid administration."[56] The clauses of the narrative portions, on the other hand, most often have a syntactical structure typical of western Aramaic (predicate followed by object).[57] This significant contrast between the syntax of the letters and of the narrative suggests that they derive from two different sources. The consistency of this evidence is compelling and lends support to the ambiguous lexical evidence offered by Williamson for a difference of date between the narrative and the documents. What is most striking about Polak's syntactical observations is that the documents also reflect the "syntactical register of the imperial administration."[58] Here we have, in my judgment, reasonable evidence in favor of authenticity that does not rest on deeply ambiguous lexical observations or subjective expectations of compositional practices. Taken all together, there is sufficient support for a

55. Bezalel Porten, "Elephantine and the Bible" in *Semitic Papyrology in Context: A Climate of Creativity: Papers from a New York University Conference Marking the Retirement of Baruch A. Levine*, ed. Lawrence H. Schiffman, CHANE (Leiden: Brill, 2003), 58–59.
56. Polak, "Sociolinguistics," 592–94.
57. Ibid., 595–96.
58. Ibid., 594.

presumption of at least basic authenticity of these documents, albeit always with an awareness that they have undergone scribal emendation to suit the theological perspective of the Ezra narrative.

What of the memorandum of 6:3–5 in particular? Here we find three aspects that have been taken as evidence of inauthenticity: (1) apparently incongruous literary or linguistic elements; (2) concern with the measurements and building materials of the proposed temple, as well as the promise of imperial financial support, which appear more likely to issue from a Jewish scribe than the Persian chancery; and (3) the unlikely claim that Cyrus would concern himself with the reconstruction of the temple of a local god in a small corner of his empire. The first objection can be discussed briefly, whereas the second and third, because they relate to the Persian attitude toward the temple reconstruction project, must be examined in more detail.

Torrey and others have compiled a long list of literary and lexical features of the Aramaic memorandum that suggest inauthenticity. Gunneweg claims that the date of Cyrus's memorandum "in the first year of his reign" (6:3) is a "theological" rather than a historical datum, and mirrors its use in Ezra 1:1.[59] In both cases Cyrus is seen as a *Heilskönig*.[60] Gunneweg also finds the notice that the memorandum was written on a מגלה (6:2) a good example of "Jewish coloring," as it is more likely that the memorandum would have been recorded on a tablet if it were real.[61] Finally he claims that the sudden shift from the

---

59. Victor A. Hurowitz (*I Have Built You an Exalted House: Temple Building in the Bible in the Light of Mesopotamian and Northwest Semitic Writings*, JSOTSup 115 [Sheffield: JSOT Press, 1992], 284) notes that it was considered a fitting act for a king to do an "impressive feat" on behalf of a god, such as build a temple, in his first year. This suggests that it is not necessarily the case that only Yahwists would have a theological or ideological reason for making this claim. It could just as easily be seen as *Persian* propaganda. On the other hand, as it is clear that Ezra 1–6 wishes to portray Cyrus (and then Darius) as royal builders, the assignment of this "impressive feat" to Cyrus's first year makes eminent sense as part of that overall portrayal, even if not in precisely the same the way Gunneweg supposes.

60. Gunneweg, *Esra*, 105. See also Batten, *Ezra*, 142, who suggests that "[i]t is quite unlikely that Cyrus would call 539 (or 538) his 1st year. It would be all right if put as Esd. 217 (Heb. 513), *in the first year that Cyrus was king of Babylonia*. [The redactor] may have changed the year to agree with 11" (which Batten considered authentic). Edelman cites Batten here but explains further the logic: "[T]he use of the year 1 of Cyrus in v. 3 presumes his first year as king over Babylonia. This was not his first year as king of Persia, however, and it is likely that Cyrus' regnal years would have been calculated from his assumption of the throne of Persia and that any official document promulgated at his court in his name would have used the Persian reckoning of his regnal years" (*Origins*, 182).

61. Gunneweg, *Esra*, 107. This objection of course relates more to the account surrounding the memorandum than to the document itself.

third to the second person in v. 5 (ותחת בבית אלהא) is not possible in an authentic edict, and can only be taken to reflect the work of the composer of Ezra.[62] Torrey also noted the use of the late form דכרונה, whereas the earlier form of זכרן, such as is found at Elephantine, would be more likely in an early Persian-period document.[63] Further objections could be related, but these suffice to indicate the kinds of arguments brought to bear on the question. It is noteworthy that a number of these objections have not been answered in the scholarship, particularly those that posit a "Jewish coloring" to the text of the memorandum, and it is undeniable that this document does fit the perspective of the larger Ezra account to a remarkable degree. It is reasonable to suspect that the document is not being presented in its original form. Whether the document is entirely fictional or whether an authentic record has been "edited" to bring it in line with the Ezra account is difficult to judge.

Turning from linguistic and literary features to the content of the memorandum, we find objections that the attention to the details of the measurements and materials of the temple is implausible for an authentic Persian document. Batten, for example, noted that the specifics of the building method and materials ("three courses of cut stone for each one of timber") seems to derive from 1 Kings 6:36, with the implication that it therefore must have been the creation of a Jewish scribe.[64] Commenting on the presence of the dimensions of the temple in the text, Edelman suggests that Cyrus would not have been aware of either these or, for that matter, of the specifics of the building methods.[65] The presence of such details are thus seen as far-fetched or derived from earlier texts and therefore inauthentic.

In response to these objections concerning the details of the build-

---

62. Gunneweg: "Daß das in einem authentischen Edikt nicht wohl möglich ist, bleibt unbestritten" (*Esra*, 108). He is perhaps correct in this statement, insofar as no one has (to my knowledge) attempted to answer this objection. However, it has been suggested that the text he cites is corrupt and that the second person form ותחת should be emended. Torrey (*Ezra Studies*, 193ni) claims that "the second person is out of the question here" and suggests reading the form as the *hophal* 3rd masc. sing. imperfect (וינחת). This reading, supported by the Greek (οὗ ἐτέθη) and the Vulgate (posita sunt), is also proposed by *BHS*. Suggesting that the versions reflect the "facilitation of a syntactical difficulty," *BHQ* retains the MT, citing 4QEzra [4Q117] in support (ותחת).

63. Torrey, *Ezra Studies*, 192nd.

64. ויבן את החצר הפנימית שלשה טורי גזית וטור כרתת אזרים; Batten, *Ezra*, 142.

65. Edelman, *Origins*, 183–84.

ing, Williamson suggests, in the first place, that Cyrus would hardly have ordered the reconstruction of a temple that he knew nothing about. It is likely, he argues, that the edict for the restoration of the temple was a response to a Jewish petition, rather than a spontaneous initiative of the Persians.[66] This memorandum would then reflect specifically permission to restore or replace the old temple and no more, in which case it would be appropriate to include such details in order to specify what was being permitted. As for the objection that such measurements would not have been known by Cyrus or his administration, Williamson suggests that if anyone of the administration wanted such measurements, they could have been rather easily discovered.[67]

Williamson further defends the plausibility of the details by noting that if the Persians were paying for the reconstruction, as the memorandum indicates, they would have been interested in specifying the size and composition of the temple for which they were paying. This observation, while reasonable enough, is nevertheless based on the assumption that the notice of imperial financial support in the memorandum is authentic. A number of scholars have found this improbable. Grabbe, for example, finds the very idea a "fantasy"; it was Persian policy to tax temples, not to finance them.[68] In response to such objections, Williamson notes that such Persian generosity would not have been without parallel, citing several instances given by de Vaux of Persian support during the reigns of Cambyses and Darius. Further, bricks with the name of Cyrus on them show that the buildings in which they were used were state-supported.[69] These may represent specific instances of Persian generosity or support, but as Bedford has shown, minor cults were usually expected to support themselves financially and there is little reason to think that the Jerusalem temple would have been an exception.[70]

---

66. Williamson, *Ezra*, 80–81. Bedford (*Temple Restoration*, 151) also suggests that the permission would have probably only been given in response to a petition; otherwise the Persians would simply have ignored the cult.

67. Williamson, *Ezra*, 80–81.

68. Lester L. Grabbe, "'Mind the Gaps': Ezra, Nehemiah and the Judean Restoration," in *Restoration: Old Testament, Jewish, and Christian Perspectives*, ed. James M. Scott, JSJSup 72 (Leiden: Brill, 2001), 91; "Persian Documents," 535, 540–41.

69. Williamson, *Ezra*, 80–1; de Vaux, "Decrees of Cyrus," 92–93. See also Steiner, "Archival Search Report," 646.

Here we come to the question of main interest: if the Persians did give permission to rebuild the temple in Jerusalem, what would have been their attitude toward it? Did they simply give permission for it to be rebuilt, perhaps in response to a petition? Or in giving permission did Cyrus take responsibility for the temple, in effect undertaking to be its royal patron (as the Hebrew and Aramaic documents suggest)?

If Cyrus took responsibility for the cult as its royal patron, then the concern for the measurements and the promise of financial support are only to be expected. Ezra certainly paints Cyrus as the royal builder and patron of the Jerusalem temple. Royal patrons in the ANE rebuilt temples—or said they did so—at the command or with the permission of the relevant deity. Thus if Cyrus did give permission to rebuild the temple, he would assure posterity that he did it with the approval of its god. Accordingly, Ezra 1 has him claiming he was commanded by YHWH to rebuild. Further, if Cyrus did consider himself the royal builder, he would have an interest in the original dimensions of the temple. Builder-kings were anxious to ensure that the temple plans were acceptable to the gods and so when rebuilding often considered it safe to build according to older plans, not deviating from the original foundations or patterns, which were presumed to have already proven acceptable to the gods, or even decreed by them, and so "safe."[71] If those "plans" are reflected in 1 Kings 6, then that text (if it had been composed by the time of Cyrus) would logically have served as the source of the memorandum dimensions. If Cyrus did give permission to rebuild the temple, and therefore took on the role of builder-king, it is not impossible to credit his apparent concern with what may appear to modern commentators as mere details of the building plan for the reconstructed temple, unlikely to be of interest to a great monarch. On the contrary, ancient kings would have been greatly concerned with such things.

As royal patron, Cyrus would have understood his role to entail underwriting the expenses of reconstruction. It would hardly have befitted him to take on the role but not the expense of a builder-king. This is not to deny that he would later have taxed the temple or

---

70. Bedford, *Temple Restoration*, 144–45. He cites the examples of Elephantine, Xanthos, and Teima.
71. Henri Frankfort, *Kingship and the Gods: A Study of Ancient Near Eastern Religion as the Integration of Society and Nature*, Oriental Institute Essays (Chicago, IL: University of Chicago Press, 1948), 269–71.

imposed the cost of maintenance on the local populace; patronage and economic exploitation were not mutually exclusive.[72]

The presence of the concern for measurements, as well as the promise of financial backing of the reconstruction, are fully consistent with a portrayal of Cyrus as the royal builder of the Jerusalem temple. If Cyrus did in fact consider himself the royal patron, then these details might be authentic elements of a genuine memorandum.

There is, however, very little to support the claim that Cyrus considered himself the designated builder of the temple. The fact that it was not completed for years after he is reported to have given permission indicates he and his administration cared little or nothing about the temple in Jerusalem. If Cyrus considered himself the royal patron of the temple, enough to concern himself with its details and to finance it, it is unlikely that he would have allowed the project to simply lapse or never get off the ground in the first place. This suggests that the elements of the Aramaic memorandum designed to support the image of Cyrus as royal benefactor and patron of the Jerusalem cult are the work of the editors of Ezra and not of the Achaemenid chancery. Is this enough to discount the possibility of an authentic document underlying the edited version? Despite all this, can we still suppose that Cyrus gave permission and resources to have the temple rebuilt without caring whether or not the project came off? If the documents are just as likely to be "doctored" as not, is there anything else to support the claim that Cyrus gave permission for the temple to be rebuilt?

Recognizing the weakness of the Ezra evidence, commentators have often asserted that even if the edicts in Ezra are not authentic, the claim that Cyrus gave permission is at least consistent with what we "know" about Persian policy regarding local cults. This alleged knowledge of early Achaemenid policy is based almost entirely on an interpretation of the significance of the Cyrus Cylinder. This text's claim that at the behest of Marduk Cyrus reinstated the cult of the deities in Babylon and other cults farther afield has been taken to indicate a stance toward all cults within Cyrus's domains. Blenkinsopp states that although the Hebrew edict is a "free composition," it nevertheless

---

72. Bedford, *Temple Restoration*, 144 (citing Muhammad A. Dandamaev and Vladimir G. Lukonin, *The Culture and Social Institutions of Ancient Iran*, trans. Philip L. Kohl and D. J. Dadson [Cambridge: Cambridge University Press, 1989], 362–65).

"is in general consonant with early Achaemenid policy."[73] Likewise, Michaeli sees in the Cylinder an "attitude de large tolérance religieuse qui ordanna de rétablir les sanctuaires étrangers," which means that the Aramaic memorandum "non contient donc rien d'invraisemblable en lui-même, mais s'accorde au contraire parfaitement avec ce que nous savons par ailleurs de l'histoire perse."[74]

The Cyrus Cylinder corresponds in physical shape and literary genre to Mesopotamian deposits placed in foundations of temples at the time of construction or rebuilding. Such texts, couched in standardized language, always represent the king as having acted piously toward the relevant god.[75] In this case, the god is Marduk, whose cult has been restored by Cyrus upon his conquest of Babylon. Of particular interest is the notice that besides reinstating the cult of Marduk in Babylon, Cyrus restored the images of gods to other sanctuaries:

> From [Ninev]eh (?), Ashur and Susa, Agade, Eshnunna, Zamban, Meturnu, Der, as far as the region of Gutium, I returned the (images of) the gods to the sacred centers [on the other side of] the Tigris who sanctuaries had been abandoned for a long time, and I let them dwell in eternal abodes. I gathered all their inhabitants and returned (to them) their dwellings. In addition, at the command of Marduk, the great lord, I settled in their habitations, in pleasing abodes, the gods of Sumer and Akkad, whom Nabonidus, to the anger of the lord of the gods, had brought into Babylon. (lines 30–34)

He then asks that all these gods he has resettled "ask daily of Bel and Nabu that my days be long and may they intercede for my welfare."[76]

This text—along with bricks stamped with the name of Cyrus found at Uruk (the Eanna temple of Ishtar) and at Ur (the Enunmah temple of Sin), as well as a foundation cylinder at the latter which can probably also be attributed to Cyrus—forms the basis of the theory that Cyrus instituted a benevolent religious policy throughout the empire that included the restoration of local cults.[77] The mention in the final lines

---

73. Blenkinsopp, *Ezra-Nehemiah*, 74.; Rudolph, *Esra*, 6–7. This idea has made it into the popular ideas about the significance of the CC and the portrayal of Cyrus as an ancient proponent of "religious freedom."

74. Michaeli, *Chroniques*, 255. Clines (*Ezra*, 34) likewise derives from the Cylinder the general conclusion that "restoration of holy places was especially important to Cyrus; cf. the last two paragraphs of the Cyrus cylinder, lines 28–36)."

75. Amélie Kuhrt, "The Cyrus Cylinder and Achaemenid Imperial Policy," *JSOT* 25 (1983): 88.

76. "Cyrus Cylinder," translated by Mordechai Cogan (*COS* 2.124:314–16).

of the text of the return of various gods to their sanctuaries has been taken to suggest that Cyrus acted according to a general policy and that, therefore, there could have been other cults reinstated in other parts of the imperium. This assumption of a wider policy has led scholars to argue that it is plausible that Cyrus also took care to see that the cult of YHWH in Jerusalem was restored at the beginning of his reign. The documents in Ezra may not be real, but they *could have been* because Cyrus did elsewhere the sort of thing they claim he did in Jerusalem. The difficulty with this argument is that the premise is flawed.

There are two problems with this reading of the cylinder. The first is a failure to acknowledge the limited scope of the actions it reports. In her analysis of the text, Kuhrt observed that the text as a whole is concerned specifically with Marduk, who orders the restoration of the other gods to their sanctuaries. These gods are subject to Marduk, and therefore their restoration is an element of Cyrus's claim to be acting piously toward the head god. This text, then, is about pleasing Marduk; the reference to the restoration of the other gods is related to that. These gods are returned to specific places, most of which are close to or within Babylonia, which further supports the idea that these gods are understood to be within the Babylonian pantheon supervised by Marduk and therefore included only because of their relationship to him.[78] Kuhrt concludes from these observations that the text cannot be taken as evidence of a general policy, but because of its "Babylo-centricity" must be recognized as having only a "limited local application."[79] It is a foundation cylinder for a temple dedicated to Marduk and reflects the traditional language and concepts related to that specific occasion. Kuhrt's argument that the cylinder does not constitute evidence of a general (which is to say, indiscriminate) empire-wide policy regarding local and national cults has been accepted in a number of recent studies.[80]

---

77. De Vaux, "Decrees of Cyrus," 64–78. In his study of the inscriptional evidence of the activities of Cyrus (and of Cambyses and Darius I), de Vaux concluded that the "religious policies of the first Persian kings are sufficiently illustrated by these documents. . . . Everywhere, whether it be in Asia Minor, Egypt, or Babylonia, they respected and even encouraged local customs so long as they did not run contrary to public order" (77).
78. Kuhrt, "Cyrus Cylinder," 87–88.
79. Ibid., 93.

The second methodological problem is the assumption that the Persians treated all political entities alike. It seems rather that they regarded certain centers such as Babylon and Egypt as more politically and culturally important and treated their cults accordingly. Kuhrt suggests that in these major centers the Persian rulers wished to appear as "active upholders of local cults in order to ensure control of the wealthy sanctuaries and the adherence of their staff."[81] In such important locales, Cyrus and his successors could be expected to give permission for the restoration of a destroyed temple because it would serve their interests to do so. A smaller, less important center such as Jerusalem could not expect the same consideration, at least not automatically.[82] Kuhrt suggests, however, that as early as Cyrus the Persians may have had a policy of restoring smaller cults when it was considered politically or militarily expedient. Drawing on the work of Harmatta, she argues that the Cylinder appears to have been modeled on the rebuilding texts of Assurbanipal, and suggests that this may be evidence that Cyrus adopted the policy of neo-Assyrian kings regarding cults in strategically important areas: "What has emerged, however, rather tentatively is that Cyrus followed a policy similar to that of some earlier Assyrian rulers, whereby cities occupying a key-position in troublesome areas or areas where there was likely to be international conflict had their privileges and/or exempt status reinstated and guaranteed by the central government."[83] She thus suggests that "one could envisage" Cyrus or another Persian ruler not only supporting but encouraging the rebuilding of the Jerusalem temple as part of a politically and militarily pragmatic policy of establishing loyalty from the local populace.[84] This would only be the case, however, if Jerusalem and Yehud were thought already in the time of Cyrus to be "near a frontier in a politically sensitive zone" (such as Egypt).[85]

Yet once again we come up against the fact that the temple was not

80. Bedford, *Temple Restoration*, 142; Grabbe, *Ezra - Nehemiah*, 126; Gunneweg, *Esra*, 105–6.
81. Kuhrt, *Ancient Near East*, 2.699.
82. Bedford, *Temple Restoration*, 142. Bedford also suggests that a temple such as that of YHWH in Jerusalem, destroyed in the course of suppressing a rebellion against imperial rule, "would not have been an obvious or natural candidate for restoration under Cyrus."
83. Kuhrt, "Cyrus Cylinder," 93.
84. Ibid., 94.
85. Ibid.

completed until years later. This observation alone strongly suggests that Cyrus did not take responsibility for the Jerusalem temple. He did not take on the role of its royal patron nor did he command its reconstruction. If he had, almost certainly it would have been completed. Cyrus may have given permission for the temple to be rebuilt, but he did not command it; it was not a "Persian project."[86]

It was therefore up to the Yehudites to decide whether or not to rebuild the temple and when to do so. In the next section, we examine reasons why they would have been unwilling or unable to do so as late as 520 BCE.

Objections and Obstacles to Reconstruction

When Haggai called to rebuild the temple in 520 BCE, he needed to persuade his audience to adopt his position in the face of several potential objections or obstacles. These barriers to reconstruction, which are interrelated, can be broadly categorized as theological and socioeconomic.

Theological Objections and Obstacles

The building or repair of a temple in the ANE could only proceed once certain theological conditions had been met. It would be inconceivable to act unless it was determined that the relevant deity or

---

86. Jon L. Berquist and James M. Trotter have speculated that later in the reign of Darius I the Persians did command the temple rebuild. Berquist has proposed that they initiated reconstruction as part of their preparations to invade Egypt. A loyal temple administration would allow Darius to secure his supply lines and help increase food production for Persian troops (*Judaism in Persia's Shadow: A Social and Historical Approach* [Minneapolis, MN: Fortress Press, 1995], 53–63). Trotter extends this line of thought, suggesting that the temple would serve as an economic and political administrative center before and after the Persian army's passage through the area ("Was the Second Temple a Primarily Persian Project?" *SJOT* 15 [2001]: 289–91). These proposals suffer from a complete lack of supporting evidence. No biblical texts hint at Persian interest in the temple in the reign of Darius, instead ascribing all interest and agency to Yehudites. Archaeological evidence indicates that nearby Ramat Raḥel, not Jerusalem, served as the main Yehudite administrative and collection center (at least for liquid commodities) throughout the Persian period. See Oded Lipschits and David S. Vanderhooft, *The Yehud Stamp Impressions: A Corpus of Inscribed Impressions from the Persian and Hellenistic Periods in Judah* (Winona Lake, IN: Eisenbrauns, 2011), 759–61; "Yehud Stamp Impressions in the Fourth Century B.C.E: A Time of Administrative Consolidation?" in *Judah and the Judeans in the Fourth Century B.C.E.*, ed. Oded Lipschits, Gary N. Knoppers, and Rainer Albertz (Winona Lake, IN: Eisenbrauns, 2007), 89–90; Oded Lipschits, "Persian-Period Judah: A New Perspective," in *Texts, Contexts and Readings in Postexilic Literature*, ed. Louis Jonker, FAT 2/53 (Tübingen: Mohr Siebeck, 2011), 202–7.

deities approved. Such assurance could be communicated mantically.[87] To work without confirmation of divine approbation was to court disaster.[88] Building inscriptions frequently refer to the concern not only to affirm whether the gods desire a particular project, but also to build according to whatever instructions the gods have given.[89] In the case of a temple understood to have been destroyed because of the anger of a deity, indication would also be needed that the divine anger that led to the destruction of the temple in the first place had passed.[90] In accordance with both Israelite tradition as revealed in the biblical texts and broader ANE conceptions, there would typically also be an expectation that a temple would be built during a time of peace and prosperity. These irenic conditions signaled not only the goodwill of the god toward the people but also the victory of that god over enemies. Finally, also in accordance with ANE temple ideology, one would normally expect a royal builder to complete a significant sanctuary.[91]

87. Hurowitz, *Exalted House*, 143–54.

88. In addition to famine and other natural disasters, signs of divine disapproval could include failure to complete the project or the collapse of the new temple shortly after completion (Hurowitz, *Exalted House*, 137).

89. The literature on this is extensive and will be drawn upon as necessary at various points in this study. The primary discussions can be found in Richard S. Ellis, *Foundation Deposits in Ancient Mesopotamia*, YNER 2 (New Haven, CT: Yale University Press, 1968), 7–34, and Hurowitz, *Exalted House*, 131–67. Much scholarship on the building of the first temple by Solomon and the rebuilding of the temple in the Persian period, as well as studies of the wilderness tabernacle tradition, has drawn on the work of these and other scholars. For a recent collection of useful essays on temple building in the ANE and in the Bible from the third millennium to the Persian period, see Mark J. Boda and Jamie Novotny, eds., *From the Foundations to the Crenellations*, AOAT 366 (Münster: Ugarit-Verlag, 2010).

The concern to act precisely according to divine will could make the process fraught and productive of much anxiety for some builders. Ellis (*Foundation Deposits*, 7) calls attention to Nabonidus's fears not only of misinterpreting the will of the gods but also of missteps during the rebuilding of Ehulhul, the temple of Sîn in Harran: "I feared their august command, I became troubled, I was worried and my face showed signs of anxiety. I was not neglectful, nor remiss, nor careless" ("The Sippar Cylinder of Nabonidus," translated by Paul-Alain Beaulieu [*COS* 2.123: 311]).

90. Hurowitz, *Exalted House*, 140–41. Hurowitz notes that this motif of "reconciliation of a god with a city or temple" is a common theme in Assyrian and Babylonian texts, although he hesitates to describe it as a "universal" or "pan-Mesopotamian theme."

In the same inscription as above, Nabonidus reflects standard ANE thought when he avers that Ehulhul was originally destroyed because of Sîn's anger: "His heart became angry against that city and temple and he aroused the Mede, destroyed that temple and turned it into ruins. . . ." The temple could only be rebuilt when "in my legitimate reign Bēl (and) the great lord, for the love of my kingship, became reconciled to that city and temple and showed compassion" (Beaulieu, "Sippar Cylinder," 311).

91. Significant, that is, in the eyes of those who hold these expectations. Whether anyone else thought the temple of YHWH in Jerusalem qualified as significant is not the point. For those Yahwists who had any concern for the rebuilding of the temple it would have been an important sanctuary and, as will be discussed below, this makes it likely that for at least some of them there would have been expectations of a royal builder.

In Yehud in 520 BCE there would have been serious doubts that these conditions had been met. Zechariah 1–8 and Isaiah 66 suggest that there was disagreement or at least lack of assurance whether or not YHWH wanted his temple rebuilt at that time. Lack of clear indications that YHWH's anger had passed would have made rebuilding the temple a controversial and dangerous prospect. The social, economic, and political conditions typically associated with the (re)building of temples were not all in place and in fact could be taken as evidence that YHWH remained angry. Further, there are indications in the biblical record that the question of whether YHWH had provided a suitable royal builder for the temple was both important and debated.

Doubts about Divine Permission

It would be pointless, even dangerous, to rebuild the Jerusalem sanctuary unless YHWH had commanded or permitted its reconstruction. The motif of divine approbation of the building or repair of temples, found throughout the corpus of ANE building inscriptions, has been described by Hurowitz and others.

Building accounts from Mesopotamia attest to the importance placed on confirmation that the proposed project was approved of or truly commanded by the relevant god. Frequently the order to build or repair is described as part of the building account. For example, the Sumerian king Gudea describes the dream he had in which Ningirsu commanded him to build his temple:

> The decreed brick lifted its head toward him, stretched out its neck toward him to build the holy temple. On that day in a night vision (he saw) his king, Gudea saw the lord Ningirsu, (and) he commanded him to build his temple.[92]

The anxiety to confirm that the dream was a true revelation of the god's will leads Gudea not only to seek an interpretation from his mother, Nanshe, but also to incubate a second dream, before which he prays, "Ningirsu, I would build your temple for you, (but) I do not have

---

92. "The Cylinders of Gudea," translated by Richard E. Averbeck (*COS* 2.155: 419).

my signal."[93] Ningirsu obliges Gudea by promising and providing a signal.

Repair of a temple destroyed because of divine wrath obviously demanded confirmation that the god permitted it. In the inscription commemorating the rebuilding of the Ebbabar temple in Larsa by Nebuchadnezzar II, the king records that Marduk "specifically ordered me, Nebuchadnezzar, king of Babylon, the servant who worships him, to restore that temple."[94] Such examples of the motif of divine command or permission to build or repair temples could be multiplied.[95]

As these examples attest, the decision to carry out such a project might be initiated by the god, or a king could decide to build and take measures to determine if the plan met with a deity's approval. The divine will was commonly conveyed through dreams, but it could also be expressed through omens (often but not exclusively celestial or meteorological) or through an intermediary.[96] Although by far the most common mode of revelation in the biblical literature, this last is less common in the inscriptions from the surrounding cultures.

Gods did not always grant permission to build or repair. It was the divine prerogative to reject or simply ignore requests. Building inscriptions from completed projects occasionally note that previous kings had not been successful, the reason for the divine disapproval only sometimes being given. Aside from building inscriptions, literary texts also recount the failure of kings to gain permission. Both inscriptions and literary texts indicate that at times the kings simply failed to receive from the gods the necessary information to begin the project, such as the location of the original foundations or the layout of the temple. The withholding of such information constituted an implicit rejection of the project.[97]

Israelite literature reflects not only the typical concern to establish

---

93. Averbeck, "Cylinders of Gudea," 423.
94. "Nebuchadnezzar II's Restoration of the Ebabbar Temple in Larsa," translated by Paul-Alain Beaulieu (*COS* 2.122: 309).
95. See, for example, Hurowitz, *Exalted House*, 135–67; Ellis, *Foundation Deposits*, 6–7; Moshe Weinfeld, *Deuteronomy and the Deuteronomic School* (Oxford: Clarendon, 1972), 249–50; Richard E. Averbeck, "Temple Building among the Sumerians and Akkadians (Third Millennium," in *From the Foundations to the Crenellations: Essays on Temple Building in the Ancient Near East and Hebrew Bible*, ed. Mark J. Boda and Jamie Novotny, AOAT 366 (Münster: Ugarit-Verlag, 2010), 16–19; and many others.
96. Hurowitz, *Exalted House*, 143–53; Averbeck, "Temple Building," 16–19.
97. Hurowitz, *Exalted House*, 160–63.

that a sanctuary has been approved by YHWH, but also that YHWH could refuse the proposal to build. It is widely recognized that the present account of the building of the tabernacle in the wilderness is an Israelite reflex of ANE building accounts.[98] The requisite divine command to build receives extensive treatment in the detailed instructions for the structure, materials, and appurtenances of the sanctuary according to the pattern (תבנית) revealed to Moses on Sinai (Exod 25:1–31:11).

The account of the building of the first temple in Jerusalem is also another version of ANE temple building accounts, and accordingly reveals the same concern to articulate the divine approval of Solomon's project.[99] The process begins with a divine refusal. The stated reason for rejecting David's seemingly pious desire to build a "house" for YHWH is that YHWH has not asked for one, being content to dwell in the tabernacle (2 Sam 7:5–7). In the same oracle, however, YHWH announces that David's son will build a house "for my name" (2 Sam 7:13). Years later, Solomon is ready to build the temple. Here the reason given for David's "failure" to build the temple was that YHWH had not yet made him victorious over his enemies. But now that YHWH has given Solomon "rest all around" it is time to build the temple:

> Now YHWH, my God, has given me rest all around, without adversary or misfortune. So I intend to build a house for the name of YHWH, my God, according to what YHWH said to David, my father: your son whom I will put in your place on your throne—he will build the house for my name. (1 Kgs 5:18–19)

As Solomon is carrying out the promise given to his father, he is essentially acting on the command of YHWH, bringing this account into

---

98. See, for example, Victor A. Hurowitz, "The Priestly Account of Building the Tabernacle," *JAOS* 105 (1985): 21–30; *Exalted House*, 110–13; Arvid S. Kapelrud, "Temple Building, a Task for Gods and Kings," *Orientalia* 32 (1963): 61. Questions about the sources and ideological perspective of the Priestly account of the tabernacle have been and remain much discussed. These debates have no bearing on the present topic. Regardless of what one thinks about the formation and intention of the tabernacle materials, Hurowitz's argument that the Exodus and Leviticus materials reflect wider ANE temple building motifs is cogent. The account is concerned to demonstrate that the tabernacle was designed by and built at the behest of YHWH.

99. For the ANE background of the Dtr account, see, for example, Victor A. Hurowitz, "'Solomon Built the Temple and Completed It': Building the First Temple according to the Book of Kings," in *From the Foundations to the Crenellations: Essays on Temple Building in the Ancient Near East and Hebrew Bible*, ed. Mark J. Boda and Jamie Novotny, AOAT 366 (Münster: Ugarit-Verlag, 2010), 281–302; Kapelrud, "Temple Building," 59–61; Weinfeld, *Deuteronomy*, 147–50.

line with the expected avowal of divine orders or permission to build a sanctuary.[100] The rest of the narrative contains numerous parallels with other ANE temple building accounts.

The accounts of the building of the tabernacle and of the first temple feature the divine command (and, for David, refusal) being conveyed through or to a prophet, rather than through omens or dreams.[101] The Israelite preference for prophetic mediation of divine will is also seen in Ezekiel's temple vision (Ezekiel 40–48).[102]

As I will show in the following chapters, the book of Haggai indicates that the there was disagreement about whether YHWH wanted his temple rebuilt in the early Persian period. Other biblical texts also point to disagreement. Zechariah 1–8 suggests that not everyone was willing to accept the authenticity of prophetic claims that YHWH had commanded his temple be rebuilt (Zech 2:13; 4:9–10; 6:15) and Trito-Isaiah claims explicit divine rejection of the reconstruction project (Isa 66:1–2).

Several oracles of Zechariah 1–8 assert that YHWH will soon be returning to Jerusalem, where his temple will be rebuilt (1:16a). Soon YHWH will come to Daughter Zion and "dwell in your midst" (2:14, 15b). When this happens, the people will know that the prophet has

---

100. Hurowitz, "Priestly Account," 23.

101. Although Kapelrud ("Temple Building," 59–61) suggests that in the original account the process really began with Solomon's dream at Gibeon (1 Kgs 3:4–5), but that the connection between 1 Kgs 3 and 1 Kgs 5–9 was broken at some point. The present form of the account obscures whatever original connection there may have been.

102. Whether this text constitutes, however implicitly, a divine command to build a temple at a later time is doubtful; only a few argue this. See, for example, Paul M. Joyce, "King and Messiah in Ezekiel," in *King and Messiah in Israel and the Ancient Near East: Proceedings of the Oxford Old Testament Seminar*, ed. John Day, JSOTSup 270 (Sheffield: Sheffield Academic, 1998), 195; John T. Strong, "Grounding Ezekiel's Heavenly Ascent: A Defense of Ezek 40–48 as a Program for Restoration," *SJOT* 26 (2012): 202–3. It seems more likely that it is a vision of an "eschatological temple" rather than the prophetic mediation of divine plans for a material temple. See Walther Eichrodt, *Ezekiel*, trans. Cosslett Quin, OTL (Philadelphia: Westminster, 1970), 542; Walther Zimmerli, "Planungen für den Wiederaufbau nach der Katastrophe von 587," *VT* 18 (1968): 234; Iain M. Duguid, *Ezekiel and the Leaders of Israel*, VTSup 56 (Leiden: Brill, 1994), 54; Robert G. Hamerton-Kelly, "The Temple and the Origins of Jewish Apocalyptic," *VT* 20 (1970): 4–13. Tuell suggests it is neither material or eschatological, but intended to be a "verbal icon." See Steven S. Tuell, "Divine Presence and Absence in Ezekiel's Prophecy," in *The Book of Ezekiel: Theological and Anthropological Perspectives*, ed. Margaret S. Odell and John T. Strong, SBLSymS 9 (Atlanta, GA: Society of Biblical Literature, 2000), 116; "Ezekiel 40–42 as Verbal Icon," *CBQ* 58 (1996): 649–64. Some scholars have suggested that the vision constitutes a prophetic rejection of any possible plans for a "brick-and-mortar" temple after the period of judgment. If the text does intend to convey a divine "rejection" of a physical temple, it does so in an extremely subtle way and cannot really be taken as evidence of divine rejection of any possible plans to rebuild the temple in Jerusalem.

been sent by YHWH (2:15c). Between these two oracles is the proclamation that those who oppress YHWH's people will "become plunder for their servants." Once again, when this happens the people "will know that YHWH of hosts has sent me" (2:13). In an oracle referring to the rebuilding of the temple by Zerubbabel, the prophet proclaims once again that when this happens, the people will know the prophet was sent by YHWH (4:9). Finally, an oracle claims that "those who are far off will come and build the temple of YHWH. Then you will know that YHWH of hosts has sent me to you" (6:15).

All four oracles contain the phrase, "Then you will know that YHWH of hosts has sent me to you" (וידעתם כי יהוה צבאות שלחני אליכם). Three of the oracles are directly related to the completion of the reconstruction of the temple. YHWH will dwell in the midst of Zion when people have come from afar to build his dwelling, and it is Zerubbabel who will surely finish the project. When this happens, "you will know that YHWH of hosts has sent me." The "me" is almost certainly the prophet, and this suggests that there was some question about whether YHWH of hosts had indeed "sent" him.[103] Why else insist three times that when these things are accomplished the authority of the prophet will be recognized?[104] Such avowals make most sense as a response to claims that Zechariah was not speaking for YHWH when he proclaimed among other things that the temple would be rebuilt. As these oracles constitute a prophetic claim that YHWH *wanted* his temple rebuilt, doubts about the authenticity of the prophet reflect or lead to doubts about the truth of that claim.

The insistence on the authenticity of the prophet is closely related to the *completion* of the temple, particularly in the Zerubbabel oracle

---

103. Although it is difficult to disentangle the speakers in 2:10–17, most commentators agree that the speaker of this phrase is the prophet, not one of the messengers of YHWH. As Horst puts it, "nur er konnte an Aussagen dieser Art ein Interesse haben" (*Zwölf kleinen Propheten*, 226).

104. Most commentators note that the use of this phrase four times in the book is intended to support the prophet's claims and therefore his own authenticity. Not all who note this go on to suggest why the prophet felt the need to argue for his credentials, but those who do suppose that it is because the outrageously utopian content of his oracles left his audience incredulous (see, for example, Petersen, *Haggai*, 178; Chary, *Aggée*, 69–70). That is, they doubt his claim that YHWH will carry out such a complete reversal. I do not know of anyone who has suggested it is because they doubt his claim that YHWH wants his temple rebuilt. This is understandable in light of the fact that most commentaries on Haggai and Zechariah fail to take into account the clear evidence and likelihood that the Yehudite community was so strongly divided over the question of the temple that the proclamations of the prophets were not necessarily received as authentic.

(4:9). One of the traditional signs that a deity did not approve of a temple building project was the failure to complete it.[105] In their building inscriptions, Warad-Sin, Samsu-iluna, Nebuchadnezzar, and Nabonidus all claim that previous kings had been unable to finish their temples because the gods had prevented them from doing so.[106] Failure to complete a temple could be understood as a sign of divine disapprobation. It is not unlikely, then, that the insistence by Zechariah that completion of the temple would substantiate his prophetic credentials is a response to accusations that he falsely proclaimed YHWH's desire that the temple be rebuilt.

The evidence of Zechariah is indirect and inferential. More explicit evidence that some in the early Persian period claimed YHWH did not approve of the proposed temple is found in Isaiah 66:1–2a:

כה אמר יהוה

השמים כסאי והארץ הדם רגלי

אי זה בית אשר תבנו לי ואי זה מקום מנוחתי

ואת כל אלה ידי עשתה ויהיו כל אלה נאם יהוה

On the face of it, these verses appear to express a divine objection to rebuilding the Jerusalem temple.[107] A number of scholars, however, have argued that the larger context of Isaiah 56–66 displays a positive attitude toward the temple, which makes it implausible that these verses oppose temple restoration. The more immediate context sug-

---

105. Hurowitz, *Exalted House*, 137.

106. Ibid., 160.

107. There is a near-universal consensus that vv. 1–2a stem from the last decades of the sixth century, based on the assumption that these verses are written in response to a temple building project, of which that of the Jerusalem temple is the most obvious and likely candidate. Only a small number of scholars have suggested on the basis of larger redactional studies of Isaiah 56–66 that these verses originated in a later period, but they have been unable to offer a plausible account of the circumstances to which the argument of these verses might apply. See, for example, Bernhard Duhm, *Das Buch Jesaia*, 5th ed. (Göttingen: Vandenhoeck & Ruprecht, 1968), 481; Blenkinsopp, *Isaiah 56–66*, 51–54; Odil H. Steck, *Studien zu Tritojesaja*, BZAW 203 (Berlin: de Gruyter, 1991), 257; *Der Abschluß der Prophetie im Alten Testament: Ein Versuch zur Frage der Vorgeschichte des Kanons*, BTSt 17 (Neukirchen-Vluyn: Neukirchener Verlag, 1991), 91, 197 (but Steck does suggest the verses may reflect earlier Persian-period disputes); Wolfgang Lau, *Schriftgelehrte Prophetie in Jes 56–66*, BZAW 225 (Berlin: de Gruyter, 1994), 117; Alexander Rofé, "Isaiah 66:1–4: Judean Sects in the Persian Period as Viewed by Trito-Isaiah," in *Biblical and Related Studies Presented to Samuel Iwry*, ed. Ann Kort and Scott Morschauser (Winona Lake, IN: Eisenbrauns,1985), 212.

These verses could have been incorporated into their present context later, but insofar as they constitute a response to a temple building project it is unlikely that they originated after the temple was completed.

gests, rather, that the objection is not to the temple or the rebuilding *per se*, but to a certain attitude toward the temple. Because so many commentators have rejected what appears to be the plain sense of these verses, and have offered diverse alternative readings, it is necessary to analyze vv. 1–2a in some detail.

Isaiah 66:1–2a is a short argument with three elements: premises, claims based on the premises, and warrants for making those claims on the basis of the premises. In these verses, the premises are the statements about YHWH in vv. 1a and 2a. The claim of the argument is stated indirectly in the form of two parallel, rhetorical questions that are obviously expected to draw from the audience a negative response.[108] The warrants for deriving the claim are unstated.[109] Arguments *may* also contain within them "rebuttals" or "qualifiers." Rebuttals serve to anticipate possible objections to the argument by recognizing that under certain conditions the claim will not hold. Qualifiers mitigate the force of the claim, suggesting, for example, that the claim is "probably" true rather than certainly true.[110] These verses do not contain any rebuttals or qualifiers. This means that the argument as it is stated does not acknowledge any exceptions to or mitigations of its claim. It is possible that some of the material that immediately follows these verses should also be considered part of the argument and may, therefore, contain rebuttals or qualifiers. We will examine that possibility after analysis of the argument of vv. 1–2a.

The first premise YHWH offers in the argument is that "the heavens are my throne and the earth is my footstool." This statement can sustain various interpretations that are not mutually exclusive. The significance may be simply that YHWH's presence extends throughout the cosmos.[111] In this case, "throne" and "footstool" function as a merism signifying his omnipresence. Related to this may be the implication

---

108. A rhetorical question can be defined as a question designed to promote "self-persuasion." The rhetor expects a certain, or "predicted," answer. "If the listener responds as the questioner predicted, the listener proves to himself what the questioner wanted." The strategy of the rhetorical question fails if the audience gives a non-predicted answer (Carroll C. Arnold, *Criticism of Oral Rhetoric* [Columbus, OH: Merrill, 1974], 207–8). Our concern here is not whether the strategy in this particular instance was or would be successful, or how it might be countered, but only to identify it as a strategy.

109. An argument may be defined as "movement from accepted data [premises], through a warrant, to a claim." (Wayne Brockriede and Douglas Ehninger, "Toulmin on Argument: An Interpretation and Application," *QJS* 46 [1960]: 44).

110. Brockriede and Ehninger, "Toulmin on Argument," 45.

that YHWH is transcendent.[112] More specifically, throne and footstool may represent YHWH's sovereign rule, which, being situated in heaven and earth extends throughout the cosmos. Beuken and others have noted that often YHWH's throne or enthronement is simply a figurative way of speaking of his rule. Psalm 103:19, for example, speaks of YHWH's throne in heaven in parallel with the claim that his dominion extends over all. Although the idea of the earth as YHWH's footstool is not found elsewhere in the HB, it is clearly related to the traditions concerning YHWH's throne, and can be readily understood to signify and contribute to the same idea of his universal sovereignty.[113] In a related, but somewhat more literal or material sense, one may see in the reference to heavenly throne and earthly footstool the notion of the place from which YHWH rules or in which he dwells. In this case, the idea would be that YHWH "dwells" in the cosmos and rules from within that cosmos, in which case the cosmos would serve as YHWH's "house" or "temple."[114]

The second premise of YHWH's argument is that "my hand made all these things." This adds to the first the notion of YHWH's status as creator. The reference to "all these things" is usually taken to mean the heavens and the earth, and also possibly the throne and footstool themselves.[115] This is fairly straightforward, but the next hemistich is

111. Georg Fohrer, *Das Buch Jesaja, 3. Band: Kapitel 40-66*, ZBK (Zurich: Zwingli-Verlag, 1964), 271; Japhet, "Temple in the Restoration Period," 235.

112. Paul A. Smith, *Rhetoric and Redaction in Trito-Isaiah: The Structure, Growth and Authorship of Isaiah 56-66*, VTSup 62 (Leiden: Brill, 1995), 159.

113. Willem A. M. Beuken, "Does Trito-Isaiah Reject the Temple? An Intertextual Inquiry into Isa. 66.1-6," in *Intertextuality in Biblical Writings: Essays in Honour of Bas van Iersel*, ed. Sipke Draisma (Kampen: Kok, 1989), 55.

114. Fohrer, *Jesaja*, 271; John N. Oswalt, *The Book of Isaiah: Chapters 40-66*, NICOT (Grand Rapids, MI: Eerdmans, 1998), 666–67; Matthias Albani, "'Wo sollte ein Haus sein, das ihr mir bauen könntet?' (Jes 66,1):Schöpfung als Tempel JHWHs?" in *Gemeinde ohne Tempel = Community without Temple: Zur Substituierung und Transformation des Jerusalemer Tempels und seines Kults im Alten Testament, antiken Judentum und frühen Christentum*, ed. Beate Ego, Armin Lange, and Peter Pilhofer, WUNT 118 (Tübingen: Mohr Siebeck, 1999): 37–56; Klaus Koenen, *Ethik und Eschatologie im Tritojesajabuch: Eine literarkritische und redaktionsgeschichtliche Studie*, WMANT 62 (Neukirchen-Vluyn: Neukirchener Verlag, 1990), 183–86; Jon D. Levenson, "The Temple and the World," *JR* 64 (1984): 295–96; Martin Metzger, "Himmlische und irdische Wohnstatt Jahwes," *UF* 2 (1970): 153–54.

115. R. N. Whybray, *Isaiah 40-66*, NCB (London: Oliphants, 1975), 281; Claus Westermann, *Isaiah 40-66: A Commentary*, trans. David M. G. Stalker, OTL (Philadelphia: Westminster, 1969), 411; Shalom M. Paul, *Isaiah 40-66*, ECC (Grand Rapids: Eerdmans, 2012), 613; Karl Pauritsch, *Die neue Gemeinde: Gott sammelt Ausgestossene und Arme (Jesaja 56-66)*, AnBib 47 (Rome: Biblical Institute Press, 1971), 199–200; Japhet, "Temple in the Restoration Period," 235. Pierre Bonnard, who takes the reference to be to potential offerings, is one of a few who offer a different interpretation (*Le second Isaïe, son disciple et leurs éditeurs: Isaïe 40-66*, Etudes bibliques [Paris: Gabalda, 1971], 485).

less so. The MT has ויהיו כל אלה ("and all these came to be"), which would simply serve as a restatement of the first hemistich. Some commentators, following the lead of the OG (και εστιν εμα), would emend the text to ולי היו.[116] In this case, the parallelism would be such that the second phrase "completes the thought" of the first phrase: my hand made all these things and therefore they belong to me.[117] This reading is really just making explicit what is implicit in YHWH's status as creator and, although it may contribute a certain rhetorical emphasis, it does not alter the content of the premise. Consequently, it is not necessary for the analysis of the argument to choose one reading over another.

Verses 1b and 2a together comprise the premise of the argument, which can be summarized as: YHWH is the sovereign creator of the cosmos, throughout which his presence and rule extends. One may go further and see here the assertion that his throne and footstool are "found" in heaven and earth, such that the cosmos constitutes YHWH's dwelling or temple. These premises are not contingent or subject to qualification. YHWH either made the cosmos or he did not. He is either omnipresent and "omnisovereign" or he is not. The cosmos serves as his "dwelling" or it does not.

If one accepts these premises as stated, then the obvious conclusion the audience is meant to draw is that it is not necessary, possible, or desirable, under any circumstances, for humans to build a house or place of resting for YHWH. This claim is not stated directly, but asserted in the form of two rhetorical questions (v. 1c):

אי זה אשר תבנו לי ואי זה מקום מנוחתי

The form אי זה is sometimes taken here to mean "where," its most common meaning elsewhere in the HB. The word זה is then understood to be used for emphasis.[118] If the question is understood in this locative

---

116. For example, Bonnard, *Second Isaïe*, 485; James D. Smart, *History and Theology in Second Isaiah: A Commentary on Isaiah 35, 40–66* (Philadelphia: Westminster, 1965), 287.

117. James L. Kugel, *The Idea of Biblical Poetry: Parallelism and Its History* (Baltimore: Johns Hopkins University Press, 1981), 8–12.

118. See, for example, 1 Sam 9:18; Jer 6:16; Job 28:12, 20; 38:19, 24. Jill Middlemas, "Divine Reversal and the Role of the Temple in Trito-Isaiah," in *Temple and Worship in Biblical Israel*, ed. John Day, LHBOTS 422 (London: T&T Clark, 2005), 178; Paul, *Isaiah 40–66*, 612; Brooks Schramm, *The Opponents*

sense, the claim being advanced through the questions would be that a house or place of resting for YHWH could not be built in any earthly location. Others take the form אי זה to mean "what sort of," a sense that is less common in the HB, but possible.[119] If the question is taken to be qualitative, the claim then would be that there is no sort of house or place of resting that could be built for YHWH. Lau rightly fails to see any great distinction between the locative and the qualitative readings, both of which are viable and appropriate.[120] The force of the claim is the same however we understand אי זה: the idea of building a house or place of resting for YHWH is inappropriate, even ludicrous. There is implied here an indignation or sarcasm that is perhaps best captured by the translation of Watts: "What is this? A house that you would build for me? What is this? A place of my rest?"[121] This sardonic or mocking tone conveys a finality to the conclusion. It is inescapable.

The movement from the premise that YHWH is sovereign creator of the cosmos to the claim that there is no place that one can build a house or place of resting for him, or that there is no sort of house that can be built for him, can only be made by accepting one or more warrants for coming to that conclusion. None of these are stated, but some possible warrants would be: "a God whose presence extends throughout the cosmos cannot be localized, 'housed,' or come to 'rest' in any single place," or "since YHWH inhabits the entire cosmos, that cosmos is, in effect, his 'house' or 'place of resting' and so any building for that purpose is unnecessary," or "if YHWH's throne is in heaven then his throne is not in a temple, yet the purpose of a temple is to provide a place for a god's throne, therefore. . . ." Any number of other warrants could be articulated that would allow one to draw the conclusion from the premises that there is no need to build a house for YHWH, or that it is inappropriate, or even blasphemous to think that the creator of heaven and earth would need humans to build a temple for him.

---

of Third Isaiah: Reconstructing the Cultic History of the Restoration, JSOTSup 193 (Sheffield: Sheffield Academic, 1995), 164.

119. For example: Eccl 2:3; 11:6; perhaps Isa 50:1. Beuken, "Trito-Isaiah," 56–57; Oswalt, Isaiah, 663; Koenen, Ethik und Eschatologie, 183.

120. Lau, Schriftgelehrte Prophetie, 170; see also Paul Volz, Jesaia II: Kapitel 40–66, KAT 9/2 (Leipzig: Scholl, 1932; repr. Hildesheim: Olms, 1974), 289.

121. John D. W. Watts, Isaiah 34–66, WBC 25 (Waco, TX: Word, 1987), 350; similarly: Smart, History and Theology, 287, and David L. Petersen, "The Temple in Persian Period Prophetic Texts," in Second Temple Studies I: Persian Period, ed. Philip R. Davies, JSOTSup 117 (Sheffield: JSOT Press, 1991), 139.

We can conclude this analysis by noting that the claim advanced via the rhetorical questions in its turn serves as a warrant for making the final claim implied by the argument: since one cannot or need not build such a house or place of resting for YHWH, then any plans to do so are misguided and should not be pursued. This is a fairly straightforward implication of the argument as it is presented in vv. 1–2a.[122] Such an argument is most plausibly seen as being articulated during the early years of the Persian period, before or perhaps even for some time after the completion of the temple. It offers a theological objection to any proposed building of the temple.

Although it is likely that any Yahwist would have accepted most if not all of the stated premises about YHWH, it is not necessarily the case that everyone would have accepted the warrants needed to arrive at the conclusion that it is not required or possible to build a house for YHWH. My point is not that the argument could not be rejected or refuted, but that the argument itself does not leave room for this. There are no qualifiers or rebuttals in the argument that would suggest that under certain conditions the claim may not hold, or that it is possibly or likely to be true. This means that the author or editor of the text was not offering a qualified statement about the temple or YHWH's attitude toward it.

I have emphasized this last point about qualification and rebuttal because there are a number of scholars, perhaps the majority in recent years, who have suggested that vv. 1–2a do not in fact reflect a rejection of the reconstruction of the Jerusalem temple. It is true, they admit, that taken out of the larger context opposition to temple building appears to be the aim of the verses. But the larger context in which they are found makes it unlikely that this is the actual meaning of the verses.[123] Rather, the positive attitude toward the temple in Isaiah

---

122. Including Fohrer, *Jesaja*, 271–73; Volz, *Jesaia II*, 288–89; Paul, *Isaiah 40–66*, 608, 611; Koenen, *Ethik und Eschatologie*, 183–86; Paul D. Hanson, *The Dawn of Apocalyptic: The Historical and Sociological Roots of Jewish Apocalyptic Eschatology*, rev. ed. (Philadelphia, PA: Fortress Press, 1979), 168–69; Lau, *Schriftgelehrte Prophetie*, 170; Japhet, "Temple in the Restoration Period," 233–36; Levenson, "Temple and the World," 295–96.

123. Middlemas, "Divine Reversal," 178; Rofé, "Isaiah 66:1–4," 212–13; Blenkinsopp, *Isaiah 56–66*, 294; Smith, *Rhetoric and Redaction*, 158–59; Oswalt, *Isaiah*, 665; Schramm, *Opponents of Third Isaiah*, 164; Anne E. Gardner, "Isaiah 66:1–4: Condemnation of Temple and Sacrifice or Contrast between the Arrogant and the Humble?" *RB* 113 (2006): 509–10. Norman H. Snaith ("Isaiah 40–66: A Study of the Teaching of the Second Isaiah and Its Consequences," in *Studies on the Second Part of the Book of Isaiah*, VTSup14 [Leiden: Brill, 1967], 241–43), takes the second question ("Where is to be my rest-

56–66 suggests that the intention here is not to argue against the temple rebuilding project *per se*, but against a particular attitude or complex of attitudes *about* the temple or the project to rebuild it. According to this view, one has to examine the immediate context of the verses to recognize what it really being argued here. It is of course true that taking into account context is important for interpretation. But without saying as much, these scholars are claiming that the argument of vv. 1–2a is effectively rebutted or qualified by elements of its context. For this to be true, that context will have to contain elements that will suggest either that the premises themselves or the warrants necessary to move from premises to claim are not true, or not always true. In other words, elements of the context would have to *undermine or qualify* the argument of vv. 1–2a. Not only must this be true, but it would also have to be established that those elements that undermine or qualify the argument of these verses would have to be part of the same argument, not an answer to the argument. We are looking, then, for contextual evidence of "intra-argument" rebuttal or qualification.

Objections to the "anti-temple" reading of vv. 1–2a arise primarily from the fact that they are found in Isaiah 56–66, which is thought to reflect a generally positive attitude toward the temple.[124] All of this makes it implausible, many argue, that the intention of 66:1–2a is to reject the idea of rebuilding the Jerusalem temple. The true intention of these verses can only be understood when they are read along with the material that immediately follows, especially 66:2b, or 2b–4. When interpreted with these verses in mind, it is claimed, vv. 1–2a are seen to reject not the temple or the building project *per se*, but rather certain attitudes about the temple or motivations for building it. Many suggest that the text is arguing against the idea that building the temple or offering sacrifices is somehow "doing something" for YHWH, is necessary or sufficient to please YHWH (in contrast to being appropriately humble and obedient), or will "automatically" bring prosperity or otherwise solve the economic and other problems of Yehudite society.[125]

ing place?") to be not rhetorical but quasi-imperative, and understands these verses to constitute an urgent call to build the temple. While this reading satisfies the need to make the verses cohere with the "pro-temple" perspective of the rest of Isaiah 56–66, to my knowledge it has not garnered any adherents.

124. Such as 56:4–7; 60:7, 13, as well as frequent mentions of "my holy mountain" and "Zion." Explicit references to the temple or altar are few.

These interpretations rely to a great extent on reading vv. 1–2a in conjunction with vv. 2b–4, or portions of them:

> This is the one whom I regard:
>> the afflicted one, broken in spirit,
>> who trembles at my word.
> The one slaughtering the ox, striking a man,
>> sacrificing the lamb, breaking the neck of a dog,
>> making an offering of the blood of a pig, burning incense,
>> bending the knee to wickedness:
> indeed these who have chosen their ways
>> and in their abominations they have found pleasure.
> But indeed I will choose their ill-treatment
> and what they fear I will bring upon them.
> Because when I called there was no one who answered;
>> I spoke but they did not listen.
> They did evil in my eyes and that which did not please me they chose.

As stated above, in order for these verses to modify the clear claim of vv. 1–2a, which calls on theological grounds for a rejection of the temple building project, they would have to include some element(s) that called into question or qualified the truth of the premises or disputed the warrants necessary to arrive at the claim. Yet there is nothing in these latter verses that does that. The additional information of v. 2b, that YHWH looks with favor on the lowly and those who tremble at his word, does not contradict any part of vv. 1–2a, and it is not entirely clear what relationship this half-verse is intended to have with them. The initial ואל זה, which seems to be a parallel to the אי זה the preceding verse, has suggested to some that a contrast is intended. For example, Blenkinsopp proposes that "attachment to the temple is contrasted with the attitude of lowly social status." He rightly notes that

---

125. For example, Blenkinsopp, *Isaiah 56–66*, 86, 294; James D. Smart, "A New Interpretation of Isaiah lxvi 1–6," *ExpTim* 46 (1934/1935): 421; Smith, *Rhetoric and Redaction*, 195; Bonnard, *Second Isaïe*, 481. Others suggest that the text means to argue against the notion that YHWH can be locally present in, confined by, or exclusively tied to a particular building. For example, Jon D. Levenson, "From Temple to Synagogue: 1 Kings 8," in *Traditions in Transformation: Turning Points in Biblical Faith*, ed. Baruch Halpern and Jon D. Levenson (Winona Lake, IN: Eisenbrauns, 1981), 158–59; Paul, *Isaiah 40–66*, 611. Certainly they are correct that one can take these verses to be an argument against the attitude that YHWH can be confined or localized in the temple. There is nothing to suggest, however, that as long as this attitude is absent or modified, building the temple is acceptable. That option, as reasonable as it may seem to some, is not made available by the terms of the argument. There is no basis for this interpretation, except for the conviction of the commentator that these verses simply cannot be rejecting the temple *tout court*.

this contrast has led more than one commentator to assume that the intention is to complete the argument against the temple building project. I am not persuaded, however, that this verse was part of the *original* argument. It is difficult to see any contrast being presented here, for example. Verses 1–2a are not concerned with anything whose contrast is lowliness or "trembling" at YHWH's word, nor are they concerned with persons. The two sections have no term, concept, stance, action, or anything in common at all. One may take v. 2b to be meant as a contrast, but it requires a certain amount of creativity to do so. In any case, even if its placement here (perhaps by a later editor?) is meant to offer a contrast, it certainly does not support the idea that the objection here is to a certain attitude toward the temple, and not the act of rebuilding itself. The premises and warrants of vv. 1–2a are not qualified or rebutted here at all.

The same is true for vv. 3–4, which are often taken as part of this section. The point of v. 3 is difficult to determine. It has been read as a polemic against legitimate sacrifices or against syncretistic sacrifices. In either case, they are taken to be part of the polemic against the temple. Yet here again, because such a rejection of the temple appears so incongruent as to be implausible, commentators take the verses to indicate that the objection is to certain attitudes toward the meaning or priority of sacrifice. The variations on this interpretation are numerous. But once again there is not here—or anywhere—a rebuttal or qualification of the argument of vv. 1–2a.

As Smart pointed out some time ago, the argument against building the temple is so clearly stated in Isaiah 66:1–2a that any suggestion that these verses cannot mean what they appear to mean can only be based on the assumption that contradictory messages cannot be present in the same biblical text.[126] Such a thing is of course quite possible, and there are plenty of examples throughout the HB. This conviction cannot serve as evidence against the clear claim of the argument, a claim that is nowhere qualified or rebutted within the argument itself. This means that it is very likely that we have in Isaiah 66:1–2a the articulation of one objection to the rebuilding of the temple in the early Persian period.

126. Smart, "New Interpretation," 420.

Concerns that the Period of Judgment Had Not Ended

Hurowitz notes that in the Mesopotamian texts the reconciliation of a god with a city or temple destroyed because of divine anger often takes place only after a predetermined period. Of particular relevance are Esarhaddon's inscriptions related to the rebuilding of Babylon, whose destruction had been ordered by Marduk. Although the length of this judgment was decreed to be seventy years, Esarhaddon claims the god had mercy and reduced the sentence to eleven years.[127] As not only the destruction but also the length of time Babylon would lay in ruins had been declared by the god, reconstruction before the completion of that period or without clear signs that the period had been divinely shortened was out of the question. Although it was perhaps not always the case that a period of divine anger was thought of in terms of a preordained length, in some cases it was.

The destruction of Jerusalem and its temple was thought (at least by those who produced the biblical texts) to be the result of YHWH's anger and a judgment on his people.[128] Haggai 1:2 suggests that the timing of the reconstruction was a question in at least some Yehudite circles in the reign of Darius, although the text does not indicate what those who claimed that "the time has not come" to rebuild the temple (לא עת בא עת בית יהוה להבנות) meant by this phrase. It is not necessarily the case that they had a particular time span in mind.[129] Other biblical

---

127. Hurowitz, *Exalted House*, 141. Recension B of the inscription reads: "Until the days were elapsed that the heart of the great lord Marduk should be appeased and he would find peace with the country against which he had raged, 70 years were to elapse, but he wrote [11] years (instead) and took pity and said: Amen!" Recensions A and D: "He (Marduk) had written 70 years as the quantity of its (the city's) exile (lit: lying fallow) but merciful Marduk – soon his heart was appeased and he turned into the lower (figure) so that he decreed its settlement for 11 years" ("Esarhaddon," translated by William W. Hallo [*COS* 2.120: 306]). Hurowitz notes further examples from Assurbanipal, Merodachbaladan, Nebuchadnezzar, and Nabonidus.

128. For example: 2 Kgs 21:10–15; 23:26–27; 24:20; Ps 79:1–4; Lam 1:12; 2:1, 3, 21–22; 3:1, 43; 4:11; Ezek 5:13; 7:8, 13; 8:17–18. It is perhaps easy to forget that not necessarily every Judahite subscribed to this theological explanation of the historical events. Those responsible for the present biblical texts clearly believed, or at least claimed, that the destruction could only have occurred because YHWH commanded or allowed it. But we must allow for the possibility that there were other Yahwists, not necessarily of the "YHWH-only" persuasion represented in the biblical texts, who understood YHWH to have been defeated by stronger gods, or who accounted for reality in other ways entirely. Nevertheless, for those who did hold the perspective represented in the biblical texts, it would have been necessary to satisfy themselves that YHWH's judgment had come to an end.

129. This will be discussed more fully in the analysis of the text in the next chapter.

texts, however, suggest that some may have conceived of YHWH's judgment in terms of a specific time frame. A perception that this divinely ordained period had not yet elapsed would constitute one objection to rebuilding the temple.

The relevant texts are Jeremiah 25:11–12; 27:7; 29:10 and Zechariah 1:12, 7:5. The first two Jeremiah texts speak of only a limited period of Babylonian dominance, after which that power will be brought down. The third, 29:10, specifically links the conclusion of this period with the restoration of YHWH's people by bringing them back to the land: "For thus says YHWH: When seventy years are completed for Babylon I will attend to you. I will fulfill for you my good word—to return you to this place."

These verses stem from either Jeremiah himself or an exilic editor.[130] It is also generally agreed that they reflect a standard ANE idiom and are not meant to be taken "literally."[131] The important question here is not what the prophet or editor meant but how this "timetable" was understood in the early Persian period. At least some circles took it to refer to a specific time frame. Although the references in 2 Chronicles 36:21 and Daniel 9:2 stem from later periods, they show that the ongoing interpretation of the Jeremiah texts involved the number seventy specifically, even if in the case of Daniel it had to be reinterpreted in terms of "weeks of years" (9:24–27). The composers of these texts do not appear to have considered the number to be merely an idiomatic indication of "a long time."

---

130. There has been some discussion about what decades the 70-year range was meant to cover. To find its end in the reign of Cyrus, as 2 Chr 36:21 does, would require the calculus to go back to the beginning of Babylonian power around the time of the Battle of Carchemish in 605 BCE, or perhaps even earlier to the destruction of Nineveh in 612 BCE. If the calendar was thought by some to begin only with the first deportation in 597 BCE or as late as the destruction of Jerusalem and the temple in 586 BCE, then period would not come to an end until after Cyrus, making it impossible to begin to rebuild the temple. Only in the reign of Darius, as the seventy years calculated from the disaster approached their completion, could rebuilding be considered. Meyers and Meyers (*Haggai*, 117) have suggested that the anticipated end of the seventy years was the impetus for the sudden interest in getting the temple built in the first years of Darius.

131. Lester L. Grabbe, "'They Shall Come Rejoicing to Zion' – or Did They? The Settlement of Yehud in the Early Persian Period," in *Exile and Restoration Revisited: Essays on the Babylonian and Persian Periods in Memory of Peter R. Ackroyd*, ed. Gary N. Knoppers, Lester L. Grabbe, and Deirdre N. Fulton, LSTS 73 (London: T&T Clark, 2009), 119; Jack R. Lundbom, *Jeremiah 21-36*, AB 21B (New York, NY: Doubleday, 2004), 248; Winfried Thiel, *Die deuteronomistische Redaktion von Jeremia 26-45*, WMANT 52 (Neukirchen-Vluyn: Neukirchener Verlag, 1981), 17; Wilhelm Rudolph, *Jeremia*, KAT 12 (Tübingen: Mohr Siebeck, 1968), 184.

From closer to the time of reconstruction of the temple two references in Zechariah refer to "seventy years":

> The messenger of YHWH answered, saying: O YHWH of hosts, for how long will you not have compassion for Jerusalem and the cities of Judah, with whom you have been angry these seventy years? (1:12)

> Speak to all the people of the land and to the priests: When you fasted and mourned in the fifth and seventh months these seventy years, was it really for me that you fasted? (7:5)

Although it is sometimes suggested that these are allusions to the Jeremianic period of judgment, there is nothing to suggest this is the case. Rather than referring to the Jeremiah texts, or any preordained timetable, these verses may simply be indicating that it has been (roughly) seventy years since the period of punishment began, more if the author is calculating from 597 BCE. If it does refer to a divine timetable, however, it constitutes evidence that someone in the early Persian period was thinking about the reconstruction of the temple with this in mind. But in this case the period is understood to have elapsed and the question now is why YHWH has not done what was promised. The latest one could reasonably calculate the beginning of the seventy years, taken literally, would surely be 586 BCE. By the time of Darius that period would be almost over and the question of whether Jeremiah's seventy years, understood literally, had not yet elapsed would be probably moot.

It is possible that in the reigns of Cyrus and Cambyses some read the Jeremiah texts to indicate that a full seventy years must elapse before YHWH would be reconciled to Israel, and that those years had not yet passed. This may account for the fact that temple reconstruction did not begin in those first decades of the Persian period. But this objection would not have remained in force in the reign of Darius. So concerns about a specific timetable would not have constituted a plausible objection to rebuilding the temple in 520 BCE.

Whether YHWH remained angry with Israel would nevertheless have remained an open question. Bedford notes that several texts from the early Persian period reveal "a painful ignorance of when Yahweh will have a change of heart," and the anxiety of not being able to discern if the period of divine anger has passed.[132] This "ignorance" arose at least in part from a failure to see expected signs that YHWH was prepared to take up residence again in Jerusalem. For those familiar with and assigning authority to Israel's prophetic tradition, the end of punishment, YHWH's return to Jerusalem, and the beginning of a new era of divine favor were to be signaled by some or all of the following: repatriation of the exiles, blessing of the people and the land, destruction of enemies, reestablishment of the Davidic monarchy, and reunification of Judah and Israel.[133] It would have been obvious in 520 BCE that these last two had not come to pass, and although Babylon had been conquered by Cyrus, it could hardly be argued that Israel's "enemies" had all been vanquished, leaving Israel triumphant. Although there is evidence of some repatriation in this period, the high numbers given by Ezra are widely acknowledged to be impossible and the archaeological evidence (discussed below) suggests there was little population growth in Yehud in this period.[134] Finally, we see little indication that Yehud in the last decades of the sixth century could be characterized by even the most optimistic as the recipient of divine blessing.

Texts from the first half of the Persian period give the impression of a struggling community. Isaiah 56–66, Malachi, and Zechariah 9–14 all reflect social, economic, and religious problems.[135] A primary claim

---

132. Peter R. Bedford, "Discerning the Time: Haggai, Zechariah and the 'Delay' in the Rebuilding of the Jerusalem Temple," in *The Pitcher Is Broken: Memorial Essays for Gösta W. Ahlström*, ed. Steven W. Holloway and Lowell K. Handy, JSOTSup190 (Sheffield: Sheffield Academic, 1995), 82–84 (citation: 83–84). He cites Pss 74:9, 10–11; 79:5; 89:47; Isa 63:7–64:11; Zech 1:12. Bedford suggests that the question "how long?" (עד מתי) found in so many of these is not merely standard language of lament, and therefore "rhetorical," but also reveals a genuine confusion about when YHWH will in fact bring judgment to an end.

133. Bedford, "Discerning the Time," 84 (citing Sigmund Mowinckel, *He That Cometh: The Messiah Concept in the Old Testament and Later Judaism* [trans. G. W. Anderson; Nashville, TN: Abingdon, 1954], 136–49). Mowinckel gives a long list of various elements of the "national and political restoration," all of which are related to the ideology of the kingship of YHWH: "the political and national deliverance of Israel, the restoration of the dynasty and kingdom of David, the reunion of the two kingdoms, the destruction of heathen powers, the return of the Diaspora, the religious and moral restoration of the people . . . marvelous, even paradisal fertility of land, people, and cattle, peace among the nations, the transformation of wild animals, the restoration and glorification of Jerusalem as the religious and political centre of the world. . . ." (146).

134. Ezra 2:64–67 claims nearly 50,000 returned along with their horses, mules, camels, and donkeys. Oded Lipschits notes that this large and relatively sudden biblical "return to Zion" failed to leave any archaeological traces ("Demographic Changes in Judah between the Seventh and the Fifth Centuries B.C.E," in *Judah and the Judeans in the Neo-Babylonian Period*, ed. Oded Lipschits and Joseph Blenkinsopp [Winona Lake, IN: Eisenbrauns, 2003]), 365. See also Grabbe, "They Shall Come Rejoicing," 117.

135. Malachi is generally dated to the first half of the fifth century. See Andrew E. Hill, *Malachi*, AB 25D

of Trito-Isaiah is that divine judgment on the community's behavior explains the failure of the expected blessings to materialize. Behind the book of Malachi lies a community afflicted by a weak economy, poverty, hardship, and social divisions.[136] As with Trito-Isaiah, there is a clear sense that expectations of plenty have not been realized, leading to a pervasive discontent.[137] The oracles of Deutero-Zechariah reflect "a lachrymose view of reality," concerned as they are with the unfinished business of the "restoration," particularly the gathering of the dispersed and the still-to-be-hoped-for flourishing of Jerusalem and Judah.[138] All of these texts leave the reader with the sense that Yehud and Jerusalem in the first several decades of the Persian period simply failed to thrive.

This impression is confirmed by archaeological data, which reveals Yehud and Jerusalem in these decades to be poor and with a low population. Immediately after the destruction of 586 BCE Judah experienced a sharp decrease in population, primarily in urban settlements.[139] Lipschits estimates for Jerusalem and environs a population decline of approximately 89 percent (from 25,000 to 2,750) between 586 BCE and the beginning of the Persian period.[140] This significant population decrease did not rectify itself for several centuries. It is only in the

---

(New Haven, CT: Yale University Press, 1998), 77–84. Dates for Deutero-Zechariah have in the past varied widely, but recently there has been more of a tendency to date it from the late sixth to the middle fifth centuries. See Carol L. Meyers and Eric M. Meyers, *Zechariah 9–14*, AB 25C (New Haven, CT: Yale University Press, 1993), 22–23, 27; David L. Petersen, *Zechariah 9–14 and Malachi*, OTL (Louisville, KY: Westminster John Knox, 1995), 4–5; Andrew E. Hill, "Dating Second Zechariah: A Linguistic Reexamination," *HAR* 6 (1982): 105–34.

136. Hill, *Malachi*, 75.

137. Beth Glazier-McDonald, *Malachi: The Divine Messenger*, SBLDS 98 (Atlanta, GA: Scholars Press, 1987), 17.

138. Meyers and Meyers, *Zechariah 9–14*, 23–26 (citation: 23).

139. Several scholars have noted that the area of Benjamin emerged from the Babylonian destruction relatively intact. With this exception, though, the rest of the former kingdom of Judah underwent demographic decline. There remains a strong debate among biblicists and archaeologists about the extent of the demographic changes in the immediate aftermath of the Babylonian destruction. Barstad and Carroll, for example, have argued that most people were not affected by the "exile" and that the idea of an "empty land" is nothing more than a "myth." Their claim that the period was marked more by continuity than discontinuity has been challenged by Vanderhooft, Oded, and Faust. Lipschits, while certainly seeing more continuity in the rural areas than Faust would allow, nevertheless seems to take a slightly more moderate position that Barstad and others, suggesting that core settlements were destroyed or abandoned while surrounding areas continued to exist almost unchanged (Oded Lipschits, "The Rural Settlement in Judah in the Sixth Century B.C.E.: A Rejoinder," *PEQ* 136 [2004]: 99–107). Faust has continued to maintain that the land was indeed devastated and virtually empty during the sixth century (Avraham Faust, *Judah in the Neo-Babylonian Period: The Archaeology of Desolation*, ABS 18 [Atlanta, GA: Society of Biblical Literature, 2012]).

Hellenistic period that we find evidence of substantial recovery in the region.[141]

Jerusalem itself was devastated and along with the rest of the region recovered only very slowly. At the beginning of the Persian period the city probably had a population of around 1000, a number which grew to only 1,250 or 1,500 by the end of the fifth century.[142] Late in the period only a narrow portion of the historical city of David was occupied, roughly 15 percent of the earlier settlement; at the end of the sixth century this would have been even smaller.[143]

Along with the demographic depletion, Yehud and Jerusalem experienced profound economic diminishment from which they emerged very slowly, with only minor changes in material culture over the entire Persian period.[144] The paucity of "rich tombs," stamp impressions, and other material remains indicates that Jerusalem did not become a large, thriving urban center until the Hasmonean period. Instead, it remained "wretchedly poor, not just in the period after the Babylonian destruction, but also at the height of the Persian period."[145]

There is no doubt that when Darius came to the throne Yehud was an underpopulated and poor region. Its former capital was devastated

140. Oded Lipschits, *The Fall and Rise of Jerusalem: Judah under Babylonian Rule* (Winona Lake, IN: Eisenbrauns, 2009), 270.

141. Avraham Faust, "Settlement Dynamics and Demographic Fluctuations in Judah from the Late Iron Age to the Hellenistic Period and the Archaeology of Persian-Period Yehud," in *A Time of Change: Judah and Its Neighbours in the Persian and Early Hellenistic Periods*, ed. Yigdal Levin, LSTS 65 (London: T&T Clark, 2007), 49–50.

142. Charles E. Carter, "The Province of Yehud in the Post-Exilic Period: Soundings in Site Distribution and Demography," in *Second Temple Studies II: Temple Community in the Persian Period*, ed. Tamara C. Eskenazi and Kent H. Richards, JSOTSup 175 (Sheffield: JSOT Press, 1994), 134–35.

143. Oded Lipschits, "Judah, Jerusalem and the Temple 586–539 B.C.," *Transeu* 22 (2001): 133; "Persian Period Finds from Jerusalem: Facts and Interpretations," *JHebS* 9 (2009): 10. Lipschits notes that this estimation of the extreme contraction of Jerusalem throughout the period is shared by "all scholars working in this area" ("Persian Period Finds," 17).

144. Lipschits, "Persian-Period Judah," 194–95; Charles E. Carter, *The Emergence of Yehud in the Persian Period: A Social and Demographic Study*, JSOTSup 294 (Sheffield: Sheffield Academic, 1999), 249, 256, 294; Faust, "Settlement Dynamics," 49–50; *Neo-Babylonian Period*, 246. Faust suggests that economically "the region was simply wiped off the map of the flourishing Mediterranean trade" of the sixth century (*Neo-Babylonian Period*, 245). The Babylonians were apparently not interested in remedying the economic decline and so it remained throughout the Babylonian period into the Persian period. For this see David S. Vanderhooft, *The Neo-Babylonian Empire and Babylon in the Latter Prophets*, HSM 59 (Atlanta, GA: Scholars Press, 1999), 106–9.

145. Oded Lipschits, "Achaemenid Imperial Policy, Settlement Processes in Palestine, and the Status of Jerusalem in the Middle of the Fifth Century B.C.E.," in *Judah and the Judeans in the Persian Period*, ed. Oded Lipschits and Manfred Oeming (Winona Lake, IN: Eisenbrauns, 2006), 31. Regardless of their various positions regarding the relative emptiness of the land after 586 BCE, no one disagrees with this estimation of the status of Jerusalem for centuries after the destruction.

and sparsely settled. The advent of Cyrus may have brought about the defeat of Babylon, but conditions on the ground remained unchanged. Those who looked to the words of the prophets, or even to classic ANE ideology about divine punishment and reconciliation, would have found it difficult to argue that the present situation indicated that the period of YHWH's anger had come to an end and that a new era had begun. The reality of life in Yehud would have constituted an argument against the idea that YHWH had been reconciled to his people and was now ready to return to Jerusalem and a reconstructed temple.

Lack of a Royal Builder

In the ANE, the building and renovation of temples was understood to be the duty as well as the prerogative of kings.[146] This was especially true in the case of major or national temples.[147] As the "royal administrator" of a god's territory, the king had a particular obligation to oversee the cult, including the building and restoring of temples. The temple and its associated cult constituted part of the royal administration of the country and were part of "the essence of the state."[148] The symbolic role of the temple as a sign of a stable, divinely approved monarchy required that the reigning king be recognized by the people and the gods as willing and able to serve as vigilant caretaker of sanctuaries.[149] Thus building inscriptions often feature kings professing

---

146. There are instances where individuals other than reigning kings undertook to build temples. Madeleine Fitzgerald mentions other royal figures such as queens, as well as priests or priestesses, who commissioned the building or restoration of temples in the Old Babylonian period ("Temple Building in the Old Babylonian Period," in *From the Foundations to the Crenellations: Essays on Temple Building in the Ancient Near East and Hebrew Bible*, ed. Mark J. Boda and Jamie Novotny, AOAT 366 [Münster: Ugarit-Verlag, 2010], 45–47). Hanspeter Schaudig notes examples from Uruk of governors or other officials who undertook restoration during periods when the monarchy was weak ("The Restoration of Temples in the Neo- and Late Babylonian Periods: A Royal Prerogative as the Setting for Political Argument," in *From the Foundations to the Crenellations: Essays on Temple Building in the Ancient Near East and Hebrew Bible*, ed. Mark J. Boda and Jamie Novotny, AOAT 366 [Münster: Ugarit-Verlag, 2010], 142–43).

147. "Major" is a relative term. In this case, it is the perspective of the devotees of a particular god that is relevant. The theological expectations of a given population would depend on what that population considered a "major" shrine, regardless of whether anyone else would agree with this characterization. Smaller local shrines or outdoor altars dedicated to a god or gods, even a "national" god, would certainly not have required royal patronage in any substantive sense.

148. Gösta W. Ahlström, *Royal Administration and National Religion in Ancient Palestine*, SHANE 1 (Leiden: Brill, 1982), 4–8 (citation: 4).

149. Jean de Fraine, *L'Aspect religieux de la royauté israélite: L'Instutition monarchique dans l'Ancien Testament et dans les textes mésopotamiens*, AnBib 3 (Rome: Pontifical Biblical Institute, 1954), 297–99; Stephanie Dalley, "Temple Building in the Ancient Near East: A Synthesis and Reflection," in *From*

their care for the cult of their divine patrons and their ardent desire to see to the repair of dilapidated sanctuaries and the reconstruction of destroyed temples either with the gods' permission or under their orders.

It was not only the duty but the privilege of kings (and gods) to build temples, a privilege often earned by the defeat of enemies.[150] Building inscriptions as well inscriptions on other offerings such as statues regularly associate temple building and restoration with military victories; the temples and offerings are a gesture of gratitude for divine aid.[151] Temple building and repair could also serve to legitimate the rule of a usurper after successfully attaining the throne as a public sign not only that he was pious but also that his rule was approved by the gods, who allowed the work to come to completion.[152] In some texts the successful conquest by a king is taken as a sign that an angry deity has given him victory and accordingly given him the privilege of restoring destroyed cult and temples.[153]

Ultimately this means that temples were typically built or restored by kings who had, or claimed to have, brought peace and stability to a region. This was often achieved through military victory, although it could also be secured by wise management of the state in times of peace. Stable, divinely approved, successful monarchies built temples in honor of the gods who had supported them.

The temple in Jerusalem had historical ties not only to kings but to a specific dynasty that tradition held had built and maintained it for four hundred years before its destruction. As we have seen, the temple building account in 1 Kings is a Judean version of the genre, in which Solomon, the divinely appointed king, undertakes to build the temple, but only after being given victory over his enemies and "rest all around" (1 Kgs 5:18). According to this account, it was "the battles

---

the Foundations to the Crenellations: Essays on Temple Building in the Ancient Near East and Hebrew Bible, ed. Mark J. Boda and Jamie Novotny, AOAT 366 (Münster: Ugarit-Verlag, 2010), 242.

150. Kapelrud, "Temple Building," 56–62. The Baal cycle and the *Enuma Elish* are classic mythic examples of the relationship between the god's defeat of enemies and the building of his palace/temple. The historical or human analog to this is the building of a temple by a victorious king, once again emphasizing the divine patronage of the king.

151. Fitzgerald, "Temple Building," 43–44. See, for example, such wide-ranging examples as the Mesha inscription (*COS* 2.23:137–38), the cone inscriptions of Rim-Sin of Larsa (*COS* 2.102A:252–53; 2.102C:253), and the foundation tablets of Iahdun-Lim of Mari (*COS* 2.111:260–61).

152. Schaudig, "Restoration," 141–64.

153. Bedford, "Discerning the Time," 77. The Cyrus Cylinder is perhaps the best known example of this.

that surrounded him" that prevented his father David from building the temple in his time (1 Kgs 5:17). The construction of the temple is associated here not only with a king but with a victorious king, as we would expect given the ANE ideology of temples and kingship.[154]

The Deuteronomistic account portrays the relationship between the Jerusalem temple and the Davidic monarchy as indissoluble. Solomon begins his temple dedication speech by referring to the selection of David to rule the people and of Jerusalem "for the building of my house" as a single choice:

> Since the day that I brought my people Israel out of Egypt I have not chosen a city from all the tribes of Israel to build a house for my name. But I have chosen David to be over my people Israel. (1 Kgs 8:16)

As successor of his father, "as YHWH has spoken," Solomon is now fulfilling his royal task of building "a house for the name of YHWH, the God of Israel" (1 Kgs 8:20).[155] The temple in Jerusalem is ideologically as well as historically tied to a single dynasty, chosen by YHWH to build and maintain it. It is not difficult to imagine, therefore, that a significant objection to any proposal to rebuild the temple in the early Persian period would be the lack of a suitable (Davidic) royal builder.

It is clear that the question of the relationship of a reconstructed Jerusalem temple to the monarchy occupied the minds of some in the sixth century, although the answers differed. For some the historical relationship between the Davidic monarchy and the temple still obtained and the reconstruction of the temple was closely associated with that family. For others, a new temple could be rebuilt by someone other than a Davidide. For those who assumed the need for a royal builder, the victorious Cyrus presented himself as an obvious candidate.

In the sixth century, Deutero-Isaiah proclaimed of Cyrus: האמר לכורש רעי וכל חפצי ישלם ולאמר לירושלם תבנה והיכל תוסד (Isa 44:28). According to the text, YHWH has commissioned Cyrus, his "anointed"

---

154. Deuteronomy 12:9–11 states that only when YHWH has given Israel rest from their enemies in the land will they come to the place that YHWH will choose as the dwelling place for his name.

155. According to 1 Kings, the succession of Solomon to the throne was attended by intrigue and violence. It is not difficult to see in Solomon's actions and words another example of the legitimating role of the temple for a king whose right to rule was in question.

(45:1) for this purpose, "for the sake of Jacob, my servant" (45:4a). It is through this royal figure, and not David or his descendants, that YHWH will see to the restoration of his city and his house.[156] The role that tradition would be expected to assign to a Davidide has now been transferred to Cyrus, YHWH's royal builder.[157] This choice of Cyrus is readily understandable, given that his defeat of Babylon was ascribed to YHWH (45:1-6). As YHWH's chosen instrument, whose military victories must be attributed to him, Cyrus had not only the prerogative but the duty to rebuild YHWH's temple, in accord with ANE traditions. Regardless of how we understand the role assigned to Cyrus in the rest of Deutero-Isaiah, in 44:24–45:7 it is clear that he is designated by YHWH as the royal builder of the temple in Jerusalem.[158] The temple building account in Ezra 1-6, which stems from a later period, also assigns the role of royal builder to Cyrus and then to his successor, Darius.[159] This, rather than historical reality, explains why this text alone insists that the Persians offered such overwhelming financial support for the temple (1:7-11; 3:7; 6:8-9). The temple was not in reality a Persian project, but the ideology of temple reconstruction required, at least for some, that the Jerusalem temple have a royal builder, effectively making it a Persian project. If that builder was a Persian king, he

---

156. The single mention of David in chapters 40-66 (55:3) has nothing to do with the temple.

157. Roddy L. Braun, "Cyrus in Second and Third Isaiah, Chronicles, Ezra and Nehemiah," in *The Chronicler as Theologian: Essays in Honor of Ralph W. Klein*, ed. M. Patrick Graham, Steven L. McKenzie, and Gary N. Knoppers (New York, NY: T&T Clark, 2003), 162-64.

158. The other oracles in Deutero-Isaiah (42:5-7; 45:11-13; 48:12-15) often thought to refer to Cyrus are, in fact, anonymous. Drawing on the redaction-critical work of a number of scholars (Kratz, van Oorschot, Berges, Merlitz), Rainer Albertz has argued that the first edition of Deutero-Isaiah stems not from the middle of the 6th century but from the beginning of the reign of Darius. ("Darius in Place of Cyrus: The First Edition of Deutero-Isaiah (Isaiah 40.1-52.12) in 521 BCE," *JSOT* 27 [2003]: 371-83). It was only in this period, and not earlier, that the hopeful vision of the repatriation of exiles and the restoration of Jerusalem and its temple would have had any chance of realization. These anonymous oracles, then, refer to Darius and not Cyrus. The oracle that does name Cyrus stems from that figure's ascendancy, except for the reference to rebuilding the city and the temple (44:28b). This portion was added in the time of Darius, Albertz says, updating the oracle "by an order that Cyrus should have given for the reconstruction of Jerusalem and the temple" (378). That this expedient is incredible, and that Darius is nowhere named in Deutero-Isaiah, leaves this suggestion without any apparent support.

159. This much is clear from the "Cyrus Edict" alone (1:2-4). For a detailed comparison of the Ezra account with standard ANE temple building motifs, see Lisbeth S. Fried, "Temple Building in Ezra 1-6," in *From the Foundations to the Crenellations: Essays on Temple Building in the Ancient Near East and Hebrew Bible*, ed. Mark J. Boda and Jamie Novotny, AOAT 366 (Münster: Ugarit-Verlag, 2010), 319-38. She makes a number of good observations, although her claim that the Cyrus Edict itself is probably taken from the foundation inscription for the new temple is not persuasive.

would also support the temple financially as part of his royal obligation.[160]

We cannot assume that the claim that Cyrus (and then Darius) was YHWH's chosen builder was accepted by everyone. Many have suggested that behind the insistence in Isaiah 45:9–13 on the sovereign prerogative of YHWH to act as he sees fit lies an objection (or anticipated objection) to YHWH's choice of Cyrus as his instrument. The standard interpretation of this passage is that it is directed toward those Israelites who cannot accept the "pagan" Cyrus as YHWH's "anointed." In response, YHWH rejects the notion that Israel can question his decisions or the modes by which he chooses to "treat the work of my hands." The placement of this otherwise ambiguous and obscure text immediately after the explicit announcement that Cyrus is YHWH's "shepherd" and "anointed," who will destroy Babylon and rebuild Jerusalem and the temple, suggests this is the point.[161] If this is in fact the attitude that lies behind the passage, it contains within it a potential objection to the idea that Cyrus is a suitable royal builder for the Jerusalem temple. If this was the case in the middle of the sixth century, it would have probably have remained an objection in the reign of Darius. But are commentators correct to see behind this text a refusal to accept the claim that YHWH has chosen a Persian as his instrument?

A few scholars have argued that the addressee of this divine reprimand is not Israel but the nations. The textual details do not support the widespread assumption that it is directed toward Israel, who is spoken, not *to*, but *about*:

> For thus says YHWH, the Holy One of Israel and his fashioner (יֹצְרוֹ): Do you question me about things concerning my children? Command me concerning the works of my hands? (45:11)[162]

160. To the extent that the producers of Ezra and Nehemiah considered the Persians the divinely appointed custodians of Israel, they would also have considered them the designated royal builders and caretakers of the temple. For the Persians as YHWH's chosen custodians of Israel in Ezra-Nehemiah, see, for example, Sara Japhet, "Sheshbazzar and Zerubbabel: Against the Background of the Historical and Religious Tendencies of Ezra-Nehemiah," *ZAW* 94 (1982): 73–75; "Temple in the Restoration Period," 241.

161. For this standard reading, see for example, Jan L. Koole, *Isaiah 40–48*, HCOT (Kampen: Pharos, 1997), 1.448–49; Bruce D. Naidoff, "The Two-Fold Structure of Isaiah XLV 9–13," *VT* 31 (1981): 184; Ulrich Berges, *Jesaja 40–48*, HThKAT (Freiburg: Herder, 2008), 414; Whybray, *Isaiah 40–66*, 107; Bonnard, *Second Isaïe*, 174–75; Watts, *Isaiah 34–66*, 157–58; Oswalt, *Isaiah*, 208; Joseph Blenkinsopp, *Isaiah 40–55*, AB 19A (New Haven, CT: Yale University Press, 2002), 252; Paul, *Isaiah 40–66*, 260–63; Duhm, *Jesaia*, 343–45.

Instead, it is claimed, the rebuke is directed toward the nations in response to their supposed objection to the way YHWH has treated his people or, according to Leene, their objection that Deutero-Isaiah is too "nationalistic." It is true that, within the conceit of the passage, Israel is not directly addressed. But of course the intended audience of the oracle is Israel, not "the nations," who cannot have been expected by the author to actually read or hear the text. If the nations are the "narrative audience," they are not the "authorial audience," to whom the author is actually directing the text.[163] In the same way that oracles against the nations are meant for Israelite consumption, although addressed to non-Israelites, so this text—if it is addressed to "the nations" on one level—is really meant to be read "in-house."[164] Despite the language of the text, Israel *is* being addressed in the oracle, which constitutes a response to some Israelite objection. In its present context, the passage suggests that the objection is to Cyrus who, although not named explicitly, is nevertheless referred to in v. 13 and who is designated by YHWH as the one who will "rebuild my city." This passage suggests, then, that in the sixth century not all Yahwists accepted the notion that Cyrus (and, we may presume, Darius) was a legitimate royal builder of the Jerusalem temple.

In addition to the fact that the Persians did not worship YHWH, and on that count alone were doubtful candidates to build his temple, they were also not Davidides. The historical and theological ties between the house of YHWH and the house of David made it likely that at least some would have insisted that the only legitimate royal builder of YHWH's

---

162. Brevard S. Childs, *Isaiah*, OTL (Louisville, KY: Westminster John Knox, 2001), 354; Westermann, *Isaiah 40-66*, 164-65; Henk Leene, "Universalism or Nationalism? Isaiah XLV 9-13 and Its Context," *Bijdr* 39 (1974): 320-21; Karl Elliger, *Deuterojesaja in seinem Verhältnis zu Tritojesaja*, BWANT 4/11 (Stuttgart: Kohlhammer, 1933), 179-83.

163. The "narrative audience" or the "narratee" is the audience to whom the narrator or speaker in the text is supposed to be speaking. This audience is entirely imaginary, as opposed to the "authorial audience," which, though a hypothetical construct of the author, nevertheless is the "rhetorical" audience of the text in question, the audience for whom the text is written, which is not entirely imaginary. See Peter J. Rabinowitz, "Truth in Fiction: A Reexamination of Audiences," *CritInq* 4 (1977): 125-34; Gerald Prince, "Introduction to the Study of the Narratee," in *Essentials of the Theory of Fiction*, 2nd ed., ed. Michael J. Hoffman and Patrick D. Murphy (Durham, NC: Duke University Press, 1996), 214, 216.

164. See John H. Hayes, "Usage of Oracles against Foreign Nations in Ancient Israel," *JBL* 87 (1968): 81-92; Paul R. Raabe, "Why Prophetic Oracles against the Nations?" in *Fortunate the Eyes That See: Essays in Honor of David Noel Freedman in Celebration of His Seventieth Birthday*, ed. Astrid B. Beck et al. (Grand Rapids, MI: Eerdmans, 1995), 248-52.

temple in Jerusalem was a descendant of David. The appearance on the Yehudite scene of Zerubbabel, apparently a Davidide, seems to have raised the possibility for some that he could be a royal builder designated by YHWH.[165] The text that most obviously portrays Zerubbabel as a royal builder is Zechariah 4:6–10. Here it is claimed that Zerubbabel will bring forth האבן הראשה, a term Petersen has suggested is cognate with the Akkadian *libitu maḫrītu*, "first or former brick," which in building inscriptions refers to a brick removed from the former temple building during the *kalû* ritual and placed in the new building by the builder king to preserve continuity between the old temple and the new.[166] Not only this parallel, but also the claim that Zerubbabel is the one who laid the foundations and will see the process through, portray him acting as a royal builder.[167]

The obvious objection would be that Zerubbabel, though a Davidide, was hardly a king. While Zechariah 1–8 might portray him in royal terms, his actual royal status would have been debatable in the early years of Darius.[168] Avowals that he was the Davidic royal builder sent to Yehud by YHWH (not the Persians) to oversee the reconstruction of the temple would have had to face the skepticism of those who failed to see any evidence of the validity of such claims. As discussed above,

165. The biblical materials all attest that Zerubbabel is of Davidic descent, although exactly how varies with the source. Those texts that refer to him according to his patronym call him "son of Shealtiel" (Ezra 3:2, 8; 5:2; Neh 12:1; Hag 1:1, 12, 14; 2:23). Shealtiel is identified in 1 Chr 3:17 as the son of Jeconiah. But 1 Chr 3:19 identifies Zerubbabel as the son of Shealtiel's brother, Pedaiah. For further, see the discussion of the figure of Zerubbabel in chap. 4.
166. David L. Petersen, "Zerubbabel and Jerusalem Temple Reconstruction," *CBQ* 36 (1974): 367–69; *Haggai*, 241. See also Ellis, *Foundation Deposits*, 20–26, 170–72 for a description of this ritual. In a similar vein, Petersen understands האבן הבדיל in v. 10a to refer to a tin tablet, also a foundation deposit (*Haggai*, 243).
167. It might be possible to see this portrayal of Zerubbabel as royal builder made even more explicit in the reference to the צמח who will build the temple and then be enthroned as ruler (Zech 6:12-13). But the identification of the Zemah with Zerubbabel here is not secure. Although several have argued that Zerubbabal is the צמח (Mowinckel, Beyse, Chary, Carroll, Petersen, Marti, Mitchell, Beuken), perhaps an equal number claim he is not Zerubbabel but a future royal figure (Rose, Tollington, Rudolph, Van der Woude, Meyers and Meyers, Smith). See Wolter H. Rose, *Zemah and Zerubbabel: Messianic Expectations in the Early Postexilic Period*, JSOTSup 304 (Sheffield: Sheffield Academic, 2000), 17–21. The historical and rhetorical roles of Zerubbabel will be discussed in more detail in the next chapter.
168. The arguments of Liver, Sacchi, and Bianchi that Yehud was a vassal kingdom, which would make Zerubbabel a king, have not been found persuasive. Nor has André Lemaire's modified position that Yehud was a "province proche d'un royaume vassal" ("Zorobabel et la Judée à la lumière de l'épigraphie (fin du VIe s. av. J.-C," *RB* 103 (1996): 53). See Nadav Na'aman, "Royal Vassals or Governors? On the Status of Sheshbazzar and Zerubbabel in the Persian Empire," *Henoch* 22 (2000): 35–44, for a refutation of their arguments.

it seems clear that not everyone accepted Zechariah's insistence that YHWH wanted the temple rebuilt and the fact that Zerubbabel was not a real king would have only contributed to doubts about the prophet's authenticity.

Ancient Near Eastern ideology understood temples to be closely associated with state and monarchy. This had also been the case in Judah before 586 BCE. Calls to rebuild the temple in 520 BCE would have had to contend with the fact that Yehud was not a state with a king (at least not an indigenous one). Without a royal builder, who could legitimately reconstruct the temple? Claims that Cyrus or Zerubbabel was YHWH's designated royal builder were clearly accepted by some but not by all.

To summarize: in the early years of Darius there would have been several theological or ideological reasons to oppose any plans to rebuild the temple in Jerusalem. The poor economic and demographic conditions could easily be interpreted as signs that Israel remained under judgment. Apart from this, indications that YHWH wanted a temple built were slight and some circles argued explicitly that YHWH did not want a "house." These objections, as well as the absence of a viable royal builder, would have contributed together or separately to skepticism about YHWH's attitude toward any proposed reconstruction. Without assurance that the project was approved by YHWH, it would be dangerous to heed any call to rebuild.

Socioeconomic Objections and Obstacles

The perspectives just discussed are discovered largely in texts, the products of scribal circles and the institutions that supported them. The concerns about a royal builder (let alone whether he was a Davidide or not), exact determination of when or if the period of divine judgment had ended, and other theological and ideological concerns reflected in them did not necessarily extend beyond the relatively small number that produced them.[169] It is unlikely that most Yehudites

169. As some of the most educated members of their societies, who possessed "high literacy," scribes comprised a small group in Israel or Yehud, just as in any polity of the ANE. See, for example, Karel van der Toorn, *Scribal Culture and the Making of the Hebrew Bible* (Cambridge, MA: Harvard University Press, 2007), 10–11; Christopher A. Rollston, *Writing and Literacy in the World of Ancient Israel: Epigraphic Evidence from the Iron Age*, Archaeology and Bible Series 11 (Atlanta, GA: Society of Bibli-

paid more than scant attention to these issues, if they knew anything of them. Certainly most of them were not familiar with the texts that articulated them. At least until the Hellenistic period, access to texts was probably limited largely to the same circles that produced them.[170] Even if they had been aware of these issues or texts, one wonders how relevant "average Yehudites" would have found these questions.

Whereas the temple occupies a central place in the texts, reflecting the biases and occupations of the elite, almost certainly it occupied a much smaller space in the imaginations of other Yehudites (or Israelites in other places). Bedford observes that the fact that the temple was important to many of those who produced the texts does not mean anyone else really cared.[171]

Yet it would have been necessary to gain at least the acquiescence if not the enthusiastic support of this great majority of Yehudites. They were the ones who would be expected to actually build the temple. Unless those who favored the temple were willing or able to enslave workers to get it built—and this does not appear to have happened—the cooperation of the "average Yehudite" was vital for the project to get beyond the planning stages.

There were socioeconomic reasons, however, why these Yehudites may have been indifferent or even hostile to a new temple in Jerusalem. How many of them would have felt a real need for such a structure and its attendant apparatus? Lack of interest combined with a consideration of the potential impact on the present religious practices as well as the economic implications of the project could lead to opposition. And although the more developed theological and ideological arguments we have examined may not have entered into their

cal Literature, 2010), 127–35; Ehud Ben Zvi, "The Urban Center of Jerusalem and the Development of the Literature of the Hebrew Bible," in *Aspects of Urbanism in Antiquity*, ed. Walter E. Aufrecht et al., JSOTSup 244 (Sheffield: Sheffield Academic, 1997), 194–209.

170. Martti Nissinen, "How Prophecy Became Literature," *SJOT* 19 (2005): 157–59; K. L. Noll, "Was There Doctrinal Dissemination in Early Yahweh Religion?" *BibInt* 16 (2008): 398–401, 419–20; Emanuel Tov, "The Writing of Early Scrolls: Implications for the Literary Analysis of Hebrew Scripture," in *Hebrew Bible, Greek Bible, and Qumran: Collected Essays*, TSAJ 121 (Tübingen: Mohr Siebeck, 2008), 206–20; Ehud Ben Zvi, "The Prophetic Book: A Key Form of Prophetic Literature," in *The Changing Face of Form Criticism for the Twenty-First Century*, ed. Marvin A. Sweeney and Ehud Ben Zvi (Grand Rapids, MI: Eerdmans, 2003), 293–94; "Urban Center," 200; van der Toorn, *Scribal Culture*, 147–48; David M. Carr, *Writing on the Tablet of the Heart: Origins of Scripture and Literature* (New York, NY: Oxford University Press, 2005), 150–51.

171. Bedford, *Temple Restoration*, 161.

considerations, certainly the Yehudites would have wanted to avoid offending YHWH, as they would any deity. If it seemed even possible that YHWH did not want this temple built, this too would contribute to their rejection of the project. In this final section of the chapter, we will investigate the likely sources of opposition or indifference to the temple reconstruction from the religious and economic perspectives of "average Yehudites."

Religious Practices

Our knowledge of the religious practices of residents of Judah after the destruction of the temple is limited. Archaeological data are scant; no sanctuaries or cult objects have been found that can be securely dated to the Babylonian or early Persian periods.[172] We are left to develop on the basis of biblical texts—some of which are ambiguous—and archaeological data not immediately pertaining to cultic behavior a *general* and *probable* idea of the religious scene in Judah in the middle of the sixth century.

It is clear that cultic worship of YHWH took place before the construction of the temple by Solomon, and the biblical texts indicate that once the temple was completed Judahites worshiped in many other locations. There are many references throughout the DtrH and other texts to the במות, cultic sites of an undetermined nature where sacrifices were regularly offered.[173] Under the reigns of Hezekiah and Josiah,

---

172. Ephraim Stern, *The Assyrian, Babylonian, and Persian Periods (732–332 BCE)* (vol. 2 of *Archaeology of the Land of the Bible*, ABRL [New York, NY: Doubleday, 2001]), 347.

173. The literature on these cultic sites is extensive and the discussion has tended to focus on what exactly they were. Because no archaeological remains have so far been recovered that can conclusively be said to represent an ancient במה we are left only with biblical texts as evidence. Menahem Haran has insisted that במות have nothing to do with temples or other cultic buildings, but rather fall under the general category of altars; a במה was "just a large altar," not associated with a temple but found in the open (*Temples and Temple Service in Ancient Israel: An Inquiry into Biblical Cult Phenomena and the Historical Setting of the Priestly School* [Winona Lake, IN: Eisenbrauns, 1985], 23–25). On the basis of a study of biblical language about the sites, however, W. Boyd Barrick has argued that the way במות are spoken of in the texts suggests they were usually urban installations, capable of being "built" (or "made," "burnt," "torn down"), *in which* sacrificial acts are performed. (The preposition used with במות is usually -ב, which in any other context would mean "in." Because they are typically understood to be "high places," the preposition is often assumed to me "on," but this is incorrect.) All of this suggests they were probably complexes very similar to temples ("What Do We Really Know about 'High-Places'?" *SEÅ* 45 (1980): 52–57). Whether they were open-air sanctuaries or temple-like structures or complexes, they appear to have been widespread and frequented cultic sites that offered an alternative or complement to worship at the Jerusalem temple.

we are told, these sites were destroyed or defiled and sacrificial worship of YHWH confined to the Jerusalem temple.[174] There has been disagreement among scholars about the historical value of these reports.
It is often suggested that Josiah's reform, for example, is largely fictional, or at least that the extent and success of the effort has been
enhanced by the editors of the DtrH.[175] Whatever the nature or reality
of the reform, its accomplishment may have been short-lived. Jeremiah
and Ezekiel report worship apart from the temple (Jer 44:15–19; Ezek
8:5–18).[176] Logic also leads one to suspect that, if there was an effort to
abolish virtually overnight local sites of worship with their attendant
religious traditions and practices, it would not have met with large or
lasting success.

If this was the case before the temple was destroyed, it is clear
that cultic worship at במות or other sites continued afterwards.[177] It is
implausible to suppose that people, even those who had been accustomed to bring offerings to Jerusalem, simply stopped offering sacrifices. Some have suggested that the altar at the temple site continued
to function, although this is debatable.[178] Even if this were the case
there is no reason to suppose other cultic sites that almost certainly
were functioning before the destruction of the temple did not continue
to receive offerings after 586 BCE.[179]

174. Hezekiah, we are told in 2 Kgs 18:4 "removed" (הסיר) the במות. Josiah shut down the practices
going on at the במות (2 Kgs 23:5), "defiled" (יטמא) the במות from Geba to Beersheba, and tore
down (נתץ) the במות at the entrance to the Gate of Joshua (v. 8). The fact that Josiah is reported to
have defiled rather than torn down the במות from Geba to Beersheba suggests that they remained
standing, possibly to be used again. See, however, the next footnote.

175. The reasons for the disagreement and the evidence brought to bear on the question are not relevant here. For recent examples of the various positions, see Rainer Albertz, "Why a Reform Like
Josiah's Must Have Happened," in Good Kings and Bad Kings, ed. Lester L. Grabbe, LHBOTS 393, European Seminar in Historical Methodology 5 (New York, NY: T&T Clark, 2005), 27–46; Christoph
Uehlinger, "Was There a Cult Reform under King Josiah? The Case for a Well-Grounded Minimum,"
in Good Kings and Bad Kings, 279–316 (with extensive bibliography); Niels Peter Lemche, "Did a
Reform Like Josiah's Happen?" in The Historian and the Bible: Essays in Honour of Lester L. Grabbe, ed.
Diana V. Edelman and Philip R. Davies, LHBOTS 530 (New York, NY: T&T Clark, 2010), 11–19, and
others.

176. Ackroyd, Exile and Restoration, 40–41; Albertz, History of Israelite Religion, 2:233; Susan Ackerman,
Under Every Green Tree: Popular Religion in Sixth-Century Judah, HSM 46 (Atlanta, GA: Scholars Press,
1992), 213–17.

177. Texts from the Persian period such as Isa 57:3–13; 65:3–7; 66:17 indicate that even after the temple
was rebuilt other sacrificial cultic sites were operative. It seems clear that for centuries Israelites
worshipped at local shrines regardless of any attempts to curb such activity.

178. See, for example, Douglas Jones, "The Cessation of Sacrifice after the Destruction of the Temple in
586 BC," JTS NS 14 (1963): 12–31.

179. Unfortunately, we have no archaeological evidence of cultic structures in the region from this

Blenkinsopp has argued that either Mizpah or Bethel, or both, served as a cultic center in the Babylonian period and early Persian periods. His argument rests both on the status of Mizpah as an administrative center and two biblical texts that, he argues, probably refer to Bethel or Mizpah as cultic sites (Jer 41:5; Zech 7:1–6).[180]

The biblical record indicates that after the destruction of Jerusalem and the Judahite kingdom, the administrative center for the area was moved to Mizpah, now identified as the modern Tell en-Naṣbeh.[181] Archaeological investigation of this site indicates it flourished well into the fifth century, with buildings that appear to be administrative structures and residences of officials.[182] Nehemiah 3:15, 19 indicate that it was still some sort of administrative unit in the mid-fifth century. Given that the area and its population survived the Babylonian destruction relatively unscathed, it is likely that this flourishing center would have had a cultic site at or near it in the succeeding decades, such as the ancient site of Bethel.[183]

Two biblical passages may offer textual support for this supposition. Jeremiah 41:4–5 reports that the day after the assassination of

period. Stern (Assyrian, Babylonian, and Persian Periods, 347) mentions one such structure at Bethel, the date and function of which remained unclear at the time of publication (2001). But there are no archaeological reports of such a structure and James Leon Kelso specifically notes that there was no cultic building excavated at Beitin (The Excavations of Bethel, 1934-1960 [Cambridge, MA: American Schools of Oriental Research, 1968], 192). Avraham Faust has also noted that apart from the temple at Arad and possibly the installation at Dan, both of which date from much earlier than the period in question, there have been no Iron II buildings built for cultic purposes unearthed in Judah/Israel despite vigorous attempts to find them ("The Archaeology of the Israelite Cult: Questioning the Consensus," BASOR 360 [2010]: 27–30).

180. Joseph Blenkinsopp, "The Judaean Priesthood During the Neo-Babylonian and Achaemenid Periods: A Hypothetical Reconstruction," CBQ 60 (1998): 25–31; "Bethel in the Neo-Babylonian Period," in Judah and the Judeans in the Neo-Babylonian Period, ed. Oded Lipschits and Joseph Blenkinsopp (Winona Lake, IN: Eisenbrauns, 2003), 93–107.

181. While it is often suggested or assumed that Gedaliah was a "governor" and that Mizpah was set up by the Babylonians as a provincial administrative center, David Vanderhooft has argued that it is unlikely that Judah was administered as a Babylonian province. In the first place, Gedaliah is never identified as a governor or with any other title; we are simply informed that he was appointed over the people (הפקיד עליהם) who remained in the land (2 Kgs 25:22; Jer 40:7), and it does not appear that he was replaced after his assassination. It appears to be only on the basis of the unfounded assumption that the Babylonians administered conquered peoples much as their Assyrian predecessors did that has led to the widespread tendency to refer to the Babylonian "province" of Judah ("Babylonian Strategies of Imperial Control in the West: Royal Practice and Rhetoric," in Judah and the Judeans in the Neo-Babylonian Period, ed. Oded Lipschits and Joseph Blenkinsopp [Winona Lake, IN: Eisenbrauns, 2003], 244).

182. Jeffrey R. Zorn, "Tell en-Naṣbeh and the Problem of the Material Culture of the Sixth Century," in Judah and the Judeans in the Neo-Babylonian Period, ed. Oded Lipschits and Joseph Blenkinsopp (Winona Lake, IN: Eisenbrauns, 2003), 444.

183. Blenkinsopp, "Judaean Priesthood," 29.

Gedaliah, eighty men were on their way from Shechem, Shiloh, and Samaria with grain offerings (מנחה) and incense to the house of YHWH (להביא בית יהוה). Whereas some commentators have presumed that the men were on their way to Jerusalem, others claim that there is nothing in the text that makes this absolutely necessary. The term בית יהוה does refer almost exclusively to the temple in Jerusalem, although it also refers to the wilderness tabernacle (Josh 6:24) and the sanctuary at Shiloh (1 Samuel 1), as well as—possibly—a northern shrine in Hosea 8:1; 9:4.[184] Nevertheless, in Jeremiah the term is used several times for the Jerusalem temple, making it seem as if the reference offered here without comment is to the same. Despite this, Blenkinsopp suggests that it is not likely that pilgrims from the north would be heading to the destroyed temple where, in any case, the altar was probably out of commission. It is more likely that they are going to Mizpah or perhaps Bethel.[185]

That Bethel may have continued to function as a cultic center in the early Persian period is suggested, according to Blenkinsopp, by Zechariah 7:1–4, a text which presents textual difficulties precisely in its reference to Bethel. The scene takes place in the fourth year of Darius (vv. 2–3):

וישלח בית אל שר אצר ורגם מלך ואנשיו לחלות את פני יהוה לאמר אל הכהנים
אשר לבית יהוה צבאות ואל הנביאים לאמר האבכה בחדש החמשי הנזר כאשר
עשיתי זה כמה שנים

The difficulty is understanding how the phrase בית אל functions syntactically. Three main solutions have been offered: (1) it is the subject of the sentence, in which case "Bethel" stands in for "the men of Bethel," who have sent a certain Sar-ezer and Regem-melek to the

---

184. What the text means here by בית יהוה is difficult to know. Commentators generally agree it does not refer to the Jerusalem temple. While it may refer to YHWH's land this is not a completely satisfying solution. Hosea 9:4 in particular seems to be referring to a temple, as Francis Andersen and David Noel Freedman note (*Hosea*, AB24 [Garden City, NY: Doubleday, 1980], 528). James Mays suggests it is an addition by a Dtr editor, as it makes no sense in Hosea's northern context and it, apparently, cannot refer to a northern shrine (*Hosea*, OTL [Philadelphia: Westminster, 1969], 127).

185. Blenkinsopp, "Judaean Priesthood," 26–27; "Bethel," 95. See also Ernst Axel Knauf, "Bethel: The Israelite Impact on Judean Language and Literature," in *Judah and the Judeans in the Persian Period*, ed. Oded Lipschits and Manfred Oeming (Winona Lake, IN: Eisenbrauns, 2006), 305; Patrick M. Arnold, "Mizpah," *ABD*, 4.880.

priests of the "house of YHWH of hosts," understood to be the Jerusalem temple;[186] (2) it is the first part of a name, thus, "Bethel-sar-ezer" sent Regem-melek to the priests;[187] or (3) Bethel is the destination, in which case the house of YHWH is the sanctuary in Bethel. This last is Blenkinsopp's suggestion.[188] Despite the claim of Meyers and Meyers that "the context makes it quite clear that Bethel is the subject of the verb 'sent'," there is nothing in the context that necessitates this solution and in fact such a reading appears forced. In the first place, as Blenkinsopp observes, this amounts to the personification of the city, a literary device that, while common in poetic contexts, is not found elsewhere and would be an odd choice for referring to the "men of Bethel."[189] The fact that the message sent to the priests is an inquiry whether "I" should weep and fast as "I" have been doing for many years also does not accord well with this reading. On the other hand, as in the text from Jeremiah, it seems unlikely that a text that elsewhere refers to the temple in Jerusalem as the house of YHWH of hosts (8:9) or as "my house" (1:6; 3:7) would use that same language to refer to another sanctuary, particularly when that text is focused on the rebuilding of the Jerusalem temple. Of the three options, the compound name appears to be the most viable.

Despite the ambiguous textual evidence brought to bear on his thesis, Blenkinsopp is correct that cultic, sacrificial worship took place apart from the temple in Judah in the Babylonian and early Persian periods. Bethel and Mizpah are good candidates, but they are not the only possible places that altars could have been erected or maintained. The evidence suggests that Judahites worshiped in sites other than, or in addition to, the Jerusalem temple while it still existed, and so we may safely presume that once it was destroyed cultic behavior persisted elsewhere, even if some did continue to bring offerings to the temple site. Whatever religious developments were occurring in Babylon during the middle of the sixth century, "back home" religious life was either going on as before or taking its own developmental course.

186. Meyers and Meyers, *Haggai*, 379, 382–83; Rudolph, *Haggai*, 135–36; Smith, *Micah- Malachi*, 221.

187. Wellhausen, *Kleinen Propheten*, 186; James P. Hyatt, "A Neo-Babylonian Parallel to Bethel-Sar-Eṣer, Zech 7:2," *JBL* 56 (1937): 87–94; Ackroyd, *Exile and Restoration*, 207; Petersen, *Haggai*, 281.

188. Blenkinsopp, "Judaean Priesthood," 32–33. He notes along with many others that this reading is reflected in OG, Syr, and Tg.

189. Ibid., 33.

There is a strong consensus that the majority of Yehudites in the early Persian period were not those who had returned from Babylon but rather the descendants of those who had remained in the land. This means that most Yehudites had an established religious life apart from the temple in Jerusalem and religious imaginations that did not give it central place, making it doubtful that they would have automatically or easily supported plans for its reconstruction. They would have had to be *persuaded* that it was in their best interest to see the temple rebuilt and its cultic life resumed.

This might not have been an easy task. Many Yehudites may have been not only indifferent to the temple but outright hostile to it. If the reports of Josiah's reform have any historical value, the memory of the effort to suppress local cultic sites with their attendant traditions might have raised fears that the same thing would happen again. While for some the temple may have become a strong symbol of a unified and purified Yahwistic faith, for others it may have been a symbol of repression. This is speculative, of course, but not improbable if in fact life under the first temple had led to the shutting down of local sites. Especially hostile to the possibility of such centralizing and "purifying" efforts would have been any priestly circles associated with Bethel or other worship sites, who faced the possibility of having their cults shut down or their livelihoods diminished.[190]

Economic Factors

This last observation leads to a consideration of possible economic objections to the temple. It is worth emphasizing that here we are interested not in what economic impact the temple ultimately did have, but in what concerns it may have raised among Yehudites before it was built. Such considerations would have been based on common understandings of the economic role and impact of temples in general and the former Jerusalem temple in particular. It is these concerns that would have influenced their perspectives on reconstruction.

Temples played an important economic role in the ANE, although the nature and extent of that role varied. While larger temples could

---

190. Ibid., 34–43.

partially finance their operations through their landholdings, all temples required the support of the community to survive. The major source of income for all temples, no matter the size, was primarily but not exclusively tithes and taxes paid in produce, wood, silver, clothing, livestock, or other commodities. These offerings could be voluntary or compulsory. In return, temples offered various services in addition to the strictly cultic, such the training of scribes for government and business, administration of laws, employment, care for the indigent, banking, tax collecting for the crown, and loans of grain. Overall, they could exercise a positive and stabilizing influence in the economic life of a community. This was particularly true of the most important temples in Mesopotamia and Egypt.[191]

Smaller temples in areas such as Asia Minor and the Levant also played a role in the economic life of their communities, but as Bedford has noted, the scale, range of activities, and overall economic importance was very different from that of the great Mesopotamian temples.[192] One significant difference was that these smaller temples tended not to have extensive land holdings, which required them to be supported almost entirely through voluntary or obligatory contributions.[193]

This would be true also for a new temple in Jerusalem. Although it is possible that it would have held some lands, its major source of income would necessarily be contributions from the Yehudites. As I argued above, the Persian government was not a sponsor of the temple and almost certainly did not contribute any significant amount to the cost of its building or its upkeep. Whether it used the temple once it was

---

191. J. N. Postgate, "The Role of the Temple in the Mesopotamian Secular Community," in *Man, Settlement and Urbanism: Proceedings of a Meeting of the Research Seminar in Archaeology and Related Subjects, Held at the Institute of Archaeology, London University*, ed. Peter J. Ucko, Ruth Tringham, and G. W. Dimbleby (London: Duckworth, 1972), 813–14; Dandamaev and Lukonin, *Culture and Social Institutions*, 360–62; Muhammad A. Dandamaev, "State and Temple in Babylonia in the First Millennium B.C.," in vol. 2 of *State and Temple Economy in the Ancient Near East*, ed. Edward Lipiński (Louvain: Department Oriëntalistiek, 1979), 589.

192. Bedford, *Temple Restoration*, 140–46. His point is that the differences are significant enough that the economic nature and role of Mesopotamian temples offers little help in discerning the same for the temple in Jerusalem.

193. The relationship between temple and palace was complex, not only politically but also economically. As this element of temple economics is not particularly relevant for the second temple, it will not be discussed. On the economy of temple and crown in the Neo-Babylonian and Achaemenid periods see, for example, Dandamaev, "State and Temple," 593–96; Dandamaev and Lukonin, *Culture and Social Institutions*, 362–65.

built for the collection of imperial taxes or assigned other fiscal roles to it is not known, but there is no evidence to suggest that the Persians took any more interest in the temple after it was completed than before.[194] Suggestions that the Persians used the temple as a means of economic as well as social or political control of Yehud are not supported well by the existing evidence.[195]

Because the cost of the temple reconstruction and future upkeep would have to be borne by the Yehudites, they would have held some opinions about it. Much of the burden would have fallen on the non-elites and we can expect some opposition in those quarters because of this. This is especially true if many or most of them would have had no reason to expect considerable benefit from the temple once built.

It is true that one perceived benefit may have been employment during construction. The economic situation was poor in Yehud in this period and many may have welcomed the chance to work on the project.[196] In some temple building accounts we hear of wages paid in barley, bread, beer, oil, and other goods.[197]

On the other hand, we hear much more often in the biblical and extrabiblical texts of levied or forced labor. Compulsory or corvée labor, whether paid or not, was a regular feature of public building,

194. Melody D. Knowles, *Centrality Practiced: Jerusalem in the Religious Practice of Yehud and the Diaspora in the Persian Period*, ABS 16 (Atlanta, GA: Society of Biblical Literature, 2006), 117–19. Knowles points out here what we have already observed above: it seems that the installation at Ramat Rahel, not Jerusalem, served as the main administrative center of the region during this period. Peter Bedford also argues that the temple would not necessarily have been used for the collection of taxes for the crown, noting that there is no clear evidence that all temples in the empire were used in this way ("The Economic Role of the Jerusalem Temple in Achaemenid Judah: Comparative Perspectives," in *Shai le-Sarah Japhet: Studies in the Bible, Its Exegesis and Its Languages*, ed. Moshe Bar-Asher et al. [Jerusalem: Bialik Institute, 2007], 15*–16*, 19*). He thus disagrees with Schaper's thesis because the Jerusalem temple appears to have acted as a foundry, it must have served as a treasury for the empire. For this thesis, see Joachim Schaper, "The Jerusalem Temple as an Instrument of Achaemenid Fiscal Administration," *VT* (1995): 528–39. For the Jerusalem temple as treasury in the Persian period, see Charles C. Torrey, "The Foundry of the Second Temple at Jerusalem," *JBL* 55 (1936): 247–60 and Joachim Schaper, "The Temple Treasury Committee in the Times of Ezra and Nehemiah," *VT* 47 (1997): 200–206.

195. See, for example, the claim of Samuel Balentine that the temple effectively represented the Persian presence. He also states that the temple, as an arm of the Persian government, was used by it to "shape the ritual world celebrated in Yehud." As evidence for these claims, he cites the reconstructions of Berquist noted above (120n347) as well as Plöger and Hanson ("The Politics of Religion in the Persian Period," in *After the Exile: Essays in Honour of Rex Mason*, ed. John Barton and David J. Reimer [Macon, GA: Mercer University Press, 1996], 141–42).

196. The work force for the first temple was reported to be "large and variegated": skilled and unskilled workers, transporters, foremen, masons, carpenters, metal workers, master artisans, etc. (Hurowitz, *Exalted House*, 289).

197. Fitzgerald, "Temple Building," 44–45.

including temples, in the ANE. Gudea reports that he imposed a levy throughout the land for workers to build his temple.[198] Texts from Alalaḫ, Ugarit, and Amarna all attest to a well-known and active institution in the Levant in the second half of the second millennium.[199] Such conscription was not voluntary and was not popular.[200]

Biblical and extrabiblical sources attest that the system was also used in Israel. Second Samuel 20:24 identifies a certain Adoram in David's administration as the one in charge of the compulsory labor (על חמס), suggesting the adoption of the institution began already with that king. The account of the building of Solomon's temple indicates that the work was done by compulsory labor, beginning with the acquisition of materials (1 Kgs 5:27):

ויעל המלך שלמה מס מכל ישראל ויהי המס שלשים אלף איש

Although 1 Kings 9:22 claims that Solomon did not impose this labor on any Israelites, that verse is widely understood to be a later apologetic addition to the account.[201] The fact that the "rebellion" against the house of David by the northern tribes revolves around the question of compulsory labor and that, when Rehoboam sent out Adoram, "all Israel" stoned him to death (1 Kgs 12:18), makes it impossible to believe that Solomon only forced non-Israelites to work. The story, and the felt need by later editors to claim that Solomon did not in fact force Israelites to work, indicates how unpopular the system was. That compulsory, even unpaid, labor could be used by Judahite kings even down

198. Gudea Cyl. A xiv 7–28.
199. See J. Alberto. Soggin, "Compulsory Labor under David and Solomon," in *Studies in the Period of David and Solomon and Other Essays: Papers Read at the International Symposium for Biblical Studies, Tokyo, 5-7 December, 1979*, ed. Tomoo Ishida (Winona Lake, IN: Eisenbrauns, 1982), 267; Amson F. Rainey, "Compulsory Labour Gangs in Ancient Israel," *IEJ* 20 (1970): 192–95; Isaac Mendelsohn, "On Corvée Labor in Canaan and Ancient Israel," *BASOR* 167 (1962): 32–33; Nadav Na'aman, "From Conscription of Forced Labor to a Symbol of Bondage: *mas* in the Biblical Literature," in *"An Experienced Scribe Who Neglects Nothing": Ancient Near Eastern Studies in Honor of Jacob Klein*, ed. Yitzchak Sefati et al. (Bethesda, MD: CDL, 2005), 746–58.
200. Na'aman, "Conscription of Forced Labor," 756.
201. Mordechai Cogan, *I Kings*, AB 10 (New Haven, CT: Yale University Press, 2001), 309; Volkmar Fritz, *1 & 2 Kings*, trans. Anselm Hagedorn, CC (Minneapolis, MN: Fortress Press, 2003), 114; Nili Sacher Fox, *In the Service of the King: Officialdom in Ancient Israel and Judah*, HUCM 23 (Cincinnati, OH: Hebrew Union College Press, 2000), 138n239; Soggin, "Compulsory Labor," 265–66; Rainey, "Compulsory Labour Gangs," 200–202.

to the end of the monarchy is suggested by Jeremiah's complaint about Jehoiakin's injustices (Jer 22:23):[202]

היו בנה ביתו בלא צדק ועליותיו בלא משפט ברעהו יעבד חנם ופעלו לא יתן לו

Extrabiblical evidence also attests that forced labor was used in Israel. A seal of unknown provenance dated by Avigad to the seventh century bears the name of a certain Pela'yahu, who is identified as one אשר על חמס.[203] This is the same designation assigned to Adoram/Adoniram (2 Sam 20:24; 1 Kgs 4:6, 5:28, 12:18). The seal indicates that the office, and therefore the institution, was in place in the last years of the Judahite kingdom. A Hebrew ostracon from Meṣad Ḥashavyahu, dating from the reign of Josiah, also suggests that some form of compulsory labor was in place at that time. The text is a request by a reaper to an officer, asking him to intervene with the former's superintendent, who is accused of taking the reapers's garment unjustly. Pardee has suggested that the reaper is a member of a labor gang, each member of which is responsible for harvesting and placing in safety an assigned portion. The supervisor has apparently accused the reaper of not fulfilling his obligation and taken his garment. If Pardee is correct in his analysis, the ostracon offers evidence, albeit ambiguous, of conscripted labor in Judah at that time.[204]

The biblical texts and material finds indicate that compulsory labor was a feature of Israelite society just as it was in the wider ANE. The construction of public buildings including temples was routinely if not always undertaken by conscripted workers. Soggin has suggested that such labor was not performed to earn a living or out of a desire to contribute public service, but rather it was compulsory precisely because the projects were unimportant to the laborers.[205] Such compul-

202. Fox, *Service of the King*, 139; William L. Holladay, *Jeremiah 1: A Commentary on the Book of the Prophet Jeremiah Chapters 1-25*, ed. Paul Hanson, Hermeneia (Philadelphia, PA: Fortress Press, 1986), 594; Lundbom, *Jeremiah 21-36*, 134–35; Leslie C. Allen, *Jeremiah*, OTL (Louisville, KY: Westminster John Knox, 2008), 250.

203. Nahman Avigad, "The Chief of the Corvée," *IEJ* 30 (1980):170–73. The seal reads on side A: לפלאיה ו מתתיהו. Side B reads: לפלאיהו אשר על המס.

204. Dennis Pardee, "The Judicial Plea from Meṣad Ḥashavyahu (Yavneh-Yam): A New Philological Study," *Maarav* 1 (1978): 33–66. Mendelsohn also considered this ostracon evidence of corvée labor in late seventh-century Judah ("On Corvée Labor," 33–34).

205. Soggin, "Compulsory Labor," 259.

sory labor could inflict economic damage on families who needed able-bodied men to work farms or otherwise support their families. The combination of economic hardship and lack of interest in the building project would lead to the discontent and hostility reflected in 1 Kings 12. As compulsory labor appears to have been the normal and common means of constructing temples, Yehudites would have had every reason to suspect they would be conscripted to build the temple in Jerusalem. There is no evidence that this happened, but the possibility would have been enough to raise objections to the reconstruction of the temple by those who risked being forced off their farms to collect the materials, clear the site, and rebuild the structure.

The cost of the temple, if reconstructed, would also be felt by Yehudites in the contribution of tithes (מעשר) and other offerings (תרומה and נדבה), first to finance the construction and then for the upkeep of its personnel. The support of temples through tithes and taxes was an ancient and ubiquitous feature of ANE life.[206] Particularly for non-landholding temples, such as in Jerusalem, tithes and other offerings would have constituted almost the entire income in support of the sacrifices and the cultic personnel.[207] Several biblical texts refer to tithes and other obligatory or expected offerings.[208] Even taking into account the idealized nature of many of these texts, we can assume they reflect at least generally standard practices in the ANE.

Even without a reconstruction of the temple, offerings would have been brought to local sanctuaries, which also needed communal sup-

---

206. Henk Jagersma, "The Tithes in the Old Testament," in *Remembering All the Way . . .: A Collection of Old Testament Studies Published on the Occasion of the Fortieth Anniversary of the Oudtestamentisch Werkgezelschap in Nederland*, OtSt 21 (Leiden: Brill, 1981), 116; Dandamaev, "State and Temple," 96; Marty E. Stevens, *Temples, Tithes, and Taxes: The Temple and the Economic Life of Ancient Israel* (Peabody, MA: Hendrickson, 2006), 168–70.

207. Knowles, *Centrality Practiced*, 105–6. Stevens (*Temples, Tithes, and Taxes*, 82–84; 92–93) notes that the debate about whether the first Jerusalem temple did own land is unresolved, but argues that in rainfall economies such as in the Levant and in Greece, temples do not appear to have held land, at least to the extent seen in the great temples in the irrigation economies of Egypt and Mesopotamia. Joel Weinberg brings together textual evidence suggesting that the first temple did have land, but also recognizes that this was really state-owned land (*The Citizen-Temple Community*, trans. D. L. Smith-Christopher, JSOTSup 151 [Sheffield: JSOT Press, 1992], 95–98). He also notes that the second temple in Jerusalem did not own land from the sixth to the fourth centuries (103). Even those who supported Weinberg's *Gemeinde* hypothesis, which ultimately depends on the temple owning land, were not able to provide evidence of this. See Peter R. Bedford, "On Models and Texts: A Response to Blenkinsopp and Petersen," in *Second Temple Studies I: Persian Period*, ed. Philip R. Davies, JSOTSup 117 (Sheffield: JSOT Press, 1991, 157).

208. For example, Exod 35:29; Lev 27:30–33; Num 28:20–32; Deut 12:6, 11; 14:22–29.

port. But in the event of the restitution of the Jerusalem cult, one could readily expect that those local offerings would be either diverted to the temple or additional offerings imposed or at least expected.[209]

As the tithe was usually assessed on animals and produce, the burden would have fallen largely on farmers, who would be expected to offer the animals for sacrifice as well as whatever else could be given to provide food, clothing, and shelter to priests and other cultic personnel.[210] As we have seen, the economy of Yehud in the early Persian period was weak. Additional tithes for a large new temple would have constituted a burden for most Yehudites. Knowles is surely right to suggest that "[i]n a situation where most members of the population of Yehud were subsistence farmers living in small unwalled villages, these individual offerings were probably small, so the temple would need the support of a large number of people."[211] It is doubtful this support would have been readily forthcoming.

That this supposition is correct is borne out by Persian-period biblical texts that point to difficulties getting the Yehudites to support the temple financially, which they were clearly expected to do. Nehemiah 10:33–40 has the people making a vow not to neglect the house of YHWH, and to be sure to keep up their offering of grain, oil, wine, wood, and so forth. While Nehemiah 12:47 claims that "all Israel" supported the gatekeepers, singers, and Levites with their offerings, Nehemiah 13:10–11 has Nehemiah reporting that when he returned to Jerusalem a second time he discovered that the temple was being neglected:

> I learned that the portions of the Levites were not given, and that the Levites and singers who serve in the temple had gone off to their own fields. So I reproached the officials, asking them, "How is it that the house of God is neglected?" So I gathered them together and set them up at the their posts.

One also suspects that the vow that "we will not neglect the house of

209. Although we cannot assume the practice was ever implemented during the monarchy, Deut 14:22–28 legislates that the tithe was to be brought to the Jerusalem temple not to the local community except every third year. Albertz, *History of Israelite Religion*, 1.208.
210. Stevens, *Temples, Tithes, and Taxes*, 94–97.
211. Knowles, *Centrality Practiced*, 117. See also Jagersma ("Tithes," 125–27) on the burden a new temple would have placed on a rural farming population.

our God" reported in 10:33–40 is either in response to or in expectation of problems in this respect. Malachi 3:8 also reflects difficulties getting the people to support the temple and its functionaries; YHWH accuses the people of robbing him of his "tithes and contributions" (המעשר והתרומה). In a difficult period for Yehud, when most of its inhabitants were struggling, the clear possibility that a new temple would impose financial burdens on them both now and ever afterwards cannot have been met with enthusiasm. This appears to have been precisely the situation even after it was completed.

Conclusion

In this chapter we have examined important elements of the background of the book of Haggai. The decision whether and when to rebuild the temple in Jerusalem was entirely in the hands of the Yahwists of Yehud (and any coreligionist supporters elsewhere). It was not a project commanded or opposed by the Persian Empire. Although it may have been possible theoretically to begin reconstruction as early as the reign of Cyrus, no work was begun until the reign of Darius I. There were several possible reasons for this. Theological reasons included doubts that YHWH had commanded his house be rebuilt, that the period of divine anger had truly passed, and that YHWH had failed to provide an expected royal builder. Among the Yehudite populace, whose religious practices had continued for decades during the Babylonian period without the temple, there can have been little perceived need or desire for its reconstruction. The real possibility that such a project would bring economic burdens in the form of compulsory labor or financial obligations would have strengthened resistance. All of these objections or obstacles to reconstruction would need to be addressed to persuade the Yehudites to begin work. Rhetorical analysis of the Haggai Narrative examines the rhetorical strategies employed by the prophet to overcome them and illumines the depth and persistence of Yehudite resistance to the project.

4

Rhetorical Analysis of Haggai 1

Introduction

The prophet Haggai urged temple reconstruction in the second year of Darius by addressing initial and subsequent objections to the project through argumentation and other rhetorical strategies. The composer of the Haggai Narrative further supported the project through rhetorical strategies in the narrative framework.

The controversy over the temple was essentially a policy dispute. The Yehudite community, we are told, had adopted a policy of waiting, maintaining that it was not the time to come and rebuild the temple (1:2). The prophet Haggai proposed an alternative policy, which was to build the temple immediately. As I will show, this proposal was accepted by some but not all members of the community. Even after work began on the temple, doubts remained about the propriety and feasibility of the project. The prophetic oracles and narrative portions in the balance of the HN are intended to answer and suppress those doubts regarding Haggai's policy proposal. The entire HN may thus be analyzed as a rhetorical artifact of this policy dispute.

All policy disputes involve areas of potential disagreement that rhetoricians call "stock issues." Advocates for the adoption or change of policy must address these issues successfully before an audience will accept their proposals. Because all policy disputes—no matter what the specific circumstances— involve them, stock issues provide a "taxonomy, a system of classifying the kinds of questions that can be at issue in a controversy."[1] This makes them a useful tool for rhetorical analysis of a text that reflects or plays a role in a policy dispute.

The concept of stock issues was originally developed to aid in the formation of legal argumentation. Later it was adapted to deliberative disputes by Hultzén, whose work, though usually modified by other rhetoricians for greater analytical precision, remains the standard approach to stock issues. Hultzén referred to four stock issues (or frames of reference) in deliberative analysis: *ill* (or *harm*), *reformability* (now usually called *cause* or *blame*), *remedy,* and *cost* (or *consequences*). Within each of these frames of reference lies one or more potential points of disagreement in a policy dispute. To persuade an audience to accept a policy proposal, advocates must be prepared to address each frame of reference, overcoming any points of disagreement or resistance that may emerge during the course of controversy. If they fail to do so, it will be difficult if not impossible to persuade their audience to adopt the policy.[2]

The analysis of a rhetorical text from a policy dispute may be developed according to these stock issues, providing "a systematic methodology for breaking the [debate] proposition down into its vital component parts."[3] This has the advantage of offering a thorough, relevant approach to the analysis while leaving room for further analysis of suasory elements of the text that are not peculiar to policy disputes (such as appeals to *ethos* or figures and tropes).

As the language and concepts of stock issues in policy debates inform the rhetorical analysis of the HN, it will be helpful to explain each of them here before proceeding.

---

1. Fahnstock and Secor, "Grounds for Argument," 137. The modern rhetorical concept of "stock issues" in deliberative speech is derived from the classical idea of *stasis* (*status* in the Latin tradition) in forensic disputes. The concept, attributed to Hermagoras in the second century BCE, refers to the situation in which a claim of a disputant in a legal case is opposed or denied by the opposition. This applies specifically to a process of argumentation, which comes to a halt (thus, *stasis*) when a claim in the chain of reasoning is disputed. Until the dispute is resolved, the case cannot proceed (Jasinski, *Sourcebook*, 528).

2. Hultzén, "Status," 108–23.

3. Ziegelmueller, Kay, and Dause, *Argumentation*, 39. Cited in Jasinski, *Sourcebook*, 532.

An *ill* or *harm* is the perceived presence of an undesirable situation in or affecting the public realm, which creates an urgent and significant problem.[4] It is the perception of the ill that leads to proposals of policies, policy changes, or other courses of action to remedy it. Advocates suggest to a relevant audience that "the existing way of doing things results in serious internal problems or fails to achieve certain goals."[5] Unless the audience already agrees that such an ill exists, the advocates will be obliged to convince them of it. Disagreements over the existence or quality of an ill may arise at various points. Opponents may deny the "facts" of the situation as described by policy advocates, suggesting they have misrepresented or misunderstood them. They may accept the facts as stated but reject the conclusion that they constitute a harm. Or they may accept that there is a problem, but deny that it is significant or urgent enough to require action. If the audience believes that an advocate's definition of the ill is incorrect at any of these points, it will have no reason to accept the proposed course of action. The initial rhetorical aim, therefore, must be to convince the audience that there is an urgent, significant ill requiring its attention and action.

Rhetorical texts from policy disputes will usually show evidence of an advocate's attempt to define the ill and, if it is controversial, to defend that definition or forestall potential objections to it. In cases where the existence or seriousness of a problem is not controversial, and the harm is recognized by all, a text will reveal little concern on the part of the advocate to meet or overcome opposition regarding the ill. The text may nevertheless devote considerable attention to the harm, not to persuade the audience of its existence, but rather to increase the cognitive or emotional "presence" of the harm as a strategy to motivate action to remove the harm.

The stock issue of *cause* or *blame* is concerned to determine the source of the ill once it has been acknowledged. A policy will not be adopted unless the audience is persuaded that the proposal will

---

4. See Hultzén, "Status," 111; Jasinski, *Sourcebook*, 532. This makes it very similar to an "exigence," a key component in a rhetorical situation that gives rise to a rhetorical text. Exigence has been defined by Bitzer as "an imperfection marked by urgency . . . a thing which is other than it should be" ("Rhetorical Situation," 6).
5. George W. Ziegelmueller and Jack Kay, *Argumentation: Inquiry and Advocacy*, 3rd ed. (Boston, MA: Allyn & Bacon, 1997), 173.

address the underlying cause of the harm.[6] Advocates of a policy have two persuasive obligations here. First, they must convince their audience that they have correctly identified the source or cause of the harm. Disputes over policy often hinge on the identification of cause. Second, they must persuade their audience that without a policy change, the underlying cause of harm cannot or will not be overcome.[7] If the audience accepts an advocate's definition of the cause of the ill, but nevertheless believes that action is unnecessary to address it (by hoping, for example, that it will "go away" on its own somehow), they will be less likely to adopt the policy. "In other words, the advocate of change has the obligation to prove that the harms in the present system are inherent—that the solution of harms or achievement of goals is precluded by" the present policy.[8]

The stock issue of *remedy* is concerned with the proposed policy or course of action. Even once an advocate's position on the harm and its cause has been accepted, there remains potential for disagreement about the efficacy of the proposal. An audience has no reason to adopt a course of action that is not expected to bring a solution. Thus advocates may be obliged to convince them that the policy will in fact remedy the harm.[9] Does the policy promise to address the cause of the problem? Will this, therefore, solve the problem itself? Finally, is the policy feasible? Even if the audience agrees that the proposed course of action will address the cause and solve the problem, if it believes that the course will be impossible to undertake because of, for example, lack of material or other resources, the policy will not be adopted. Advocates for a policy must persuade their audience that it will be both efficacious and feasible.

The stock issue of *cost* or *consequences* addresses the potential disadvantages to adopting the proposed policy. An audience may be persuaded of the efficacy of a course of action to remedy a harm, but may nevertheless identify disadvantages, "side effects," or negative consequences of a proposal.[10] Advocates must therefore be prepared to per-

6. Hultzén, "Status," 112.
7. Ziegelmueller and Kay, *Argumentation*, 174.
8. Ibid.
9. Ibid., 176. See also Hultzén, "Status," 112–13; Jasinski, *Sourcebook*, 535.
10. Jasinski, *Sourcebook*, 535; Ziegelmueller and Kay, *Argumentation*, 177; Hultzén, "Status," 113–14.

suade their audience that any perceived costs or burden imposed by the policy do not exist, are not as significant as supposed, or are less serious than the cost of not adopting the policy.[11]

These stock issues provide a helpful framework for understanding the persuasive aim, strategies, and dynamic of the HN, as reflected in the reported oracles of the prophet and the narrative additions of the composer.

Context of the Controversy

The opening verses present the historical context and major figures of the HN, as well as the controversy that informs it. The figures presented are Darius the king; YHWH; Haggai the prophet; Zerubbabel ben Shealtiel, the פחה of Yehud; Joshua ben Jehozadak, the high priest; and "this people" (העם הזה).

Darius the King

The HN is structured according to a series of specific dates on which the prophet speaks or is commanded to speak or act by YHWH (1:1; 2:1, 20), or on which significant events occur (1:15a; 2:18). These dates root the narrative in an identifiable historical context in which the temple controversy occurs. The opening verse of the HN informs us that the events take place "in the second year of Darius the king." Four specific dates within that year are given in the course of the narrative: the first day of the sixth month (1:1), the twenty-fourth day of the same month (1:15a), the twenty-first day of the seventh month (1:15b–2:1a), and the twenty-fourth day of the ninth month (2:10, 18, 20).[12] The time frame

---

11. Ziegelmueller and Kay, *Argumentation*, 178.
12. The months are counted beginning with the spring new year, according to the Babylonian calendar, which came into use during the Babylonian period. We see this clearly in Zechariah 1–8, which refers to the ninth and eleventh months by their Babylonian names, Kislev (7:1) and Shebat (1:7). We may assume that the composer of HN, whose dating system is otherwise virtually identical to Zechariah 1–8, follows the same calendar.

The sixth month is Elul. The first date, according to the Gregorian calendar, is therefore August 28 or 29, 520 BCE. (Richard A. Parker and Waldo H. Dubberstein, *Babylonian Chronology 626 B.C.–A.D. 45*, BUS 19 [Providence, RI: Brown University Press, 1956], 30). To my knowledge, the month and day are undisputed among scholars.) This means that the HN narrative, which ends in the ninth month (December), covers a period from the dry season at the end of the summer well into the rainy season. The rainy season in the Levant is normally mid-October to March. See

for the HN is thus a little less than four months, all within the second year of Darius the king.[13]

Darius is the king of Persia. There were three Persian kings named Darius: Darius I (522–486); Darius II (425/4–405/4); and Darius III (335–330). It is almost universally accepted that the Persian king of Haggai (and Ezra and Zechariah) is Darius I.[14] Scholars generally take his second year to be 520 BCE. This date is based on the assumption that the composer is following the Babylonian system of calculating regnal years, which were counted beginning with the first full year after accession. This system was in place during the Neo-Babylonian period, and so would have been used in Judah at that time. As the Persians adopted this system in the west, for the composer of the HN, "it would be most natural, when referring to the Achaemenid monarch, to use the system of dating commonly in use in the empire."[15]

By the second year of his reign, Darius had quelled two successive rebellions in Babylonia. Thus, although his early reign had been marked by unrest, at the time the HN commences there would have been relative peace in the empire.[16]

Philip J. King and Lawrence E. Stager, *Life in Biblical Israel*, LAI (Louisville, KY: Westminster John Knox, 2001), 86.

13. Although the narrative is structured according to these specific dates, it is also occasionally temporally ambiguous. For example, the 1:1–2 states that on the first day of the sixth month YHWH spoke to Zerubbabel and Joshua "through" Haggai. This is immediately followed by a second statement that "the word of YHWH came through Haggai," but there is no date. The verse is introduced only by ויהי, an ambiguous temporal indicator. The composer thus gives no clear indication whether or not Haggai spoke to "this people" (the implied addressee of 1:4–11) on the same day or later. The same ambiguity is present in 1:12, which also begins with a *wayyiqtol* form. Did the leaders and "the remnant of the people" respond to the prophetic command to build immediately, or was it some time later? The brief narrative of 1:12–15a ends with the notice that the leaders and the remnant of the people began to work twenty-four days after Haggai first spoke to the leaders about "this people," but we are not told the chronological details of the intervening events. However noteworthy it may be, I do not find this ambiguity rhetorically significant.

14. For arguments that the "Darius" referred to in Haggai is not Darius I, but a later king, see n. 1 at the beginning of chap. 3.

15. Kessler, *Haggai*, 81. See also Ackroyd, "Historical Problems," 13–15; Elias Bickerman, "Calendars and Chronology," *CHJ*, 1:60–69. For the Babylonian dating system, see Parker and Dubberstein, *Babylonian Chronology*. Those who reject this near-consensus argue that the second year of Darius refers to 519. Leroy Waterman argued that the composer of Haggai used the older Judean system of counting regnal years from the time he assumed the throne ("The Camouflaged Purge of Three Messianic Conspirators," *JNES* 13 [1954]: 73–78). Elias Bickerman posited that Darius would have counted his reign from the death of Cambyses, ignoring and delegitimizing the brief period under Gaumata ("En marge de l'écriture," *RB* 88 (1981): 19–23. For critiques of these positions, see Ackroyd, "Historical Problems," 15–19; Kessler, *Haggai*, 82–85.

16. This has potential relevance for understanding the prophetic speech in 2:6–9 and the oracle of 2:21–23, which will be explored in chap. 5. For a detailed history of the early reign of Darius, see Briant, *Cyrus to Alexander*, 107–38.

Darius is mentioned in three date formulas (1:1, 15b–2:1a; 2:10). The first two refer to him as "Darius the king" and the last simply as "Darius." Except for one instance in Jeremiah (52:12), dates calculated according the reign of a foreign monarch are found only in Haggai and Zechariah 1–8.[17] The date formulas in these two books are also notable for including months and days. In this they depart from other prophetic books, except Jeremiah, which includes months, and Ezekiel, which includes months and days. Yet all of these books reflect the standard practice of those prophetic texts that explicitly date the activities of the eponymous prophets, which is to temporally locate them within the reigns of monarchs.[18] If the HN composer wished to include a detailed dating scheme, it is not surprising that he should include a monarch. Lacking a Judean king, he turned to Darius. By doing so, the composer appears to implicitly acknowledge Persian domination and the legitimacy of Darius as king of Yehud. There is no hint of resentment at the rule of a foreign monarch, nor is there an attempt to qualify that rule by, for example, pointedly noting that he is "king of Persia" (and not Yehud). Darius is simply "the king" or even "Darius."[19] When the prophet looks forward to the "shaking of the nations" and indicates YHWH's election of Zerubbabel, we should not assume that main point is that YHWH plans to replace Darius with Zerubbabel while "liberating" Yehud from the empire. It is more likely that the aim of these oracles is to support the reconstruction of the temple rather than the deconstruction of the existing political order. (We will return to this in chapter 5.)

YHWH

The next figure mentioned in the opening verses is YHWH, to whom most speech is attributed in the HN. In both narrative portions and reported words of Haggai, it is insisted that he speaks the word of

---

17. The narrator dates the destruction of Jerusalem in the "nineteenth year of the king Nebuchadrezzar, the king of Babylon."
18. Only the books that lack dated superscriptions or incipits omit this information: Joel, Obadiah, Jonah, Nahum, Habakkuk, and Malachi. We may also include here large texts that, while part of books with dated superscriptions or incipits, are widely considered later additions: Second Isaiah, Third Isaiah, and Zechariah 9–14. None of these include dates either.
19. Rudolph, *Haggai*, 31; Meyers and Meyers, *Haggai*, 5; Kessler, *Haggai*, 115.

YHWH. Only his part of the dialogue with the priests in 2:12–14 is presented as the words of Haggai himself, and even here the prophet's words shade into a declaration of YHWH.

In the thirty-eight verses of the HN, the deity is referred to thirty-four times, always by his personal name, YHWH. Twice in one verse he is also referred to in the third person as "YHWH their God" (1:12). Eighteen times he is called simply "YHWH," fourteen times "YHWH of hosts."[20]

The term "YHWH of hosts" is an ancient epithet that is associated with a complex of cultic and divine kingship traditions.[21] It first appears in the biblical narrative in connection with the shrine at Shiloh and the ark.[22] In accounts of the early monarchy the epithet is associated with YHWH's kingship and presence in the Jerusalem temple, where he sat "enthroned upon the cherubim."[23] The term thus connotes the sovereign rule of YHWH, who resides in his temple-palace.

Scholars have generally seen the association of "YHWH of hosts" with divine kingship and cultic presence as the explanation for its prevalence in Haggai, as well as in Zechariah 1–8 and Malachi. All three texts are concerned in some way with the temple as YHWH's dwelling, and so the ancient association of the term with the Jerusalem cult makes it a particularly apt epithet. As the term also connotes divine rule, its use in these early postexilic texts is seen as an implicit asser-

---

20. YHWH: 1:1, 2, 3, 8, 12, 13 (2x), 14 (3x); 2:1, 4 (2x), 10, 14, 15, 17, 18, 20, 23. YHWH of hosts: 1:2, 5, 7, 9, 14 ("YHWH of hosts, their God"); 2:4, 6, 7, 8, 9 (2x), 11, 23.

21. For the antiquity, origin, and possible meaning of the epithet see, among others, William F. Albright, Review of *L'Épithète divine Jahvé Seba'ôt: Étude philologique, historique et éxégétique*, by B. N. Wambacq, *JBL* 67 (1948): 377–81; Frank Moore Cross, *Canaanite Myth and Hebrew Epic: Essays in the History of the Religion of Israel* (Cambridge, MA: Harvard University Press, 1973), 69–71; Patrick D. Miller, Jr., *The Divine Warrior in Early Israel* (Cambridge, MA: Harvard University Press, 1973), 152–55; Zobel, "צבאות," *TDOT* 12:215–32; Daniel F. O'Kennedy, "The Use of the Epithet יהוה צבאות in Haggai, Zechariah and Malachi," *JNST* 33 (2007): 80–84. For additional discussions of the epithet, see B. N. Wambacq, *L'Épithète divine Jahvé Seba'ôt: Étude philologique, historique et éxégétique* (Paris: Desclée de Brouwer, 1947); James L. Crenshaw, "*YHWH Ṣeba'ôt Šemô*: A Form-Critical Analaysis," *ZAW* 81 (1969): 156–75; Tryggve N. D. Mettinger, *The Dethronement of Sabaoth: Studies in the Shem and Kabod Theologies*, ConBOT 18 (Lund: Gleerup, 1982), 19–37; Tryggve N. D. Mettinger, "YHWH SABAOTH—The Heavenly King on the Cherubim Throne," in *Studies in the Period of David and Solomon and Other Essays*, ed. Tomoo Ishida (Winona Lake, IN: Eisenbrauns, 1982), 109–38; Manfred Görg, "Ṣb'wt: Ein Gottestitel," *BN* 30 (1985): 15–18.

22. 1 Sam 1:3, 11; 4:4.

23. 1 Sam 4:4; 2 Sam 6:2; 2 Kgs 19:15; Isa 37:16; Pss 80:2; 99:1. Although the formula does not appear in the book of Ezekiel, the imagery in ch. 10 of the כבוד of YHWH enthroned on the cherubim as he departs the temple reflects this tradition.

tion of YHWH's sovereignty, despite the current political situation, in which a Persian monarch, not YHWH or a Yahwistic king, ruled.[24]

In the HN, the epithet has no particular rhetorical function. Certainly in the narrative the concern for the temple is paramount, and the use of the epithet is consistent with the assertion that YHWH intends to return to Jerusalem. But beyond this general use the term plays no discernible rhetorical role. The epithet is used in formulaic phrases (messenger, speech report, and oracle formulas) in the HN slightly less frequently than in other texts where the epithet appears.[25] In the non-formulaic portions of the HN, יהוה צבאות appears only once (1:14), whereas יהוה alone appears fourteen times. Overall, the HN uses the epithet less frequently than any other prophetic book except MT Jeremiah.[26] As the HN shows less or comparable preference for the epithet than most other prophetic texts in which יהוה צבאות frequently appears—nor is it used in any distinctive way—its presence very likely reflects larger trends in the prophetic literature rather than a particular persuasive strategy.

Haggai the Prophet

The main human character in the HN is Haggai. This figure appears only here and in the book of Ezra, where he is credited—along with

---

24. See, for example, Meyers and Meyers, *Haggai*, 18–19; Verhoef, *Haggai*, 52–53; Tollington, *Tradition*, 65–70; O'Kennedy, "Epithet," 92–93; Kessler, *Haggai*, 122.

25. This judgment is based on the ratio of the instances of the use of the epithet in a formula to the total number of instances of that formula in a given book. For example, the messenger formula appears in the HN five times. All five times it uses יהוה צבאות, giving a ratio of 1 (or 100%). On the other hand, of the twelve occurrences of the oracle formula, six use יהוה צבאות and six use only יהוה, yielding a ratio of .5. A comparison of the ratios of epithet to total occurrences in the prophetic texts in which יהוה צבאות occurs regularly reveals shows that frequency of the epithet in formulas is lower than in Zechariah 1–8, Malachi, and Zechariah 9–14, but much higher than in Isaiah 1–39 and MT Jeremiah:

Book	Formulaic	Book	Formulaic
Hag	13/20 (.65)	Mal	21/26 (.81)
Zech 1–8	28/36 (.78)	Isa 1–39	12/41 (.29)
Zech 9–14	6/7 (.86)	MT Jer	56/321 (.17)

26. This count includes the occurrences of the *Wortereignisformel*, as well as any other occurrences of the Tetragrammaton apart from the three formulas attributed to the prophetic speakers (messenger, speech report, and oracle).

Book	Non-formulaic	Book	Non-formulaic
Hag	1/15 (.07)	Mal	3/22 (.14)
Zech 1–8	19/59 (.32)	Isa 1–39	44/230 (.19)
Zech 9–14	7/41 (.17)	MT Jer	17/387 (.04)

the prophet Zechariah—with bringing the temple reconstruction to completion (5:1; 6:13). Nothing is known of the historical Haggai. Ezra and the HN offer only his name; he is one of the few prophets in the prophetic books who is introduced without patronymic or at least place of origin.[27] It is impossible to know, for example, if he was a returned exile or one of the Yehudite "locals."[28]

The composer introduces YHWH's spokesperson in v. 1 as "Haggai the prophet" (חגי הנביא). This designation recurs throughout the narrative (1:3, 12; 2:1, 10), although at times he is called simply "Haggai" (2:13, 14, 20) or, once in 1:13, "the messenger of YHWH" (מלאך יהוה). Kessler suggests that by referring to Haggai as "the prophet," the composer ascribes to him a social role "with real status" and thus an "authority and dignity" on par with Zerubbabel and Joshua.[29] Undoubtedly the role of נביא held status within the scribal community that produced the text, or the composer of the HN would not have applied the term to his eponymous hero. And for the composer, Haggai possesses authority that not only equals but exceeds that of the leaders. It is he, not the leaders, who has access to the mind of YHWH, whose word is mediated by the prophet. It is Haggai who exhorts the leaders, along with others, to work on the temple and it is he who delivers an oracle to Zerubbabel at the end of the narrative. There can be no doubt that for the composer Haggai is an authentic prophet of YHWH. It is another question, though, whether the community that Haggai addressed would have accorded him the same authority the composer does.[30] We will return to that question later in this chapter.

---

27. Most of the eponymous prophets bear patronymics: Isaiah ben Amoz, Jeremiah ben Hilkiah, Ezekiel ben Buzi, Hosea ben Beeri, Joel ben Pethuel, Jonah ben Amittai, Zechariah ben Berechiah ben Iddo. The genealogy of Zephaniah is unusually long, going back four generations: Zephaniah ben Cushi ben Gedaliah ben Amariah ben Hezekiah. Three prophets are introduced without patronymic but with place of origin: Amos of Tekoa, Micah of Moresheth, and Nahum of Elkosh. Only Obadiah, Habakkuk, Haggai, and Malachi are without patronymic and place of origin.
28. Most scholars have not concerned themselves with this question. Of those that have, most have also noted that there is no evidence to support either position. See, for example, Amsler, *Aggée*, 15; Petersen, *Haggai*, 18–19; Verhoef, *Haggai*, 6–7.
29. Kessler, *Haggai*, 118.
30. Wolff's assertion that Haggai "impressed the postexilic community as being a prophet with extraordinary authority" may be overconfident (*Haggai*, 17).

Zerubbabel ben Shealtiel

Zerubbabel was an official representative of the Persian empire who exercised leadership in Yehud in the years leading up to the reconstruction of the temple. Although Ezra 2:2 and Nehemiah 7:7 have him returning in the early years, we can be confident only that he was a leader in Yehud in the reign of Darius.[31] He is referred to or addressed several times throughout the book, usually as both "son of Shealtiel" (1:1, 12, 14; 2:2, 23) and פחת יהודה (1:1, 14; 2:2, 21).[32] Of the two, the rhetorically significant element for the HN is the patronymic, which suggests that Zerubbabel, despite his Babylonian name, is a Davidide.[33] According to 1 Chronicles 3:17, Shealtiel was the son of Jehoiachin, the Judahite king exiled by Nebuchadnezzar in 597 BCE.[34] This same text, however, states that Zerubbabel was the son of Shealtiel's brother, Pedaiah (3:19). All other references to Zerubbabel with a patronymic agree with Haggai in calling him son of Shealtiel (Ezra 3:2, 8; 5:2; Nehemiah 12:1). Some scholars have tried to account for the apparent discrepancy by suggesting that Zerubbabel was the son of both: Pedaiah was his biological father, who begat him in a levirate arrangement on behalf of his older brother Shealtiel, who had died childless.[35] A less harmonistic approach posits an error in the MT of 1 Chronicles 3:19.[36]

31. As clearly stated in Haggai and Zechariah, and implied in Ezra 5:2. As noted in the previous chapter, the historical details of Ezra 1–6 are sometimes difficult to reconcile. Although Ezra has Zerubbabel returning in the reign of Cyrus and participating in the restoration of the altar "in the seventh month" of (presumably) the first year of the "return" (Ezra 3:1–2), it also suggests that Sheshbazzar was the local leader at that time (Ezra 1:8, 11b; 5:16). There is no need to reassess the historical problems posed by Ezra here. The important point, which no one contests, is that sometime before 520 BCE Zerubbabel was appointed פחה of Yehud, and that he held that position during the early years of the reconstruction of the temple. For further discussion, see Japhet, "Sheshbazzar and Zerubbabel," 66–98; "Sheshbazzar and Zerubbabel," *ZAW* 95 (1983): 218–29.
32. On two occasions the patronymic is missing (2:4, 21), the title is absent on three (1:12; 2:4, 23). The title is never found in the speeches attributed to the prophet. On the title and its distribution, see Lipschits and Vanderhooft, "Yehud Stamp Impressions," 77–80.
33. The name is of Akkadian origin, probably from *Zēr-Bābili*, meaning "offshoot of Babylon" or "seed of Babylon." See Wolff, *Haggai*, 38; Meyers and Meyers, *Haggai*, 9; and others.
34. 2 Kgs 24:12, 15; Jer 24:1; 27:20. 1 Chronicles refers to the king as "Jeconiah" (1 Chr 3:16, 17). 2 Chronicles refers to him as "Jehoiachin" (2 Chr 36:8, 9). The book of Jeremiah refers to him both as "Jeconiah" (Jer 24:1; 27:20; 28:4; 29:2) and as "Coniah" (Jer 22:24, 28; 37:1).
35. Japhet ("Sheshbazzar and Zerubbabel," 72) cites Rudolph, *Esra*, 18, and L. H. Brockington, *Ezra, Nehemiah and Esther*, NCB (London: Nelson, 1969), 53. Williamson (*Ezra*, 32) and Albertz (*Israel in Exile*, 107, 107n210) also hold this out as a possibility. Blenkinsopp (*Ezra-Nehemiah*, 84) dismisses this harmonizing expedient as "pure speculation."
36. Japhet notes this without advocating it as a solution ("Sheshbazzar and Zerubbabel," 72). The OG has Σαλαθιηλ (= Shealtiel), but this could be harmonizing by the translator.

Despite the discrepancy between 1 Chronicles and the other sources, almost all scholars agree that Zerubbabel was, or was understood to be, a Davidic descendant.[37]

The Davidic ancestry of Zerubbabel is a key rhetorical element in the HN because it identifies him as a royal figure. Although this royal identity is only implicit throughout most of the narrative—being "stated" only through the patronymic—in the final oracle, as we will see, it is made explicit and confirmed. As a divinely recognized representative of the Davidic line, Zerubbabel furnishes the temple project with a royal builder. The project thus gains legitimacy through his close association with it throughout the narrative. He is addressed by the prophet in the first oracle (1:1), he obeys the call to rebuild (1:12) and works on the temple (1:14), and he is addressed again in a second oracle (2:2, 4). Zerubbabel is never shown actually doing or saying anything, but he nevertheless plays a crucial role in the HN simply by being a recognized Davidide associated with the rebuilding of the temple.[38]

Apart from his Davidic patronymic, Zerubbabel is also designated by his official title, פחת יהודה. This is usually translated as "governor of Yehud," although there is some question whether "governor" is the most appropriate term.[39] Whatever the exact nature of his office, or the political status of Yehud, Zerubbabel's title clearly reflects his official role as a representative of the Persian empire. This title is placed alongside the Davidic patronymic without tension in the narrative, which

---

37. Most scholars maintain that Zerubbabel was in fact a Davidide, and Japhet appears to be correct in stating that almost no one questions this ("Sheshbazzar and Zerubbabel," 71). J. Maxwell Miller and John H. Hayes, however, reject this claim, observing that Zerubbabel's supposed Davidic identity is nowhere explicitly noted in Ezra, Nehemiah, Haggai, or Zerubbabel. The Chronicler, they suggest, gave Zerubbabel a member Davidic lineage to emphasize the continuity between preexilic and postexilic leadership (*A History of Ancient Israel and Judah*, 2nd ed. [Louisville: Westminster John Knox Press, 2006], 518). If this were the case, though, one would expect the Chronicler to follow the others in making him the son of Shealtiel, rather than Pedaiah, since both of them are already in the Chronicler's genealogy (Shealtiel is listed as the oldest son of Jehoiachin in 1 Chr 3:17). See also Lipschits and Vanderhooft, "Yehud Stamp Impressions," 79.

38. In Zechariah he plays a much more prominent and explicit role in the reconstruction (Zech 4:6–10 and, if צמח is meant to refer to Zerubbabel, 6:12–13). The identification of צמח with Zerubbabel is disputed. Ackroyd (*Exile and Restoration*, 174n12), Petersen (*Haggai*, 276), and others identify Zerubbabel as צמח. Wolter H. Rose rejects this identification ("Messianic Expectations in the Early Postexilic Period," in *Yahwism after the Exile: Perspectives on Israelite Religion in the Persian Era*, ed. Rainer Albertz and Bob Becking, STR 5 [Assen: Van Gorcum, 2003], 169–72).

39. "Governor" implies that Yehud was a province in 520 BCE, which is disputed. See, for example, Japhet, "Sheshbazzar and Zerubbabel," 80–84; Lemaire, "Zorobabel," 49, 55–56; Na'aman, "Royal Vassals," 53; Petersen, *Haggai*, 45–46; Wolff, *Haggai*, 39. The question of the precise political status of Yehud in 520 BCE is not relevant for the present analysis.

suggests that, for the composer, the two identities were not in conflict. This juxtaposition further raises the possibility that, regardless of what the historical prophet may have thought, the composer had no dispute with Persian rule over Yehud.[40] This is an observation that must be taken into account when assessing the rhetorical function of the final oracle of the HN. I will explore this question further in chapter 5. Apart from these implications, I find no explicit rhetorical function in the composer's use of this title throughout the narrative.

Joshua ben Jehozadak

Ezra and Nehemiah state that Joshua the high priest, son of Jehozadak, arrived with Zerubbabel and was involved in the earlier and later work on the altar and temple in Jerusalem.[41] Whether or not we can take the claims of Ezra and Nehemiah at face value, as with Zerubbabel, we can be confident that Joshua was in Yehud and held the position of high priest in 520 BCE.

Joshua is invariably referred to in the HN by both his patronymic and his title (1:1, 12, 14; 2:2, 4).[42] The patronymic suggests that he was considered a descendant of Zadok, and therefore of Aaron (according to the genealogy of 1 Chr 5:37–41). Most scholars presume that his father Jehozadak is the son of Seraiah mentioned in 1 Chronicles 5:40–41, who was taken into exile after his father was put death in 587 (2 Kgs 25:18–21; Jer 52:24–27).[43] Joshua's lineage as the direct heir of the Zadokite priesthood would qualify him for the highest cultic office in Yehud, הכהן הגדול. It is possible that this title only began to be used

---

40. In the prophetic speeches, Zerubbabel is never referred as פחה. The title only occurs in the narrative framework (1:1, 14; 2:2, 21). In 2:2 and 2:21, the title is mentioned in speech attributed to YHWH, who commands Haggai to "speak to the governor of Yehud, Zerubbabel." It is possible that the historical prophet deliberately avoided referring to Zerubbabel by his official Persian title, preferring instead to refer to him simply by name (2:4) or by his Davidic patronymic (2:23). Whatever the implications of that may be for understanding the historical prophet's attitude toward the Persian empire, the object of study here is the HN, which betrays no concern with the title or Zerubbabel's position as representative of the empire.

41. Ezra 2:2; 3:2, 8–9; 4:3; 5:2; Neh 7:7. In Ezra and Nehemiah, he is called ישוע rather than יהושע, and his father is named יוצדק rather than יהוצדק (Ezra 3:2; 5:2). He is also never referred to by a title in these books, whereas in Haggai and Zechariah he is referred to as הכהן הגדול (see Zech 3:1, 8; 6:11). No one seriously questions the assumption that the Joshua of Haggai and Zechariah 1–8 is the same person as the Jeshua of Ezra and Nehemiah.

42. Except for 2:4, all references to Joshua are the narrative framework. In 2:4 his is named in the prophetic speech.

43. See, for example, Tollington, *Tradition*, 126; Wolff, *Haggai*, 39; Kessler, *Haggai*, 120–21.

in this period; Seraiah is referred to as הכהן הראש.[44] Although scholars have discussed the cause and implications of the change in terminology, such questions need not detain us here.[45] The term clearly designates him as the head of the official Jerusalemite cult (see also Zech 3:1–10).

In the HN, Joshua is always mentioned along with Zerubbabel, except for the last oracle, which is addressed to the latter only. The rhetorical role of Joshua is difficult to discern, as he never stands out as an individual figure, but always appears alongside Zerubbabel. Like Zerubbabel, he never actually does or says anything, but is nevertheless intimately connected to the temple project from the beginning. Like the Davidide, Joshua lends a legitimacy to the project by his presence. Without an authorized cultic apparatus the temple could not function. As its representative, Joshua signals that the official cultic establishment supports its reconstruction. His constant presence in the HN, as well as the claim that he along with Zerubbabel and "the remnant of the people" participated in the rebuilding (1:12, 14; 2:2) implies his endorsement of Haggai's policy proposal.

Rhetorical Analysis of Haggai 1:1–11

A. Haggai 1:1–4—Introducing the Dispute

The narrative begins with the notice that on the first day of the sixth month (Elul) the word of YHWH came "through" (ביד) Haggai the prophet, and was directed to Zerubbabel and Joshua.[46] The *Wortereignisformel* (היה/ויהי דבר יהוה) is attached to a specific date, which is com-

---

44. 2 Kgs 25:18; Jer 52:24.

45. For detailed discussion see, for example, Tollington, *Tradition*, 126–31; Beuken, *Haggai*, 309–16; James VanderKam, *From Joshua to Caiaphas: High Priests after the Exile* (Minneapolis, MN: Fortress Press, 2004), 1–42; John W. Bailey, "The Usage of the Post Restoration Period Terms Descriptive of the Priest and High Priest," *JBL* 70 (1951): 217–25.

46. Commentators have noted that the beginning of the month, the new moon, is associated in the HB with sacrifice (Num 28:11–15; Ezek 46:6–7), Sabbath rest (Amos 8:5; Isa 1:13–14; 2 Kgs 4:23), or other observances (Ps 81:3–4). If the populace was accustomed to gather and celebrate a new moon festival, the reminder that there was no functioning temple may have prompted Haggai to begin his building campaign. (See, for example, Petersen, *Haggai*, 44; Wolff, *Haggai*, 36–37.) This suggestion assumes, though, that the date is precisely accurate, which cannot be taken for granted. The new moon plays no part in Haggai's attempts to persuade the Yehudites to build. In fact, the only time cultic matters are raised is in 2:10–14, and the role they play there has nothing to do with the new moon. Nor does the composer make anything of this or any of the other dates.

mon in Ezekiel and in Zechariah 1–8, but not elsewhere.[47] The distinctive feature of the formula in the HN is its use of ביד rather than אל, which is the preposition used in this formula in every other occurrence in the MT: היה/ויהי דבר יהוה אל. . . .[48] The term ביד, while never associated with the *Wortereignisformel* outside of the HN, is frequently used to describe the prophetic mediation of Moses, although less often apart from him.[49] The phrase here as elsewhere emphasizes the prophet as agent of YHWH.[50] Rather than placing the focus on the prophet as receiver of a divine message, it brings to the fore his role as intermediary, the conduit, between YHWH and the leaders.[51] This implies that the message Zerubbabel and Joshua receive is the word of YHWH, not Haggai's or his interpretation of what he received from YHWH. The distinctive use of the ביד thus has rhetorical implications. It contributes to the textual representation of the prophet as authentic, insisting that what Haggai says is not his own version of reality but YHWH's.[52] This is especially important when we consider that only YHWH can authorize the building of his temple, and so Haggai's position in the policy dispute to follow must be seen as grounded in the deity's preferences, not Haggai's. In effect, it is not his personal policy, but YHWH's, that is being presented.

The current policy regarding the temple—not to rebuild it yet—is

47. The *Wortereignisformel* itself is uncommon outside of Jeremiah, Ezekiel, Haggai, and Zechariah 1–8: Gen 15:1; 1 Sam 15:10; 2 Sam 7:4; 1 Kgs 6:11; 13:20; 16:1; 17:2, 8; 18:31; 21:17, 28; Dan 9:2; 2 Chr 11:2; 12:7. In the prophetic literature, it occurs once at Isa 38:4 and twice in Jonah (1:1; 3:1), otherwise it is confined to the four books mentioned.
    The formula is associated with a specific date several times in Ezekiel (1:3; 26:1; 29:17; 30:20; 31:1; 32:1, 17), although most instances occur within a narrative sequence without a date (ויהי דבר אל . . .). In Zechariah it is attached to a date in 1:1, 7; 7:1 and, again within a narrative sequence without a date, at 4:8; 6:9; 7:4, 8; 8:1, 18). The *Wortereignis* formula occurs several times in MT Jeremiah, but usually not in association with a date (except 1:2, 4; 32:1; 49:34), but these dates are more general than the dates associated with the formula in Ezekiel, Haggai, and Zechariah 1–8.
48. The formula occurs five times in the HN (1:1, 3; 2:1, 10, 20). Of these, the first three have ביד, while the last two use the more standard אל.
49. The phrase ביד משה occurs throughout Exodus–Deuteronomy and a few times elsewhere (30x). It is only occasionally used to refer to the mediation of prophets in general (2 Kgs 12:13; Ezek 38:17; Zech 7:7, 12), or specific prophets other than Moses, such as Nathan (2 Sam 2:25), Abijah (1 Kgs 12:15), Isaiah (Isa 20:2), Jeremiah (Jer 37:2; 50:1), and Malachi (Mal 1:1).
50. Michael H. Floyd, *Minor Prophets, Part 2*, FOTL 22 (Grand Rapids, MN: Eerdmans, 2000), 280; Kessler, *Haggai*, 116; Tollington, *Tradition*, 65. The expression is used several times in the HB in reference to prophets as intermediaries for YHWH, most especially Moses. Examples are too numerous to cite here, but they occur in the dozens.
51. Kessler, *Haggai*, 116–17.
52. As noted by, for example, Tollington, *Tradition*, 65; Kessler, *Haggai*, 117.

presented in the next verse. The speaker in the verse is YHWH of hosts and the addressees are, as we know from v. 1, Zerubbabel and Joshua. Using the messenger formula, Haggai presents the words of YHWH, who informs the leaders of the position of "this people" regarding the temple: העם הזה אמרו לא עת בא עת בית יהוה להבנות.[53] Three elements of the verse are rhetorically significant: the distinction created between the leaders and העם הזה, the referent of the term and implications of its use, and the possible content or rationale of the "policy" of העם הזה.

Verses 1 and 2 make a clear distinction between the leaders and "this people." It is the leaders who are directly addressed here, not the people along with the leaders. YHWH speaks to Zerubbabel and Joshua about the people, who are referred to in the third person, and there is no indication that the leaders are considered part of העם הזה. As we will see, it is העם הזה who come in for critique; the leaders are presented in neutral or positive terms. Historically, Zerubbabel and Joshua may well have shared the people's hesitation to rebuild, but here it is the position of the people, separated in the text from the leaders, that is being examined. The point of quoting the people is not to inform the leaders of a situation of which they are unaware, but to present rhetorically the position of העם הזה in order to challenge it.

The only thing we are told here about "this people" is their apparent position regarding the temple. We do not know, for example, whether they represent returnees, locals, or a mix of both. Scholarly claims that העם הזה must be the locals because all the returnees to Yehud would have been in favor of the temple cannot be sustained.[54] This argument assumes, in the first place, the historicity of the claim in Ezra that those who returned to the land from Babylon or elsewhere did so for the purpose of rebuilding the temple, a position few hold today.[55] More importantly, there is no mention here or anywhere in Haggai of a distinction between returnees and locals. Haggai does distinguish between groups, as we will see, but on the basis of other criteria. For the same reason, suggestions that "this people" must refer to the returnees must also be

---

53. For discussion of text-critical issues and the translation of this verse, see chap. 2, pp. 24–25.
54. See, for example, Steck, "Zu Haggai," 375–76; Rudolph, *Haggai*, 32. Few scholars support this position today.
55. See the discussion of the historical problems regarding Ezra and the temple reconstruction in chap. 3.

rejected for lack of evidence. Today most assume that YHWH is referring to the whole community (except the leaders), although this too is uncertain.[56] The social composition of the group cannot be known from the text, and there is probably a good reason for this. It is, as far as Haggai is concerned, irrelevant. Where the people come from, their historical experience, their current social location—these are unimportant. The only relevant factor is their position on the temple. This is what gives them their "rhetorical identity." For Haggai, anyone who suggests that now is not the time to rebuild the temple is העם הזה.

The epithet itself contributes to the rhetorical identity of this group. As many have noted, in prophetic literature especially the term "this people" is often used to refer to a group being subjected to criticism, relating the displeasure, reproach, and judgment of the speaker (often, but not always, YHWH).[57] This usage is found especially in Jeremiah, where the term is often used by YHWH to describe a people who has rejected or disobeyed him.[58] The rhetorical force of this term lies in what it connotes about those who say it is not time to build the temple. Even before we hear the divine response to this position, we suspect that those who hold it have incurred divine displeasure. The term encourages the audience to see העם הזה not just as misguided or mistaken in their appraisal of the time for rebuilding, but as wayward. Because this people has decided (for whatever reason) not to build the temple, they have set themselves in opposition to YHWH. When this term reappears later in the HN (2:13), the implications of this characterization of העם הזה will become clearer.

What is the policy that העם הזה has adopted? All we are told is that they claim that it is not time for the temple to be rebuilt. We are not given the basis or rationale for this determination. Nevertheless, scholars have offered some possibilities. The reference to "time" suggests to some a concern with a divinely-ordained timetable, and the one that has come to mind is Jeremiah's seventy years.[59] Tadmor, for exam-

56. Amsler, *Aggée*, 23; Hallaschka, *Haggai*, 17n14; Kessler, *Haggai*, 123; Meyers and Meyers, *Haggai*, 19.
57. Verhoef, *Haggai*, 55; Hallaschka, *Haggai*, 17; Chary, *Aggée*, 19; Mitchell, *Haggai*, 45; Wolff, *Haggai*, 40; Adrian Graffy, *A Prophet Confronts His People: The Disputation Speech in the Prophets*, AnBib 104 (Rome: Biblical Institute Press, 1984), 99.
58. See, for example, Jer 5:14; 6:19, 21; 7:16; 9:14; 11:14; 14:10; 16:15; 35:16, and others. See also the use of this term in similar circumstances in Exod 17:4; 32: 9, 21, 31; Isa 6:9–10; 8:6; 29:13.
59. For more details about this, see the discussion in chap. 3, pp. 111–17.

ple, considers the phrase quoted to be a "popular slogan" reflecting the belief that the seventy years had not yet come to pass.[60] Similarly, Meyers and Meyers suggest that Haggai thought the seventy years had actually come to pass (thus his call to rebuild), but the people were unaware of this.[61]

Other scholars, noting that there is no mention of such a timetable in the book, have argued that the reluctance to rebuild probably stemmed from an interpretation of the current situation. Japhet and Bedford have suggested that poor economic conditions and other troubles were interpreted by the people as a sign that they remained under YHWH's judgment. Until there were positive signs that the divine anger had abated and YHWH was once again ready to bless the people and dwell among them, it was not "time" to rebuild the temple.[62] This position, which was discussed in the previous chapter, has merit. But Kessler has contested it, arguing that if this were the basis for the people's position, there would be evidence of it in Haggai's response, which does not answer this sort of argument. Instead, the emphasis later on the economic conditions in the land (vv. 6, 9–11) suggests that Haggai is responding to a "sapiential" judgment that the time is not "propitious." In other words, the basis for the claim that it is not time to rebuild is not theological but prudential.[63] Kessler's view is based on

---

60. Hayim Tadmor, "'The Appointed Time Has Not Yet Arrived': The Historical Background of Haggai 1:2," in *Ki Baruch Hu: Ancient Near Eastern, Biblical and Judaic Studies in Honor of Baruch A. Levine*, ed. Robert Chazon, William W. Hallo, and Lawrence H. Schiffman (Winona Lake, IN: Eisenbrauns, 1999), 402–8.

61. Meyers and Meyers, *Haggai*, 20–21, 38.

62. Sara Japhet, "'History' and 'Literature' in the Persian Period: The Restoration of the Temple," in *Ah, Assyria . . .: Studies in Assyrian History and Ancient Near Eastern Historiography Presented to Hayim Tadmor*, ed. Mordechai Cogan and Israel Eph'al (Jerusalem: Magnes, 1991), 178–79; Bedford, "Discerning the Time," 74–86. Bedford has rightly noted that all we really have access to here is how Haggai (and his editors) wish the reader to understand "this people" and their reasons for their opposition to the temple. What the reality was may be quite a different thing. While this may seem like an obvious observation, until recently most commentators appear to have assumed not only that Haggai accuses the people of being disingenuous when they say it is not the time to rebuild the temple, but also that this was historically accurate, and that in reality the reason the people made this claim was because they *were* too selfish to rebuild the temple. Despite Kessler's argument, just above, for another reason the people may believed it was not time to rebuild the temple, he has come around to Bedford's position that the portrait of the people in this text may not be an accurate reflection of reality. ("Building the Second Temple: Questions of Time, Text, and History in Haggai 1.1–15," *JSOT* 27 [2002]: 250–53.)

63. Kessler, "Le temps," 556–57; "Building," 245; *Haggai*, 125–27. Hallaschka agrees with this reading (*Haggai*, 18–20). Kessler explains the distinction between the position of Bedford and Japhet and his by characterizing theirs as "theological" and his as "sapiential" (*Haggai*, 125). In both scenarios the people are interpreting their current situation. The "theological" interpretation is that

the precarious assumption that Haggai's response in v. 4 is, as he puts it, a "reformulation" of the people's belief.[64] As we will see, Haggai's response is not intended to reflect or reformulate the beliefs of the people, but is strategically oriented toward *redefining* the situation. We cannot presume, therefore, that his response reflects the actual beliefs of the people or the reason they have determined that the time has not come to rebuild.

The rationale for the people's claim that "it is not the time for coming, the time for the house of YHWH to be rebuilt" cannot be known with any certainty. The suggestions of Bedford and Japhet are certainly plausible, as are Kessler's, even if one does not accept his assumption that Haggai has "reformulated" the people's position. It is even possible that there was a question of a preset timetable. There were any number of reasons why the people believed that the time was not right to rebuild the temple. As I argued in the previous chapter, these reasons could have been theological or material or both, and they were probably well-entrenched. Haggai's (or YHWH's) quotation of the people indicates only in the broadest outlines their position regarding the temple: it was not the time for it to be rebuilt.

The position of העם הזה is presented as a quote, suggesting that Haggai is reporting their actual words.[65] Many commentators have taken this to be the case. But it is a mistake to assume that the quote accurately or completely reflects the position of the Yehudites who opposed the building of the temple. This quote is given not in a simple act of reportage, but as part of a persuasive effort. Haggai would not be the only rhetor in history to represent the opposing side's position

---

YHWH remains angry and therefore Yehud remains under judgment. The "sapiential" interpretation assumes no such conclusion, but merely that the current circumstances indicate it is not prudent to build. It makes no assumptions about YHWH's attitude. The distinction Kessler makes is anachronistic: "sapiential" logic would have been theological in ancient Israelite thought. Much of the argument about this question rests on how various commentators determine the connotation if the word עת, which is difficult to do here without falling into circular reasoning.

64. Kessler, "Le temps," 556–57.
65. The syntax indicates that what is being offered is meant to be understood as a quote, or direct speech, rather than report of indirect speech. Direct quotations are not integrated into the syntax of the sentence in which they are found (the "matrix sentence"). Indirect speech, on the other hand, is almost always syntactically integrated into the matrix sentence through "syndetic sentential complements" such as כי or, less commonly, אשר. See Cynthia L. Miller, *The Representation of Speech in Biblical Hebrew Narrative: A Linguistic Analysis* (HSM 55; Atlanta, GA: Scholars Press, 1996), 74–81, 97–141. This syndetic sentential complement is missing here, which makes it unlikely that the reported speech of the people is indirect.

in terms that are favorable, or at least not unfavorable, to his own. In other words, we cannot assume that the quotation accurately or fully represents the range of reasons or rationales for believing that the temple should not be built at that time. It is not in Haggai's interest to consider the details or nuances of the position, or present them for the consideration of leaders.[66] It is more rhetorically effective to consolidate "this people's" position into a short quote that, while presenting the basic stance, is not intended to emphasize the actual reasons for it. The assumption that Haggai has faithfully, fully, and accurately represented the views of those he opposes is naïve in that it fails to take fully into account that this is a rhetorical text.

Once the people's policy position has been stated for the benefit of the leaders, the prophet changes audience. The *Wortereignisformel* introduces a new scene in the same narrative.[67] This allows for a change of addressee, without explicitly indicating who the new addressee is. But it is obvious from the deictic elements of the following verses that it is "this people," not the leaders. The speech in vv. 4–11 addresses an audience in the 2mp. While syntactically the addressees could be or include the leaders, the context makes this impossible. These verses constitute a refutation of the position taken by העם הזה, not the leaders, and it is "this people" who are now the addressees. The *Wortereignisformel* allows for this change of addressee while continuing to stress that it is YHWH speaking through the prophet, now directly to the people in order to persuade them to adopt a different policy.

At this point in the text we only know of a policy advocated by העם הזה. We have not been given a clear idea what this means or the theological or material basis of the position. YHWH's response in v. 4 is a retort in the form of a rhetorical question that makes it clear that he rejects their policy: העת לכם אתם לשבת בבתיכם ספונים והבית הזה חָרֵב. This response sheds no light on the opposing position because YHWH chooses not to refute their reasons. Instead, he "reframes" the question by focusing on the contrast between the houses of the Yehudites and his. He critiques the discrepancy rather than the reasons for not

---

66. Nor would it be in the interest of the composer of the HN to do so for his readers.

67. Although the formula typically introduces a speech with a new topic, or one only loosely related to the previous one, in some places it introduces a new prophetic saying as a continuation of a particular story. See, for example, Isa 38:4; Jer 13:8; 18:5; 32:26; Ezek 17:11; 21:6; Zech 4:8; 7:4, 8.

rebuilding. YHWH is not interested in their reasons. He is interested in the fact that the Yehudites have functioning houses in which to dwell, while he does not.

Rhetorical questions act as "pseudo-assertions," enabling a speaker to imply rather than directly state a claim.[68] The interrogative form itself induces the hearer to infer the desired answer. It is the audience rather than the speaker who actually (mentally) articulates the desired statement. Rhetorical questions are persuasive—and not just stylistic—also because they lead to agreement with the speaker's position by making it seem obvious. Further, people are inclined to accept more readily a conclusion they have drawn for themselves.[69] An added benefit of rhetorical questions is that they relieve the rhetor of the obligation to actually substantiate his assertion. A claim that has been implied, rather than actually stated, is not subject to the same scrutiny as one that is made explicitly.[70] YHWH's rhetorical question asks whether it is "time" for his house to sit deserted while the Yehudites

---

68. The term is from Jürgen Schmidt-Radefeldt, "On So-Called 'Rhetorical' Question," *JPragmat* 1 (1977): 377.

69. "A rhetorical question is a question used as a challenging statement to convey the addresser's commitment to its implied answer in order to induce the addressee's mental recognition of its obviousness and the acceptance, verbalized or non-verbalized, of its validity" (Cornelia Ilie, *What Else Can I Tell You? A Pragmatic Study of English Rhetorical Questions as Discursive and Argumentative Acts*, SSE 82 [Stockholm: Almqvist & Wiksell, 1994], 128). This definition addresses the *intention* of the rhetorical question. Cognitive and psychological studies of persuasion have shown that the potential for persuasive *effect* of rhetorical questions is complex and depends on a variety of factors and the circumstances in which the message is received. For example, rhetorical questions tend to be effective in raising the level of interest in a persuasive message for audiences who do not initially perceive the relevance of the message. On the other hand, they have less persuasive potential for those who already have an interest in a topic or who are already engaged with the message. This suggests that rhetorical questions can be most effective at the beginning of a persuasive message as a strategy for gaining a hearing from the audience. This is what we see in Hag 1:4. See Dolf Zillmann, "Rhetorical Elicitation of Agreement in Persuasion," *JPSP* 21 (1972): 159–65; Dolf Zillmann and Joanne R. Cantor, "Rhetorical Elicitation of Concession in Persuasion," *JSP* 94 (1974): 223–36; Richard E. Petty, John T. Cacioppo, and Martin Heesacker, "Effects of Rhetorical Questions on Persuasion: A Cognitive Response Analysis," *JPSP* 40 (1981): 432–40; David R. Roskos-Ewoldsen et al., "What is the Role of Rhetorical Questions in Persuasion?" in *Communication & Emotion: Essays in Honor of Dolf Zillmann*, ed. Jennings Bryant, David Roskos-Ewoldsen, Joanne Cantor, LEA Communication Series (Mahwah, NJ: Lawrence Erlbaum Associates, 2003), 297–321; Kevin L. Blankenship, "Rhetorical Question Use and Resistance to Persuasion: An Attitude Strength Analysis," *JLSP* 25 (2006): 111–28.

70. "Negative" political ads use rhetorical questions regularly, allowing them make claims through innuendo and inference rather than direct statements: "My opponent used to work for company X, who polluted the environment and then laid off hundreds of people. Do you want someone who would do that to be your governor?" The question implies, but does not state, that the opponent was responsible for polluting the environment and laying off employees. The hoped-for inference, which is almost certainly inaccurate and misleading, does not have to be defended because it is made in the mind of the audience, not stated directly by the maker of the ad.

enjoy their finished, occupied houses. The question is intended to force the Yehudites themselves to provide the answer: "No, of course not." If they do so, they accept YHWH's claim that this state of affairs constitutes a problem that they have not previously believed existed.[71]

There is not necessarily a *logical* connection between the state of the Yehudites houses and YHWH's house. Haggai creates a *rhetorical* relationship verbally by describing both habitations with the same word, בית. Use of the same word for two different realities is a tacit persuasion strategy that implies "a natural affinity between objects or concepts which logically possessed none."[72] Haggai capitalizes on the standard way of conceiving and describing a deity's temple as a בית to suggest such an affinity. If the houses of the Yehudites and of YHWH are conceptually commensurate, then so are their respective conditions. These conditions and their comparability are verbally represented in structural parallelism:

your houses—finished![73]   בבתיכם ספונים

this house—desolate!   הבית הזה חרב

The audience is meant to draw the conclusion that the state of YHWH's house is appropriately considered in terms of their own.

Once the audience has been induced to compare the state of their houses with that of YHWH's, Haggai can count on them to provide the missing premise, namely the cultural belief that a deity's house should never be in worse shape than a human's house (unless it was the deity who caused the destruction of his or her house). In the rhetorical tradition, this unstated premise is a commonplace, a commonly held belief or value that serves as a warrant for moving from a fact to a conclusion.

Haggai could have had YHWH state, "It is not right that you have

---

71. Or, if one wished to suggest that they did know this was a "problem" but didn't really care, then Haggai is forcing them to acknowledge and admit the problem. Either way, the question is intended to induce agreement that the current situation is unacceptable.

72. Richard A. Lanham, *Analyzing Prose* (New York, NY: Scribner's Sons, 1983), 125.

73. It makes little difference whether we understand ספונים to mean "paneled" or "roofed." The scholarship has made it clear that both translations are viable. (See the discussion in chap. 2, p. 26.) Probably the term is meant to convey the idea that houses are both completed and rather nice (although this would possibly be an exaggeration given what we can surmise about the economic conditions at the time).

houses but I do not." But such a straightforward statement would lack the persuasive force of a rhetorical question that induces agreement. He would also have found it necessary to *argue* that this inequality was relevant to their claim that it was not time to rebuild the temple. The people could have responded that, while it may true that their houses are ספונים and YHWH's is חָרֵב, the fact remained that it was not time for the temple to be rebuilt. By phrasing YHWH's rhetorical question in terms of "time," Haggai implies that the two issues—when to rebuild the temple and the state of the respective houses—are somehow related. As with the use of בית, the double use of "time" suggests a stronger connection than exists in reality between the policy regarding the temple and YHWH's observation about the state of the Yehudites' houses. Haggai *implies without stating* that there is a logical connection between the disparate conditions of the houses and the policy he opposes.

The use of "time" also lends to YHWH's response a sarcastic tone that indicates a disdain not only for the claim that it is not time to build the temple, but also for the people themselves, which echoes his reference to them in v. 2 as העם הזה. I have observed that the use of "time" is meant to suggest a connection between the policy and the current unacceptable contrast between human and divine houses. The tone of the question also suggests that YHWH's question is an indirect *ad hominem* argument, aimed at the policy *through* those who maintain it.[74] The argument is indirect because Haggai is not attacking the people themselves. He is instead implying that their motivation for not rebuilding the temple may be selfish, and therefore that their claim

---

74. *Ad hominem* arguments have traditionally been labeled fallacies by dialecticians, but have been considered effective persuasive strategies by rhetoricians. Recent scholarship in argumentation studies has led to a more nuanced appreciation of *ad hominem* argumentation by dialecticians, many of whom now acknowledge that depending on the circumstances *ad hominem* can be a "valid" argumentation scheme. ("Valid" is a term that rhetoricians would hesitate to apply to any argumentative strategy. They would prefer to ask whether or not the strategy is "effective.") For a lengthy treatment of *ad hominem*, see Douglas Walton, *Ad Hominem Arguments* (Tuscaloosa, AL: University of Alabama Press, 1998). Walton develops a typology of *ad hominem* arguments and a norm for evaluating their validity in argumentation. For various positions on the validity and effectiveness of *ad hominem* in argumentation and rhetoric, see, for example, Audrey Yap, "Ad Hominem Fallacies, Bias, and Testimony," *Argumentation* 27 (2013): 97–109; Michael Leff, "Perelman, ad Hominem, and Rhetorical Ethos," *Argumentation* 23 (2009): 301–11; Douglas Walton, "Argumentation Schemes and Historical Origins of the Circumstantial Ad Hominem Argument," *Argumentation* 18 (2004): 359–68; Frans H. Van Eemeren, Bert Meuffels, and Mariel Verburg, "The (Un)reasonableness of Ad Hominem Fallacies," *JLSP* 19 (2000): 416–35.

that it is not time for the temple to be rebuilt is a rationalization rather than a principled stance.[75] The implication that the people have been concerned more with themselves than with YHWH's house is formally represented by the threefold reference to the second person: "Is it time for *you yourselves* to dwell in *your* houses—finished! But this house—desolate!" One can almost hear the theatrical exasperation at the sheer lunacy of the Yehudites' impertinence.

This short response, then, is rhetorically complex, seeking to persuade through the use of a rhetorical question, *ad hominem* innuendo, suggestive juxtaposition and comparison, and tacit connections between concepts. One further strategy is Haggai's framing of the question as the direct speech of YHWH. This is not the prophet's personal response to the policy, but YHWH's. Although Haggai does not address the reasons the people have for claiming that now is not the time to build the temple, his use of divine speech renders any reasons the people may have moot. YHWH's resentment of the fact that they have houses while he does not effectively nullifies any theological reasons העם הזה may have expressed for not building. YHWH, after all, is the final arbiter of all things theological. As for any non-theological reasons for not rebuilding, these are *a fortiori* invalid in the face of divine displeasure.

What does Haggai hope to accomplish with his retort? He wishes to signal that there is a problem with the present policy position that it is not time for the temple to be rebuilt. YHWH himself challenges this position in terms that suggest resentment if not anger. For the moment he does not elaborate, but he *implies* that this displeasure has do with the fact that the temple has not been rebuilt and that the people have been more concerned with their own houses than his. Whatever their *stated* reasons may be for claiming that it is not time to build the temple, perhaps their real motivation can be seen in the fact that their

---

75. Direct *ad hominem* attacks are intended to raise suspicions about the opponent himself, his intelligence, character, morals, etc. Indirect attacks throw suspicion on the opponent's motives for holding his position by implying that reasons he gives for his position are really just rationalizations. In both cases, though, the merits of the position are not addressed. The focus is instead on the one who holds the position. In the case of Hag 1:4, the rhetorical question is intended to raise doubts about the reasons the Yehudites claim it is not the time for the temple to be rebuilt. This, of course, may have implications for their character, but that is secondary. See Frans H. van Eemeren and Rob Grootendorst, *Argumentation, Communication, and Fallacies: A Pragma-Dialetical Perspective* (Hillsdale, NJ: Lawrence Erlbaum Associates, 1992), 111–12.

houses are functional. But this all works through innuendo. As the passage progresses, what is implied here will become explicit.

B. Haggai 1:5–7—Defining the Ill

Haggai now begins to make his case for rebuilding YHWH's house by drawing attention to an ill that currently plagues the community (vv. 5–7). He will then briefly present his proposal to rebuild the temple (v. 8) before returning to the ill, whose cause he will connect to the people's failure to attend to YHWH's house (vv. 9–11). In stating a causal relationship between what the community is experiencing and its current policy regarding the temple, Haggai will suggest—without actually claiming it—that *his* policy will effectively address that ill.

The prophet begins by calling the people to consider very carefully the present state of affairs: ועתה כה אמר יהוה צבאות שימו לבבכם על דרכיכם. This section is introduced with yet another messenger formula, reiterating that the speech is YHWH's, not the prophet's. This messenger formula not only imbues what follows with divine authority, but also signals that YHWH is aware of the problems facing the community. What he speaks of he knows well, not because he has observed it, but (as will soon be evident) because he has caused it. This tightens the rhetorical connection between the ill soon to be articulated and the cause of that ill.

The section is introduced by ועתה, which is often translated as "now" or "and now."[76] The particle is followed by the imperative שימו, and is intended to exhort the audience to heed the imperative. It is better, then, to see ועתה functioning here as a cohortative: "Come now!"[77] Although the messenger formula intervenes between ועתה and the imperative שימו לבבכם על דרכיכם, the import of the particle is to call attention not to the fact that YHWH now speaks, but to what YHWH wants the people to do.[78]

---

76. Petersen, *Haggai*, 41; Verhoef, *Haggai*, 44; Rudolph, *Haggai*, 28 ("und nun"), and others. This reflects Reventlow's comment that the particle signals a new thought, not the continuation of the foregoing (*Haggai*, 12). Wolff's suggestion (*Haggai*, 43) that it reflects the idea of urgency (a beginning on the temple should be made *now*) is perhaps not far off, but only in the sense that the urgent need here is to שים לב. The call to build has not been made yet.

77. Brongers notes several instances where the particle, when followed by an imperative, has the sense of "Komm doch," "Ach," "Wohlauf," or "Auf!" He gives as examples Exod 10:17; 2 Kgs 1:14; 3:15; Isa 5:3; and many others ("Bemerkungen," 294–95).

YHWH begins by exhorting the people: שימו לבבכם על דרכיכם. The idiom שים לב occurs in combination with different prepositions and carries a number of connotations, most of them having to do with paying attention, being concerned about, or taking into consideration.[79] Where it occurs in the same form as in Haggai 1:5, 7 (שים לב על), the context suggests it means to "take note of" or "take into consideration" (Job 1:8; 2:3; and possibly Judg 19:30[80]). In Haggai 1:5, 7, too, the context indicates the audience is being asked to notice or consider something.

YHWH is drawing to the people's attention their דרכים. This word is often used metaphorically to describe customary conduct, habitual ways of acting.[81] If the term is used here in that sense, YHWH is calling the people's attention to their typical way of doing things, their customary actions. What will emerge, however, is a depiction not just of the habitual actions of the people but also the consistently meager results of those actions. The word "experience" captures what will emerge for consideration: the relationship between customary activities and habitual results. The Yehudites, we will see, find themselves not in a static "situation" as much as they find themselves experiencing an apparently futile dynamic of action-and-lack of results. As he enters into his bid for a new policy, Haggai thus begins by having YHWH draw the attention of the Yehudites to their present reality: "Come now . . . consider carefully what you are experiencing."

What they are experiencing is a serious ill. Through content, form, and lexical choices the prophet now defines and makes vividly present an urgent harm. Thus depicted in v.6, the ill will serve rhetorically as both *evidence* of a need for a new policy and *motivation* to adopt that policy immediately.

זרעתם הרבה והבא מעט אכול ואין לשבעה שתו ואין לשכרה
לבוש ואין לחם לו והמשתכר משתכר אל צרור נקוב

---

78. A similar use is found in Jer 44:7, which is introduced by ועתה כה אמר אלהי צבאות אלהי ישראל. What follows is a series of questions ("Why inflict such a great evil upon yourselves," "why provoke me," "have you forgotten," etc.) that functions as an appeal to the Yehudites to come to their senses. Much the same intention is present in Hag 1:5.

79. See, for example, שים לב על (Exod 9:21), where it means to "heed" or "listen"; שים לב ל (Ezek 40:4), where it means to "pay attention to"; שים אל לב ל (1 Sam 9:20; 2 Sam 13:33), where it means "give a thought to" or "concern oneself with."

80. The MT has here שימו־לכם. The suggested emendation is שימו לבבכם.

81. "דרך," *HALOT*, 232.

The troubles afflicting the Yehudites, with the exception of the last, are set out formally in a series of antitheses.[82] The first element reflects action taken, while the second element presents the result, which is the opposite of what would be desired or expected from the action:

You have	sown much	but brought in little
	eat	but there is no fullness
	drink	but there is no inebriation
	dress	but there is no warmth for anyone
The wage earner	earns wages	for a bag with holes in it

The antithetical structure emphasizes the relationship between action and result. The point is not simply that the Yehudites have harvested little, but that this has happened despite the fact that they have sown much. Their hunger, thirst, and lack of warmth exist in spite of their attempts to alleviate them. Although he works, the worker has nothing to show for it. The ill that afflicts the community is not simply a failure to flourish. It is the inability to meet basic needs despite all efforts. Haggai defines the experience of the Yehudites as one of *frustrated expectations*. Antithesis not only defines the ill, but heightens its effect. Aristotle notes, for example, that the antithetical form is rhetorically effective "because the significance of contrasted ideas is easily felt, especially when they are put side by side."[83] This effect is strengthened by the list form—one thwarted effort after another is presented. The form of the verse seems designed to heighten the audience's sense of disappointment and frustration. This not only brings to consciousness the ill but, more importantly, it elevates the desire to alleviate it.[84]

---

82. Antithesis, a common rhetorical figure, is "the juxtaposition of contrasting ideas, often in parallel structure" (Edward P. J. Corbett, and Robert J. Connors, *Classical Rhetoric for the Modern Student*, 4th ed. [New York, NY: Oxford University Press, 1999], 429). Corbett and Connors cite an example from Samuel Johnson that is similar in style and structure to v. 6: "Though studious, he was popular; though argumentative, he was modest; though inflexible, he was candid; and though metaphysical, yet orthodox." (Dr. Johnson is describing the character of the Rev. Zacariah Mudge, in the *London Chronicle*, May 2, 1769.)

83. Aristotle, *Rhet.* 3.9.20, 1410a.

84. Richard Whately (*Elements of Rhetoric*, 7th ed. [New York, NY: International Debate Education Society, 2009], 237) stated in his classic work on rhetoric: "There can be no doubt that this figure [antithesis] is calculated to add greatly to Energy. Every thing is rendered more striking by contrast." He also notes that antithesis permits the rhetor to express much in relatively few words. This conciseness contributes to the Energy. He gives as an example "When Reason is against a

The activities presented here are comprehensive and the disappointing results serious. These are not minor concerns or a lack of luxuries; the basic necessities of life are going unmet or barely met. (One necessity missing from the list is shelter. But Haggai has already noted that he believes this particular need is being met—all too well.) This makes the ill not only frustrating but urgent. The list makes clear that the Yehudites are suffering from grave problems that cannot go on indefinitely. This urgency also contributes to the motivation to act immediately to resolve the ill, once that decision has been made.[85]

Scholars have often noted that what Haggai presents here closely resembles the classic "futility curses" of biblical and extrabiblical literature, and have drawn the conclusion that the prophet has these in mind. Hillers, for example, saw in v. 6 "clear examples" of such curses.[86] Petersen, who agrees that Haggai is drawing explicitly on covenant curses for his material, infers that the prophet means to suggest that curses have been brought on the community because of "an abrogated covenant," which implies for Petersen that Haggai considers the reconstruction of the temple a covenant duty.[87] There are indeed similarities. Parallel examples of covenant futility curses can be found in the HB for all of the elements of v. 6, with the exception of wage earning.[88]

The difficulty with this interpretation is that Haggai nowhere refers to a covenant or to the temple reconstruction as a covenant obligation. In fact, Haggai will later explicitly cite the cause for the current prob-

---

man, he will be against Reason," and notes that "it would hardly be possible to express tis sentiment not Antithetically, so as to be clearly intelligible, except in a much longer sentence."

85. Wolff (*Haggai*, 30) and Floyd (*Minor Prophets*, 266) suggest that the point of this recital of actions and results is to call the people to consider "the causal relationship between [their] choices and their general welfare" (Floyd). But there is no such causal relationship, as vv. 9–11 make clear. The people are not being chastised for trying to feed and clothe themselves, as if these were culpable actions. There is no indication in this passage that YHWH is upset because the people have sought to eke out a living for themselves. The divine displeasure is related to the fact that while doing that they have not attended to his house.

86. Delbert R. Hillers, *Treaty-Curses and the Old Testament Prophets*, BibOr 16 (Rome: Pontifical Biblical Institute, 1964), 29. See also, for example, Petersen, *Haggai*, 50; Verhoef, *Haggai*, 63; Wolff, *Haggai*, 43–44.

87. Petersen, *Haggai*, 50. Petersen notes that if Haggai does see temple reconstruction as a covenant duty, his "view represents a significant reformulation of the covenant norms, a focusing on the cult per se, something that is markedly absent from other covenant stipulations preserved in the Hebrew Bible." See also Kessler (*Haggai*, 153–55), who supports the view that the prophet is referring specifically to covenant curses.

88. Wolff (*Haggai*, 44) notes the following: *sowing* (Mic 6:15; Lev 26:16; Deut 28:38), *eating* (Hos 4:10; Mic 6:14; Lev 26:26), *drinking* (Amos 5:11; Mic 6:15; Deut 28:39), *clothing oneself* (Deut 28:48). Hillers notes many of the same (*Treaty-Curses*, 29).

lems, and will say nothing about an abrogated covenant. It is therefore difficult to accept that he wants the Yehudites to understand that by failing to rebuild YHWH's house they are in breach of covenant. It is true that he has chosen to describe the Yehudites' experience in a way that is reminiscent of the content and form of treaty futility curses, which include a protasis ("You will do this . . .") and an apodosis (". . . but this will happen").[89] But the content of v. 6 is derived from the actual experience of the people, not from the treaty curses (and of course the content of treaty futility curses is drawn from human experience in the first place). The protasis-apodosis form is also not necessarily derived from treaty futility curses, since it is not limited to them. We find the same form used in the sapiential literature, for example, to describe the difference between hopes or expectations and reality: "Then they will call upon me [i.e., Wisdom], but I will not answer; they will seek me, but they will not find me" (Prov 1:28).[90] The form is basically antithetical, and its presence in proverbs suggests it was a common way of making a point. We should therefore consider the futility curse form a variation of the more general form, common to many contexts. This is the form that Haggai is drawing upon to frame the content of the ill he wishes his audience to consider carefully.

Nevertheless, there is no doubt that the content and form of v. 6 resembles treaty futility curses. Even if Haggai does not mean to argue that the Yehudites have actually breached the terms of a covenant, the resemblance has its rhetorical advantages. To those familiar with the treaty form, it could imply that Yehud lies under a curse, whether for covenant violations or not. This would only strengthen Haggai's claim, which he will make in vv. 9–11, that the cause of the current problems lies in YHWH's anger for the failure to rebuild his house. Indeed, before Haggai ever spoke the Yehudites were likely to have inferred that their failure to thrive was a sign of YHWH's displeasure. *That* they were under a curse would probably not have been a controversial claim. The question would have been *why*. We will return to this below.

The verb forms in v. 6 are rhetorically significant. Through them

---

89. Hillers, *Treaty-Curses*, 28. He describes the protasis as the description of the activity and the apodosis as the frustration of that activity.
90. For other examples, see Job 19:7; 23:8; 30:20; 31:8; Pss 18:42; 22:3; 69:21. Particularly noteworthy is the use of אין in Job 19:7; 23:8; Ps 18:42.

Haggai defines the ill as persistent and intransigent. Six verbs appear in the series. The first, זרעתם, is in the perfect. The next four (לבוש, הבא, אכול, שתו) are absolute infinitives, and the final verb (משתכר) is an active participle. The perfect form of the first verb grounds the series in the past, but not solely in the past. It is clear from the context that the effects of the sowing continue into the present.[91] The problems depicted here reach into the past and have persisted until now.

The absolute infinitives that follow serve several rhetorical purposes at once. Although they function as finite verbs, formally they are atemporal and they lack explicit subjects. The choice of infinitives "releases" the verbs from temporal constraints, allowing them to reflect not just past, but also present realities.[92] The people not only "have harvested little," but continue to "harvest little." They have eaten, etc., and continue to eat, drink, dress.[93] The infinitives suggest a timeless, persistent situation.[94] Because they do not take an explicit subject, the infinitives suggest a global situation.[95] It is not just "you" who eat, drink, etc. Everyone is harvesting little, eating, drinking, and dressing. The use of לו as an "individualizing singular" in an impersonal construction (לבוש ואין לחם לו) also contributes to the generalizing ten-

---

91. In which case, the verb is an example of what Waltke and O'Connor (*IBHS*, 487) refer to as the "persistent (present) perfective," which "represents a single situation that started in the past but continues (persists) into the present."

92. Joüon (§123x) suggests that especially in later texts, such as Haggai, the inf. abs. is often the equivalent of the preceding form. Thus he reads the infinitives in v. 6 as perfects ("one has eaten . . ."). Craig E. Morrison also notes that when the inf. abs. follows participles and finite forms, "it takes its aspect from the preceding verb" ("Infinitive: Biblical Hebrew," *EHLL*). He cites Hag 1:6 as an example. Gesenius notes that the form is used "to emphasize the idea of the verb *in the abstract*, i.e. it speaks of an action (or state) without any regard to the agent or to the circumstances of time and mood" (GKC §113a; emphasis in the original). Muraoka likewise emphasizes that when the inf. abs. is used in this and similar constructions, "a given verbal idea is set apart and made distinct in abstracto, namely without any indication of person, number, etc. In this way it is stressed that the writer or the speaker has especially intense interest in, or demands special attention of the hearer or the reader to what he expressed by the verbal form" (*Emphatic Words*, 88). Muraoka's observation expresses well one of the rhetorical functions of the inf. abs. in v. 6.

93. Thus Meyers and Meyers: ". . . you keep eating . . . you keep drinking . . . you keep putting on clothes . . ." (*Haggai*, 3).

94. Absolute infinitives can function in a number of ways, and can indicate past, present, or future. (Joüon, §123 u–x). Several commentators have also noted that the use of the infinitives here gives the list, as Gesenius puts it (GKC §113y), a "hurried or otherwise excited style" that "intentionally contents itself with this infinitive, in order to bring out the verbal idea in a clearer and more expressive manner."

95. Joüon §123x: "sometimes the author wished to use a form with a vague subject like *one* or *they*." (Emphasis in the original.)

dency of the infinitival forms.[96] The problem is not only persistent, it is widespread, extending beyond any specific subjects.

The final verb form is an active participle, which also indicates an ongoing situation.[97] This contributes to the temporal trajectory that the antitheses set out. The list begins in the past with a suffix-conjugation, extends through a series of formally timeless infinitives, and ends with an active participle indicating a situation that is persistent. The subject here is "the" wage earner, indicating that not one particular earner, but all earners are struggling.[98]

Taken together the verbal forms in the list suggest an enduring condition of thwarted efforts extending from the past into the present. The audience can readily infer from this dynamic that unless something is done, the situation will continue indefinitely into the future. The Yehudites have found themselves, these verb forms suggest, in an endless, antithetical cycle of effort and lack of results.

The idea of "lack" is brought to the fore through the use of the particle אֵין. The results of the Yehudites' efforts are phrased in terms of the absence of concrete results: "there is no fullness," "there is no inebriation," "there is no warmth."[99] The force of this lexical choice is the emphasis on the *non-existence* of the desiderata.[100] The people are simply never able to experience fullness or warmth; it is absent from Yehud. The rhetorical stress on absence and lack also serves to motivate to action.

The formal, lexical, and substantive elements of v. 6 work together to produce substantial "presence." The rhetorical concept of "presence" refers to the "discursive effect" through which "some phenomenon, idea, concept, process, or person is made vivid, tangible, and/or proximate to an audience."[101] It is achieved through a combination of

---

96. See chap. 2, n. 188, on the translation of this phrase in chap. 2.
97. "The *participle active* indicates a person or thing conceived as being in the continual uninterrupted *exercise* of an activity" (GKC §116 a; emphasis in original).
98. Determination of a noun with the article can indicate "the sum total of individuals belong to a class (which may, however, be done just as well by the plural)." (GKC §126m; emphasis in the original). Joüon (§137i) and Waltke and O'Connor refer to this as the "generic" use of the article (*IBHS* 13.5.1f).
99. For discussion of the syntax of ל אֵין-, see chap. 2, n. 187.
100. Muraoka (*Emphatic Words*, 109) states that אֵין can simply negate a statement or indicate "non-existence or absence." He believes that indicating non-existence is the primary or original syntactic function.
101. Jasinski, *Sourcebook*, 456.

form, substance, and stylistic strategies. As Jasinski notes, presence is particularly useful for the advocate of a policy: "A central task in advocacy is to make the problem or *ill* that one wants to address present to the audience."[102] Through presence, the proponent seeks to persuade the audience that the ill is *urgent, persistent, severe, significant,* and *immediate.*[103] The rhetorical strategies Haggai employs in v. 6 are designed to do just this. Haggai has defined the current experience of the Yehudites as one of ongoing frustration in obtaining the concrete necessities of life, an ill—it is implied—that will not go away on its own. The vivid presence of this ill is intended to capitalize on the feeling of frustration by raising in the minds of Haggai's audience a desire to alleviate it as quickly as possible. This naturally leads to the hope or expectation that Haggai will propose a remedy.

In v. 7 the people are again exhorted to consider their experience: כה אמר יהוה צבאות שימו לבבכם על דרכיכם. This exhortation is introduced, as in v. 5, by a messenger formula. This formula would seem to indicate the beginning of a new unit, but the verse forms with v. 5 an inclusio around v. 6, framing it and emphasizing the gravity of the Yehudites' experience and the need to think carefully about it. At the same time, from a form-critical perspective, the messenger formula seems naturally to introduce what follows in vv. 8–11. From a rhetorical perspective, either option is plausible. The exhortation can both conclude the previous section—thus emphasizing its importance—and introduce what follows, implicitly urging the audience to form an association between the ill just portrayed and Haggai's new policy proposal. In speech or written on a scroll without an editorial "layout" that assigns the verse to one unit or another, the verse can easily be understood as a hinge or bridge related to and connecting what precedes with what follows.[104]

---

102. Jasinksi, *Sourcebook*, 457 (emphasis in the original). See also Chaim Perelman and L. Olbrechts-Tyteca, *The New Rhetoric: A Treatise on Argumentation*, trans. J. Wilkinson and P. Weaver (Notre Dame, IN: University of Notre Dame Press, 1969), 118.

103. Jasinski, *Sourcebook*, 457. For further discussion of presence, see Thomas F. Mader, "On Presence in Rhetoric," *CCC* 24 (1973): 375–81; Louise A. Karon "Presence in *The New Rhetoric*," *Ph&Rh* 9 (1976): 96–111; Charles Kauffman and Donn W. Parson, "Metaphor and Presence in Argument," in *Argumentation Theory and the Rhetoric of Assent*, ed. David C. Williams and Michael D. Hazen, Studies in Rhetoric and Communication (Tuscaloosa, AL: University of Alabama Press, 1990), 91–102; Robert E. Tucker, "Figure, Ground and Presence: A Phenomenology of Meaning in Rhetoric," *QJS* 87 (2001): 396–414.

C. Haggai 1:8—Proposing the Remedy

The call to "consider your experience" is immediately followed by the exhortation to rebuild the temple: עלו ההר והבאתם עץ ובנו הבית. As Graffy has observed, Haggai does not have YHWH state *explicitly* that there is a connection between the dismal circumstances in Yehud and the fact that the temple has not been rebuilt, but the arrangement of material is clearly intended to lead the audience to draw that conclusion.[105] An implied critique related to הבית הזה (v. 4) is followed immediately by a vivid description of the bad state of affairs, which is then juxtaposed with a call to rebuild הבית. Although no explicit connections have been made between these three elements, the "house" language of vv. 4 and 8, which forms a conceptual envelope around the litany of woes in v. 6, strongly suggests a relationship. This inference is further strengthened by the repetition of the exhortation to the people to consider their experience, immediately preceding the command to build.

With their present futile experience firmly in mind, the people are then exhorted to make preparations to rebuild "the house." The call to gather wood is specific, the first step perhaps in the process of rebuilding. Kessler suggests that this order to go to the hills functions as a synecdoche for all of the work required to build the temple, which is certainly a possible reading, although not necessary to understand the rhetorical force of the command.[106] This rhetorical force resides in the concrete nature of the order, whose specificity lends itself to a call to action ("here is a real, tangible thing to do") and that suggests that work can, and should, begin right away ("so go do it").

The command to rebuild is stated in two words: בנו הבית. This is the new "policy initiative" toward which Haggai is directing his persuasive efforts. The exhortation is straightforward and has been anticipated in vv. 2 and 4. Now the prophet must convince the people that they

---

104. As we find, for example, in *BHQ* and in the earliest extant manuscript of the text, Murabaʿat 88.
105. Graffy, *Prophet Confronts*, 100–101.
106. Kessler, *Haggai*, 133–34. Mark J. Boda ("From Dystopia to Myopia: Utopian (Re)Visions in Haggai and Zechariah 1–8," in *Utopia and Dysopia in Prophetic Literature*, ed. Ehud ben Zvi [Helsinki: Finnish Exegetical Society; Göttingen: Vandenhoeck & Ruprecht, 2006], 232) notes also that the command to gather wood echoes a consistent motif in the ANE traditions about temple building, the gathering of materials for construction. He cites Hurowitz's discussion of this in *Exalted House*, 205–20.

should build and motivate them to do so. He has prepared the groundwork for this in v. 6, but he has not made the connection between the present experience of the people and building the temple. He will do this later, in vv. 9–11. For the moment he expresses the deity's attitude toward the proposal.

Haggai assures his audience that YHWH will be pleased with his house once it is built: וארצה בו ואכבד אמר יהוה. The syntax here (imperative cohortatives) indicates that YHWH's pleasure in or acceptance of the temple, as well as his being honored or glorified, are the purpose or the intended (promised?) result of the reconstruction.[107] This is a significant claim, as the command to rebuild the temple is being offered as a counter policy to the current decision to wait until the right "time."

The phrase וארצה בו ואכבד requires a nuanced reading. The syntax allows us to understand that the people should build the temple "so that" or "with the result that" YHWH will be pleased by it and be glorified. There is no great difference in meaning; they both indicate that YHWH wants and will approve of the temple. Such an assurance would be potentially meaningful for those in the community who opposed the temple for theological reasons, that is, out of a belief that YHWH did not want the temple built at this time. The assurance that YHWH does want the temple built and will take pleasure in it is intended to allay concerns in this regard and to clear away at least some possible objections to Haggai's proposal.

The prophet's choice of words also contributes to this strategy. As several commentators have noted, the verb רצה is often found in cultic contexts, where its basic meaning of "to be pleased" takes on the connotation of "acceptance" or "recognition" of offerings.[108] Haggai intends the audience to hear in this phrase a promise that once the

---

107. Thomas O. Lambdin, *Introduction to Biblical Hebrew* (Upper Saddle River, NJ: Prentice Hall, 1971), 119; *IBHS*, 577–78; Joüon §116 a–b. Joüon notes that in this construction the distinction between purpose and intended result cannot always be sharply drawn, and this is probably not intended to be so. Where one wishes to make it clear that one is speaking of purpose rather than result, other options are available, such as ל inf. const. or למען, etc.

108. See, for example, Barstad, "רצה," *TDOT* 13:620–21, 626–27; Petersen, *Haggai*, 51; Wolff, *Haggai*, 45. Petersen cites 2 Sam 24:23; Jer 14:10, 12; Ezek 20:40, 41; 43:27; Mal 1:10, 12; Pss 51:18; 119:108; Mic 6:7; Amos 5:22.

temple is built YHWH will "accept" it.[109] Those who currently oppose the temple on theological grounds have nothing to fear.

At the same time, YHWH states that he will be honored or glorified by, or perhaps in, the temple. Although some commentators have taken this statement to mean that YHWH's glory will appear and therefore read it as an assurance of divine presence, others understand אכבד to mean what it usually means, "to be honored or glorified."[110] It is not necessary to rule out either reading. The audience can hear both that YHWH will be glorified and honored in or by the temple, and that he is assuring them of his presence in it once completed. In either case the rhetorical force is the same as the promise to accept the temple. YHWH's presence or glorification—they both signal divine acceptance of the house.

Haggai has offered a proposal in the form of a divine assurance—spoken by YHWH in the first person—that if the people build the temple he will accept it and be present in it. The context makes it clear that Haggai is presenting the temple reconstruction project as a remedy for the ill plaguing the community. But Haggai has not actually voiced this claim. He has left it to his audience to infer what is so obviously implied. The prophet has suggested in v. 4 that YHWH disapproves of the present discrepancy between the finished houses of the Yehudites and his own deserted house. He has also held up in v. 6 for the community's consideration the frustratingly meager results of its ongoing efforts to provide for most of its basic needs. Now he has presented a command to rebuild the temple with the associated promises from YHWH's own mouth that he will accept it once completed. Without articulating the logical relationship between any of these elements (except that YHWH will be pleased with the temple), Haggai nevertheless enables the audience to draw the conclusion that building the temple will remedy the ill.

---

109. So Kessler, *Haggai*, 134–35; Petersen, *Haggai*, 51; Amsler, *Aggée*, 25; Verhoef, *Haggai*, 67; Ackroyd, *Exile and Restoration*, 160; Wolff, *Haggai*, 45.

110. Those who read here an assurance of the presence of YHWH's glory or a manifestation of his sovereignty include Amsler, *Aggée*, 25; Gary A. Anderson, *Sacrifices and Offerings in Ancient Israel: Studies in Their Social and Political Importance*, HSM 41 (Atlanta, GA: Scholars Press, 1987), 93–95; Meyers and Meyers, *Haggai*, 28; Rudolph, *Haggai*, 34; Wolff, *Haggai*, 46. Those who read it as an indication that YHWH will be honored or glorified by the temple include Elliger, *Zwölf kleinen Propheten*, 87; Reventlow, *Haggai*, 14. See chap. 2, p. 27, for discussion of the text-critical issues related to this word.

The Yehudites might do this, but only if two persuasive aims are met. The first is acceptance of the truth of Haggai's claim that YHWH will be pleased with the temple. It is not a foregone conclusion that the audience will take Haggai at his word when he claims to speak for YHWH. This raises the question of Haggai's *ethos* or perceived authority. This is a significant question that will be addressed below. The Yehudites must also be convinced that building the temple will address the root *cause* of the ill that plagues them. Unless they believe that building the temple will affect the cause of their problems, they do not necessarily have a new, compelling motivation to build it. The prophet now turns to the question of the cause of the community's troubles.

D. Haggai 1:9–11—Defining the Cause of the Ill

So far Haggai has implied a relationship between the community's problems and the current state of the temple. In the final section of his first speech, he explicitly articulates the relationship in terms of *cause*. The exasperating state of affairs in Yehud has been brought about by YHWH because he is offended that the Yehudites have attended to their own houses while ignoring his. Once he has stated the cause of the ill, Haggai will leave it to his audience to infer that building the temple immediately will remedy that ill.

The prophet resumes, in v. 9a, his discussion of the ill afflicting the Yehudites with a summary statement: פנה אל הרבה והיה למעט והבאתם הבית ונפחתי בו.[111] This interweaving of temple and problems continues throughout the passage, structurally reinforcing the impression that the two issues are inextricably related.

vv. 2, 4	temple
vv. 5–7	ill
v. 8	temple
v. 9a	ill
v. 9b	temple
vv. 10–11	ill

111. See the text-critical discussion in chap. 2, pp. 27–28, for the emendation from הנה to היה.

The antithesis that begins with an inf. abs. contributes to the sense that the problem is both ongoing and comprehensive: "[You] expected much, but it has turned out to be little." This sentiment summarizes the point of v. 6.[112] Not only are the Yehudites having problems, but the problems persist despite efforts to alleviate them.[113] This resumptive statement brings attention back to the ill so that Haggai can establish its cause.

Haggai moves closer to disclosing the root cause of their problems by having YHWH state that it is he who is "blowing away" everything they bring to their houses. What little harvest they manage to get is destroyed before they can profit from it.[114] Haggai not only reveals that the agent of their problems is YHWH, he also emphasizes that it is precisely at those בתים ספונים that YHWH acts against them. YHWH's destructive acts against the people are localized specifically at each person's "house." Once again a verbal connection is made between the house of YHWH and the houses of the Yehudites. In one phrase Haggai juxtaposes the woes of the community, the agent of those woes, and what will soon be revealed to be the reason for those woes: houses.

To introduce this reason, Haggai has YHWH pose a question and then answer it: יען מה נאם יהוה צבאות יען ביתי אשר הוא חרב ואתם רצים איש לביתו. We have now come to the central issue, upon which Haggai's proposal to rebuild the temple hinges. As we will see, it also a highly debatable assertion of the cause of the ill. It is therefore introduced with the solemn oracle formula נאם יהוה צבאות.

YHWH asks and then immediately answers his own question. This makes the question quasi-rhetorical, as YHWH does not expect his audience to answer it.[115] The question serves to heighten the curiosity of the audience and to draw attention to what follows. The solemn oracle formula serves as a rhetorical indicator that what follows is not only important, but assuredly the true word of YHWH.[116] This oracle for-

---

112. Noted also by Wolff, *Haggai*, 46–47; Meyers and Meyers, *Haggai*, 28.

113. Verhoef (*Haggai*, 69–70) and others note that the emphasis here is again on the disappointment of the people.

114. See chap. 2, n. 190, for a discussion of the meaning of נפחתי. Regardless of how one decides to translate the word, the point is obvious: YHWH is the agent of their troubles.

115. The difference is that, as noted above when discussing v. 4, rhetorical questions generally are not actually answered. Asking and then immediately answering one's own question is a common rhetorical figure called *hypophora*.

116. As in the other prophetic books, in the HN the oracle formula occurs within statements and at

mula occurs twelve times in the HN, each time punctuating a statement that is potentially disputable or at the center of a particular unit's persuasive function, usually both. The placement and the unusually high frequency of the formula in this short text suggest that the prophet (or the composer) anticipated or was aware that his claims pertaining to the reconstruction of the temple would be disputed.[117] Haggai's controversial claim needed to be bolstered through as many traditional rhetorical devices as possible, including this solemn divine declaration formula.[118]

YHWH's answer to his own question has already been alluded to in v. 4. YHWH has caused the calamity because *YHWH's* house is desolate (חָרֵב) while the Yehudites run, each to his own house.[119] Here, even more than in v. 4, it is clear that what YHWH finds so disagreeable is not simply that his house is deserted. What angers him especially is the contrast between his house and those of the Yehudites. The pleonastic pronoun emphasizes the fact that it is *YHWH's* house that is abandoned (and not the Yehudites' houses): ביתי אשר הוא חרב.[120] It is, in

---

their conclusions, in some cases both in the same statement. Eising ("נאם," *TDOT*, 9:110–12) notes that very often the formula emphasizes not only the divine origin of the message, but the truthfulness of a divine declaration or oath. Because the formula occurs most often in Jeremiah, its function there has received specific attention, but the results of those investigations apply to the HN also. See Rolf Rendtorrf, "Zum Gebrauch der Formel *ne'um jahwe* im Jeremiabuch," *ZAW* 66 (1954): 27–37; Friedrich Baumgärtel, "Die Formel *ne'um jahwe*," *ZAW* 73 (1961): 277–90.

117. The formula occurs in three forms (נאם יהוה [צבאות], נאם עדני, נאם העדן יהוה) a total of 357x in the MT, almost half of them in Jeremiah (175x). In the rest of the prophetic books, only Isaiah (25x), Ezekiel (85x), Amos (21x) and Zechariah (20x) have more instances of the formula than the HN. To gain a sense of how disproportionately high the frequency of this formula is in HN, we can compare ratios of formula counts per book/verses per book. We discover: Jeremiah (175/1364 = .13), Ezekiel (85/1271 = .07), Isaiah (25/1291 = .02), Amos (21/146 = .14), Zechariah (20/211 = .09), Haggai (12/38 = .31).

118. Claus Westermann suggests that the increased use in later periods of formulas that "identify the word of the prophet as God's word"—such as we see in Jeremiah, Ezekiel, Haggai, and Zechariah—indicates "that in the course of its history the prophet's speech ceased being self-evident and self-understandable (*Basic Forms of Prophetic Speech*, trans. Hugh Clayton White [Louisville, KY: Westminster John Knox, 1991], 187–88). The legitimation of the prophetic word as God's word thus became more and more necessary and thus the words of legitimation in the framework accumulated." My argument is that the truth of Haggai's claims regarding YHWH's desire to see the temple built was not "self-evident," and is therefore rhetorically bolstered, as Westermann suggests, by the abundant use of formulas to identify the prophet's words with YHWH's.

119. See chap. 2, n. 192, for the meaning of this word, which is best understood here to connote desolation or desertion.

120. The pleonastic pronoun plays an important role here. It is resumptive, but the resumption is not grammatically necessary for the verse to make sense. The following would be perfectly good Hebrew: יען ביתי אשר חרב. Robert D. Holmstedt notes that Hag 1:9 is one of 32 cases in the HB of non-obligatory pleonastic resumption in a verbless relative clause. He suggests as "a plausible

other words, unconscionable that YHWH's house lies unattended while the Yehudites are so concerned about their own, a concern referred to hyperbolically (and sarcastically) as "running." Whereas in v. 4 the contrast drawn was between the state of the houses themselves (deserted vs. finished), here it is between the attention each receives. The difference is one of emphasis only; both contrasts serve as an indictment of the Yehudites' neglect of the temple while assiduously attending to their own affairs.

The explicit individuation highlights that each member of the community is culpable. It is not "this people," lumped together in a vague, general way, that is responsible for the current state of affairs. It is each member of the community, understood as individuals. The rhetorical force of laying the blame for YHWH's indignation on every member of the community, not simply on some abstract notion of "this people," is the emphasis it places on each member's responsibility to remedy the ill caused by his own negligence.

Haggai does not state that the Yehudites' neglect of YHWH's house in favor of their own is unacceptable, culpable behavior. He assumes that the discrepancy is so obviously disordered it does not need to be argued or even asserted. He is relying on the audience to come to this same conclusion. If so, they should have a strong "moral" motive for accepting Haggai's proposal to build the temple, in addition to whatever more narrowly defined self-interest could lead them to support reconstruction.

Regardless of whether or not the Yehudites agree with Haggai's assumption that it is wrong for YHWH's temple to be desolate, it is clear that YHWH takes great offense, enough to cause all of the problems that Haggai has made so vividly present to them:

---

explanation" for these non-essential pleonastic pronouns that they are *kontrastive*. In pragmatics, *Kontrast* is a kind of focus that directs the listener or reader to mentally establish a "membership set" defined by the predicate, and to place emphatically the focused item referred to by the pronoun within that membership set. ("The Relative Clause in Biblical Hebrew: A Linguistic Analysis" [PhD diss., University of Wisconsin-Madison, 2002], 100, 220, 284–85). See also Robert D. Holmstedt, "Relative Clause: Biblical Hebrew," *EHLL*.

In other words, in a verbless relative clause, the non-obligatory resumptive pronoun indicates that the subject is emphatically a member of the group described by the predicate, and not outside of that group. In the case of Hag 1:9, the pronoun focuses attention on the fact that YHWH's house belongs to the "membership set" of houses that are desolate. The irony, given the context, is that it is a membership set of one, and this is the point. *Only* YHWH's house is desolate, all the others in Jerusalem are functioning and populated.

על כן עליכם כלאו שמים טלם והארץ כלאה יבולה ואקרא חֹרב על הארץ ועל
ההרים ועל הדגן ועל התירוש ועל היצהר על אשר תוציא האדמה ועל האדמה ועל
הבהמה ועל כל יגיע כפים[121]

The prominent place of עליכם highlights the fact that Yehudites have only themselves to blame for their problems: "Therefore, on your account. ..." YHWH may be the agent of their difficulties, but their negligence is the true cause. The skies have withheld water and the earth crops because YHWH has called forth a comprehensive חֹרב. The verbal connection between the desolation of YHWH's house (חָרֵב; vv. 4, 9) and the desolation of the land (חֹרב) strengthens the causal connection being drawn here. It is because of חָרֵב that there is חֹרב. The word play also suggests the condign nature of the judgment. The devastation wrought by the חֹרב called forth by YHWH is fitting in light of the חָרֵב he sees when he looks at his house.[122]

This חֹרב is comprehensive and devastating. The fields and mountains have been affected, leading to a loss of grain, wine, oil—all staples. Everything that comes forth from the earth, humans, animals—everything that the Yehudites touch or try to do (כל יגיע כפים) is ruined. The comprehensive depiction of the desolation indicates the depth of YHWH's anger at the neglect of his house and serves to make the ill facing the Yehudites vividly present to them. They are reminded yet again that the problems they are facing are urgent, persistent, severe, significant, and immediate. Now that they know the cause, the people are left to infer the obvious benefit of accepting Haggai's proposal to rebuild the temple.

E. Conclusions

As a rhetorical unit, Haggai 1:1–11 can be divided into two main sections. In 1:1–4 the controversy at the center of the HN is revealed as a dispute between "this people," who claims that it is not the time to rebuild the temple, and Haggai (speaking in the name of YHWH), who insists that the Yehudites begin building immediately. In 1:5–11

121. See chap. 2, p. 29, for discussion of emendation of MT to טלם.
122. Lanham, *Analyzing Prose*, 125: the similarity of sounds suggests "a natural affinity between objects or concepts" whether one exists logically or not.

the prophet presents his case. The entire passage reflects a genre of disputation known as a policy dispute. Using the four stock issues of such disputes—ill, cause, remedy, and cost—as analytical frames, we can make the following observations about the persuasive aims and strategies of Haggai 1:1–11.

The controversy revolves around whether or not "now is the time" to build the temple. "This people" claims that it is not. Haggai implies in v. 4 that it is time to build, and makes the claim explicit in v. 8, when YHWH exhorts the people to gather wood and build. As noted above, we cannot know exactly what reason(s) the people have for their position. Although some scholars have been willing to entertain the possibility that the people's position was based on principled theological or ideological considerations, it is a testament to the persuasive force of the HN that others have assumed that the statement quoted in v. 2 was, as the prophet implies, merely a rationalization of selfish neglect.[123]

The prophet gives considerable attention to the *ill* afflicting the community. In vv. 6 and 9a he depicts this ill as a frustrating experience of thwarted efforts and the Yehudites' failure to rise above chronic economic and agricultural problems. These problems are further described in vv. 10aβ–11 in terms of a comprehensive and devastating חֹרֶב that is currently upon the land, affecting produce, animals, humans—everything the Yehudites are attempting to do, all the work of their hands. In vv. 5 and 7, the Yehudites are exhorted to consider carefully all of these problems. Thus in the portion of the passage devoted to Haggai's argument in favor of building the temple, vv. 5–11, all but vv. 8 and 9b–10aα concern the ill. This suggests that the prophet ascribes considerable rhetorical significance to this stock issue. This could be because the ill constitutes a point of potential or actual disagreement between Haggai and his opponents, such that he is obliged to address it. Or the emphasis on the ill could serve a different persuasive purpose.

---

123. For example, Mitchell (*Haggai*, 45) states, "At first sight this objection [i.e., that the time has not come for the temple to be rebuilt] would seem to mean that those who made it were waiting for the expiration of the seventy years of Jeremiah's prophecy. *The answer given to it shows that it was dictated by selfishness*, which manifested itself also in the comparatively trivial personal affairs to the neglect of the larger issues that ought to interest all the members of the community" (emphasis added). Wolff (*Haggai*, 41) likewise states that in v. 4 Haggai "shows up their egoism for what it is."

In a policy dispute, the ill may be a point of contention if the opponents disagree with the advocate about the facts of the situation, the claim that these facts actually constitute an ill or harm, or the insistence that the ill is significant enough to require action. Haggai almost certainly did not face opposition from "this people" regarding any of these. The prophet's description of the problems plaguing the community is deliberately designed to increase the sense of frustration in his audience, and so is probably somewhat hyperbolic. But it would have to be grounded in the experience of the people to be credible; he could not completely misrepresent the conditions in Yehud. And his depiction of the ill is supported by biblical and extrabiblical evidence that suggests that the economic conditions in Yehud from the beginning of the Babylonian period through the early Persian period were indeed poor.[124] It was therefore unlikely that his audience would have disputed Haggai's claim that they were struggling. Even if we allow for a certain amount of prophetic exaggeration, we may also presume that the Yehudites would have agreed that the conditions constituted a harm or problem significant enough to address. It is likely, therefore, that Haggai's audience would have accepted his claim that they faced a serious and urgent ill that called for action. Haggai's rhetorical emphasis on the ill is not offered, then, primarily to persuade the community that it has a problem.

Haggai places so much emphasis on the ill to motivate the Yehudites to accept his proposal. The vivid portrayal of frustration and suffering is intended to heighten the desire to find a solution to chronic problems. Haggai is thus appealing to the self-interest of his audience to motivate them to rebuild the temple. This is to be expected, as appeal to advantage or interest is the primary persuasive strategy of deliberative rhetoric.[125] It is nevertheless ironic that Haggai appeals to the material concerns of the Yehudites while simultaneously reproaching them for attending to their own "houses" at the expense of YHWH's. It is true that this appeal to interest is implicit—a point I will develop

---

124. See the discussion of the evidence for this in chap. 3, pp. 111–17, 131–38.

125. Aristotle (*Rhet.* 1.3.3, 1358b23–26): "The political [i.e., deliberative] orator aims at establishing the expediency or the harmfulness of a proposed course of action; if he urges its acceptance, he does so on the ground that it will do good; if he urges its rejection, he does so on the ground that it will do harm; and all other points, such as whether the proposal is just or unjust, honourable or dishonourable, he brings in as subsidiary and relative to this main consideration."

below—but it is there nonetheless.[126] Why else dwell so much and in such detail on an ill that was probably undisputed, if not to prepare the audience to accept quickly and wholeheartedly the proposal that (Haggai will imply) promises to remedy it?

In comparison to his emphasis on the problems facing the people, Haggai spends very little time on the *cause* of that ill. Only in v. 9b does he explicitly state the reason the people are suffering such exasperating deprivations (although v. 4 foreshadows this, and the following verses develop it, albeit by focusing on the deprivations themselves). The cause of the ill, according to Haggai, is that YHWH is displeased that his house remains deserted while the people attend to their own. This assertion requires some further discussion.

Because the stock issue of cause forms the logical connection between ill and remedy, it is a crucial element for the advocate to establish. Opponents to a policy may deny that the advocate has correctly identified the cause of the ill. Even if they are convinced of the cause, the advocate must still persuade the audience that the ill will only be resolved if they attend to the cause (hopefully by adopting the advocate's policy recommendation). In other words, the audience must believe both that some thing or person is the cause of the problem and that the problem will not go away unless that person or thing is eradicated or otherwise addressed.

Haggai claims that the cause of the persistent poor results of the Yehudites efforts is not only that YHWH is angry, but that he is angry specifically because the temple has not been built. There are therefore two elements to the cause, and they do not necessarily enjoy the same persuasive force. It is likely that the people would accept the claim that their agricultural and economic problems had their source in YHWH's anger. They would not necessarily have accepted the further assertion that the reason for YHWH's anger was the state of the temple. It is this latter claim that forms the crucial bridge from ill to remedy, and which very likely presented the greatest rhetorical problem for the prophet.

It was a well-established belief in the ANE that agricultural and other material problems were punishment sent from the divine realm. The

---

126. In fact, the self-interest for which the prophet reproaches the people will be the main weapon in his rhetorical arsenal.

prophets consistently rely on this belief to argue that Israel lies under YHWH's judgment, or is being warned to "turn back" to him lest they suffer such a fate. The specific reasons offered for the (threatened) punishment vary according to circumstance, but the basic belief that such things come from the hand of YHWH was taken for granted. The Yehudites did not need Haggai to inform them that their problems could be traced to divine anger. In fact, as Bedford and others have suggested, the chronic economic and other challenges faced by the community may have contributed to the sense that the judgment brought on Judah in 586 BCE continued unabated, which in turn led to the belief that "it is not the time for coming, the time for the house of YHWH to be rebuilt."[127]

It is one thing to acknowledge that the ill stems from YHWH's displeasure. It is another to agree on the reason YHWH is angry. The Yehudites could surmise explanations for divine judgment that had nothing to do with the temple, and could therefore dispute Haggai's claim that YHWH's anger could be traced specifically to the failure to rebuild. The evidence for judgment was apparent in the problems facing the community, but the reason for that judgment was not. There was no way for Haggai to prove beforehand that the desolate temple was the cause of the community's problems. He can only assert this. This poses a significant rhetorical challenge because the only basis for accepting an assertion about the divine will is trust that the individual proclaiming it is an authentic prophet. Without this trust Haggai has little hope of persuading the people to accept his proposal. His entire argument depends on the Yehudites' acceptance of his prophetic authority.

The problem of trust and authority is captured in the rhetorical concept of *ethos*, which refers to an audience's perception of the credibility of a speaker (or writer). Aristotle suggested that a rhetor's *ethos* "may almost be called the most effective means of persuasion he possesses."[128] It is not enough, he notes, to present a plausible argument.

---

127. See the discussion of this in chap. 3, pp. 111–24.
128. Aristotle, *Rhet.* 1.2.1, 1356a13. Studies in recent decades have tended to confirm this insight. Although the specific perceptions that lead an audience to conclude that a source is credible may vary across cultures, the necessity of a perception of source credibility appears to be universal. If audiences question the expertise or qualification of a source to address a topic, or if they doubt his trustworthiness ("the degree of confidence in the communicator's intent to communicate the

One must also inspire confidence in one's *ethos* by evincing good sense (φρόνησις), good moral character (ἀρετή), and goodwill (εὔνοια).[129] Good sense may also include competence or expertise.[130]

In the case of the prophet Haggai, expertise translates into audience perception of his authority to speak for YHWH.[131] The repeated claim that Haggai is a conduit for YHWH's speech indicates that this is a concern for Haggai or the composer of the HN. I have already noted the implications of the use of ביד in vv. 1 and 3. In addition, we find the messenger formula כה אמר יהוה צבאות in vv. 2, 5, and 7. The explanation of the ill in v. 9b is preceded by נאם יהוה צבאות. The entire speech in vv. 5–11 is presented as YHWH's, a conceit that is accentuated by the consistent use of the first person in vv. 8–11, the section of the passage that deals specifically with the cause of the problems and their implied remedy. Haggai, the audience is given to understand, is speaking the words of YHWH. What he says is therefore credible and trustworthy.

How likely is it that Haggai's audience would have readily accepted his claim to be speaking in the name of YHWH? We know nothing about this prophet apart from the HN and Ezra 5:1 and 6:14, which give us no additional information. We have no direct evidence to tell us how Haggai was perceived by his Yehudite audience, whether they accepted him as a prophet or not.[132] But we can say something about how indi-

---

assertions he considers most valid"), they tend to be very resistant to persuasion, no matter how "logical" the arguments presented (James B. Stiff and Paul A. Mongeau, *Persuasive Communication*, 2nd ed. [New York, NY: Guilford, 2003], 104–7; quotation: 105).

129. Aristotle, *Rhet.* 2.1.1, 1378a7–9.

130. Michael S. Kochin, *Five Chapters on Rhetoric: Character, Action, Things, Nothing, and Art* (University Park, PA: Pennsylvania State University Press, 2009), 34–35.

131. "Goodwill" can also be thought of as empathy or shared values or concerns. One issue that I do not explore here is the question of the historical audience's perception of how concerned Haggai really is with the problems of the Yehudites. Although he emphasizes these problems in vv. 5–11 he appears to do so primarily to motivate his audience to accept his call to build the temple. One easily gets the sense from the indignant tone of vv. 4 and 9a that what he places greater value on is the honor of YHWH. While this may be a shared value with his audience, they may not feel it as strongly as he does. Thus the audience may suspect that his emphasis on their problems is more strategic than "heartfelt." The fact that in this section he never actually promises that once work on the temple is begun the situation will improve, but strongly implies it, could also lead a careful listener to suspect the same.

132. Although the composer of the HN refers to Haggai as a prophet, it is not evident that everyone in Yehud at that time would have done the same. Thomas W. Overholt (*Channels of Prophecy: The Social Dynamics of Prophetic Activity* [Eugene, OR: Wipf & Stock, 1989], 23) notes that "prophet" is a social role and therefore those who claim to be prophets must be recognized as such to be effective. The private revelatory experiences of these individuals are the "primary source of their authority" and "[t]hese essentially private experiences from the theological justification for prophetic activity." But others beside the would-be prophet must acknowledge that these revelations are real:

viduals who claimed to be prophets of YHWH were perceived in Yehud around this time, and also on what bases the reliability of prophets was generally established.

In the ANE in general, and in Israel in particular, the authenticity of a prophet was not taken for granted, at least until that prophet had developed a reliable "track record." The trust a society was willing to place in prophetic figures varied. In Mari, for example, prophetic claims were entertained, but were usually subjected to confirmation through forms of divination such as extispicy, whereas in the Neo-Assyrian records we see no such concern for confirmation.[133] The biblical record also reflects the desire to confirm the reliability of prophets.[134] Individuals may suspend judgment on the reliability of putative prophets until they have shown themselves to be "men of God" through deeds (see, for example, Elijah and the widow of Zarephath: 1 Kgs 17:24). The story of the prophet Micaiah (1 Kgs 22:5–28) also reflects the anxiety attendant upon taking prophets at their word. This story ends with Micaiah's statement to the effect that his audience would only know after the fact whether he spoke the truth or not. Indeed, this appears to be the primary way of knowing whether an individual was a true prophet or not. The classic expression of this is Deuteronomy 18:21–22: וכי תאמר בלבבך איכה נגע את הדבר אשר

"[A] more public aspect of prophetic authority displays itself in various reactions to their message by the people to whom it is addressed. Because the act of prophecy must necessarily take place in a social context, these reactions are both inevitable and critically important. Prophets seek to move their audiences to action, and audiences may be said to attribute authority to prophets insofar as they acknowledge and are prepared to act upon the 'truth' of their message." Audiences do not always attribute authority to those who claim to speak for the divine.

133. In Mari, "the validity of the prophetic oracle was often controlled by extispicy" out a "need to check and exclude the possible misinterpretations and other faults resulting from the vulnerability of the intermediary and the often tangled process of communication" (Martti Nissinen, *Prophets and Prophecy in the Ancient Near East*, Writings from the Ancient World 12 [Atlanta, GA: Society of Biblical Literature, 2003], 16). Thus the frequent scribal inclusion at the end of prophetic reports that hair and the fringe of a prophet's garment are being sent along, for use in divination. For the social role of prophets in the Neo-Assyrian empire, see Martti Nissinen, "The Socioreligious Role of the Neo-Assyrian Prophets," in *Prophecy in Its Ancient Near Eastern Context*, ed. M. Nissinen, SBLSymS 13 (Atlanta, GA: Society of Biblical Literature, 2000), 89–114.

134. For discussion of confirmation of one "mantic act" by "undertaking a second mantic act of a different method" in the biblical literature, see Jeffrey L. Cooley, "The Story of Saul's Election (1 Samuel 9–10) in the Light of Mantic Practice in Ancient Iraq," *JBL* 130 (2011): 247–61 (citation: 249). As examples, Cooley notes Judges 6–7; 1 Samuel 9–10; and 1 Sam 23:2–4. See also Jack M. Sasson, "Oracle Inquiries in Judges," in *Birkat Shalom: Studies in the Bible, Ancient Near Eastern Literature, and Postbiblical Judaism Presented to Shalom M. Paul on the Occasion of His Seventieth Birthday*, ed. Chaim Cohen et al. (Winona Lake, IN: Eisenbrauns, 2008), 149–68 (cited by Cooley).

לא דברו יהוה אשר ידבר הנביא בשם יהוה ולא יהיה הדבר ולא יבוא הוא הדבר אשר לא דברו יהוה בזדון דברו הנביא לא תגור ממנו. Only if a prophet's word comes true can one be certain that he speaks in the name of YHWH. The corollary to this is that only after a prophet had established a record of speaking the truth would his word be accepted without need for verification. We have no indication in the biblical texts that Haggai had established such a record.

Although it had always been a concern, the problem of establishing prophetic authority may have been a particularly acute in the Persian period. Scholars have noted that, while prophecy as a social institution did not "dry up" in this period, evidence suggests that it suffered a crisis of authority as early as the time of Jeremiah. Blenkinsopp, for example, maintains that a significant problem, triggered by such public displays of prophetic disagreement as we see in Jeremiah, contributed to

> the inability of the prophets' audience to distinguish between conflicting claims and predictions, leading not only to a breakdown of prophetic authority in general but to widespread questioning of the religious premise on the basis of which the prophetic message claimed a hearing. The contribution of optimistic prophets [Jeremiah's opponents] to this crisis is easier to assess, since it could be argued, *post factum*, that they had deceived the people into fatally misreading the contemporary political situation.[135]

Blenkinsopp notes that the "impossibility of discriminating between true and false prophecy on the basis of objective and verifiable data" never went away.[136] As one example from the Persian period, we find three times in Zechariah the insistence that once certain things come to pass, "you will know that YHWH sent me," a claim one would expect to hear in response to doubts in this regard.[137] Wilson notes that although the earlier prophetic warnings of judgment had come to pass, the accompanying promises of restoration had not. Consequently,

---

135. Joseph Blenkinsopp, *A History of Prophecy in Israel*, rev. and enl. ed. (Louisville, KY: Westminster John Knox Press, 1996), 157.
136. Blenkinsopp, *History of Prophecy in Israel*, 158.
137. Zech 2:15; 4:9; 6:15. These verses were briefly discussed in chap. 3.

for the general population the delay in the fulfillment of the preexilic and exilic prophetic promises simply raised doubts about the authority of prophets themselves. . . . For this reason, people may have grown increasingly unwilling to acknowledge the authority of the prophets of any sort.[138]

This unwillingness apparently led to the cessation of traditional prophecy. Cross argued that social prophecy (as opposed to "literary prophecy") was coterminous with the Israelite monarchy, such that when the latter institution ceased, so did the former.[139] Overholt, drawing on the work of Petersen and Harrelson, has also argued that beginning in the Babylonian period Yahwistic prophecy experienced a crisis of authority and social viability that eventuated in the apparent cessation of classical prophecy.[140]

The repeated insistence on the divine origin of his message through the use of נאם יהוה צבאות, his inability to authenticate his claim to that effect, and the apparent decline in confidence in prophecy in the sixth century all suggest that the question of Haggai's *ethos* would have been a difficult obstacle to acceptance of his claim to speak for YHWH. His message about the temple would not have been automatically received as authentic, not without some sort of indication that he truly spoke for YHWH. Yet we hear of none. This is a rhetorical problem, because his prophetic *ethos* is the sole support for Haggai's assertion that the reason the Yehudites were suffering was the unreconstructed temple. We must question, therefore, how likely it was that Haggai's claim regarding the cause of the ill was accepted by all "this people."

Haggai has exhorted the Yehudites to consider the ill afflicting them, and asserted its cause is YHWH's anger that they have neglected his temple. The *remedy* for this ill obviously is to rebuild the temple immediately (v. 8). Yet even if his definition of the cause is accepted (at least by some), Haggai faces two potential objections to his proposal: that

---

138. Robert R. Wilson, *Prophecy and Society in Ancient Israel* (Philadelphia, PA: Fortress Press, 1980), 307. For a more recent argument that supports and develops this position, see Benjamin D. Sommer, "Did Prophecy Cease? Evaluating a Reevaluation," *JBL* 115 (1996): 31–47.

139. Cross, *Canaanite Myth*, 223. He notes in another place that "Haggai and Zechariah are the only apparent exceptions" to this (343). We have to take this to mean that the scribal circles who preserved their memories, not necessarily the "general public," considered them exceptions.

140. Overholt, *Channels of Prophecy*, 150–61.

building the temple will not address the cause of the ill, and that it is not feasible or possible to rebuild the temple at this time.

Haggai asserts clearly that if the Yehudites build the temple, YHWH will be pleased, accept it, and be glorified or honored by it. There is a subtlety at play here. Those who have accepted the claim regarding *cause* can be expected to accept rebuilding as the logical *remedy* for the *ill*. As I have noted several times, however, Haggai never explicitly states that once the temple is built the ill will be resolved, that the economic and agricultural problems will cease. It is obvious that he expects the audience to draw this conclusion once he has stated that the cause of the ill is linked to the deserted temple. It is logical to assume that those Yehudites who did accept Haggai's proposal to rebuild the temple expected that once the cause was addressed the ill would be resolved. As we will see in the next chapter, it appears the implied and expected recovery from the ill was not forthcoming even after work on the temple began.

Haggai does not address in this passage the second question related to remedy, its feasibility. Yet, as I argued in chapter 3, the temple project would certainly pose ideological and material challenges. Two significant objections would be that the community could not afford to build, equip, and maintain the temple, and that YHWH had not provided the requisite royal builder for this central shrine. Yehud was small and poor and, as Haggai himself takes pains to point out, struggling economically. Material resources would be difficult to obtain. Yehud was also without a king or royal figure to fulfill the traditional role of royal builder. Given these realities, it could be objected that it was not *possible* to build the temple. Furthermore, the apparent failure of YHWH to provide the necessary resources could be taken as evidence that Haggai was wrong to assert that the deity wished his house to be rebuilt. Although Haggai does not anticipate these potential objections in this passage, he does address them later in the HN, which suggests that they were in fact raised.

Finally, although advocates must generally anticipate objections that the advantages of a policy are outweighed by its disadvantageous consequences, this consideration is entirely absent in the HN. It unlikely that those Yehudites who accepted Haggai's claims about the cause and remedy of the ill would argue that, nevertheless, there were significant disadvantages to building. If YHWH wanted the temple built, the disadvantage of *not* building would undoubtedly outweigh any putative disadvantages to reconstruction. This stock topic would not have been a point of dispute for those who accepted Haggai's claims regarding the ill, its cause, and its remedy.

Rhetorical Analysis of Haggai 1:12–15a

The narrative that follows Haggai's first speech records the initial Yehudite response to his call to rebuild the temple. The notice is brief, but complex: the leaders and a portion of the community respond positively; others experience a fear of YHWH, who responds through the prophet with a word of assurance; YHWH then awakens the "spirits" of those who have responded positively and they begin to work on the temple. The unit ends by noting the date on which this work commences.

The narrative of vv. 12–15a is not "argumentative" in the narrow sense. There is no deliberation, presentation of evidence, or exhortation to act. Yet the narrator's depiction of the effects of the prophet's preaching serves three rhetorically significant functions. First, it indicates that the response to Haggai was divided. Some members accepted, at least provisionally, his claim to speak for YHWH, while others remained unsure or unconvinced. This division within the community forms the background for the material in the second chapter of the HN. The second rhetorical function is the continued insistence that Haggai is an authentic messenger of YHWH, and that YHWH does indeed want the temple to be rebuilt, despite whatever doubts may remain about this. The third rhetorical function of the unit is seen in the designation of those who obeyed the call to rebuild as "the remnant of the people," a term that defines this element of the community as the true, faithful continuation of YHWH's people. These last two functions in particular are argumentative, broadly speaking, and contribute to the persuasive aims of the HN as a whole.

The narrative can be divided into three units: the report of the obedience of the leaders and "the remnant of the people" (1:12a); the notice that "the people" feared YHWH, and YHWH's response

(1:12b–13); and the report that YHWH awakened the "spirits" of leaders and the "remnant" such that they came and worked on the temple.

Haggai 1:12a—The Positive Response

וישמע זרבבל בן שלתיאל ויהושע בן יהוצדק הכהן הגדול וכל שארית העם בקול
יהוה אלהיהם ועל דברי חגי הנביא כאשר שלחו יהוה אלהיהם

There are two rhetorically significant elements in this half-verse: the use of the term כל שארית העם, and the emphasis on the authority of the prophet.

Zerubbabel and Joshua, again named individually with patronymics, respond to the prophetic exhortation to rebuild. This result has never really been in doubt, given the narrator's original choice to have Haggai point out to the leaders the errant attitude of העם הזה. This implies that the leaders did not share "this people's" attitude toward reconstruction. It has been implied from the beginning that Zerubbabel and Joshua were not part of "this people."

Along with the leaders, a group referred to as כל שארית העם also listens to the voice of YHWH.[141] The significance of the phrase כל שארית העם has been understood in different ways in Haggai scholarship. A small minority of commentators has read the term שארית only in its most fundamental sense of "the rest," which would suggest that the point here is simply that the leaders "and all the rest of the people" obeyed YHWH.[142] The difficulty with this reading is that it fails to take into account the clear distinction that has been made by the composer between the leaders and "this people" in 1:1–4.[143] There the prophet is

---

141. Commentators have occasionally perceived a strongly Deuteronomistic flavor in the statement that the leaders and "listened to the voice of YHWH their god." Beuken, in particular, argued that this—in association with the motif of futility curses in the book—indicates that what is happening here is a covenant renewal (*Haggai*, 33). Others have also seen here at least allusions to the covenant: Petersen, *Haggai*, 60; Amsler, *Aggée*, 26; Kessler, *Haggai*, 142–43. Meyers and Meyers simply note that the narrator is using "standard biblical language" for obedience to YHWH (*Haggai*, 34). How one decides this question is not, in my judgment, rhetorically relevant.

142. Reventlow, *Haggai*, 17; Eric W. Heaton, "The Root שאר and the Doctrine of the Remnant," *JTS* NS 3 (1952): 31. Mitchell too reads it this way (*Haggai*, 53–54), but also recognizes that the term connotes "remnant" as well. But he ascribes no significance to its use here beyond a reflection that the population of Yehud is now smaller than in the past. It is a "remnant" in that numerical sense only.

143. For a discussion of the redaction of the book of Haggai, see chap. 2, pp. 39–63.

shown speaking to Joshua and Zerubbabel about the people as if they were separate from them, and addresses the people separately from the leaders.[144] It is therefore unlikely that 1:12 should read "Zerubbabel . . . Joshua . . . and all the rest of the people," as if the leaders were part of העם. As further analysis of the HN will suggest, the term העם functions in the narrative as more than a convenient term for the population of Yehud. Already we have seen that "this people" connotes for Haggai specifically those who have culpably delayed building the temple, rather than the Yehudite community as a whole. The rhetorical and exegetical implications of this will become apparent as analysis of the HN continues.

Rather than understand שארית simply as "the rest," most commentators have recognized the theological connotation of the term and translated the phrase כל שארית העם as "all the remnant of the people" or its equivalent.[145] The composer has chosen this word intentionally to characterize theologically or ideologically those who responded to the prophet. As "all the remnant of the people," this group shares in the concept of "the remnant" that had become by the early Persian period something of a "fixed expression" in scribal circles, denoting those who had survived YHWH's judgment.[146] But in the prophetic literature the term connotes more than just those who have been delivered, or the "divinely chosen survivors of disaster."[147] The remnant, especially

144. In v. 2, "this people" is referred to in the 3mp, whereas they are addressed in the 2mp in vv. 4–11. See the discussion above.

145. Wolff, *Haggai*, 28; Petersen, *Haggai*, 55; Verhoef, *Haggai*, 79; Kessler, *Haggai*, 106; Floyd, *Minor Prophets*, 270; Mitchell, *Haggai*, 54; Ackroyd, *Exile and Restoration*, 162. The German *Rest* and the French *reste* reflect both the idea of "the rest" and "the remnant." In this sense they mirror the ambiguity of the Hebrew. Reventlow is, to my knowledge, the only German-language scholar who does not see at least an allusion to the concept of "remnant" here. Meyers and Meyers translate the phrase as "all the rest of the people," suggesting that "it may be unwarranted to accept a specialized theological intent of the compiler." Just a few lines later, however, they state that the "use of a loaded word such as 'remnant,' which is clearly intentional, perhaps does reveal something about the point of view of Haggai's compiler" (*Haggai*, 34).

146. Verhoef, *Haggai*, 81. It is helpful to remember in this regard that all of the references to שארית in Haggai are found in the narrative framework, which is the work of the scribal circle responsible for the text. It is not necessarily a term that the historical prophet used or a term that his historical audience of Yehudites would have understood in any theological or ideological sense. Here we are concerned only with what the scribes would have understood by this term. Almost certainly they would have recognized levels of meaning in the term, one of which would be theological.

147. Ackroyd, *Exile and Restoration*, 163. For more extensive and detailed discussion of the concept of remnant, see also Roland de Vaux, "Le 'reste d'Israël' d'après les prophètes," *RB* 44 (1933): 526–39; Gerhard F. Hasel, *The Remnant: The History and Theology of the Remnant Idea from Genesis to Isaiah*, AUMSR 5 (Berrien Springs, MI: Andrews University Press, 1972); Werner E. Müller and Horst Diet-

in such texts as Zephaniah 3:12–13; Jeremiah 23:1–8; 31:7–14; 50:20; and Zechariah 8:6–12, constitutes a new community built by YHWH and characterized by greater fidelity, confidence, and trust in him.[148] As such, the remnant is the recipient of YHWH's blessing and carrier of the promises to Israel.

The composer has chosen to describe those who responded positively to the prophetic call as "all the remnant of the people." The phrase functions rhetorically, then, to characterize the respondents as the faithful remnant foreseen in the prophetic literature composed and maintained in scribal circles. As Ackroyd notes, in agreeing to build the temple, this group shows itself to be "the remnant," opening the way for divine blessing and to becoming the new community of YHWH.[149]

But who is it, exactly, who has responded in obedience and so now constitutes כל שארית העם? Most scholars have argued or assumed that it refers to the entire community addressed by Haggai. Verhoef claims that the leaders and the people "unanimously decide to resume work on the temple."[150] Meyers and Meyers take the verse to mean that the response of "all sectors" of the community was "immediate and unanimous."[151] Tollington asserts that the former opposition "collapsed very easily."[152] Almost all other commentators suggest or assume the same thing.[153] The basis for this judgment is rarely stated in the scholarship, and one gets the impression that the reason it goes unexplained so often is because it is a judgment that has come to be largely taken for

---

rich Preuß, *Die Vorstellung vom Rest im Alten Testament* (Neukirchen-Vluyn: Neukirchener Verlag, 1973).

148. Hasel, *Remnant*, 402–3. See also Heaton, "Doctrine of the Remnant," 39.

149. Ackroyd, *Exile and Restoration*, 162–63. He also notes that the same sort of language is found more fully developed in Zechariah, and suggests that it would be natural for Haggai's redactor to be reflecting the same ideas here. It is particularly striking that in Zech 8:6, 11, 13 we find the phrase שארית העם הזה used to describe the faithful community. For similar evaluations of the use of "remnant" here, see Amsler, *Aggée*, 26; Kessler, *Haggai*, 142; Floyd, *Minor Prophets*, 281.

150. Verhoef, *Haggai*, 80.

151. Meyers and Meyers, *Haggai*, 43–44. Although they acknowledge that there may have been some residual dissent, which (they claim) we do not hear about, nevertheless the prophet's argument was apparently so powerful and his message so completely accepted that there was "full compliance."

152. Tollington, *Tradition*, 54.

153. See, for example, Kessler, *Haggai*, 153; Petersen, *Haggai*, 55; Wolff, *Haggai*, 54; Ackroyd, *Exile and Restoration*, 167; Chary, *Aggée*, 21; Rudolph, *Haggai*, 37; Mitchell, *Haggai*, 54; Elliger, *Zwölf kleinen Propheten*, 88; Reventlow, *Haggai*, 16–17; Elie Assis, "To Build or Not to Build: A Dispute between Haggai and His People (Hag 1)," *ZAW* 119 (2007): 523.

granted. The few scholars who do explain their reasons for stating that the entire population responded positively point to the word כל before שארית. They also assume that the composer is using the phrase כל שארית העם and העם later in the same verse to mean the same population. In other words, כל שארית העם is just a different way the composer chooses to refer to the people in general, albeit one with a theological connotation.[154]

This widespread assumption that 1:12a indicates that the entire Yehudite population accepted Haggai's policy proposal to rebuild the temple does not withstand scrutiny. To begin, it is unlikely that Haggai's preaching could have had the effect these scholars ascribe to it. For the reasons I have outlined in the previous section regarding the prophet's *ethos*, as well as the strong, entrenched, and varied sources of potential opposition to the temple that existed in Yehud at the time (see chapter 3), it is historically implausible that Haggai's argument was persuasive enough to sway the entire community. If this is what the text is claiming, it can hardly be taken at face value, as so many commentators have done.[155]

But is it true that the composer is claiming that the entire community was persuaded by Haggai? The word "remnant," besides carrying a theological connotation, suggests that only a portion of "the people" responded in obedience. "The remnant of the people" is not the whole people, but only part of it, which means that the entire community did not "obey YHWH." Amsler and Floyd appear to be the only two commentators to make this observation. Amsler notes that only a subset of the people formed this "cercle des fidèles."[156] Floyd finds here an indication that the prophet had only "limited success."[157] Kessler rejects

---

154. See, for example, Kessler (*Haggai*, 141), who states that the composer "allowed the phrase 'remnant of the people' (v. 12, 14) to stand alongside the shorter designation 'the people', (cf. 1:2) referring to those who fear Yahweh and to whom Yahweh speaks in vv. 12b and 13. *Thus the redactor saw the two designations as coextensive, and inclusive of the entire community*" (emphasis added). Kessler's logic here seems to be that because the terms (שארית העם and העם) "stand alongside" each other they must refer to the same group of people. But this is an assumption only.

155. Kessler (*Haggai*, 141n270) acknowledges that there may be some discrepancy between what he takes to be the textual claim of full obedience and the historical reality, although he does not appear to draw any implications for reading the text from this possibility. He merely notes that "whatever the historical realities may have been, this is how the reader is meant to perceive the situation." (See also "Building," 250–53.) As I will argue below, I think he is wrong about the intended reader perception.

156. Amsler, *Aggée*, 26.

Floyd's reading, however, claiming that the word כל indicates that the remnant is the whole community.[158] But in the phrase כל שארית העם, "all" modifies שארית, not העם. It is "all the remnant," not "all the people," that obeys YHWH. Unless we assume (*contra* Kessler) that שארית means "the rest of the people," the phrase can only mean that a portion of the people responded to the prophet.[159]

Nevertheless, it was the entire portion. The presence of כל here conveys the sense that *all* of the remnant obeyed. This is a significant point: the remnant—YHWH's new, faithful community—is coextensive with those who concur in the need to rebuild and support the project. There is no member of the remnant that is not part of this group because for the composer, the "remnant" is defined by this act of obedience. This remnant is able to respond to Haggai's call because they recognize that YHWH has sent him: "all the remnant of the people obeyed the voice of YHWH their God, that is to say, the words of Haggai the prophet, because YHWH their God had sent him." This final statement is meant not only to strengthen the *ethos* of the prophet but also to indicate that *the remnant* recognized Haggai as an authentic prophet. It is because of this that they are able to respond in obedience and thus show themselves to be the true remnant.[160]

---

157. Floyd, *Minor Prophets*, 269. He claims later, though, that "there was no opposition from those who still did not support the project" (277). This may be true to the extent that no Yehudites actively opposed, or tried to stop the building project (but we do not know this did not happen). But as I will show here and the next chapter the text itself gives evidence of ongoing concerns and opposition, or at least resistance. Despite what all commentators appear to assume, the controversy was *not* immediately and completely resolved in Haggai's favor.

158. Kessler, *Haggai*, 141n270. In assessing Floyd's claim, he objects the idea that the difference in language between 1:12a and 1:12b is meaningful: "this kind of distinction is too subtle, and the difference between the two groups [the "remnant" and "the people"] overdrawn." Yet in another place he notes, in speaking about the significance of the narrator's choice of the term "remnant," that "[m]inor variations may be highly significant in narrative" (142).

159. A minority of scholars have supposed that the term is meant to refer specifically to the גולה, as opposed to the locals. It is the returnees only, then, who are involved in the building project. See, for example, Galling, *Studien*, 75, 136; Wolff, *Haggai*, 52; Chary, *Aggée*, 21. This argument assumes that the term שארית connotes the same thing it does in Ezra 3:8; 4:1; 6:16, an *assumption* that, as many have pointed out, is unjustified.

160. Rex Mason (*Preaching the Tradition: Homily and Hermeneutics after the Exile* [Cambridge: Cambridge University Press, 1990], 192), who assumes along with almost everyone else that that "this people" in 1:1 and "the remnant" in 1:12 refer to the same group, suggests that the reason they are only now called "the remnant" is because it is only by obedience that they have shown themselves to be "the remnant." Similarly, Beuken (*Haggai*, 30) sees the difference in language only as a reflection of the redactor's tone or attitude. Whereas before they were "this people," now those same people are "the remnant." I agree with both Mason and Beuken that the language reflects the redactor's evaluation of the respective groups. I disagree that both groups are identical otherwise.

Haggai 1:12b–13—The Negative Response

After noting that the leaders and the remnant of the people obeyed YHWH and his prophet, the composer immediately informs us that "the people" were afraid of YHWH, who responds with words of assurance:

וייראו העם מפני יהוה ויאמר חגי מלאך יהוה במלאכות יהוה לעם לאמר אני אתכם נאם יהוה

Commentators have struggled to understand the relationship between 1:12a and 1:12b, and therefore the meaning of the phrase וייראו העם מפני יהוה. As I noted above, scholars have generally assumed that "the people" in v. 12b are the same as "the remnant of the people" (as well, perhaps, as their leaders) in v. 12a, and have tried to reconcile the claim that they were obedient yet afraid. Harmony is most easily achieved when the fear is understood as a "reverential awe" or "respect for the authority of YHWH."[161] This expedient is not satisfying, however, because the phrase ירא מן primarily denotes fright or alarm in the face of an actual or potential threat.[162] The verb with מפני is always used in that sense.[163] Accordingly, most have understood the phrase to mean that העם are *afraid of YHWH*. And because they assume that העם is the same as שארית העם, they are left wondering why the obedient remnant of the people should be afraid of YHWH, whom we are told they have just obeyed.

Some scholars have supposed that the people expect punishment for their disobedience, and they are afraid of YHWH because of that.[164] This reading makes little sense because in his speech Haggai had made

They have failed to take into account that the claim is not that "the remnant" obeyed YHWH, but that "the remnant of the people" did so.

161. Mitchell, *Haggai*, 54, and Amsler, *Aggée*, 26, respectively. Chary's claim (*Aggée*, 21) that they are experiencing "un réveil de la foi" is not quite the same, but equally implausible in here.

162. Louis Derousseaux describes it as "la peur de Dieu" (*La crainte de Dieu dans l'Ancien Testament*, LD 63 [Paris: Cerf, 1970], 73, 296). Joachim Becker describes it as "sich furchten vor" (*Gottesfurcht im Alten Testament*, AnBib 25 [Rome: Pontifical Biblical Institute, 1965], 59, 81). See also Fuhs, "ירא," *TDOT*, 6.295.

163. See, for example, Exod 9:30; 1 Sam 7:7; 18:29; 21:13; 1 Kgs 1:50; 2 Kgs 19:6; 25:26; Isa 37:6; Jer 41:18; 42:11; Neh 4:8.

164. Becker, *Gottesfurcht*, 207–8; Ackroyd, "Studies in the Book of Haggai," 168; Reventlow, *Haggai*, 16; Rudolph, *Haggai*, 37.

clear that the current suffering of the Yehudites was chastisement or punishment for not rebuilding the temple. Now that they have obeyed the call to rebuild, why would they expect further punishment? Other commentators have taken וייראו העם מפני יהוה to mean that the people have realized, to their horror, that they have been disobedient all along and now they are feeling "dread and anguish" in recognition of this.[165] But this is not the same as being "afraid of YHWH," a phrase that suggests fear of a potential or actual threat. What are they expecting YHWH to do to them? Still others have seen here a "paralysis" or a "paralyzing angst." Assis suggests that the positive response in v. 12a is "only apparent." In fact, the people do not know how to respond to Haggai's message. They remain worried that YHWH has rejected them, and therefore that they should not build the temple. It is only after the oracle of assurance in the next verse that they are no longer afraid.[166] The suggestion that "the people" are afraid to respond has some merit, as I will argue further below, but it does not cohere with the clear statement that they have responded in obedience in v. 12a. Unless we make the doubtful assumption that the obedience indicated here should be understood as merely psychological, that the people "wanted to obey" but were unable to fully commit, Assis's solution makes little sense. None of these attempts to understand why the obedient remnant of the people should nevertheless be afraid of YHWH is convincing.

A more compelling reading lies at hand if we take seriously the composer's choice of words. In v. 12a, he has referred to those who obeyed (along with the leaders) as כל שארית העם. The words are deliberately chosen to convey that only a portion of the people responded, and these are referred to as "the remnant." This leaves those who did not respond, those who continued to resist the prophetic call. In 1:2 those who opposed rebuilding were called "this people." I suggest that the composer has retained this term to refer to those who remain resistant or opposed, and it is this group only who is afraid of YHWH. Verse 12, then, records two disparate responses to Haggai's argument: that of the leaders and the "remnant" of the people (who obeyed), and that of the people (who did not).[167] As we will see in the analysis of 2:10–14, the

---

165. Elliger, *Zwölf kleinen Propheten*, 86–88; Verhoef, *Haggai*, 83; Beuken, *Haggai*, 206.
166. Assis, "To Build," 522–26.
167. The syntax of the verse supports reading 12a and 12b as antithetical (". . . but the people"). While

HN will again use the language of "this people" for those who remain "disobedient." The language is consistent across the entire text and coheres with a carefully developed rhetorical strategy.

It is "the people" who have not accepted the prophet's call, and who are afraid of YHWH. This fear is the reason for their failure to respond to Haggai; perhaps they do not believe that "YHWH their God had sent him." Instead, they are afraid of what YHWH will do if they accept the call of a doubtful prophet and build a temple against YHWH's will. Fear of rebuilding temples without the permission of the gods is a consistent theme in ANE accounts of temple building. Ellis notes, for example, how fearful Nabonidus was in this regard: "I feared their august command, I became troubled, I was worried and my face showed signs of anxiety."[168] Centuries earlier, Gudea of Lagash had been initially reluctant to rebuild the temple of the god Ningirsu out of fear that he might have misunderstood the divine messages he had received. He was afraid to build lest he anger the god.[169] It is entirely consistent with what we know of ancient concepts of temples and gods that there would be a segment of the population of Yehud that, not being sure of Haggai's prophetic credentials, was afraid of YHWH and what he would do if they built his temple against his wishes.

It is to "the people" who are afraid to build, then, and not to the entire population or to the "remnant," that the oracle in v. 13 is directed. The text indicates that the message of YHWH (מלאכות יהוה) is specifically לעם, "to the people" or, better, "for the people." This message is a traditional "priestly" *Heilsorakel*, intended to assure those who are afraid that YHWH is with them.[170] In this case, the fear is that YHWH will be angry with them for rebuilding the temple without his

---

it is true that typically the *wayyiqtol* form indicates temporal or logical succession, at times the context makes it clear that two situations are being contrasted. In Gen 32:31; Judg 1:35; 2 Sam 3:8; Job 32:3, contrasting notions are connected with the *wayyiqtol* form of a verb. See *IBHS* 33.2.1d; Joüon §172f; GKC §111d. Gesenius notes that the "imperfect consecutive sometimes has such a merely *external* connexion with an immediately preceding perfect, that in reality it represents an antithesis to it, e.g. Gen 32:31 *and (yet) my life is preserved*" (emphasis in original).

168. Ellis, *Foundation Deposits*, 7. The citation here is from Beaulieu, "The Sippar Cylinder of Nabonidus," *COS* 2.123: 311. See also Dalley, "Temple Building," 246; Frankfort, *Kingship and the Gods*, 269.

169. Frankfort, *Kingship and the Gods*, 255–56. See Averbeck, "Gudea Cylinder A," *COS* 2.155: 419–20.

170. See, for example, Joachim Begrich, "Das priesterliche Heilsorakel," *ZAW* 52 (1934): 81–92; Horst D. Preuss, ". . . ich will mit dir sein!," *ZAW* 80 (1968): 139–73; Fuhs, "ירא," *TDOT*, 6.305. Most commentators assume this is the intent of the oracle here: Horst, *Zwölf kleinen Propheten*, 206; Verhoef, *Haggai*, 83–85; Meyers and Meyers, *Haggai*, 35; Mitchell, *Haggai*, 54–55; Amsler, *Aggée*, 26–27; Petersen, *Haggai*, 57–58; Kessler, *Haggai*, 148.

permission, a fear that stems perhaps from the conviction that YHWH has not yet decided to return to Yehud and the community. The oracle is intended to quell their doubts that the temple project is divinely sanctioned.[171] By affirming for those who are afraid to build because they fear the divine response that YHWH is indeed "with them," Haggai signals that it is appropriate to build. YHWH would not be with them if he opposed the building project.

The oracle is couched in the strongest terms as an authentic message of YHWH, as if to assure "the people" that Haggai truly does speak for him.[172] It is only here that Haggai is referred to as מלאך יהוה, who speaks to the people מלאכות יהוה, a message of YHWH. Haggai is a messenger of YHWH who speaks a message of YHWH. The choice of מלאך emphasizes more than the term נביא the divine origin of the message. The term, which is only rarely used for prophets (Isa 44:26; Ezek 30:9; 2 Chr 36:15–16; possibly Mal 1:1) is associated with messengers sent from human or divine courts.[173] The rhetorical intention here is to underline the authority of Haggai.[174] The close connection between the prophetic identity as messenger and the message itself is signaled by the use of nearly identical words: מלאך יהוה במלאכות יהוה. The word מלאכות does not occur elsewhere and may be a neologism. In any case, the close affinity between מלאכות, מלאך, and מלאכה, the word for work on the temple in the next verse, suggests the three words were chosen to express the close relationship between the prophet, his message, and work on the temple.[175] Finally, the oracle is concluded with the second oracle formula, נאם יהוה. Of course, we may wonder how convincing this would be for those who already were inclined to disbelieve Haggai's claim to be an authentic spokesman for YHWH. The text does not record that they were dissuaded from their fear by this *Heilsorakel*.

---

171. Elie Assis says as much, although he believes that "the people" and "the remnant of the people" refer to the same group ("A Disputed Temple [Haggai 2, 1–9]," *ZAW* 120 [2008]: 589).

172. Assis ("To Build," 526) notes that this is related to doubts about authenticity.

173. Freedman-Willoughby, "מלאך," *TDOT*, 8.309, 315–16.

174. Meyers and Meyers, *Haggai*, 44; Verhoef, *Haggai*, 84; Kessler, *Haggai*, 148; Petersen, *Haggai*, 56; Horst, *Zwölf kleinen Propheten*, 206.

175. Meyers and Meyers propose the choice of מלאכות may have been influenced by its similarity to מלאכה (*Haggai*, 35), but I am indebted to David S. Vanderhooft for the suggestions that מלאכות may be a neologism invented by the prophet and that all three words work together rhetorically.

Haggai 1:14–15a—YHWH Rouses the Obedient to Work

Despite the failure of some Yehudites to respond positively to Haggai's policy initiative, others did, and so this unit ends with the notice that, on the twenty-fourth day of the sixth month, Zerubbabel, Joshua, and all the remnant of the people came and began to work on the temple:

ויער יהוה את רוח זרבבל בן שלתיאל פחת יהודה ואת רוח יהושע בן יהוצדק הכהן הגדול ואת רוח כל שארית העם ויבאו ויעשו מלאכה בבית יהוה צבאות אלהיהם ביום עשרים וארבעה לחדש בששי

The composer turns his attention back to those who responded to the prophetic call. Once again the leaders are listed individually along with the remnant of the people. The רוח of each one (the remnant being conceived as a single entity) is "stirred" or "aroused" by YHWH, causing them to come and "do work" on the house of YHWH of hosts, their God. The idiom of "awakening the spirit" is used elsewhere of individuals who become instruments of YHWH's will: the Medes and the Persians (Jer 51:11), Tiglath-pileser III (called "Pul" in 2 Chr 5:26), and Cyrus (Ezra 1:1, 5; 2 Chr 36:22). The רוח represents the "disposition" or "capacité de décision," which is then moved to do something YHWH desires.[176] Often the verb עור presupposes a condition of inactivity which is then brought to an end.[177] This is clearly the case here. The "dispositions" or wills of the leaders and the remnant of the people are being "awakened" from a period of inactivity to one of "doing work" on the house of YHWH. The repetition of רוח with each "individual" emphasizes that all three were impelled by YHWH to work, and that they did participate in the project.

The rhetorical function of this verse is to emphasize, once again, that work done on the temple was at the instigation and under the impulsion of YHWH. If there is any doubt that YHWH desired the temple to be rebuilt, the reader is told that the actual work began under the impetus of YHWH. Not only did YHWH send his messenger Haggai to persuade the people to build the temple, he also "awakened" the dis-

---

176. See Charles A. Briggs, "The Use of רוח in the Old Testament," *JBL* 19 (1900): 136; Daniel Lys, *"Rûach"*: *Le souffle dans l'Ancien Testament*, EHPR 56 (Paris: Presses Universitaire de France, 1962), 230–31.

177. Schreiner, "עיר," *TDOT*, 10.570. See, for example, Judg 5:12; Isa 51:9; Ezek 23:22; Zech 13:7; Ps 7:7.

positions of the leader and the remnant of the people to get the project started.

The unit ends with the notice that this happened on the twenty-fourth day of the same month that Haggai offered his "policy proposal." It was on this day that YHWH moved the leaders and the remnant to begin work. The date formula, along with the triple emphasis on YHWH's awakening of the רוחות of the obedient, marks the date as significant.

Conclusions

Haggai 1:12–15a functions rhetorically in three ways: (1) it provides a narrative conclusion to the prophet's first speech, indicating that his policy proposal had a mixed response; (2) it continues to argue for Haggai's prophetic authenticity; and (3) it creates a link between the theological concept of "the remnant" and the building of the temple.

Haggai's initial argument in favor of a "policy reversal" was accepted only by some members of the community. There is no indication whether or not "the remnant of the people," along with the leaders, constituted the majority of Yehudites, but the number and influence of those who did respond positively was apparently enough get the project off the ground. The HN suggests that other members of the community, designated by the narrator as "the people," remained unconvinced of Haggai's claim to speak for YHWH, and were therefore afraid to offend the deity by building his temple against his wishes.[178] This

---

178. This suggestion that the Yehudite community was divided over the question of the temple is not new, although it has had little influence on interpretation of Haggai. Hanson, for example, argued that there was a "bitter struggle" in the early Persian period between a "hierocratic" or Zadokite party that supported the temple and a prophetic "visionary" party that rejected it. Both Haggai and Zechariah brought prophetic legitimation to the "hierocratic temple program" by bringing an "infusion of the prophetic spirit" into the hierocratic cause (*Dawn of Apocalyptic*, 245). Morton Smith posited "at least three parties in Jerusalem: a local party, and two important groups of former exiles" (*Palestinian Parties and Politics That Shaped the Old Testament* [New York, NY: Columbia University Press, 1971], 80–81). The former exiles, including Haggai, supported the temple against the locals, who did not. Hanson's thesis that Yehud was divided between hierocrats and visionaries has been criticized, but his contention that the temple was contentious and a source of division is sound. Smith's suggestion that Haggai was a former exile cannot be supported by the evidence, nor can it be assumed that all who returned were in favor of rebuilding in 520 BCE or that the locals uniformly opposed it. My argument is that the community was divided over whether or not to rebuild the temple and that there was a variety of reasons for this, but the evidence of Haggai does not allow one to determine if this resulted in "parties" or what the exact make-up of such parties would have been.

textual indication of a divided response accords well with what probably was the historical reality. It is implausible that the brief preaching of an individual, apparently with no previously recognized prophetic "credentials," would be sufficient to persuade the entire population of Yehud to rebuild the temple. Rather than try to whitewash or ignore this reality, the text acknowledges it. Contrary to the assumptions of most commentators, the policy dispute that began the HN is not resolved by the end of the first chapter. This is an important observation, as the dispute informs the rest of the narrative, recognition of which can illumine otherwise obscure or confusing aspects of the second chapter of Haggai.[179] This narrative therefore sets the stage for the next chapter, in which Haggai will continue to address challenges to the reconstruction project.

The *ethos* of the prophet remains an ongoing rhetorical concern. The divided response presumes that not everyone accepted that Haggai spoke for YHWH. Thus we continue to see textual assertions that he is an authentic spokesperson for the deity. Indeed, the composer draws on new language to emphasize this, particularly when the attention is focused on the people who remain afraid to build. In v. 13 the prophet is referred to specifically as מלאך יהוה, who delivers a מלאכות יהוה לעם. The lexical change serves to underscore that Haggai has been sent by YHWH, as the remnant of the people and the leaders have already recognized. He brings a special message for those who remain afraid. This brief *Heilsorakel* is concluded with the oracle formula. This formula, which we have already seen once in 1:9, will become increasingly prominent in the rest of the HN, where it occurs ten more times, a statistic which itself may attest to the difficulty the prophet and his editors had in getting his credentials accepted by the populace.[180] In addition, the narrator insists that it was YHWH who roused the workers to their task, but only after they had accepted Haggai "because

---

179. Kessler, then, is correct to state that "[t]he content of this section is utterly essential to the rest of the book." He goes on to explain, however, that this is so "since all of what follows presupposes a restored relationship between Yahweh and his people, and a building whose reconstruction is in process" (*Haggai*, 153). Certainly the building project does begin, but not everyone has subscribed to it. There is a portion of the population that, from the narrator's perspective, does *not* enjoy "a restored relationship" with YHWH. The rest of the HN presupposes this division and comments on it.

180. Hag 2:4 (3x), 8, 9, 14, 17, 23 (3x). See n. 117 for statistics about the frequency of this formula in Haggai relative to other prophetic books.

YHWH their God had sent him." This brief narrative, then, is filled with assertions regarding the authenticity of Haggai as YHWH's prophet and of the divine origin of his efforts to get the temple built.

Finally, the narrative creates a link, not previously found in the prophetic literature, between the building of the temple and notion of the "remnant" of his people that YHWH will form into a new, more faithful community. By referring to those who "obeyed YHWH" as "all the remnant of the people," the narrator essentially defines this new community precisely and exclusively as those who participate in the project. The argumentative function of this definition is *epideictic*.

One of Aristotle's three genres of oratory (along with deliberative and forensic), epideictic rhetoric, as it is understood today, is argumentative insofar as it defines events, persons, actions, etc., in terms of communal values; aims to strengthen adherence to those values; and shapes the community that holds those values by defining them against those who do not. The narrator's use of the term "remnant" functions in all three ways.

By associating those who build the temple with the concept of "remnant," the composer defines the act of reconstruction in terms not only of obedience to YHWH but also of participation in the promised future relationship with him.[181] The decision to participate in the temple project, according to the composer of the HN, is a decision to join YHWH's community, the faithful remnant who will carry forward the future of Israel. If one values membership in that community, then one must help rebuild the temple. This is all implied in the use of the phrase "all the remnant of the people" for those who, along with the leaders, listen to Haggai, YHWH's prophet.

This definition of the builders as the remnant and the remnant as the builders is closely related to another function of epideictic rhetoric: it "strengthens the disposition toward action by increasing adherence to the values it lauds."[182] In this case, the value being praised is obedience to YHWH. This obedience, specifically obedience to the call to rebuild the temple, is what defines the new community. As we will see,

---

181. The definitional function of epideictic, according to Celeste M. Condit, allows it "to explain a social world" by explaining a "troubling issue in terms of the audience's key values and beliefs" ("The Functions of Epideictic: The Boston Massacre Orations as Exemplar," *CommQ* 33 [1985], 288).

182. Perelman and Obrechts-Tyteca, *New Rhetoric*, 50.

even those who initially accepted the prophetic call to build appear to have later expressed concerns about its validity. There was thus a need to "strengthen the disposition toward action," and one way to do this was by insisting that only obedience to the prophetic call allows one to *remain* a member of the remnant. The concept of the remnant essentially argues for adherence to the value of obedience, in particular to the call to build the temple.

Epideictic also serves to shape communities by helping members define themselves in contrast to others. Those who adhere to certain values, extolled by the rhetor, are comfortably within the group, while those who do not hold those values are outside.[183] The composer of Haggai has defined the true community of YHWH—the remnant—in terms of obedience to the call to build the temple. Those that do so are "in," those that do not are "out." Thus to decide not to build is to effectively place oneself outside the community. This epideictic function will be operative again in 2:10–14, where the prophet will assert that those who do not participate in the temple project are not members of YHWH's new people.

This brief narrative unit thus proves to be a rhetorically rich and significant conclusion to the first part of the HN, as well as providing an important context for second part, which we will examine in the next chapter.

---

183. "Definitions of community are often advanced by contrast with 'others' outside the community. . . . In giving a speaker the right to shape the definition of the community, the audience gives the speaker the right to select certain values, stories, and persons from the shared heritage and to promote them over others" (Condit, "Functions of Epideictic," 289). This is precisely what the narrator of Haggai is doing here by defining obedience to the call to rebuild in terms of the remnant, and the remnant in terms of obedience to the call to rebuild.

5

Rhetorical Analysis of Haggai 2

After presenting Haggai's initial argument in favor of temple reconstruction and the divided response to it, the HN continues with three oracles (1:15b–2:9; 2:10–19; 2:20–23), each of which addresses actual or potential objections to the project. The ongoing agricultural problems in Yehud, which the temple rebuilding was intended to address, have now called into question the legitimacy and therefore efficacy of Haggai's proposal.

Rhetorical Analysis of Haggai 1:15b–2:9

Haggai 1:15b–2:2—Setting of Oracle

This unit begins with a *Wortereignisformel* dated to the twenty-first day of the seventh month (Tishri). This is approximately seven weeks since the first reported speech to the people (1:1) and less than four weeks since work began, according to the date in 1:15a. It is unlikely that much could have been accomplished in the intervening weeks, but by this time the community would have had the opportunity to assess the amount and quality of resources available for the project.

YHWH commands the prophet to deliver a message to Zerubbabel and Joshua—both again named with patronymics and offices—and to שארית העם. Haggai is commanded, then, to speak to those who have heeded his call to rebuild the temple, not to the Yehudite community as a whole.[1] Verses 3–9 comprise a single message.

This message relates to the policy dispute about the temple by addressing the stock issue of *remedy*. For a policy to be accepted as a remedy for an acknowledged ill, its proponent must counter any doubts about the *possibility of its implementation* or its *effectiveness in relieving the ill* if implemented.[2] The present oracle attends to both of these concerns: it asserts that despite the meager resources currently available to the community the temple project is feasible and that once his house is completed YHWH will bring the expected well-being and prosperity (שלום) to Yehud (v. 9). The position of this argument in the HN suggests that doubts about the feasibility and efficaciousness of the temple reconstruction arose early—or persisted—even among those who initially accepted the call to rebuild. Left unaddressed, such concerns would imperil the project, causing the Yehudites to abandon it at this early stage.

Haggai's response comprises two main elements, a concession regarding the prospects of the temple (v. 3) and a counterargument (vv. 4–9). The counterargument first affirms the validity of the project (v. 4), then addresses the question of the "glory" (כבוד) of the temple (vv. 5–9a), and concludes with a brief statement promising the expected benefits of the temple reconstruction (v. 9b).

Haggai 2:3—Concession of Poor Prospects for Temple

Haggai begins by asking if there are any in his audience who saw the temple in its former glory and, if so, how they see it now: מי בכם הנשאר אשר ראה את הבית הזה בכבודו הראשון ומה ראים אתו עתה. Commentators regularly note that in 520 BCE there can have been only a handful of such eyewitnesses, since the temple had been destroyed sixty-six years earlier. They nevertheless assume that such individuals did exist and that they were actually being addressed by the prophet.[3] In fact there

---

1. See my argument in chap. 4, pp. 189–93, that the phrase שארית העם refers to a subset of the Yehudite community.
2. See chap. 4, pp. 139–43, for the discussion of stock issues.

need not have been any people in his audience from before (הנשאר). Haggai's question about the state of the temple is rhetorical. He verbally conjures up הנשאר to direct his entire audience to consider the present state of the temple from the perspective of its "former glory," to which these real or imagined elders can stand as witnesses.[4] In other words, those who have been working on the temple are deliberately led to regard its present condition and its future possibilities not with reference to the state in which they found it four weeks earlier, but according to the reputed splendor of its predecessor.[5]

This comparison will not invite a favorable assessment. Rather than wait for his audience to draw the obvious conclusion that there is something lacking in the new temple, Haggai asserts it emphatically in the form of a rhetorical question: הלוא כמהו כאין בעיניכם.[6] The prophet is careful to frame this assessment in terms of the audience's perception: the temple in its present state, as well as its future prospects, must look "like nothing" *in the eyes of the witnesses.* Haggai does not explicitly agree with this presumed evaluation or affirm it as an objective fact. Nevertheless, he not only acknowledges possible disappointment with the new "house," he gives voice to it. Why this concession from such an ardent proponent of the project?

Commentators have tended to assume that Haggai's statement reflects the expressed attitude of his audience, or at least of הנשאר who actually saw the former temple. Petersen, for example, posits that the Yehudites considered the temple "a pale copy," and now that work

3. See, for example, Sara Japhet, "People and Land in the Restoration Period," in *Das Land Israel in biblischer Zeit: Jerusalem-Symposium 1981 der Hebräischen Universität und der Georg-August-Universität,* ed. Georg Strecker, GTA 25 (Göttingen: Vandenhoeck & Ruprecht, 1983), 109; Meyers and Meyers, *Haggai,* 71; Wolff, *Haggai,* 77; Verhoef, *Haggai,* 95–96; Mitchell, *Haggai,* 59.

4. Kessler, who characterizes this group as "dramatis personae only," suggests that the point of calling on them is to "heighten the affective impact" by allowing the entire audience to view the present temple through their eyes (*Haggai,* 164–65). Kessler does not explore what the point of this affective heightening might be, or why Haggai would want to call attention to the perceived deficiencies of the new "house" in the first place.

5. The "glory" (כבוד) of the temple here and in vv. 7 and 9 refers to the splendid or magnificent appearance of the temple, as well as to the quality of the materials used to build, decorate, and furnish it. In particular, the term refers to the "wealthy" appearance of the temple that, as we will see, can be seen in its decoration with gold and silver. For the use of כבוד to denote wealth or gold and silver, see, for example, Gen 31:1; 1 Kgs 3:13; Isa 10:3; 61:6; Nah 2:10.

6. Where they occur elsewhere, questions that begin with הלוא usually expect an affirmative response (Judg 5:30; Jer 26:19; 38:15; Amos 5:20; Jonah 4:2). As such, they function as exclamations or emphatic affirmations, rather than as questions. See Gordis, "Rhetorical Use," 212; GKC §150c; Brongers, "Remarks," 181–85; Wolff notes this (*Haggai,* 77).

was "well under way" the new building was not good enough. For this reconstruction of the people's perspective, Petersen moves beyond Haggai and draws on Ezra 3:12, in which the elders who had seen the former temple weep loudly—presumably in sorrow—when they see the foundation being laid for the new house.[7] Petersen ascribes historical value to the Ezra verse, claiming that it "preserves" the elders' reaction, but given the well-known problems assessing the historical reliability of Ezra 1–6, this is a doubtful claim.[8] Without depending on Ezra, others have also presumed that Haggai's words indicate that the people had developed a "derisory attitude" toward the temple and regarded it with "deep feelings of contempt."[9] In light of the exhortation in the following verse to "be strong" and keep working, some have suggested that the problem was one of morale: once the work commenced, the difficulty of the labor required to complete the project quickly dawned on the people, who become discouraged and demoralized.[10] Whether the purported problem is understood as derision or discouragement, or both, it is assumed by commentators that this was in fact the attitude of Haggai's historical audience, to which the prophet was obliged to respond.

The text offers no evidence that the prophet is responding to actual, voiced concerns. Demurrals are not cited, as in 1:2, and then rebutted. Instead, through his rhetorical questions, which are really statements, the prophet presents the current state of the temple and its meager prospects as a problem whose existence *the audience* must acknowledge: "Surely it's like nothing in your eyes!"[11] This is a strategic move, or a way of getting "out in front of the story." The statement that the temple must surely look "like nothing in your eyes" is a concession that anticipates—but does not state—potential arguments against con-

---

7. Petersen, *Haggai*, 63–64. While verb בכה may denote weeping from joy or some other emotion, is usually refers to weeping from grief or sorrow (Hamp, "בכה," *TDOT* 2.116–20). This is the sense in which most commentators, with Petersen, take it in Ezra 3:12.

8. A number of scholars suggest that Ezra 3:12–13 is actually based on Hag 2:3, a plausible position given the acknowledged historical problems associated with the Ezra 1–6. See, for example, Rudolph, *Esra*, 32; Jacob M. Myers, *Ezra, Nehemiah*, AB 14 (Garden City, NY: Doubleday, 1965), 29; Williamson, *Ezra*, 48; Blenkinsopp, *Ezra-Nehemiah*, 101.

9. Assis, "Disputed Temple," 584.

10. Wolff, *Haggai*, 76; Verhoef, *Haggai*, 97.

11. For discussion of the translation of this sentence as a statement rather than a question, see chap. 2, n. 200.

tinued work on the temple in order to defuse them by offering a counterargument.[12]

Concession is a pragmatic rhetorical strategy that allows the rhetor to accept a premise without also accepting its presumed consequences, which would be damaging to his argument.[13] Haggai does not deny that the present temple could compare unfavorably to real or imagined memories of the former temple. He concedes that possibility (without explicitly adopting it) because there is little he can do about it. It is pointless to pretend that the quality and quantity of construction materials, and the size and skill of the workforce, are equal to those thought to have been available to Solomon. The undeniable reality that the community lacks everything necessary to build a "glorious" temple is more than just a potential source of discouragement, as commentators generally suggest. The poor prospects for the temple actually pose a danger to Haggai's policy because they may lead the Yehudites to conclude that YHWH does not want the temple built after all, or that it is not appropriate to build a temple that will not adequately "glorify" YHWH. Haggai concedes that the Yehudites do not possess materials and labor to build a splendid temple, but only in order to deny such potentially damaging implications.[14]

The lack of quality materials with which to build and furnish the temple may lead to doubts about the propriety of the project for a number of reasons. First, as we saw in the previous chapter, Yehud's

---

12. Those commentators who wonder why the prophet would want to call attention to the apparently miserable state or prospects of the temple generally assume he is reflecting the actual concerns of the people and wishing to establish some sort of bond with them by acknowledging their concerns. Petersen, for example, suggests that Haggai's "tactically brilliant maneuver . . . establishes rapport with that sector of the community that is dissatisfied" (*Haggai*, 64). Mitchell, likewise, states that the prophet "sought to bring himself into sympathy with his people" (*Haggai*, 60). Without denying such a motive, I will suggest here a more explicitly argumentative strategy.

13. Elisabeth Rudolph, *Contrast: Adversative and Concessive Expressions on Sentence and Text Level*, Research in Text Theory (Berlin: de Gruyter, 1996), 124, 136–41; Marco Mazzoleni, *Costrutti concessivi e costrutti avversativi in alcune lingue d'Europa* (Florence: Nuova Italia, 1990), 123. Mily Crevels presents the logic of concession and counterarguments thus: "if *p*, then normally not *q*, nevertheless *q*" ("Concessives on Different Semantic Levels: A Typological Perspective," in *Cause—Condition—Concession—Contrast: Cognitive and Discourse Perspectives*, Topics in English Linguistics 33, ed. Elizabeth Couper-Kuhlen and Bernd Kortmann ([Berlin: de Gruyter, 2000]), 313. For concession as a strategy, see also Pereleman and Olbrechts-Tytecha, *New Rhetoric*, 486, 488–89.

14. Only rarely have commentators noted that the unimpressive prospects for the new temple constitute a potential challenge to Haggai's claim that YHWH has commanded his house to be rebuilt, a danger the prophet must address through a new argument. See Elie Assis, "Haggai: Structure and Meaning," *Biblica* 87 (2006): 539; Meyers and Meyers, *Haggai*, 71.

impoverished status was taken as a sign that YHWH remained displeased with his people. Although Haggai had presented an alternative interpretation that persuaded the leaders and the העם שארית to build, there was always the danger that as the inability to outfit sufficiently YHWH's house became more obvious, doubts about Haggai's policy would set in; backsliding was a clear possibility. Second, temple-building inscriptions and accounts from the ANE and in the HB consistently rhapsodize about the rare, costly, and luxurious decorations provided the temples by their builders. These descriptions not only testify to the piety and ardor of the builders, but also to the magnificence of the gods for whom the gold, silver, costly woods, and precious stones have been acquired. As it was the gods who were the source of prosperity in the first place, the ability to decorate their temples so extravagantly was a sign of divine power, favor, and blessing.[15] The biblical descriptions of the tabernacle and of Solomon's temple affirm that Israel shared the larger cultural assumption that the dwellings of deities should be built and furnished with the highest quality materials.[16] Thus the inability of the Yehudites to provide sufficient silver, gold, precious wood or stones to glorify YHWH's new house would have threatened to undermine their confidence that YHWH wanted or would be pleased with the temple.

To meet this threat, the prophet offers two oracles. The first (vv. 4, 5b) affirms that the community enjoys the presence of YHWH, who exhorts the Yehudites to continue to work on the temple. The second oracle (vv. 6–9) promises that at some point YHWH himself will provide

---

15. For discussions of numerous inscriptions, from Gudea to Nabonidus, see Averbeck, "Temple Building," 27–28; Schaudig, "Restoration," 155–57; Hurowitz, *Exalted House*, 244–46; Jamie Novotny, "Temple Building in Assyria," "Temple Building in Assyria: Evidence from Royal Inscriptions," in *From the Foundations to the Crenellations: Essays on Temple Building in the Ancient Near East and Hebrew Bible*, ed. Mark J. Boda and Jamie Novotny, AOAT 366 (Münster: Ugarit-Verlag, 2010), 131–35.

16. According to Exodus, the tabernacle should be made and furnished with contributions from the Israelites of gold, silver, bronze, as well as violet, purple, and scarlet yarn, linen, precious stones, acacia wood, spices and incense (25:2–7; 35:5–9). The text recounts how the people donated their jewelry and other materials, as well as their skills, for the construction and outfitting of the tabernacle (35:20–29). The historicity or plausibility of this account is not relevant. The text reflects a cultural assumption that the tabernacle should be made with the finest materials and idealizes the exodus generation's willingness to provide whatever was asked of them.

The account of Solomon's temple in 1 Kings has him making or covering the entire edifice and most of its interior furnishings and vessels with fine woods and gold, as well as decorating with carved figures of cherubim, palm trees, and flowers (6:14–36; 7:48–51). Thus Solomon is able to declare at its dedication that he has built for YHWH a זבל בית, usually understood to mean an "exalted (or magnificent, or princely) house" (8:13).

for the כבוד of the new temple and also bring שלום to Yehud. Together these oracles form a promise of restoration that serves as a counterargument to any damaging implications of the current and the less-than-glorious prospective future state of the temple.

Haggai 2:4, 5b—Counterargument:
YHWH Supports Work on the Temple

The first oracle of Haggai's counterargument (vv. 4, 5b) affirms that YHWH is present to the community and exhorts it to keep working and to be strong and unafraid: ועתה חזק זרבבל נאם יהוה וחזק יהושע בן יהוצדק הכהן הגדול וחזק כל עם הארץ נאם יהוה ועשו כי אני אתכם נאם יהוה צבאות ורוחי עמדת בתוככם אל תיראו. The logical connection between the concession of v. 3 and this oracle is signaled by ועתה at the beginning of v. 4, which should be translated "nevertheless."[17] The oracle seeks to counter a possible implication of the impoverished prospects for the temple, which is that YHWH has not commanded or approved of the reconstruction. Such a conclusion, if allowed to form, would bring a halt to the project. The oracle, introduced by "nevertheless," implicitly acknowledges the normal validity of this conclusion, but insists it does not apply here.[18] Despite appearances to the contrary, YHWH is with the people and wants them to keep building.

The oracle has three imperatives ("be strong," "act," "do not be afraid") and two forms of the affirmation that YHWH is present to the people ("I am with you," "my spirit stands in your midst"). This language is largely conventional, reflecting that found in salvation oracles and in what some have called "installation oracles."[19] The combination of these commands and assurances is not unique, as we will see, but it is unusual. In a prelude to the second oracle, this conventional language

---

17. Brongers ("Bemerkungen," 295) reads this as "dennoch" or "trotzdem." See also Reventlow (*Haggai,* 19) and Wolff (*Haggai,* 78) for a similar reading.

18. As noted above, the logic of concession and counterargument is "if *p,* then normally not *q,* nevertheless *q.*" See Crevels, "Concessives on Different Semantic Levels," 313. Concession does not dispute the normal relationship between *p* and *q,* but only its validity in a particular circumstance.

19. For a discussion of the "installation genre" or *Amtseinsetzung,* in which key figures are installed in their offices, see Norbert Lohfink, "Die deuteronomistische Darstellung des Übergangs der Führung Israels von Moses auf Josue: Ein Beitrag zur alttestamentliche Theologie des Amtes," *Scholastik* 37 (1962): 32–44; Dennis J. McCarthy, "An Installation Genre?" *JBL* 90 (1971): 31–41; Roddy Braun, "Solomon, the Chosen Builder: The Significance of 1 Chronicles 22, 28, and 29 for the Theology of Chronicles," *JBL* 95 (1976): 586–88.

of salvation not only conveys an assurance that the temple project is approved by YHWH but also serves to rebut any perception by those who oppose the rebuilding project that the time of restoration has not yet arrived.

In the oracle the prophet addresses Zerubbabel, Joshua, and כל עם הארץ. In its present context the phrase כל עם הארץ is clearly parallel with the HN composer's expression (1:12, 14; 2:2) for those who have accepted the call to rebuild, כל שארית העם. The difference in language reflects different sources rather than different referents. The introduction to the oracle (v. 2), as with 1:12 and 1:14, stems from the composer of the HN; here in the body of the oracle we probably see the prophet's own language, which he uses in a general sense to refer to the people of Yehud.[20] This suggests that Haggai himself, if this oracle is original to him, addressed it to the entire community, not only to those involved in the temple reconstruction. This exhortation to the entire community is consistent with his aim to complete the temple as quickly as possible. Here, however, the HN composer has YHWH direct the prophet to speak specifically to those who are working on the temple—and in danger of turning aside from the task.

The prophet's response begins with a triple "formula of encouragement" (*Ermutigungsformel*): חזק! The exhortation is repeated each time individually to one of the three addressees: Zerubbabel, Joshua, and כל עם הארץ. This repetition and individualization is a form of amplification, strengthening the persuasive force of the command by increasing its rhetorical presence and impressing upon the audience the central

---

20. Thus also Amsler, *Aggée*, 32–33. Most commentators consider the referent of the two phrases to be the same, although they offer different explanations for the use of עם הארץ here, if they offer an explanation at all. A. H. J. Gunneweg, for example, suggests the term hearkens back to an earlier usage in which it indicated the elite land holders. It is these Haggai is addressing in this section, since they alone could finance the temple ("עם הארץ—A Semantic Revolution," *ZAW* 95 [1983]: 437–39). Floyd proposes that the change of language reflects a "social transformation" in which the faithful "remnant," previously a minority in Yehud, has broadened to such a degree that the majority of Yehudites now support the temple reconstruction (*Minor Prophets*, 280–82).

Ernest W. Nicholson ("The Meaning of the Expression עם הארץ in the Old Testament," *JSS* 10 [1965]: 59–66) cites several instances where the obvious or most likely referent for the term עם הארץ is the general populace, including Gen 23:7, 12–13; 42:6 (כל עם הארץ); Lev 4:27; 20:2, 4; Num 14:9; 2 Kgs 15:5; 16:15; 24:14; Jer 1:18; Ezek 12:19; 33:2; 39:13 (כל עם הארץ); 45:22 (כל עם הארץ); 46:3, 9. Given these numerous examples across the biblical corpus, there is no need to assume Haggai is referring to a specific group within Yehud. He is exhorting the entire populace to work on the temple, in accordance with his rhetorical aim to garner as much support as possible for the temple project.

importance of the need to "be strong."[21] This is further emphasized by the double use of the declaration formula (נאם יהוה). When used in a command or exhortation, as here, חזק typically means to be courageous, calm, or confident.[22] It thus occurs frequently in circumstances in which the addressee faces a daunting or important task that must be accomplished despite misgivings about the possibility of success.[23] The call to be strong is Haggai's first, emphatic response to possible doubts about the propriety or feasibility of the project in light of the challenges it presents for a poor, divided community with few resources.

In accordance with similar exhortations elsewhere in the HB, the command חזק is followed by assurances of divine presence and support.[24] Here this assurance is given twice: אני אתכם and רוחי עמדת בתוככם. The first phrase repeats the assurance given in 1:13 to those who feared that YHWH did not want the temple built. Here, in the face of potential renewed doubts about the project, it functions in much the same way, but its attachment to the command עשו adds further the promise of assistance. The people are commanded to "act" and are supported and empowered to do so, כי אני אתכם.[25]

The idea of divine assistance with the reconstruction project is more clearly present in the second promise: רוחי עמדת בתוככם. YHWH's רוח represents divinely-granted skill to accomplish the task.[26] It is this same spirit that is given to the artisan Bezalel at Sinai, filling him with the "skill and understanding and knowledge in every kind of work" necessary to complete the tabernacle (Exod 31:3; 35:30–31).[27] The participle עמדת signals that YHWH's creative and supportive power is securely present to the community as it undertakes the challenging

---

21. On amplification and presence, see Perelman and Olbrechts-Tyteca, *New Rhetoric*, 175–76; Jasinski, *Sourcebook*, 12–13.
22. F. Hesse, "חזק," *TDOT* 4.302; J. Schreiner, "אמץ," *TDOT* 1.325.
23. See, for example, Deut 31:6–7; 2 Sam 2:7; 13:28; 1 Kgs 2:2; Isa 35:4; Zech 8:13 (in a text also related to the reconstruction of the temple).
24. For example: Deut 31:6; Josh 1:9; Isa 35:4.
25. See Preuss, ". . . ich will mit dir sein," 139–73. The same promise of divine presence as assistance is found in a number of texts: Gen 26:3, 24; 28:15; 31:3; Exod 3:12; Josh 1:5; 3:7; Judg 6:16; Isa 41:10; 43:2, 5; Jer 1:8, 19; 15:20; 30:11; 42:11; 46:28.
26. Kessler, *Haggai*, 171–72; Meyers and Meyers, *Haggai*, 52; Wolff, *Haggai*, 79–80; Lys, "Rûach," 229–30; S. Tengström, "רוח," *TDOT* 13.390–94.
27. ואמלא אתו רוח אלהים בחכמה ובתבונה ובדעת ובכל מלאכה (Exod 31:3). Note that מלאכה is the word used in Hag 1:14 for the work on the temple.

project.[28] As a consequence of this divine assurance, the people need not be afraid to rebuild the temple.

Between the exhortation to confidence and the assurances of divine presence is the command, עשו. In conjunction with חזק this imperative constitutes a command to act with resolve. This combination of חזק and עשה occurs only a few times in the HB, always in postexilic texts.[29] In each case, the addressee is commissioned to undertake an important but challenging duty in fidelity to YHWH. Ezra is exhorted by Shecaniah to enforce the Law (Ezra 10:4).[30] King Jehoshaphat appoints judges in Judah to ensure faithfulness to YHWH, commanding them: חזקו ועשו (2 Chr 19:11). Two texts in which the combination occurs concern the building of the first temple, and bear striking similarities in language and context to Haggai 2:4, 5b.[31] In 1 Chronicles 22:11–13, David assures Solomon that he will succeed in completing the temple, but only if he is faithful to the Mosaic covenant: "You will succeed if you are careful to do (לעשות) the statutes and decrees that YHWH commanded Moses for Israel. Be strong and steadfast; do not fear and do not be terrified (חזק ואמץ אל תירא ואל תחת)" (22:13). He immediately turns to a list of all that he (David) has prepared for the temple, gathering precious metals, wood, stones, and skilled laborers. All has been set for Solomon, who must now complete the task commanded by God: קום ועשה ויהי יהוה עמך (22:16b). In 1 Chronicles 28:10 David once again commissions Solomon in similar language: ראה עתה כי יהוה בחר בך לבנות בית למקדש חזק ועשה. David repeats the exhortation and assurance in 1 Chronicles 28:20, insisting to Solomon that God will not abandon him before he has completed the temple: חזק ואמץ ועשה אל תירא ואל תחת כי יהוה אלהים אלהי אמך.

These texts from 1 Chronicles have obvious linguistic and conceptual parallels with the Haggai oracle and therefore merit further consideration. Scholars interested in the source of the language in the Chronicles passages have suggested it was inspired by similar passages in Deuteronomy and Joshua that feature the transfer of leadership

---

28. H. Ringgren, "עמד," *TDOT* 11.183–84; Verhoef, *Haggai*, 100–1; Wolff, *Haggai*, 79–80; Meyers and Meyers, *Haggai*, 74.

29. Hesse, "חזק," *TDOT* 4.307. See Ezra 10:4; 1 Chr 28:10, 20; 2 Chr 19:11.

30. קום כי עליך הדבר ואנחנו עמך חזק ועשה.

31. This is an observation I have not found in other commentators.

from Moses to Joshua.[32] They find three elements common to the Deuteronomistic passages: the exhortation to "be strong and steadfast" (Deut 31:7, 23; Josh 1:6a, 7a, 9a), a description of the task the new leader must undertake (Deut 31:7, 23; Josh 1:7b–8), and a formula of accompaniment (Deut 31:8, 23; Josh 1:9b).[33] The same elements are present in the Chronicles passages, in which the transfer of leadership from David to Solomon involves specifically the role of royal temple builder. Solomon, like Joshua, is exhorted, חזק (1 Chr 22:13b; 28:10, 20) and אל תירא (1 Chr 22:13b; 1 Chr 28:20). The formula of divine accompaniment is present as either an indicative (1 Chr 28:20) or a volative (1 Chr 22:11, 16). In addition, we find in all three Chronicles passages the command עשה (22:16; 28:10, 20).

It is noteworthy that Haggai 2:4, 5b has the same four elements as 1 Chronicles 22:13–16 and 28:20—the encouragement formula, the command to "act," the accompaniment formula, and the command אל תיראו. The Haggai oracle is not based on the Chronicles passages, which were composed later, but it too may be deliberately drawing on and adapting the combination of elements we find in the Deuteronomistic passages, adding the command עשו.[34] The rhetorical force of this evocation of earlier material is to convey the sense that the leaders and the people are being divinely commissioned and empowered to carry out a significant but challenging task on par with the entrance into the land.

The rhetorical function of this first oracle, then, is to reassure the people that YHWH approves the reconstruction, despite doubts raised by the lack of adequate resources. The use of language found in commissions emphasizes further that the rebuilding project, although daunting, is nevertheless commanded by YHWH and will receive his support until it is completed. Thus the people have nothing to fear: the project is divinely approved and feasible.

---

32. See Lohfink, "Darstellung des Übergangs," 32–44; McCarthy, "Installation Genre," 31–41; Braun, "Solomon," 586–88.

33. The task Joshua is given in Deuteronomy 31 is to bring the people into the land. In Joshua 1 it is also to observe the covenant, which will ensure his success.

34. It is likely that the Haggai oracle is the earliest example of the use of the command in combination with the other elements, which raises the possibility that it, and not only the Deuteronomistic texts, is the model for the Chronicles material. To my knowledge this suggestion has not previously been made and deserves further exploration.

Haggai 2:6–9—Counterargument:
YHWH Will Provide for the Temple

This subunit has two rhetorical functions. First, it addresses the feasibility of the reconstruction project by asserting that YHWH will soon intervene and cause the wealth of the nations to come to Yehud to adorn the temple. The meager resources of the Yehudites will not prevent YHWH's house from attaining the appropriate glory, and thus are not an argument against continuing reconstruction. Second, the oracle attempts to alleviate ongoing concerns about the timing of the project by arguing that the period of salvation, thought to be a prerequisite for rebuilding, is already on the horizon. Once the temple is completed YHWH will bring the expected well-being and prosperity (שלום).

The oracle begins with an unusual phrase that emphasizes the imminence of YHWH's intervention while nevertheless avoiding a specific timeframe: "Once more—and soon—" (עוד אחת מעט היא).[35] The immediacy assures the Yehudites that the solution to the problem of the temple's meager prospects for "glory" lies just ahead. In addition to assuring the audience that YHWH's intervention is nigh, it seeks to reinforce confidence in the assertion by alluding to previous, unspecified acts of YHWH: he will act "once more." It is here, in the assertion that YHWH will provide for the temple's כבוד in the near future, that Haggai resolves the problem posed by the meager resources of the community. Having conceded that the Yehudites cannot possibly provide appropriately for the temple, he nevertheless refuses to allow his audience to conclude from this that YHWH does not want the temple built. The logic of such a conclusion lies in the assumption that if YHWH had wanted his house rebuilt he would have provided for it by bringing prosperity to Yehud. Haggai counters or preempts this (unspoken) argument by asserting that YHWH will indeed provide for the "glory" of the temple, not by first bringing prosperity to Yehud—as expected—but by bringing wealth directly from the nations during or after the reconstruction of the temple. The present lack of resources cannot be taken as evidence that YHWH does not want his house built, nor serve as a rationale to stop work.

---

35. See ch. 2, p. 32 and p. 66 n. 202, for discussion of this text and its translation.

The description of the imminent intervention (2:6b–7) is brief, conventional, and vague. YHWH will cause the heavens and earth, dry land and sea to "quake" (מרעיש). The language of quaking (רעש) is conventional, drawn from traditional descriptions of divine theophanies.[36] YHWH will also cause "all the nations" (כל הגוים) to quake; it is their wealth (חמדת) that will fill the new temple with a כבוד greater than that of the first temple (ומלאתי את הבית הזה כבוד). Haggai avoids details of the intervention or the mechanism by which the wealth of the nations reaches Jerusalem. Once the world and the nations have been shaken, their wealth will simply "come" (ובאו).

The vague, conventional language has led to divergent interpretations of this oracle. While some commentators have taken the expectation of divine intervention to refer to actual or hoped-for political disturbances, most have seen the description as "eschatological." YHWH's action has been imagined both as peaceful and as martial.[37] Depending on how one imagines the details of the intervention, the wealth of the nations will come to Jerusalem as voluntary offerings, tribute, the spoils of holy war, reclaimed property (namely, the temple vessels), or some combination of these.[38] No single reading has claimed broad support, except that the intervention is somehow "eschatological." The language is too vague and allusive to derive a specific image of what Haggai has in mind.

The inability to clearly imagine the nature of the imminent intervention, or the process by which the wealth of the nations will actually come to Jerusalem, is undoubtedly intentional. Kessler has suggested that the generalized, vague language was deliberately chosen by Haggai to avoid divisiveness by ignoring other traditional elements such as "the presence of non-Jews in the temple and their worship of Yahweh,

---

36. Brevard S. Childs, "The Enemy from the North and the Chaos Tradition," *JBL* 78 (1959): 187–89; Kessler, "Shaking," 159–65; H. Schmoldt, "רעש," *TDOT* 13.590–92; Meyers and Meyers, *Haggai*, 52–53; Verhoef, *Haggai*, 102–3; Kessler, *Haggai*, 175.

37. Those who see the oracle referring to contemporary historical realities include Amsler, *Aggée*, 34; Reventlow, *Haggai*, 23; Mitchell, *Haggai*, 62. Most consider it "eschatological" or related in some way to future expectations of the day of YHWH: Kessler, *Haggai*, 177–78; "Shaking," 159–65; Meyers and Meyers, *Haggai*, 52–53; Childs, "Enemy from the North," 190; Rudolph, *Haggai*, 43, and others. Although most commentators assume YHWH's intervention is martial, Wolff (*Haggai*, 81) suggests it will not be destructive, and therefore presumably peaceful.

38. Contributions: Verhoef, *Haggai*, 103; Assis, "Disputed Temple," 592; Mitchell, *Haggai*, 62. Tribute: Elliger, *Zwölf kleinen Propheten*, 92–93; Meyers and Meyers, *Haggai*, 53–54. Spoils of war: Reventlow, *Haggai*, 21–22. Reclaimed property: Petersen, *Haggai*, 69; Meyers and Meyers, *Haggai*, 54.

the subjugation of non-Jews, the return of exiles."[39] Dwelling on such issues would have taken focus away from the main concern, which was the reconstruction of the temple. Thus the vague language is designed to avoid matters with the potential to be "divisive, troubling, or not immediately relevant."[40] The suggestion that Haggai (or the HN composer) does not wish to be divisive is implausible; the language and strategies of the HN do not avoid polemic.[41] A more likely reason for conventional language and vagueness is that it suits Haggai's rhetorical purpose to provide as few details as possible. He merely needs to assure the people that YHWH will provide for the temple and that therefore they need not worry about it. He does so using traditional, recognizable language readily at hand, merely asserting that soon YHWH will act and wealth will come. The phrase "once more" at the beginning of the oracle induces the audience to accept Haggai's vague claim of imminent divine action by tying it to traditions of past actions on Israel's behalf, whatever those may be. The rhetorical strength of the oracle lies precisely in its vagueness and allusive nature, because it makes an "argument" based on traditional expectations, using traditional language, but without running the risk of presenting details that could be disputed or found improbable. The audience is left to fill in the details in any way that strikes them as plausible (much as modern commentators have done), or to simply trust that what YHWH has done in the past he will do again.

The claim that YHWH will enrich Jerusalem at the expense of the "nations" is reinforced by the insistence that this wealth belongs to YHWH in the first place: לי הכסף ולי הזהב. Commentators have deliberated whether Haggai is referring to temple vessels or other consecrated wealth that was removed by the Babylonians; to the spoils of war, proleptically in YHWH's possession; or possibly to all the silver and gold in the world, which belongs to YHWH as cosmic sovereign.[42] As in the previous verses, the language is deliberately vague and leaves

---

39. Kessler, *Haggai*, 195.
40. Ibid.
41. Rhetorical analysis of the next section, 2:10–14, will show that Haggai employs strategies of vilification and polarization.
42. Vessels: Petersen, *Haggai*, 67; Meyers and Meyers, *Haggai*, 54. Spoils: Meyers and Meyers, *Haggai*, 53–54; Reventlow, *Haggai*, 21–22. Wealth belonging to YHWH as creator and sovereign: Kessler, *Haggai*, 181–82; Rudolph, *Haggai*, 43.

room for the audience to determine, if it wishes, what exactly YHWH means. But the rhetorical force of the statement does not lie in such particulars. The focus and point of the claim is not the content or proximate source of the wealth but in the fact that it belongs to YHWH: *Mine* is the silver and *mine* is the gold. Possession implies access and control. Because "the gold" and "the silver," however conceived, belong to YHWH, he can easily dispossess the nations of it. The assertion that the wealth belongs to YHWH reinforces the main point of the oracle, which is that YHWH will cause the wealth to come to Jerusalem to adorn his house. The rhetorical aim of the statement is thus to instill confidence in this imminent arrival of wealth. YHWH can do this because he exercises full control over his silver and gold.

The oracle ends with two assertions that address the question of resources and of timing: גדול יהיה כבוד הבית הזה האחרון מן הראשון אמר יהוה צבאות ובמקום הזה אתן שלום נאם יהוה צבאות. The concluding statement presents the result of the foregoing divine intervention and "shaking" of the nations: the glory or splendor of the new temple will exceed that of its predecessor. This assertion directly addresses the issue of feasibility, answering real or potential objections that the community lacks sufficient resources to complete the project by effectively dismissing them with promise of an imminent remedy. If the audience accepts the claim that YHWH will intervene soon and bring wealth to Yehud, then they can have no objections to continuing the reconstruction.

The final assertion that once the temple is completed and glorious YHWH will at last bring שלום to Yehud relates to the overarching question of timing. The Yehudites had interpreted their lack of prosperity as a sign that the period of judgment was still in effect. Until there were signs that the restoration had begun, it was not time to rebuild the temple. Haggai first addressed this problem by arguing that the lack of prosperity was a sign of YHWH's anger at the lack of progress on the temple (1:3–11). Now he asserts that once the temple is completed, the expected restoration will commence: ובמקום הזה אתן שלום. The phrase המקום הזה certainly refers primarily to the temple itself, in accordance with the traditional association of מקום with sacred places.[43] But as

---

43. J. Gamberoni, "מקום," *TDOT* 8.37–54; Arthur Cowley, "The Meaning of מקום in Hebrew," *JTS* 17

a number of scholars have pointed out, the blessings implied by the word שלום would be expected to fall upon the city and the land and even the whole world once YHWH had again taken up residence in his house.[44] The rhetorical force of this concluding statement lies in YHWH's promise of restoration: אתן שלום. More than simply "peace," the word שלום evokes prosperity, well-being, and fertility, all of which are signs of divine favor and in this context of reversal of judgment.[45]

Conclusions

In his initial argument for temple reconstruction (1:3–11) Haggai had forcefully articulated the severe problems facing the Yehudites, which we may characterize as a lack of שלום. The aim of that first oracle was to persuade the community that this absence of שלום was the direct consequence of its failure to attend to YHWH's house. The implication there was that once reconstruction began, YHWH would reverse his judgment. Two months into the work it has become clear to the Yehudites that the results of the project will not be impressive because the community lacks resources to properly "glorify" YHWH's house, a situation that raises the possibility that Haggai was wrong to argue that YHWH wanted the temple built. Conceding only that the people see meager prospects for the house, Haggai nevertheless draws on traditional forms and language to offer a counterargument. Despite appearances to the contrary, YHWH wants his house built, and so they must keep working. As for the dismal potential of the new temple, the prophet asserts that YHWH himself will see to its כבוד by bringing the wealth of the nations to Jerusalem. This intervention will result in a temple whose glory surpasses that of the first temple. More importantly for the Yehudites, from this new temple YHWH will bring שלום.

This second argument concludes by addressing the persistent doubts about the temple project encouraged by the poor conditions. The

---

(1916): 174–76; David S. Vanderhooft, "Dwelling Beneath the Sacred Place: A Proposal for Reading 2 Samuel 7:10," *JBL* 118 (1999): 626–30.

44. For example, Kessler, *Haggai*, 183; Verhoef, *Haggai*, 107–8; Wolff, *Haggai*, 83–84.

45. F. J. Stendebach, "שלום," *TDOT* 15.26–43 (citing numerous examples throughout the HB); Rudolph, *Haggai*, 43; Mitchell, *Haggai*, 63; Meyers and Meyers, *Haggai*, 75; Kessler, *Haggai*, 183; Verhoef, *Haggai*, 107–8. Gerhard von Rad suggested that the root meaning of the term is "'well-being,' with a strong emphasis on the material side." ("שָׁלוֹם in the OT," *TDNT* 2.402).

vague yet traditional language employed throughout this section is meant to assure the Yehudites that the reconstruction project must go forward, and that it does so with YHWH's blessing and at his command. The traditional language and forms substitute for specific details, which Haggai cannot provide, yet presents the argument as fully consistent with YHWH's past actions and present capacities to carry out his will. A failure to continue working could thus be seen as a failure to trust YHWH. This is only implied, of course, but we have already seen in the previous oracle implication used as a rhetorical strategy. Haggai further seeks to advance his policy proposal by pushing the promise of שלום back from the beginning of work (implied in the first oracle) to the completion of the temple and YHWH's intervention in the near but otherwise unspecified future.

Rhetorical Analysis of Haggai 2:10–19

This section of the HN comprises two subunits. In the first, 2:10–14, the prophet is sent by YHWH to the priests for a תורה regarding the transmission of holiness and ritual defilement. Haggai uses their response to make a judgment about the defiled state of a group referred to as העם הזה והגוי הזה and of their cultic offerings. In the second subunit, 2:15–19, Haggai turns his attention again to the community's persistent agricultural problems, promising that they will soon come to an end.

The rhetorical aim of the entire unit is to strengthen commitment to the reconstruction of the temple. The first subunit reinforces the positive identity of those engaged in the project by characterizing those who worship elsewhere, who have not supported the reconstruction project, as unclean and thus "dangerous." The second subunit seeks to assure the audience—yet again—that the unimproved conditions in Yehud are not a sign that the temple reconstruction is untimely. Now that the temple is actually founded and its cult therefore operational, the expected blessings will soon flow.

Scholars have struggled to interpret this passage because the meaning of the prophet's statement regarding העם הזה והגוי הזה in v. 14 is not obvious. This difficulty has been compounded by the unclear relationship between the two subunits. The result has been a set of widely divergent readings, particularly of the "priestly torah" subunit. None of these readings has commanded agreement among a majority of scholars, primarily because each relies on assumptions that are not well founded in the text and must be supplied. The analysis that follows offers a solution to this problem by arguing that Haggai is using the principle that impurity is contagious to claim that those who do not support temple reconstruction and who worship at another site have "infected" themselves and thus threaten the wider community. It is these recalcitrant Yehudites who are העם הזה והגוי הזה.

The unit is dated to the twenty-fourth day of the ninth month, almost four months after the first oracle (1:1), exactly three months after work began on the temple (1:15a), and two months since the previous oracle (2:1). In the ninth month (Kislev) the rainy season should have been well underway.[46] Under normal weather conditions all of the autumn harvesting would have been completed by this time and the barley and wheat grain for the spring harvest sown.[47] Even if, as we will see, the harvest had been meager and it had not yet been possible to sow grain for the spring, the agrarian work during these months nevertheless would have been considerable. For those dependent on farming, the combination of the failure of the crops and the distraction of eking out a livelihood during the preceding three months of temple reconstruction would have exacerbated concerns about—or indifference to—the project. Haggai must therefore again energize and assure the Yehudites. In 2:10-14 he does this through the rhetorical strategy of vilification and polarization. In 2:15-19 he once again assures them that the promised blessings are about to appear.

Haggai 2:10–14—Construction and Vilification of Enemies

YHWH commands the prophet to seek a priestly תורה regarding the

---

46. Kislev corresponds to November–December. The rainy season in Israel began in late October with the "early rain" (יורה). See Deut 11:14; Jer 5:24; s.v. "יורה," *HALOT*; Gustaf Dalman, *Arbeit und Sitte in Palästina* (Gütersloh: Bertelsmann, 1928), 1.129; Oded Borowski, "Agriculture," *ABD* 1.96; King and Stager, *Life in Biblical Israel*, 86.

47. Oded Borowski, *Agriculture in Iron Age Israel: The Evidence from Archaeology and the Bible* (Winona Lake, IN: Eisenbrauns, 1987), 31–44 (this includes his discussion of the Gezer Calendar and its relevance for understanding the agricultural year in Israel). Only after the first rains have softened the ground can it be plowed and seed for grain sown (Borowski, *Agriculture*, 47; King and Stager, *Life in Biblical Israel*, 88).

transmissibility of holiness and cultic defilement.[48] Although Haggai begins by asking whether consecrated meat can transmit its state of holiness to other food (it cannot), it soon becomes clear that the point of the consultation lies in the following question about cultic defilement. The priests confirm that such defilement can be contracted indirectly, by coming into contact with someone who has become unclean by touching a corpse. The purpose of this exercise is not for Haggai to acquire information he does not already have. After all, he has been sent to the priests by YHWH himself, who we may presume is aware of the properties of holiness and ritual defilement. The aim of the dialogue is entirely rhetorical: through his questions Haggai establishes clearly and on priestly authority the principle that defilement can be contracted indirectly, from an intermediary who acts as a carrier and vector of impurity. It is, in other words, contagious.

Haggai now applies this principle to the situation in Yehud, presenting it as a divine oracle: כן העם הזה וכן הגוי הזה לפני נאם יהוה וכן כל מעשה ידיהם ואשר יקריבו שם טמא הוא. Clearly this is a weighty pronouncement, but its meaning is obscured by a vagueness that prompts a number of questions: Who is or are העם הזה and הגוי הזה? What are כל מעשה ידיהם? Where is this place, presumably a cult site, identified merely as שם? How and why are these things טמא? How exactly does this pronouncement relate to the priestly תורה about the transmission of impurity through an intermediary? Scholars' answers to these questions have been various and often contradictory.

The key to understanding Haggai's declaration and its rhetorical purpose lies first in the identification of העם הזה. Scholars generally agree that the phrase that follows, הגוי הזה, refers to the same group.[49] This means that Haggai is characterizing העם הזה not only as טמא but

---

48. It is not necessary for the purposes of the following analysis to enter into details about the literary, historical, or theological background of the priestly ruling in the passage, or into Israelite notions of purity and impurity in general. For such an analysis, the reader may consult the standard commentaries on Haggai. For a discussion of the responsibility of priests to make determinations of clean or unclean, see Philip John Budd, "Priestly Instruction in Pre-Exilic Israel," VT 23 (1973): 1–14.

49. In other words, the second phrase (גוי) is in apposition to the first (עם), providing additional information about it. In this case, the waw connecting the two phrases functions as a waw explicativum. The repetition of כן is for emphasis: "Thus it is for this people—thus for this nation."

also as a גוי, an observation that has complicated scholarly assessment of this passage.

Earlier commentators tended to presume that העם הזה must be non-Yehudites, arguing that the prophet would not refer to his fellow Yehudites and coreligionists as גוי. Drawing on the Ezra account in which the Yehudites reject the offer by the northern Samarians to help build the temple (Ezra 4:1–5), Rothstein tentatively suggested that Haggai was referring to these same Samarians.[50] Considering them and the cult they conduct שם (in Samaria) unclean, the prophet implicitly rejects their participation in the reconstruction project. This suggestion proved surprisingly tenacious, becoming for a while *the* interpretation of the passage, despite numerous weaknesses that even Rothstein recognized.[51]

The value of this reading was that it apparently explained Haggai's use of גוי, which could be safely ascribed to the northerners who were not considered true Yahwists by Ezra. But this advantage did not outweigh the principle problem with this reading, namely that it introduces an otherwise absent group of antagonists into the Yehudite scene by drawing anachronistically on a text that is itself historically problematic. Nowhere in the HN is Haggai shown to be concerned with anything but getting the temple built; his are not the ethnic and religious issues that exercised Ezra. Just as importantly, the assumption that an Israelite prophet would never refer to YHWH's people as a גוי is easily seen to be false, as May argued.[52] Without this assumption, the need to find a non-Yehudite referent for העם הזה can be set aside, and in recent years Rothstein's suggestion has been regarded as untenable and unnecessary by all but a few scholars.[53]

If העם הזה is not a foreign people, then it is Yehudites themselves who are both גוי and טמא. In trying to determine what point Haggai is trying to make by referring to them in these terms, commentators

50. Rothstein, *Juden und Samaritaner*, 31–36.
51. Rüdiger Pfeil, "When Is a *Gôy* a 'Goy'? An Interpretation of Haggai 2:10–19," in *A Tribute to Gleason Archer*, ed. Walter C. Kaiser Jr., and Ronald F. Youngblood (Chicago, IL: Moody, 1986), 263–66.
52. Herbert G. May, "'This People' and 'This Nation' in Haggai," *VT* 18 (1968): 190–97. The meaning and significance of גוי in this subunit will be discussed in more detail below.
53. See, for example, Wolff, *Haggai*, 92–93; Rudolph, *Haggai*, 49; Horst, *Zwölf kleinen Propheten*, 208; Elliger, *Zwölf kleinen Propheten*, 95–96; Beuken, *Haggai*, 68. For the most part, Rothstein's position was abandoned after May's article appeared.

have tended to focus on the declaration of impurity rather than on the designation גוי. Two main kinds of interpretations have emerged, which may be broadly characterized as moral and cultic.

The moral interpretation takes as its starting point the presumption that the people are being *reproached* for their uncleanness, which can be understood either as a result of their moral lapses or as a way of speaking of their moral failure itself. The prophet fails to mention, however, what offense the people have committed to warrant this judgment. The most popular candidate the commentators have produced is the previous failure to attend to the temple. This earlier lapse rendered them unclean up to the present time.[54] But this interpretation lacks textual support and, more importantly, the reproach makes little sense if directed toward Yehudites who have been working on the temple for weeks.

The cultic interpretation focuses on the role of the temple in purification from defilement. According to this reading, the people are unclean not for any particular moral reason but simply because the unfinished state of the temple has left the people without a cultic mechanism for purification from defilement.[55] Thus the people are declared טמא.

The cultic interpretation, while explaining the reason the people are unclean, nevertheless fails to account adequately for the critical tone that most scholars have discerned in v. 14. Why does Haggai refer to the people as גוי, a term with negative connotations in this context (as we will see)? If the people, through no fault of their own, are unable to achieve ritual purification, why are they being reproached? And why raise the issue in the first place? What is the purpose of pointing out to the people who are working on the temple that they are unclean? The cultic interpretation does not explain adequately Haggai's motivation

---

54. T. N. Townsend, "Additional Comments on Haggai 2:10–19," *VT* 18 (1968): 559–60. Others include David R. Hildebrand, "Temple Ritual: A Paradigm for Moral Holiness in Haggai ii 10–19," *VT* 39 (1989): 155; May, "This People," 191; Mitchell, *Haggai*, 68–69; Chary, *Aggée*, 31; Verhoef, *Haggai*, 120; Meyers and Meyers, *Haggai*, 80.

55. See, for example, Koch, "Haggais unreines Volk," 63–66; Floyd, *Minor Prophets*, 292; Japhet, "Temple in the Restoration Period," 227; Petersen, *Haggai*, 82–83. The theses of these scholars, and others who hold to a general cultic interpretation, differ in details (sometimes greatly), but they nevertheless assume that the people are cultically impure because the temple is not yet completed or because atoning sacrifice has not resumed.

for bringing the people's cultic impurity to their attention or the reason for calling them גוי.

The moral interpretation is unsupported by a specific act of disobedience or moral failing within or even suggested by the HN. The cultic interpretation cannot account for the reproachful tone of the declaration of uncleanness. And neither interpretation addresses adequately the purpose of the priestly תורה dialogue that precedes the declaration. Why go to the trouble of establishing that impurity is contagious, if that principle plays no role in what follows? If the point were merely that the people are unclean for some reason, there would hardly be a need to discuss the transmission of that uncleanness. A fresh analysis of this section, which attends not only to its content, language, and tone, but also to its rhetorical relationship to the larger concerns of the HN offers a way to resolve these interpretative difficulties.

We can begin by questioning two generally unexamined assumptions about this subunit. The first is that when Haggai speaks of העם, he is speaking of all of the Yehudites, all of whom are assiduously rebuilding the temple. As I argued in the previous chapter, not only is it historically implausible that the entire community had accepted the prophetic call to rebuild, but the text itself suggests that the response was divided. Not everyone in Yehud supported the temple project. The second assumption, which follows from the first, is that Haggai's audience and העם הזה are the same, in other words, that Haggai is calling his audience גוי and טמא. But this does not appear to be the case. In v. 14 Haggai refers to העם הזה in the third person, speaking of "the works of their hands" and "what they bring." He even refers to the place where they bring offerings as simply "there" (שם), suggesting it is distant from both him and his audience. In the next verse, v. 15, he resumes his regular practice of speaking to the Yehudites in the second person.[56] These observations indicate that the group that he refers to as העם הזה is not his audience, but someone else. If they are not his audience, and his audience—as the larger context indicates—are those who support and work on the temple, then it seems clear that העם הזה are

---

56. See 1:4-11, 13; 2:3-9. The only time Haggai (or YHWH) uses the third person in reference to the Yehudites is 1:2, in a comment he is making to the leaders about העם הזה. The same tone of reproach we find in that verse is present in 2:14.

those Yehudites who have rejected Haggai's call for reconstruction. For his audience of faithful followers, Haggai is characterizing those who have not heeded his call as גוי and טמא.

Two initial observations support this conclusion. Most obviously, it alleviates the need to speculate why without apparent warning or warrant the prophet would refer to the people working on the temple as גוי and טמא. It is not difficult to imagine why he would refer to those who rejected his call to rebuild in such negatively loaded terms. (Indeed, as we will see below, there are significant rhetorical reasons for doing so.) Further, even the term העם הזה echoes the language of 1:2, in which the term referred to those who had insisted it was not time to rebuild the temple. The same tone of reproach that the term connoted in the first oracle is magnified here by being associated with גוי and טמא. Thus the prophetic language used to refer to those who fail to work on the temple remains consistent. These initial observations are supported by a rhetorical analysis of the text, which clarifies the persuasive aim and strategies of 2:10–14.

We can begin by examining Haggai's motives for prefacing his remarks about העם הזה with the priestly תורה dialogue. As I noted above, the point of this dialogue is to establish the principle that defilement can be transmitted through an intermediary. That is, the originating source of impurity not only infects anything that comes into contact with it, but that which is infected in turn can infect anything that it contacts. This means that cultic defilement is highly infectious, capable of being contracted by individuals or groups who are far away from the originating source of the impurity.

The source of the defilement in Haggai's question is specifically a corpse (טמא נפש). Of all the possible sources and states of defilement, the prophet has chosen the most severe.[57] According to the HB, corpse contamination does not require physical contact; being in the same room with a dead body is sufficient to render one unclean for seven days. The purification process is longer and more elaborate for this form of defilement than any other. Priestly instructions emphasize

---

57. See Num 5:2–3; 19:1–22; 31:19–24 for priestly instructions regarding corpse contamination. Later rabbinic tradition (Rashi on b. Pesaḥ 14b, 17a; m. Kelim 1:1–4; Ṭohar. 1:5) referred to this form of defilement as the "father of the fathers of uncleanness" (David P. Wright, "Unclean and Clean [OT]," ABD 6.730).

that those who fail to purify themselves from corpse contamination will be cut off from the assembly of Israel.[58] Corpse contamination thus represents the most dramatic, rhetorically powerful form of defilement Haggai could choose to ask about.

Haggai's question concerns specifically the contagious properties of corpse-induced defilement. As noted above, YHWH's purpose in sending Haggai to the priests can hardly be to gain information. The point of the question is to elicit and confirm for the benefit of Haggai's audience that corpse defilement is particularly contagious, capable of being transmitted through *intermediate* vectors.[59] In a brief dialogue with the priests, the prophet raises the specter of the most severe form of cultic defilement and establishes its highly contagious nature. He now applies this image of defilement to those who oppose the temple reconstruction project, and in doing so implies that being defiled themselves they constitute a potential source of contamination for others.

Haggai states that just as whatever comes in contact with someone who has corpse contamination is defiled, "so it is with" (כן) this people—this גוי, the works of their hands, and whatever they offer שם: it is all טמא. What does he mean when he says "so it is"? What exactly is the parallel he is drawing between the people and the lesson derived from the priestly dialogue? Commentators have tended to assume that the parallel has to do with the state of impurity shared by the one defiled by a corpse and העם הזה. As we have seen, this leads to interpretations of the passage that do not adequately account for its language, tone, or purpose. It also fails to take into consideration the whole focus of the priestly dialogue, which is about—not the *state* of impurity—but the *contagiousness* of impurity. From this observation we may conclude that Haggai is drawing a parallel between the contagious role of the one who has been defiled by a corpse—or been defiled by coming into contact with corpse defilement through a vector—and העם הזה. Just as someone who has touched a corpse becomes defiled and in turn becomes a source of defilement for others who come in contact with him, "so it is" (כן) with "this people." They too have become defiled,

---

58. Num 19:13, 20.
59. The reader is never told, of course, that this interview took place in the place of witnesses. But apart from the fact that the reading audience of the HN is privy to it, the structure of 2:10–14 presumes that Haggai has the same audience throughout.

along with the works of their hands and everything they offer "there," and as such they are now a potential source of contamination. This is the lesson Haggai's audience is meant to draw from his dialogue with the priests and the divine declaration.

What is the original source of this contamination? In Haggai's analogy, what plays the role of the original defiling corpse? It is the cultic site designated simply as "there" (שם). This is the place where those who have chosen not to participate in the temple reconstruction, who have rejected the prophetic call, continue to worship. It is not the Jerusalem temple or some other cultic site approved by the prophet. This is why the prophet refers to the site merely, even dismissively, as שם.[60] This undetermined site is the source of the defilement, passed on directly to העם הזה as well as to the works of their hands and their offerings. Simply by frequenting a site Haggai considers illegitimate and therefore dangerous (the corpse), העם הזה have rendered themselves unclean. Haggai offers no warrant for determining that the other site is a source of defilement, he simply states it, using the traditional priestly "declarative formula": טמא הוא.[61] YHWH, through Haggai, declares any site other than the temple illicit for Yahwistic sacrifice and therefore unclean.

Haggai's point is not merely that those who reject the temple are טמא, but also that they are a potential source of defilement even for those who support the temple and avoid the illegitimate cult site. The obvious conclusion to be drawn is that העם הזה must be avoided, if not actively opposed, as a danger and an enemy. By characterizing as contagiously טמא those who have chosen not to support the temple

---

60. Blenkinsopp ("Judaean Priesthood," 33) suggests the prophet is referring to Bethel. Those who held to Rothstein's thesis assumed that "there" meant the Samarian worship site. Since that thesis has fallen into disfavor, most scholars assume Haggai is referring to the temple in Jerusalem. Most of these scholars do not comment on the apparently odd choice of words: why refer to the temple as "there"?

61. This phrase occurs often in priestly instructions regarding clean and unclean animals (Lev 11:4, 5, 7; Deut 14:8, 10, 19) and in instructions regarding priestly inspections of persons or things that may be or have been unclean: Lev 11:38; 13:11, 15, 36, 44, 46, 51, 55; 14:44; 15:2; Num 19:15, 20. For discussion of the priestly "declarative formula" see Gerhard von Rad, "Die Anrechnung des Glaubens zur Gerechtigkeit," TLZ 76 (1951): 129–32; Rolf Rendtorff, Die Gesetze in der Priesterschrift: Eine gattungsgeschichtliche Untersuchung (Göttingen: Vandenhoeck & Ruprecht, 1954), 74–76; Wilfried Paschen, Rein und unrein: Untersuchung zur biblischen Wortgeschichte, SANT 24 (Munich: Kösel-Verlag, 1970), 50. Milgrom states that the declaration טמא הוא "is found only in cases of impurity that are indefinite and irreversible by man." (Leviticus 1–16, 648).

reconstruction project, Haggai is engaging in a rhetorical strategy of vilification.[62] For the prophet, anyone who opposes the project is not just in disagreement with him, but also constitutes a danger to the well-being of the community by knowingly bringing defilement into its midst. This makes those who reject or simply ignore the temple project an enemy.

Haggai vilifies his opponents by designating העם הזה not only as טמא, but also as גוי. Although in its early use this term referred in a neutral way merely to "a people considered either politically or racially," often stressing "territorial affiliation," by the early Persian period the term had begun to take on negative connotations.[63] When the term is used to describe non-Israelites, it is usually frankly hostile, primarily because the גוים in question are understood to be displeasing to YHWH for religious reasons, or because they constitute a threat to YHWH's people.[64] But the term can also refer to YHWH's people, although often in contexts in which they are being reproached for infidelity to YHWH. There the term connotes not only divine disapproval but also the sense that the unfaithful people are unworthy of being distinguished from others.[65] This strongly negative connotation is clearly present in v. 14. By referring to those who do not support the temple project as גוי, Haggai asserts that they are no longer Israelites, no longer YHWH's people.[66] This diminished status is achieved, in the first place, merely by failing to support the temple reconstruction project, and is a logical consequence of it. This is fully consistent with the HN composer's insistence that only those who support the temple constitute the faithful "remnant" (שארית). Even if we do not ascribe this specific perspective to Haggai himself, his association of the non-supporters with illicit wor-

---

62. Vilification is a strategy that "delegitimizes [opponents] through characterizations of intentions, actions, purposes, and identities" (Marsha L. Vanderford, "Vilification and Social Movements: A Case Study of Pro-Life and Pro-Choice Rhetoric," QJS 75 [1989]: 166). Among other things, vilification "casts opponents in an exclusively negative light" and "magnifies [their] power" (166–67). As we will see, Haggai does just this by characterizing opponents of temple reconstruction as גוי and contagiously (and therefore dangerously) טמא.

63. R. Clements, "גוי," TDOT 2.427, 431. For a discussion of this term, see also Ephraim A. Speiser, "'People' and 'Nation' of Israel," JBL 79 (1960): 157–63; Aelred Cody, "When Is the Chosen People Called a gôy?" VT 14 (1964): 1–6; May, "'This People,'" 192–93.

64. Clements, "גוי," 432. See, for example, Deut 7:1; 18:9.

65. Cody, "Chosen People," 1–2. For examples, see Judg 2:20; Isa 1:4; 10:6; Jer 5:9; 7:28; 9:8; Ezek 2:3; Mal 3:9.

66. As Cody also notes ("Chosen People," 2).

ship explains well enough his choice of the term. By choosing to worship at a site that does not enjoy divine sanction, העם הזה have willfully and persistently engaged in behavior that renders them טמא, effectively cutting themselves off from the assembly of YHWH and making themselves a גוי. Thus Haggai vilifies them as both unclean and inauthentic Israelites. Moreover, their very presence in the community constitutes a danger, insofar as their unclean status is contagious.

When he calls טמא and גוי those who oppose or simply do not care about temple reconstruction, and implies that their proximity to the faithful constitutes a danger, Haggai engages not only in vilification, but also in the complementary rhetorical strategies of subversion and polarization. Fisher notes that "[t]he rhetoric of subversion occurs in situations in which a communicator attempts to weaken or destroy an ideology."[67] In this case, the "ideology" Haggai wishes to subvert is the notion that YHWH does not approve of the temple. Rhetorical subversion aims to discredit opponents by suggesting or claiming that their perspective, actions, or motives are not merely misguided or incorrect but evil:

> Subversive rhetoric is an anti-ethos rhetoric; that is, it invariably is an attempt to undermine the credibility of some person, idea, or institution. One of its chief modes accords with what is sometimes called the "devil theory" of persuasion. The strategy is to make a man, idea, or institution consubstantial with Satanic attributes and intentions.[68]

In the first oracle of the HN the prophet had sought to delegitimize the idea that YHWH did not want the temple built at that time by suggesting that העם הזה was motivated by selfishness (1:2–4). This was a relatively mild form of subversive rhetoric compared to the present oracle, which is harsher and more explicit: those who continue to resist the prophetic call even months later have willfully made themselves contagiously טמא and גוי, dangerous non-Israelites who are opposed to the will of YHWH and of the community. By thus characterizing his oppo-

---

67. Walter R. Fisher, "A Motive View of Communication," *QJS* 56 (1970): 137.
68. Fisher, "Motive View," 138. See also Andrew A. King and Floyd D. Anderson, "Nixon, Agnew, and the 'Silent Majority': A Case Study in the Rhetoric of Polarization," *Western Speech* 35 (1971): 244–45, 248–54.

nents, Haggai rhetorically constructs them as enemies of YHWH and his people.[69]

This is a polarizing assertion. By implication those who support the temple—whom the HN composer calls the שארית—are both clean and Israelite. Haggai's rhetoric of polarization implies a neat division of the Yehudites into the good and the bad, the clean and unclean, the Israelite and the גוי.[70] The ultimate goal here is not merely to denigrate opponents of the project, but to shore up commitment to reconstruction by unifying and solidifying the group identity of the שארית. The invocation of an enemy that poses a threat to the community—either through literal or metaphorical contamination or by simply slowing down the project—has the potential to spur the efforts of those already committed by reinforcing their virtue and the goodness of their work. This also increases resistance to defection from the project. No one would willingly place himself in a vilified population.

The rhetorical aim of 2:10–14, then, is to strengthen the commitment of those already engaged in temple reconstruction by vilifying those who have opposed it and who continue to worship in a location deemed illicit and contaminating. By asserting that העם הזה is unclean and un-Israelite, Haggai presents them as the "other" that his audience does not want to become. This other is compared to a vector of contamination, whose very presence—it is implied—constitutes a danger to the community. However else his audience may respond to this, at the very least it should cause them to think twice before falling away from the temple rebuilding project.

This rhetorical aim implies that in Yehud such defection remained a possibility at least during this early period of reconstruction. Almost certainly the main reason for this would have been persistent doubts that YHWH had commanded or approved the rebuilding of his house. As earlier sections of the HN make clear, such doubt was occasioned by

---

69. For the rhetorical construction of enemies, see Murray Edelman, *Constructing the Political Spectacle* (Chicago, IL: University of Chicago Press, 1988), 66–89. Edelman defines rhetorically constructed enemies as "identifiable persons or stereotypes of persons to whom evil intentions, traits, or actions can be attributed" (87).

70. "Polarization, as a rhetorical phenomenon, may be defined as the process by which an extremely diversified public is coalesced into two or more highly contrasting, mutually exclusive groups sharing a high degree of internal solidarity in those beliefs which the persuader considers salient." It is a strategy that promotes a "strong sense of group identity" (King and Anderson, "Rhetoric of Polarization," 244).

the continuing agricultural and economic problems faced by the Yehudites. The following unit, 2:15–19, also addresses crop failure, and thus reinforces the impression that such persistent difficulties constituted the major challenge to Haggai's temple reconstruction project, a policy proposal that was intended to solve those problems in the first place.

Haggai 2:15–19—Reassertion of Remedy for Ill

Although in this subunit the topic changes abruptly from the dangerous impurity of those who worship at another site to the ongoing agricultural problems plaguing the Yehudites, 2:15–19 is clearly a continuation of the speech begun with 2:10–14. Neither the prophet nor the narrator indicates a change of setting or audience. The date is the same: vv. 10 and 18 place each subunit on "the twenty-fourth day of the ninth month" (2:10). The unity of 2:10–19 is further supported by the narrator's notice that the following oracle (2:20–23) is a second "word of YHWH" coming on the same date: ויהי דבר יהוה שנית אל חגי בעשרים וארבעה לחדש לאמר (2:20). All of 2:10–19, which occurs on the same date, therefore constitutes the first "word."

The logical connection between the subunits, which focus on entirely different issues, is not explicitly indicated. There is no linguistic signal relating the defiled and foreign nature of those who do not support the temple reconstruction and who worship "there," and the cause or the imminent amelioration of the persistent agricultural problems. Nevertheless, as we will see, the juxtaposition of oracles concerning two segments of Yehudite society now understood to oppose each other creates a rhetorical relationship that is intended to strengthen commitment to the reconstruction project.

The subunit begins with ועתה שימו נא לבבכם. Here, as in 1:5, the particle ועתה serves as a cohortative introducing the imperative: "Come now, consider carefully. . . ."[71] As in that first oracle, Haggai asks the people to reflect on their current misery, but this time they are to remember it in the future, "from this day forward" (מן היום הזה ומעלה). Later it will become clear that "this day" is the day of the refounding of the temple (v. 18). In the first oracle of the HN, the Yehudites were

---

71. Brongers, "Bermerkungen," 294–95. See chap. 4, pp. 163–64, for previous discussion.

asked to consider carefully their misfortunes at that moment, to understand them as evidence that YHWH wanted the temple built. As they looked around at their miserable state, they were to see it as a sign of present divine displeasure. In the present oracle the crop failures will also serve as evidence, but from the perspective of the past. Haggai exhorts the community to remember in the future how things are in Yehud now. As the oracle proceeds, it becomes clear that the prophet expects that beginning on "this day" the fortunes of the community will change for the better. As they look back on the dismal past they should know precisely when—and therefore why—life in Yehud began to improve.

Haggai exhorts his audience to consider carefully what things were like for them, מטרם שום אבן אל אבן בהיכל יהוה ("before setting stone to stone in the temple of YHWH").[72] Commentators have generally assumed that by "setting stone to stone" the prophet is referring to the event occurring on that very day, which according to v. 18 has to do with the "foundation" of the temple (more on this below).[73] They are thus being asked to remember how things were before that day, several weeks after they agreed to work on the temple. But the context suggests that the prophet is referring to an earlier "moment," to the time before the prophet had persuaded the leaders and the שארית העם to begin that work. We see this as the oracle proceeds. In vv. 16–17 YHWH will remind the Yehudites what things were like and what he did to them in that time when he was "not with" them (ואין אתכם אני).[74]

---

72. See chap. 2, n. 208, for translation of מטרם. Only here and in v. 18 does Haggai refer to YHWH's temple as his היכל. The term, which can mean palace also, is often used interchangeably with בית to refer to the temple (for example: Jer 7:4; 24:1; Ezek 8:16; Jonah 2:5, 8). It can also refer to a specific part of the temple, namely the "nave," the space between the אולם (vestibule) and the דביר ("holy of holies"), as we see in 1 Kgs 6:3, 16–17. See M. Ottosson, "היכל," *TDOT* 3.382–88.

    I agree with most commentators that by היכל יהוה the prophet probably means simply "the temple of YHWH." Although Wolff (*Haggai*, 66) suggests that the prophet is referring specifically to the nave, upon which work began first, it seems unlikely that anyone would refer to a specific part of the temple as היכל יהוה. It is possible that this change of terms is merely a stylistic choice. In light of the oracle of 2:20–23, which focuses on the sovereignty of YHWH, we might wonder if the choice of a term that can also mean "palace" was intended for its allusive nuance.

73. Thus Wolff, *Haggai*, 63–64; Petersen, *Haggai*, 88; Kessler, *Haggai*, 207; Amsler, *Aggée*, 29; Galling, *Studien*, 136; Verhoef, *Haggai*, 124; Meyers and Meyers, *Haggai*, 63; Elliger, *Zwölf kleinen Propheten*, 89; Mitchell, *Haggai*, 70–71.

74. This translation and my thesis regarding what Haggai means here is based on my text critical analysis and suggested emendation of the MT (ואין אתכם אלי), which makes little sense, to ואין אתכם אני. See chap. 2, pp. 34–37.

Since in both 1:13 (when they agreed to work) and 2:4b, 5b (while they were working) the deity had assured the Yehudites that he was with them (אני אתכם), he must now be referring to the situation at the beginning of the HN, when he was angry with them and causing their misfortune. The Yehudites are being asked to remember what things were like before they agreed to rebuild the temple, not what things were like after they obeyed the prophetic call. This is an important point, because part of the rhetorical aim of this section is to prevent backsliding and abandoning the project, specifically out of fear that the ongoing problems facing the community are signs that the deity has not commanded the reconstruction of his house. To *remind* the people and ask them to remember that even up to that day—weeks after they began working on the temple—things still had not improved and that YHWH remained angry with them would be counterproductive. Rather, Haggai wants the Yehudites to remember how bad things were, and how angry YHWH was with them, before they began rebuilding, lest they reconsider and stop their work.

Briefly but vividly Haggai recalls that earlier misfortune, reiterating key ideas from 1:4-11—the lack of resources and the frustration of expectations caused by devastating and comprehensive crop failures, which had been brought on by YHWH as a sign of his displeasure. As in that first oracle the prophet emphasizes not just that the people lacked what they needed, but that their expectations were consistently frustrated. This is represented by the concrete image of visiting grain heaps and wine vats. When they would come to get grain or wine they were able to take only half (or less) than what they wanted or expected: בא אל ערמת עשרים והיתה עשרה בא אל היקב לחשף חמשים פורה והיתה עשרים. The experience of consistently frustrated expectations is made vividly present through concrete imagery and balanced antitheses, as it was in 1:6.[75] Also as in the first oracle, YHWH explains that it was he who brought about these miserable conditions: הכיתי אתכם בשדפון ובירקון ובברד את כל מעשה ידיכם. Blight, mildew, and hail have severely reduced crop yield, and once more the encompassing nature of the disaster is stressed: everything to which the Yehudites turned their hands was damaged and frustrated by YHWH.[76] All of this, Haggai has made clear

---

75. See chap. 4, pp. 163–88, for a fuller discussion of the relevant rhetorical strategies.

in the past, was because YHWH had been angry with them for failing to rebuild his house (1:9–11).

This divine displeasure, and the concomitant lack of blessing, is succinctly summarized with the phrase, "and with you I was not" (ואין אתכם אני). The placement of אין at the beginning negates the entire clause and emphasizes the negation of divine presence.[77] This construction focuses attention on the contrast between the situation of the Yehudites before they agreed to work on the temple and afterwards, when YHWH insisted he *was* with them (1:13; 2:14b, 15b). This is the greatest difference between the past (by which Haggai means the time before temple reconstruction began) and the present: before, YHWH was not with them, but now YHWH is, and has been since work began.

But now the prophet assures the people these misfortunes were all in the past, and he concludes their rehearsal by emphasizing that nevertheless they must be remembered and understood carefully with respect to the present day and event: שימו נא לבבכם מן היום הזה ומעלה מיום עשרים וארבעה לתשיעי למן היום אשר יסד היכל יהוה שימו לבבכם. The date of "this day" is now clearly identified as the twenty-fourth of the ninth month (Kislev), the same date as the command to seek a priestly תורה at the beginning of the unit. More importantly, it is the date of the "(re)founding" (יסד) of the temple of YHWH.

While the significance of the event to Haggai is evident, its exact nature is not. It is described merely as יִסַּד היכל יהוה. When used of buildings, the term יסד in the HB is always related to the idea of the foundation of a permanent structure, but its connotations vary widely depending on context.[78] In addition to the laying of the physical foundations of a building, it can refer to the beginning of work on a building, the completion of the project, or simply be a general term for construction or restoration of a building.[79] This last possibility is ruled out here because the term is associated with a single event on a specific

---

76. Blight and mildew are conventional punishments sent by YHWH for covenant disobedience (see Deut 28:22; 1 Kgs 8:37; Amos 4:9). Hail as an instrument of YHWH's judgment occurs in the exodus tradition (Exod 9:22–26).

77. GKC §152d.

78. In some cases in the HB, the term refers not to a building but to YHWH's establishment or founding of the earth (for example, Isa 48:13; 51:13, 16; Ps 104:5; Prov 3:19) or of Zion (for example, Isa 14:32; 28:16).

79. R. Mosis, "יסד," *TDOT* 6.109–21.

date.[80] It also is unlikely that the term is referring to the beginning of all work on the temple, since the HN states clearly that work began on the temple weeks before (1:14–15a).[81] Reventlow offers a plausible modification of this thesis, proposing that 24 Kislev marks the end of preparatory work begun three months before and that therefore יסד refers to the beginning of the actual construction of the temple.[82] Some scholars have suggested that the prophet is referring to the laying of the physical foundations of the temple, but others have questioned this reading on the grounds that the physical foundations of the temple would probably have survived the destruction of 586 BCE and would not need to be relaid.[83] Having accepted this logic, recent scholarship has tended to see Haggai referring to a ceremony, perhaps analogous to the Akkadian *kalû* ritual, that marks a *symbolic* refounding or rededication of the temple.[84] This may have involved purifying the site and reestablishing the temple cultus.[85] There seems to be no way to finally resolve this question on the basis of a single word (יסד); the precise nature of the event to which Haggai refers must remain ambiguous.

But its significance for Haggai is clear: the event of 24 Kislev will inaugurate a new era in Yehud, bringing to an end the misfortunes of the past. Although the prophet has emphasized that the miseries were brought about by YHWH before the leaders and the remnant of the

---

80. When the root occurs in *piel, pual* (as here), and *hophal*, it always refers to a specific moment in the construction process (Mosis, "יסד," 116).

81. Often such readings are dependent on rearranging the text or emending the date to the sixth month, neither of which is warranted (see comments on this in chap. 2). For this reading, see, for example, Wolff, *Haggai*, 63–64; Chary, *Aggée*, 24; and Rudolph, *Haggai*, 44–46 (who does not rearrange the text, but does change the month). Some earlier scholars, taking at face value the notice in Ezra 3:11–12 that the foundation to the temple was laid (הוסד) during the reign of Cyrus, assume that the term here must refer merely to the *resumption* of work. See, for example, Andrés Fernández, "El profeta Ageo 2, 15–18 y la fundación del segundo temple," *Bib* 2 (1921): 214; Francis I. Andersen, "Who Built the Second Temple?" *ABR* 6 (1958): 13; Anthony Gelston, "The Foundations of the Second Temple," *VT* 16 (1966): 232–35.

82. Reventlow, *Haggai*, 28 ("Das Datum 24. 9. bezeichnet offenbar den Tag des eigentlichen Baubeginns nach Abschluß der am 1. 6. aufgenommenen Vorarbeiten [1,14]."). Similarly, Verhoef thinks Haggai is referring to the "actual and official commencement of work on the temple" (*Haggai*, 130).

83. Mitchell (*Haggai*, 70–71) represents this view that the foundation was being relaid. Gelston ("Foundations," 235) argued that the foundation would not need to be rebuilt and suggested instead that here the term refers to repairing, restoring, or rebuilding the temple (not its foundation).

84. Galling, *Studien*, 136; Elliger, *Zwölf kleinen Propheten*, 89; Petersen, *Haggai*, 88; "Zerubbabel," 369; Kessler, *Haggai*, 207–9; Amsler, *Aggée*, 29; Meyers and Meyers, *Haggai*, 63; Halpern, "Historiographic Commentary," 171–72. For a discussion of this ritual, see Ellis, *Foundation Deposits*, 20–26.

85. Petersen, *Haggai*, 88; Kessler, *Haggai*, 207–9; Halpern, "Historiographic Commentary," 171–72.

people began to work on the temple, he has no choice but to acknowledge that they have continued up to the present moment. Kislev is well into the rainy season, and normally by this time the fields would have been plowed and the winter crop of grain growing.[86] Yet the seed remains in the grain pit: העוד הזרע במגורה.[87] By this time, too, grapes, figs, pomegranates, and olives should have been harvested, but the trees have produced nothing: ועד הגפן והתאנה והרמון ועץ הזית לא נשא.[88]

Haggai asks his audience, "Is there still seed in the grain pit, while the vine, the fig, the pomegranate, and the olive tree have not produced?" The answer, of course, is yes. In this question the prophet (or YHWH) acknowledges that despite everything that has been implied or promised about the end of the agricultural problems, things have yet to change.[89] The temple construction has been going on for months, yet apparently the drought has not ended—the Yehudites have not been able to plow their fields for grain and they have not harvested anything from their trees and vines. If the cause of all of this had been inattention to the temple, then why is it still going on? This question indicates that sustained crop failure remains a problem for Haggai and his policy of temple reconstruction. Still no rain, no grain, no fruits: it all silently argues against the prophet's implied claim that if the people start building YHWH's house, the deity will withdraw his judgment against them.

Haggai must once again counter this objection. In 2:9 he claimed that once the temple was built YHWH would bring שלום. Apparently the intervening weeks have raised further doubts about this claim, and so now Haggai seizes upon the event of the יסד of YHWH's temple as

---

86. Dalman, *Arbeit und Sitte*, 1.129; Borowski, "Agriculture," *ABD* 1.96; Borowski, *Agriculture*, 47; King and Stager, *Life in Biblical Israel*, 86.

87. The translation of this verse has proven difficult. For the discussion of my text critical analysis and translation, see chap. 2. For a reading similar to mine, in which the point of the question is to acknowledge that agricultural failure persists, see, for example, Petersen, *Haggai*, 86; Wolff, *Haggai*, 58, 66–67; Verhoef, *Haggai*, 111. Meyers and Meyers (*Haggai*, 48) take the verse to mean the exact opposite: "Is there still seed in the storehouse [which they take to mean plenty of grain left for sustenance]? Have not even the vine, the fig tree, the pomegranate, and the olive borne fruit?" This reading assumes that the promised blessings have already begun. This makes less sense in the context of the passage, and of the HN as a whole, than the reading proposed here and by others, that the blessings have still to appear.

88. Grapes were typically harvested June–September; figs and pomegranates, August–September; olives, September–November: Borowski, *Agriculture*, 37.

89. Wolff (*Haggai*, 66) notes that the "interrogative -ה" that begins the verse "expects assent" and so may be understood as a "limited admission" by the prophet.

the moment when, he assures the people (in YHWH's voice), things really will turn around: מן היום הזה אברך! Now that the temple has been "refounded," YHWH will bring an end to the poor conditions that have plagued the Yehudites for years. Now, Haggai assures the people, they will see their fortunes improve.

The persuasive aim of 2:15–19 is to alleviate ongoing concerns that the temple reconstruction is not divinely approved, as it was for 2:3–9. Haggai had sold the project as a "policy" that would bring an end to the Yehudites' economic and agricultural misfortunes, which had been sent directly by YHWH as judgment for their failure to rebuild his house. Three months into the reconstruction, and the improvement implied in the oracle of 1:4–11 has not materialized. In response to concerns that the community lacks the resources to adequately rebuild and adorn the temple, Haggai had promised that at some point in the future YHWH himself will see to this, finally bringing שלום to Yehud. One could reasonably expect that full economic and even agrarian recovery would take some time, but surely it would begin by ending the drought that YHWH had visited upon the people. Yet several weeks after work has begun and well into the rainy season, the fall harvest has failed and there has not been enough rain to permit planting of grain for the spring harvest. The signs are not in Haggai's favor and this must surely have deepened concerns that the project was ill-advised.

In response, Haggai points to the date of the "founding" of the temple as the true turning point. Yes, it is a fact that the expected change of fortune has not occurred, but now that the temple has been refounded or rededicated, YHWH will begin to bless. Such a claim would find a basis in ANE ideology, which associated temples with fertility. If the event of 24 Kislev involved the restitution of the temple cultus, as some have suggested, then Haggai's assertion that now, at last, שלום will come to Yehud would have been plausible.

But the aim of the subunit is not only to assure the people that YHWH will now bring the promised blessings. It is also to assert the validity and effectiveness of Haggai's temple reconstruction policy. The people are called upon to remember in the future that it was on "this day" that things improved. This memory will legitimize the temple project by tying the improvements to the temple policy and substantiating it. In the future, when things do improve, the Yehudites will not be able to attribute the changed conditions to anything else but to the refounding of the temple, and this will redound to Haggai's credit as a legitimate prophet. YHWH will have blessed the people solely because they heeded Haggai's call to devote their time and resources to rebuilding his house. The temple project and Haggai will be validated.

Conclusions

Both 2:10–14 and 2:15–19 are intended to shore up flagging enthusiasm for the work on the temple and to deter possible defections. The aim of 2:10–14 is to paint those who do not support the temple, and who worship at another site, as גוי and dangerously, contagiously טמא. Through vilification of his opponents, Haggai polarizes the Yehudite community into those who are true Israelites and those who are not, those who are impure and those who are in danger of becoming impure if they "contact" the "enemy." This polarization is consistent with the earlier characterization (by the narrator) of those who accepted the prophetic call as שארית העם. Vilification, polarization, and the rhetorical construction of enemies all contribute to group cohesion and therefore reinforce commitment to the temple project.

This commitment is strengthened by the positive claim that the promised result of rebuilding the temple is imminent. Whatever the nature of the event of 24 Kislev, Haggai assures his audience that from that day YHWH will bless the Yehudites, bringing an end to their persistent agricultural woes. When they look back on the difference between the time of cursing "before setting stone on stone" and the time of blessing beginning on that date, they will know that it was because they accepted Haggai's policy proposal that their troubles came to an end.

Rhetorical Analysis of Haggai 2:20–23

In this final oracle of the HN, the prophet continues to press the case for his temple reconstruction policy. Although at first glance the unit has nothing to do with the temple, it nevertheless addresses the question of the efficacy and feasibility of the project in two ways. First, it develops the earlier claims that the restored temple will lead to YHWH's bestowal of שלום and blessing by affirming that soon YHWH will publicly establish his universal sovereignty, which is both a sign and a precondition of the full restoration of Yehud and of YHWH's people. The temple also will provide the locus of YHWH's enthronement as sovereign. Second, the oracle provides the temple project with a royal builder in the person of Zerubbabel, the Davidide who is explicitly identified as YHWH's chosen royal representative.

The unit comprises two subunits: vv. 20–22, which concerns YHWH's victory over the nations, and v. 23, which announces the divine election of Zerubbabel. According to v. 21a, the entire oracle is addressed only to Zerubbabel (אמר אל זרבבל פחת יהודה לאמר), who nevertheless becomes the focus only in v. 23. While it is true that the oracle is addressed to him, its message is not intended only for him, for the claims concerning YHWH's sovereignty and his choice of Zerubbabel as his representative are relevant for the entire Yehudite community, and form part of Haggai's rhetorical strategy in support of the temple policy. If this oracle stems from the historical prophet, it almost certainly would have been intended for the same audience as all of the previous oracles, the Yehudites in general or, after the work on the temple began, those who supported the project. The specific address to Zerubbabel makes sense given the focus on him in v. 23 as well as the close connection between that verse and the affirmation of YHWH's sovereignty in vv. 21b–22.

Haggai 2:20–22—Assertion of Imminent Establishment of YHWH's Sovereignty

The unit begins with a *Wortereignisformel*: ויהי דבר יהוה שנית אל חגי בעשרים וארבעה לחדש. The language strongly suggests that what follows is closely related to the previous oracle: it is a "second word of YHWH" given to the prophet on the same date. Given on the same day as the "refoundation" of the temple and the promise that henceforth YHWH will bless, this new oracle develops the implications of that momentous event.[90] It also highlights the importance of continuing to build

90. As Verhoef (*Haggai*, 141–42) also notes.

the temple and not abandoning the project out of fear that YHWH has not yet agreed to return to Yehud.

The previous assurances that YHWH would bless and bring שלום implied more than just agricultural fecundity and concomitant economic recovery; they were to be signs and results of YHWH's forgiveness of his people and of his intention to bring about a fuller, hoped-for restoration. Whereas the prevailing expectation among the Yehudites had been that YHWH would order or allow the reconstruction of his temple only after he had withdrawn his decades-long judgment and begun the restoration of his people, Haggai has claimed that the rebuilding of the temple is in fact a prerequisite for that restoration. Only after his house is completed will YHWH bring blessing and שלום to his people. Now that the temple has been "refounded," the prophet further assures his audience that this period of restoration is beginning.

As Mowinckel noted, the Yehudites' expectations concerning YHWH's restoration of his people—informed by longstanding prophetic tradition—would have included above all else the affirmation of YHWH's kingship.[91] Tradition also suggested that this sovereignty would be accomplished through the defeat of "the nations" or other hostile powers.[92] Once he had established his kingship, YHWH would rule from the temple, the site of his enthronement. In this first part of the final oracle (vv. 21–22), Haggai assures his audience that YHWH is about to defeat and publicly establish his sovereign rule over the nations. The persuasive force of this claim is twofold: it suggests the urgency of completing YHWH's temple (or "palace" = היכל) and it provides hope that the temple project will soon bear the promised fruit of full restoration (שלום).

The subunit begins with the same theophanic language as 2:6: אני מרעיש את השמים ואת הארץ. As in the earlier oracle, the participle indicates YHWH's intervention is imminent, but apart from this no temporal information is given.[93] In 2:6–9, it was promised merely that YHWH would "shake" (הרעשתי) the nations (כל הגוים), bringing their wealth to

---

91. Mowinckel, *He That Cometh*, 143–49.
92. See, for example, Exodus 15; Isaiah 24; Obad 21; Pss 9, 10, 47, 89, 96, 98, 99.
93. The *futurum instans* use of the participle: *IBHS*, 627–28; Joüon §121e; Kessler, *Haggai*, 221.

Jerusalem to fill his house with כבוד. Here YHWH's intervention is more substantial and clearly martial: והפכתי כסא ממלכות והשמדתי חזק ממלכות הגוים והפכתי מרכבה ורכבה וירדו סוסים ורכביהם איש בחרב אחיו.

As in 2:6–9, the vagueness of this oracle, which does not identify the kingdoms or give YHWH's motivation for overthrowing them, has left it open to a variety of interpretations. A prominent reading is that Haggai is anticipating an overthrow of the Persian Empire, a "throne of kingdoms," perhaps along with other "kingdoms of the nations." The point of the oracle, then, is to assure the Yehudites that they will soon be achieving political autonomy.[94] This is certainly possible, but as we saw with 2:6–9, the prophet uses language that is meant to be "evocative" rather than referential.[95] What seems to be important is not whom YHWH will overthrow (הפך) and destroy (השמד), but that he will do so. The traditional, conventional imagery of the oracle is intended to make the point that YHWH will soon affirm his sovereignty in an expected, standard way, by defeating nations—any nations, all nations.

As a number of scholars have noted, v. 22 draws in a general way on the language of YHWH as divine warrior, holy war, the יום יהוה, and theophany, as well as related images from the exodus tradition (for example, the mention of horses and chariots).[96] The verb שמד features prominently in oracles against the nations.[97] The verb הפך, perhaps through its use as a "fixed idiom" in Genesis for the destruction of Sodom and Gomorrah, comes in other texts to "[typify] the judgment of Yahweh."[98] The final phrase, איש בחרב אחיו ("each by the sword of his fellow"), has been taken to suggest mutual destruction and panic, a

---

94. Japhet, "Sheshbazzar and Zerubbabel," 77; Elliger, *Zwölf kleinen Propheten*, 97; Meyers and Meyers raise the possibility that it may be an "oblique reference to the Persians" (*Haggai*, 67). This identification is intended to make sense of the phrase כסא ממלכות ("throne of kingdoms"), which would seem to be describing a single "throne" (emperor?) ruling over several semiautonomous "kingdoms."

95. As Kessler notes, Haggai makes use "of highly evocative language in a generalized fashion, with the result that the precise referent is difficult to determine" (*Haggai*, 235). I suggest it is not meant to be determined.

96. Chary, *Aggée*, 34; Rudolph, *Haggai*, 53–54; Petersen, *Haggai*, 98–101; Reventlow, *Haggai*, 29; Verhoef, *Haggai*, 143–45; Kessler, *Haggai*, 225–26.

97. Kessler, *Haggai*, 224; Verhoef, *Haggai*, 144; N. Lohfink, "שמד," *TDOT* 15.188. See, for example, Isa 10:7; 13:9; 14:23; 23:11; Jer 48:8, 42; Ezek 25:7; 32:12.

98. K. Seybold, "הפך," *TDOT* 3.425, 426. See Gen 19:21, 25, 29, and also Hos 11:8; Lam 4:6; Isa 34:9; Jer 20:16. Verhoef similarly notes that הפך through its use in such texts becomes a "leitmotif" in prophecies of doom (*Haggai*, 143).

motif also found in the language of YHWH's wars.[99] This traditional language lends itself to a generalized claim that soon YHWH will be bringing about the destruction of unnamed kingdoms and nations. There are no specifics, nor is there any motive given, because the defeat of the nations here is simply a standard trope designed to convey YHWH's decisive victory over (presumably) hostile powers as part of a public expression of his universal sovereignty. Haggai's rhetorical aim is not to persuade his audience that soon YHWH will defeat a particular enemy. It is to persuade them that soon YHWH will establish his kingship and exercise his sovereign prerogatives.

This becomes clear when v. 22 is seen in relation to v. 23, which (as we will see shortly) is as much about YHWH's kingship as it is about the royal identification or function of Zerubbabel. The oracle, taken as a whole, reflects the mythic narrative—familiar to all students of the ANE and the HB—of a god's defeat of hostile powers as a prelude to enthronement in a temple (palace) as sovereign. Verse 22 provides the defeat, v. 23 alludes to YHWH's sovereignty, and YHWH's house currently being built at Haggai's instigation provides the temple.[100]

Haggai uses, then, the theme of YHWH's defeat of the ממלכות to further his claim that 24 Kislev marks the turning point in Yehud's fortunes. Now that the temple has been "refounded" YHWH will soon bless his people, not just with agricultural fecundity, but with a complete restoration, referred to in 2:9 as שלום. This restoration will be possible through YHWH's universal sovereignty, made public through his military victories against unnamed kingdoms.

Haggai 2:23—Counterargument: YHWH Has Provided a Royal Builder

YHWH's defeat of the nations will establish his kingship, certainly over his people if not also over all the nations. According to Judahite tradition, YHWH's sovereignty will be "embodied" and "guaranteed"

---

99. Kessler, *Haggai*, 224. He cites as examples Judg 7:22; Isa 19:2; Jer 46:16; Ezek 38:19–21; 2 Chr 20:20–25.

100. One need only think of the Baal Cycle, the *Enuma Elish*, and biblical texts such as Exodus 15. For a classic treatment of the theme of temple building by victorious gods, see Kapelrud, "Temple Building," 56–62.

through his chosen dynasty, the Davidic kings.[101] In this final subunit of the HN, Haggai asserts that the Davidide Zerubbabel has already been chosen by YHWH and, once YHWH's kingship is publicly acknowledged, Zerubbabel will be recognized as his royal representative. Through this assertion the prophet furthers his argument for the temple reconstruction by affirming that despite appearances to the contrary, YHWH has provided a legitimate, Davidic royal builder to oversee the project.[102]

Verse 23 is temporally and logically connected to vv. 21–22 by the phrase ביום ההוא. Although some scholars have suggested that this phrase lends an "eschatological" character to the entire oracle, we need not assume that Haggai necessarily understands the events he describes in those terms.[103] "On that day" often simply indicates that two events—in this case the defeat of the kingdoms and the "taking" of Zerubbabel—occur at the same time or that the second event occurs as a consequence of the first.[104] In any case, whether or not we take YHWH's defeat of the kingdoms to be an eschatological event (whatever that may mean), the point and rhetorical force of the oracle remains the same. On the same day that YHWH establishes his kingship, and as a consequence of that, he will elevate Zerubbabel, the Davidic heir.

Unlike vv. 21–22, v. 23 directly concerns Zerubbabel, who is addressed in the second person three times: אקחך זרבבל בן שאלתיאל עבדי נאם יהוה ושמתיך כחותם כי בך בחרתי. Without mentioning David or going so far as to call Zerubbabel "king," the oracle makes it clear through the confluence of several key terms ("take," "servant," "seal," "chosen") that YHWH is acknowledging Zerubbabel as heir to the

---

101. Ackroyd, *Exile and Restoration*, 253. Ackroyd suggests that in ideas of the restoration, there was a "linkage between the new age and a central figure who both embodies divine rule and is himself the guarantee of its reality." The anticipation of this figure was based on the understanding of the role and significance of the Davidic ruler, as reflected in the royal Judahite theology of the monarchic period.

102. As some previous commentators have noted: Meyers and Meyers, *Haggai*, 83; Bedford, "Discerning the Time," 94; Boda, "Dystopia," 231; William J. Dumbrell, "Kingship and Temple in the Post-Exilic Period," *RTR* 37 (1978): 39; Antti Laato, *Josiah and David Redivivus: The Historical Josiah and the Messianic Expectations of Exilic and Postexilic Times* (Stockholm: Almqvist & Wiksell, 1992), 225–26.

103. Meyers and Meyers, *Haggai*, 67; Reventlow, *Haggai*, 30; Verhoef, *Haggai*, 145; Kessler, *Haggai*, 227.

104. Peter A. Munch, *The Expression bajjôm hāhū': Is It an Eschatological terminus technicus?* (Oslo: Dybwad, 1936), 6–10. Munch notes that of the approximately 200 instances of the phrase in the HB, only about half are clearly "eschatological." Often the phrase serves as a more mundane temporal or logical connector. See Munch, *Expression*, 10–15 for numerous examples.

Davidic throne and announcing his intention to establish him in that role once YHWH has defeated the kingdoms.[105]

Haggai establishes the Davidic lineage of the governor by referring to him as "Zerubbabel son of Shealtiel, my servant." As discussed in the previous chapter, Shealtiel was the son of the Judahite king Jehoichin, who ruled until 597 BCE, when he was exiled by Nebuchadnezzar.[106] The term עבדי likewise directs attention to Zerubbabel's roots by associating him with the election of David. Although in the HB YHWH occasionally calls others עבדי, David is the individual he most often refers to as "my servant." Indeed, it is the deity's favorite epithet for David, one he reserves almost exclusively for him among the Davidic kings.[107] Moreover, in most cases, when YHWH refers to David as עבדי, he does so within the context of David's election.[108] By having YHWH refer to Zerubbabel as "my servant," Haggai signals that the son of Shealtiel has already been elected to fulfill the royal role first assigned to David. This will be explicitly stated at the end of the promise.

Once he has established his own kingship, YHWH will "take" (לקח) Zerubbabel and make him "like a seal" (כחותם). In the HB, לקח often indicates the selection of an individual or group for a particular status or role, i.e., "to choose."[109] Several times the verb relates the choice of an individual as king. YHWH took David from the pasture to become king over Israel (2 Sam 7:8). As a consequence of Solomon's sins, YHWH announces to Jeroboam son of Nebat that he will replace Solomon as ruler of the northern tribes: ואתך אקח ומלכת (1 Kgs 11:37). Through the same idiom we are told that the Judahites confirmed and anointed Azariah and, later, Jehoahaz as kings upon the deaths of their fathers

---

105. Thus also Rex Mason, "The Messiah in the Postexilic Old Testament Literature," in *King and Messiah in Israel and in the Ancient Near East: Proceedings of the Oxford Old Testament Seminar*, ed. John Day, JSOTSup 270 (Sheffield: Sheffield Academic Press, 1998), 341–42; Petersen, *Haggai*, 103–6; Japhet, "Sheshbazzar and Zerubbabel," 77–78; Reventlow, *Haggai*, 30–31; Verhoef, *Haggai*, 146; Kessler, *Haggai*, 228–31.

106. See chap. 4, p. 149.

107. H. Ringgren, "עבד," *TDOT* 10.39. See 2 Sam 3:18; 7:5, 8; 1 Kgs 11:13, 32, 34, 356, 38; 14:8; 2 Kgs 19:34; 20:6; Ps 89:4, 21; Isa 37:35; Jer 33:4, 22, 26; Ezek 34:23, 24; 37:24, 25. Only rarely, as in 2 Sam 24:12, does YHWH refer to the king merely as "David," and not as "David, my servant." Only once is another Davidic king—Hezekiah—referred to by YHWH as "my servant," and that is in a text produced after the HN (2 Chr 32:16).

108. Ringgren, "עבד," *TDOT* 10.394–95; Curt Lindhagen, *The Servant Motif in the Old Testament: A Preliminary Study to the "Ebed-Yahweh Problem" in Deutero-Isaiah* (Uppsala: Almqvist & Wiksells, 1950), 281.

109. Wolff, *Haggai*, 104–5; H. Seebass, "לקח," *TDOT* 8.20.

(2 Kgs 14:21; 23:30). But the idiom is not limited to royal contexts. It also refers to YHWH's choice of Israel (Exod 6:7; Deut 4:20) and of the Levites (Num 3:12; Isa 66:21). When YHWH states, then, that he will "take you, Zerubbabel son of Shealtiel, my servant," the audience already suspects that the governor has been chosen to fulfill a royal role.

This is confirmed by YHWH's promise to set Zerubbabel "like a seal" (כחותם). The noun חותם refers to a seal used to affix "signatures" to documents, bullae, ceramic containers, or other items that could be impressed with a seal.[110] As such it serves as a mark of identity that represents the owner in his or her absence. As a simile or metaphor for a person the noun is used, apart from here, only twice in the HB. In Song 8:6, the lover asks to be to her beloved "as a seal upon your heart, as a seal upon your arm" (שימני כחותם על לבך כחותם על זרועך), a request that conveys her desire to be as close to her beloved as his own identity, which is represented by a seal.[111] In Jeremiah 22:24, חותם appears as a metaphor, or at least a potential metaphor, for the Judahite king Coniah (Jehoiachin): כי אם יהיה כניהו בן יהויקים מלך יהודה חותם על יד ימיני כי משם אתקנך. As a Davidic king, Jehoiachin represented the dynasty's patron deity, and so the metaphor of חותם is apt. The point in the Jeremiah text, though, is that YHWH has rejected Jehoichin as king and representative, and so will (or would) "pull him off" his hand. A few scholars have seen in Haggai's use of the metaphor a possible signal that in Zerubbabel YHWH is reversing the rejection of Jehoiachin.[112]

Given its application to humans in Song of Songs 8:6 and, especially, Jeremiah 22:24, we may assume that through his use of the image of חותם Haggai intends his audience to understand that YHWH will make Zerubbabel his representative. Given Zerubbabel's Davidic lineage, and the traditional role of that lineage as representatives of YHWH, this implies that in Zerubbabel YHWH intends to restore the Davidic monarchy.[113]

---

110. See B. Otzen, "חתם," *TDOT* 5.264–66; Wolff, *Haggai*, 105–6.

111. A. Robert and R. Tourney, *Le Cantique des cantiques: Traduction et commentaire*, Études bibliques (Paris: Gabalda, 1963), 299; J. Cheryl Exum, *Song of Songs*, OTL (Louisville, KY: Westminster John Knox, 2005), 250; Otzen, "חתם," *TDOT* 5.269.

112. For example, Japhet, "Sheshbazzar and Zerubbabel," 77; Verhoef, *Haggai*, 147; Kessler, *Haggai*, 230–31; Reventlow, *Haggai*, 30.

113. This is the position of almost scholars. Only a few suggest that Haggai does not have the restitu-

All of this will happen to Zerubbabel because he has been "chosen" by YHWH: כי בך בחרתי. Within a context of allusions to Zerubbabel's Davidic lineage, YHWH's choice of David, and the role of the Davidic monarchs as representatives of YHWH, בחר clearly signals that Zerubbabel will take his place as Davidic ruler. Like עבדי, in the context of the Judahite monarchy, בחר has close and nearly exclusive connections to the election of David. Although initially used to refer to YHWH's choice of Saul, once David replaces him, בחר is used only in reference to this final, definitive choice.[114] The term, then, is "loaded" and its use here conveys the sense that, like David, Zerubbabel has been specifically and deliberately elected to represent YHWH when the deity takes his throne in the new temple.

In the context of YHWH's announcement that he will soon demonstrate his sovereignty through the defeat of the kingdoms, his promise that at the same time he has chosen and will set his servant "like a seal" leaves little doubt that the Davidide Zerubbabel will serve as YHWH's royal representative. Yet he is never called "king" nor is it stated that he will actually rule. The oracle carefully stops short of placing Zerubbabel on the throne or giving him monarchical powers.[115] He is a royal figure, but he is not a ruler. Noting this, Verhoef suggested that Haggai is hesitant to proclaim overtly that YHWH intends to reestablish the Davidic monarchy out of fear of how it will be perceived by the Persian overlords.[116] One has to wonder, though, how much attention Persia was expected to pay to someone who claimed to be a prophet or to writings derived from his words.

A more likely explanation for Haggai's "hesitancy" to call Zerubbabel a king, even a future king, is that it was not rhetorically expedient

---

tion of the Davidic monarchy in mind, even in the "eschaton." Rose finds such an interpretation "implausible" ("Messianic Expectations," 170–73).

114. H. Seebass, "בחר," *TDOT* 2.78: "Now David and his dynasty are regarded as the chosen representative of the kingdom, and the original simple concept of choice receives an ideological component inasmuch as the purpose of the Deuteronomistic history is to show that Yahweh recognized the choice of the Davidides until Manasseh brought the dynasty to an end." G. Quell notes that "emphatic and explicit references to election of the king are limited to sources dealing with the rise of the monarchy" ("ἐκλέγομαι," *TDNT* 4.156). The claim that YHWH "chose" David is not limited to the historical narratives; see Ps 78:70, which combines the choice of David with his role as YHWH's servant: ויבחר בדוד עבדו.

115. Meyers and Meyers (*Haggai*, 68) note that the metaphor of seal and the title servant are "terms of instrumentality" that "do not suggest direct monarchic powers."

116. Verhoef, *Haggai*, 146.

or advisable to do so. Zerubbabel was manifestly not a king, and there was probably little expectation that he would soon become one. For Haggai to call him king, or to imply that he would soon become one, was to court further disbelief in all of his claims, which had already proven challenging to accept on their face. Fortunately for Haggai, he does not need Zerubbabel to actually *be* a king sitting on a throne to serve as a designated royal figure. The claim that YHWH already recognized Zerubbabel as his representative and heir to the Davidic throne was enough to provide a legitimate royal builder for the temple. Haggai cannot provide an actual king to build YHWH's house, but he can provide YHWH's choice for the office, a Davidide conveniently at hand and already associated with the reconstruction project.

Conclusions

The final oracle of the HN serves Haggai's rhetorical purpose by affirming that in the (near) future YHWH will assert his sovereignty by defeating unnamed kingdoms. As sovereign, YHWH will be enthroned in his temple, as he was in the past. Thus the Yehudites must continue to work on YHWH's house so that it will be ready for him when the time comes. At the same time that YHWH establishes his own kingship, he will publicly acknowledge Zerubbabel as heir to the Davidic throne. The man who is currently governor of Yehud, and who has been closely associated with the temple reconstruction, has already been chosen by YHWH has his royal representative. Thus, while there is no reigning Davidic king in Yehud, there is a Davidic royal builder to fulfill that traditional role. The final oracle, then, asserts the legitimacy and the necessity of the temple reconstruction project.

In the three oracles examined in this chapter, Haggai has continued to assert the feasibility and efficacy of his policy to rebuild the temple. In the first oracle of the HN (1:2–11) the prophet had proposed that the answer to the ongoing agrarian and economic problems in Yehud was to build a house for YHWH. This policy proposal was based on the claim that the misfortunes of the Yehudites had been sent by YHWH because his temple had been neglected. By rebuilding YHWH's house, the community—Haggai had implied without explicitly stating—would find relief from persistent drought and crop failure. While some, perhaps most, Yehudites accepted Haggai's claims, others remained unpersuaded and were afraid to participate in the project (1:12–14).

The oracles that follow in Haggai 2 indicate that the agricultural and economic problems persisted even after work began on the temple, and that the lack of improvement contributed to concerns about the legitimacy of the project. The drought, crop failures, and general poverty of the region belied the prophet's claim these had been caused by YHWH because his house had been neglected.

In 2:2–9, the prophet concedes that the Yehudites do not have the resources to build a temple as "glorious" as the first was reputed to have been. Rather than allow this to be taken as evidence that YHWH had not willed—because he had not provided for—the reconstruction of his house, Haggai argues that the deity is with the people in their effort, fully supporting it with his presence and his "spirit." Furthermore, YHWH himself will soon provide for the glory of his temple by "shaking" the nations and causing their wealth to come and fill his house with כבוד. When that is accomplished, the promised relief from distress, signaled by the term שלום, will flow from the new and glorious temple.

Weeks later, the situation has not improved in Yehud. Crops have failed and no rain has fallen to allow for the plowing and sowing of grain for the winter. In response, Haggai offers a single oracle. In 2:10–14, he uses a priestly instruction on the contagiousness of impurity to argue that those who still do not support the temple and who persist in offering sacrifices elsewhere ("there") are not only contaminated by their association with the illicit cult site, but their contagious contamination poses a threat to the rest of the community. Through vilification of his opponents and polarization of the Yehudites, Haggai seeks to consolidate group identification, cohesion, and commitment among those who support the temple project.

The oracle continues as Haggai reminds his audience of supporters how bad things were before they agreed to work on the temple (2:15–19). This was because YHWH was angry and not "with" them. The implication is that now, even though conditions have not improved, YHWH is with the Yehudites who are working on his house. The oracle concludes by affirming that from that day forward—the day of the ritual refounding of the temple—YHWH will indeed bless his people.

The final oracle of the HN (2:20–23) continues to argue that the reconstruction of the temple is a feasible and divinely ordained project. Once it is completed, YHWH will manifest and establish his sovereignty by defeating the "kingdoms" and acknowledging his chosen Davidide, Zerubbabel, to be his royal representative. As YHWH's chosen representative, Zerubbabel already enjoys royal status, and thus serves as the traditional royal builder of YHWH's temple.

Through this series of oracles, Haggai seeks to counter threats to the temple project, threats that derive mostly from the apparent failure of his policy to effect the ends toward which it was intended, the blessing of Yehud by its god.

6

Summary of Findings

In this study I have attempted through rhetorical analysis of the Haggai Narrative (HN) to advance understanding of both the text and the historical dispute behind it. In 520 BCE, the second year of Darius I, the prophet Haggai began to advocate for immediate reconstruction of the Jerusalem temple. The temple that had been destroyed by the Babylonians in 586 BCE remained desolate (חָרֵב), leaving its patron god, YHWH, without his house. This situation constituted for Haggai an unconscionable scandal that must be addressed at once. His call for reconstruction required Haggai to overcome resistance from Yehudites who held that it was not time to rebuild. Although his initial exhortation did lead some Yehudites to begin work on the temple, doubts that YHWH had in fact ordered his house rebuilt persisted. These doubts threatened to undermine confidence in Haggai as YHWH's prophet and thus the reconstruction project itself. The entire HN is a rhetorical artifact of Haggai's initial and subsequent attempts to persuade the Yehudites that he did speak for YHWH and that YHWH did want his house rebuilt immediately.

The HN is a record of the controversy over the timing of the rebuilding of the temple, an example of the rhetorical subgenre "policy dispute." Policies are courses of action intended to meet a need or solve a problem. Those who advocate for a particular policy must persuade others first that a need or problem exists and then that the proposed policy will effectively address that need or problem. A policy dispute arises if the advocate's construction of the problem or its solution is called into question. Because policy disputes are carried out through persuasion, they are rhetorical in the traditional sense. Records of such disputes constitute rhetorical artifacts and are thus good candidates for rhetorical analysis.

Policy disputes revolve around one or more "stock issues," points of potential disagreement that must be addressed by policy advocates through persuasion. First, advocates must establish that there is a need or problem (an *ill*) to be addressed. The existence of the ill may not be immediately obvious to others or it may be disputed. They must also persuade their audience of the *cause* of the ill; this too may be a point of disagreement. Only if agreement can be reached about the existence and cause of an ill can an advocate hope to succeed in getting the proposed policy accepted as a necessary and effective *remedy* for the ill. This will not be possible if opponents cannot be persuaded that the policy will be effective in addressing the ill or that it will be feasible to implement in the first place. Even if all these obstacles are overcome by an advocate, concerns that the policy will have unacceptably high *costs* or consequences may finally lead to rejection of the policy proposal. An advocate of a disputed policy must be prepared to address rhetorically one or more of these "stock issues."

The policy dispute over the reconstruction of the temple involved the stock issues of ill, cause, and remedy. To get them to accept his policy proposal to rebuild, Haggai had to persuade the Yehudites that the economic and agricultural problems they were experiencing were an ill whose cause lay in the fact that YHWH's house remained חרב. The remedy to this ill was to begin immediately to rebuild and provide a house for YHWH. Whereas the Yehudites would readily have agreed that their poor circumstances constituted an ill, the cause of that ill—and thus the remedy for it—were debatable. In addition, the feasibility of rebuilding the temple was questionable, and this fueled doubts about Haggai's policy proposal. As my analysis has shown, to overcome

these points of dispute, Haggai employed a variety of rhetorical strategies, as did the composer of the narrative portions of the HN.

In the second chapter, I established the rhetorical artifact to be analyzed. Although the book of Haggai has only thirty-eight verses, it
presents a number of text-critical challenges. The most important or
disputed of these were examined to determine the most likely consonantal form of the original composition, as well as the vocalization that
most plausibly reflects the intention of the composer. With few exceptions, the MT reading was accepted. Proposals to emend or remove
important texts such as שִׂימוּ לְבַבְכֶם עַל (1:2a), עֵת בֹּא עֵת בֵּית
דַּרְכֵיכֶם (1:7a), בְּמַלְאֲכוּת יְהוָה (1:13a), and עוֹד אַחַת מְעַט הִיא (2:6a) were
rejected as unnecessary or unlikely for reasons that become clear in
the course of the rhetorical analysis. Other elements were emended
as unlikely or incomprehensible, notably וְהָיָה לְמְעַט הִנֵּה לִמְעָט to הִנֵּה לִמְעַט (1:9a),
וְאֵין אֶתְכֶם אֲנִי to וְאֵין אֶתְכֶם אֵלִי (2:16a) and מָה הֱיִיתֶם to מְהִיוֹתָם (2:17a).

Proposals regarding the compositional history of the HN were examined to determine which elements, if any, are likely additions to the
original composition and thus not part of the rhetorical artifact under
analysis. Earlier proposals to remove 1:13 because of its unusual language were rejected as unnecessary; the lexical choices in this verse
can be explained as part of a rhetorical strategy employed by the HN
composer. Suggestions that 2:17 is an interpolation derived from Amos
4:9 were also not compelling. Earlier arguments that 2:15–19 are misplaced and should be restored to their original position between 1:15a
and 1:15b were found to be based on questionable assumptions. More
recent attempts to argue that the 2:6–9; 2:10–14; and 2:20–23 are not
original to the HN but were added much later as part of a larger process
of editing the "Book of the Twelve" were examined in detail and also
found unpersuasive. Only 2:5aα was determined on the basis of both
text-critical and redaction-critical grounds to be a later addition to the
text. The result of the analysis of this chapter was that the rhetorical
artifact to be examined, which I call the Haggai Narrative, is substan-
tially the same as the MT, with the exception of 2:5aα and the textual
emendations noted above.

In chapter 3 I examined Persian involvement in the reconstruction
of the temple and potential Yehudite reasons to oppose rebuilding in

the early Persian period. Both of these questions are important for understanding the nature of the policy dispute concerning the temple. If Persian permission to rebuild had been required but not given until the reign of Darius, then Yehudite failure to rebuild would not necessarily reflect internal opposition to the reconstruction. If, on the other hand, the Persians had permitted reconstruction or permission was not required, reasons for failing to rebuild until 520 BCE could be found only within the Yehudite community. This, in turn, would suggest that opposition to the project was long-standing and well-entrenched and thus difficult to overcome. Evidence that the Persians would have required permission to rebuild was found to be inconclusive. The claim in Ezra that Cyrus commanded or took responsibility for the temple is inconsistent with the fact that the temple was not completed until years later. If the Persians had wanted the temple built, it would have been, regardless of any Yehudite opposition. The most plausible scenario is that either the Persians gave permission in the reign of Cyrus or it was not required at any time. In any event, the responsibility to rebuild—or to not rebuild—lay exclusively with the Yehudites. If the temple was not rebuilt until 520 BCE, it was because the Yehudites lacked the will or the ability to rebuild.

There were several possible obstacles or sources of opposition to reconstruction in early Persian-period Yehud. A primary concern at the time would be to determine if YHWH did in fact want his temple built. To proceed without assurances of divine permission would be catastrophic. Anxiety to determine the divine will regarding temple construction or, in particular, reconstruction is evident in biblical and extrabiblical texts. Several oracles from Zechariah 1–8 suggest that prophetic claims that YHWH wanted his temple rebuilt in 520 BCE were met with skepticism. Isaiah 66:1–2a further indicates that Yahwists were not of one mind about YHWH's desire for a temple. General doubts in this regard could be supported by the economic and agricultural difficulties in Yehud, which could be—and probably were—interpreted as signs of YHWH's abiding anger. The general failure of YHWH's people to thrive even after the fall of Babylon indicated that the expected time of restoration had not arrived. Until such time as the signs that YHWH's anger had begun to abate appeared, any effort to rebuild his temple in Jerusalem would been deemed disastrously premature. Ancient Near Eastern traditions also called for a royal builder to undertake (re)construction of royal sanctuaries such as the Jerusalem temple. Calls to rebuild the temple in 520 BCE would have to contend with the fact that no such royal builder, divinely appointed to rebuild the temple, was in evidence. These "theological" concerns would have constituted strong reasons to doubt Haggai's claim that YHWH wanted his temple built.

Temple building required not just theological support, but also material support in the form of labor and funding. It would have been impossible to rebuild without the acquiescence or participation of a substantial number of Yehudites. Although the reconstruction of the temple and its attendant cultic apparatus may have been a high priority for some Yehudite elites, the "average Yehudite" may have been indifferent or hostile to the project. Both evidence and reason suggest that cultic worship of YHWH continued in the aftermath of the destruction of 586 BCE at small altars or at centers like Bethel or Mizpah. The notion that a large, expensive temple needed to be rebuilt in Jerusalem may not have been met with enthusiasm by those whose religious practices did not require such a temple. Economic factors, too, would have increased opposition. A temple project would require struggling farmers to leave their land to build the edifice. The temple would have been expensive to build and the prospect of taxation to pay for construction and then, afterwards, to maintain the cult would not have been welcomed by a poor populace. Even the fear of being forced to work on the project for little or no pay may have contributed to strong opposition. These suggestions that the Yehudites would have been unenthusiastic or hostile to the temple are borne out by evidence from Malachi and Nehemiah, which reflect the difficulty the temple had gaining financial support from the populace once it was built. These material obstacles, coupled with potential theological objections to reconstruction, form the background of the policy dispute between Haggai and the Yehudites. To get the Yehudites to accept his claim that YHWH wanted his temple rebuilt immediately, Haggai would have to meet these objections in some way.

In chapters 4 and 5, I analyzed the HN as a rhetorical artifact of the policy dispute over the temple. In 1:1–4, the dispute between Haggai and "this people" (העם הזה) is revealed. According to the prophet, the people do not believe it is time to rebuild. In 1:5–11 he attempts to persuade them they are wrong using two main strategies. First, he insinuates that their position is not principled, but rather is a rationalization of their selfish neglect of YHWH's house while attending to their own needs. Haggai couples this *ad hominem* attack with a possibly more persuasive appeal to the very self interest he is deriding. Most of the oracle is concerned with reminding the Yehudites of the depth and breadth of their economic and agricultural misfortunes. This is intended to make the *ill* of the policy dispute vividly present to them, and thus prepare them to consider his recommendation for a remedy. The reality of the ill cannot have been in dispute, but the cause of it was. Very likely, when the Yehudites say that it is not time to rebuild the temple, the poor conditions have contributed to their sense that YHWH *remains* angry with his people. The failure to rebuild the temple is not the cause of their ill. Haggai turns this on its head and asserts that the fact that the YHWH's house remains desolate and deserted is the cause of the ill. His argument implies, but does not explicitly state, that the remedy to the ill afflicting the Yehudites is to rebuild the temple. Thus in this first oracle, the prophet addresses the stock issues ill, cause, and remedy by appealing to the self interest of the Yehudites, a rhetorically compelling strategy.

The narrative section of 1:12–15a reflects the response of the community to Haggai's first argument. Verse 1:12a indicates that the leaders Zerubbabel and Joshua, and כל שארית העם responded positively to the prophet's call. I argued that although this Hebrew phrase is often understood to indicate simply that "all the rest of the people" responded along with the leaders, it should be taken to mean that the leaders and "the whole remnant of the people" responded positively the call to rebuild. The term שארית indicates only a subset of the Yehudite population, which—because it agreed to support temple reconstruction—the narrator refers to as "remnant." The use of this term signals the narrator's conviction that only those who supported the temple constituted the faithful "remnant," and thus the "true Israel." But not all of Yehud was persuaded by Haggai's argument;

they remained afraid. Verses 1:12b–13 reflect this fearful response, not by "the remnant of the people" but by simply "the people" (העם) that is, those who are not part of the remnant. Their response is recorded as one of fear, presumably fear that Haggai is not a true prophet who speaks for YHWH. In response, the prophet assures "the people" specifically that YHWH is with them. The reader is next told that the leaders and the remnant of the people began to work on the temple.

My argument that the response to the prophetic call was divided and that the failure of "the people" to accept Haggai's argument was based on fear that YHWH did not want his temple built is central to my analysis of the rest of the HN. Against almost all commentators, who take 1:12–14 to indicate that the entire Yehudite population accepted Haggai's argument, I have argued that many remained unpersuaded and thus afraid to build. The text suggests as much, and the rest of the HN reflects ongoing efforts of the prophet to shore up support by addressing concerns regarding the propriety and feasibilty of the temple policy. A divided response is also historically more plausible than a sudden and complete reversal of attitude on the basis of Haggai's preaching.

Chapter 5 examines three further oracles. In 2:3–9, Haggai confronts the objection that the impoverished Yehudites are economically incapable of providing a suitable house for YHWH. The poor prospects of the temple reinforced the notion that YHWH had yet to begin the restoration of his people. Further, if YHWH had wanted his temple built, he would surely have provided for it. Haggai is thus faced with questions regarding the feasibilty of the reconstruction policy. Although he concedes that the prospects of the temple currently are dim, he offers a two part counterargument. First, he assures the leaders and the entire Yehudite populace (כל עם הארץ) that YHWH is with them and supports the temple. Second, he addresses the problem of the temple prospects by offering a vaguely worded assurance that soon YHWH will "shake the nations" and cause their wealth to come to Jerusalem and fill his temple with "glory." Once the temple is built, YHWH will bring שלום to Yehud.

The HN then moves to a dialogue between Haggai and the priests, in which the prophet confirms a basic principle: cultic defilement is highly contagious, capable of being transmitted indirectly from its original source through human or non-human carriers to others (2:10-14). Haggai then applies this principle to an unnamed group called "this people—this nation" (העם הזה והגוי הזה), as well as to the "work of their hands," and to their offerings that they bring some-where referred to simply as "there" (שם). This section has occasioned much confusion among scholars and agreement on its meaning has been elusive. It has generally been assumed that Haggai means by "this people this nation" the people of Yehud, who are presumably all working on the temple, and by "there" the temple. This raises the question of why he would call the people and the temple "unclean" (טמא), and, in addition, call the Yehudites הגוי הזה. I have argued that the resolution to this dilemma lies in the recognition that the response to Haggai had been divided. The prophet is referring to those who have refused to support the temple but have instead continued to offer sacrifices elsewhere. By calling those Yehudites who are not engaged in reconstruction "unclean" and "nation," Haggai vilifies them and asserts that they are not true Israelites; they are the counterpart to the "remnant." The principle of contagion emphasizes that the impu-rity "this people—this nation" has contracted from its illicit cultic site ("there") has contaminated their offerings, and them, and because it is contagious, it threatens the whole community. By attending to the his-torical plausibility of a divided response to Haggai's claims about the temple, and to the rhetorical strategy of vilification and polarization, I have offered a solution to this long-standing exegetical puzzle.

The oracle of 2:15-19, delivered on the day of the "refounding" of the temple, is intended to address once again the issue of remedy. It has been several months since work began on the temple, yet there has been no improvement in agricultural conditions. Haggai assures them that now that the temple has been refounded, YHWH will bless. The oracle indicates that Haggai's implied claim that temple reconstruction policy would bring a solution to the ill of economic and agricultural problems was in doubt, and needed to be shored up.

The final oracle of the HN (2:20-23) was shown to address another objection to temple reconstruction, the lack of a royal builder. The assurance to Zerubbabel, a Davidide, that soon YHWH would establish his sovereignty and then, "on that day," take Zerubbabel as his "signet"

(חותם) is intended to show that YHWH has indeed provided a royal builder for his new temple.

Rhetorical analysis of the HN has illumined various aspects of the text, and has offered a solution to a thorny exegetical problem. It has also highlighted the need to reconsider the nature and depth of the debate around the rebuilding of the temple in the early Persian period. A number of scholars have noted that the question appears to have been contentious, but this basic insight has often not been taken sufficiently into account when reading the book of Haggai. This study invites further inquiry into the relationship between this text and this historical debate that gave rise to it. In particular, this study has raised the possibility that socioeconomic realities played a larger part in the history of the temple in the early Persian period than is typically thought. Further inquiry in this direction promises to deepen our knowledge of Persian-period Yehud.

Bibliography

Ackerman, Susan. *Under Every Green Tree: Popular Religion in Sixth-Century Judah.* HSM 46. Atlanta, GA: Scholars Press, 1992.

Ackroyd, Peter R. *Exile and Restoration: A Study of Hebrew Thought of the Sixth Century B.C.* OTL. Philadelphia, PA: Westminster, 1968.

_____. "Some Interpretive Glosses in the Book of Haggai." *JJS* 7 (1956): 163–67.

_____. "Studies in the Book of Haggai." *JJS* 2 (1951): 163–76; 3 (1952): 1–13.

_____. "The Temple Vessels: A Continuity Theme." Pages 166–81 in *Studies in the Religion of Ancient Israel.* Edited by G. W. Anderson et al. VTSup 23. Leiden: Brill, 1972.

_____. "Two Old Testament Historical Problems of the Early Persian Period." *JNES* 17 (1958): 13–37.

Ahlström, Gösta W. *Royal Administration and National Religion in Ancient Palestine.* SHANE 1. Leiden: Brill, 1982.

Albani, Matthias. "'Wo sollte ein Haus sein, das ihr mir bauen könntet?' (Jes 66,1): Schöpfung als Tempel JHWHs?" Pages 37–56 in *Gemeinde ohne Tempel = Community without Temple: Zur Substituierung und Transformation des Jerusalemer Tempels und seines Kults im Alten Testament, antiken Judentum und frühen Christentum.* Edited by Beate Ego, Armin Lange, and Peter Pilhofer. WUNT 118. Tübingen: Mohr Siebeck, 1999.

Albertz, Rainer. "Darius in Place of Cyrus: The First Edition of Deutero-Isaiah (Isaiah 40.1–52:12) in 521 BCE." *JSOT* 27 (2003): 371–83.

_____. *A History of Israelite Religion in the Old Testament Period.* 2 vols. Translated by J. Bowden. OTL. Louisville, KY: Westminster John Knox, 1994.

_____. *Israel in Exile: The History and Literature of the Sixth Century B.C.E.* Translated by D. Green. Studies in Biblical Literature 3. Atlanta, GA: Society of Biblical Literature, 2003.

_____. "The Thwarted Restoration." Pages 1–17 in *Yahwism after the Exile: Perspectives on Israelite Religion in the Persian Era*. Edited by Rainer Albertz and Bob Becking. Studies in Theology and Religion 5. Assen: Van Gorcum, 2003.

_____. "Why a Reform Like Josiah's Must Have Happened." Pages 27–46 in *Good Kings and Bad Kings*. Edited by Lester L. Grabbe. LHBOTS 393. European Seminar in Historical Methodology 5. New York, NY: T&T Clark, 2005.

Albright, William F. Review of *L'Épithète divine* Jahvé Seba'ôt: *Étude philologique, historique et éxégétique*, by B. N. Wambacq. *JBL* 67 (1948): 377–81.

Allen, Leslie C. *Jeremiah*. OTL. Louisville, KY: Westminster John Knox, 2008.

Amsler, Samuel, André Lacoque, and René Vuilleumier. *Aggée-Zacharie 1-8, Zacharie 9-14, Malachi*. CAT 11c. Geneva: Labor et Fides, 1988.

Andersen, Francis I. "Who Built the Second Temple?" *ABR* 6 (1958): 1–35.

Andersen, Francis I., and David Noel Freedman. *Hosea*. AB 24. Garden City, NY: Doubleday, 1980.

Anderson, Gary A. *Sacrifices and Offerings in Ancient Israel: Studies in Their Social and Political Importance*. HSM 41. Atlanta, GA: Scholars Press, 1987.

Aristotle. *The Art of Rhetoric*. Translated by H. C. Lawson-Tancred. London: Penguin Books, 2004.

Arnold, Carroll C. *Criticism of Oral Rhetoric*. Columbus, OH: Merrill, 1974.

Assis, Elie. "Composition, Rhetoric and Theology in Haggai 1:1–11." *JHebS* 7 (2007): article 11, available at http://purl.org/JHS and at http://www.JHSonline.org.

_____. "A Disputed Temple (Haggai 2,1–9)." *ZAW* 120 (2008): 582–96.

_____. "Haggai: Structure and Meaning." *Biblica* 87 (2006): 531–41.

_____. "To Build or Not to Build: A Dispute between Haggai and His People (Hag 1)." *ZAW* 119 (2007): 514–27.

Averbeck, Richard E. "Temple Building among the Sumerians and Akkadians (Third Millennium)." Pages 3–34 in *From the Foundations to the Crenellations: Essays on Temple Building in the Ancient Near East and Hebrew Bible*. Edited by Mark J. Boda and Jamie Novotny. AOAT 366. Münster: Ugarit-Verlag, 2010.

Avigad, Nahman. "The Chief of the Corvée." *IEJ* 30 (1980): 170–73.

Babylonian Talmud. 35 vols. Translated by Isidore Epstein. London: Soncino, 1935–1959.

Bailey, John W. "The Usage of the Post Restoration Period Terms Descriptive of the Priest and High Priest." *JBL* 70 (1951): 217–25.

Balentine, Samuel E. "The Politics of Religion in the Persian Period." Pages 129–46 in *After the Exile: Essays in Honour of Rex Mason*. Edited by John Barton and David J. Reimer. Macon, GA: Mercer University Press, 1996.

Barrick, W. Boyd. "What Do We Really Know about 'High-Places'?" *SEÅ* 45 (1980): 50–57.

Barthélemy, Dominique. *Ézéchiel, Daniel et les 12 Prophètes*. Vol. 3 of *CTAT*. OBO 50/3. Fribourg: Éditions Universitaires; Göttingen: Vandenhoeck & Ruprecht, 1992.

Batten, Loring W. *Critical and Exegetical Commentary on the Books of Ezra and Nehemiah*. ICC. Edinburgh: T&T Clark, 1946.

Bauer, Lutz. *Zeit des zweiten Tempels-Zeit der Gerechtigkeit: Zur sozio-ökonomischen Konzeption im Haggai-Sacharja-Maleachi Korpus*. BEATAJ 31. Frankfurt: Lang, 1992.

Baumgärtel, Friedrich. "Die Formel *ne'um jahwe*." *ZAW* 73 (1961): 277–90.

Baynes, Norman H. "Zerubbabel's Rebuilding of the Temple." *JTS* 25 (1924): 154–60.

Becker, Joachim. *Gottesfurcht im Alten Testament*. AnBib 25. Rome: Pontifical Biblical Institute, 1965.

Bedford, Peter R. "Discerning the Time: Haggai, Zechariah and the 'Delay' in the Rebuilding of the Jerusalem Temple." Pages 71–94 in *The Pitcher Is Broken: Memorial Essays for Gösta W. Ahlström*. Edited by Steven W. Holloway and Lowell K. Handy. JSOTSup 190. Sheffield: Sheffield Academic, 1995.

_____. "Early Achaemenid Monarchs and Indigenous Cults: Toward a Definition of Imperial Policy." Pages 17–39 in *Religion in the Ancient World: New Themes and Approaches*. Edited by Matthew Dillon. Amsterdam: Hakkert, 1996.

_____. "The Economic Role of the Jerusalem Temple in Achaemenid Judah: Comparative Perspectives." Pages 3*–20* in *Shai le-Sarah Japhet: Studies in the Bible, Its Exegesis and Its Languages*. Edited by Moshe Bar-Asher et al. Jerusalem: Bialik, 2007.

_____. "On Models and Texts: A Response to Blenkinsopp and Petersen." Pages 154–62 in *Second Temple Studies I: Persian Period*. Edited by Philip R. Davies. JSOTSup 117. Sheffield: JSOT Press, 1991.

_____. *Temple Restoration in Early Achaemenid Judah*. JSJSup 65. Leiden: Brill, 2001.

Begrich, Joachim. "Das priesterliche Heilsorakel." *ZAW* 52 (1934): 81–92.

Ben Zvi, Ehud. "The Prophetic Book: A Key Form of Prophetic Literature." Pages 276–97 in *The Changing Face of Form Criticism for the Twenty-First Century.* Edited by Marvin A. Sweeney and Ehud Ben Zvi. Grand Rapids, MI: Eerdmans, 2003.

_____. "The Urban Center of Jerusalem and the Development of the Literature of the Hebrew Bible." Pages 194–209 in *Urbanism in Antiquity: From Mesopotamia to Crete.* Edited by Walter E. Aufrecht, Neil A. Mirau, and Steven W. Gauley. JSOTSup 244. Sheffield: Sheffield Academic, 1997.

Benoit, William L. "The Genesis of Rhetorical Action." *SCJ* 59 (1994): 342–55.

Berges, Ulrich. *Jesaja 40–48.* HThKAT. Freiburg: Herder, 2008.

Berquist, Jon L. *Judaism in Persia's Shadow: A Social and Historical Approach.* Minneapolis, MN: Fortress Press, 1995.

Beuken, Willem A. M. "Does Trito-Isaiah Reject the Temple? An Intertextual Inquiry into Isa. 66.1–6." Pages 53–66 in *Intertextuality in Biblical Writings: Essays in Honour of Bas van Iersel.* Edited by Sipke Draisma. Kampen: Kok, 1989.

_____. *Haggai-Sacharja 1–8: Studien zur Überlieferungsgeschichte der frühnachexilischen Prophetie.* Assen: Van Gorcum, 1967.

Bickerman, Elias J. "En marge de l'écriture." *RB* 88 (1981): 19–41.

_____. "The Edict of Cyrus in Ezra 1." *JBL* 65 (1946): 249–75. Updated and expanded version, pages 72–108 in *Studies in Jewish and Christian History, Part One.* AGJU 9. Leiden: Brill, 1976.

Bitzer, Lloyd F. "Functional Communication: A Situational Perspective." Pages 21–38 in *Rhetoric in Transition: Studies in the Nature and Uses of Rhetoric.* Edited by Eugene E. White. University Park, PA: Pennsylvania State University Press, 1980.

_____. "The Rhetorical Situation." *Ph&Rh* 1 (1968): 1–14.

Blankenship, Kevin L. "Rhetorical Question Use and Resistance to Persuasion: An Attitude Strength Analysis." *JLSP* 25 (2006): 111–28.

Blenkinsopp, Joseph. "Bethel in the Neo-Babylonian Period." Pages 93–107 in *Judah and the Judeans in the Neo-Babylonian Period.* Edited by Oded Lipschits and Joseph Blenkinsopp. Winona Lake, IN: Eisenbrauns, 2003.

_____. *Ezra-Nehemiah.* OTL. Philadelphia, PA: Westminster, 1988.

_____. *A History of Prophecy in Israel.* Rev. and enl. ed. Louisville, KY: Westminster John Knox, 1996.

_____. *Isaiah 40–55.* AB 19A. New Haven, CT: Yale University Press, 2002.

_____. *Isaiah 56–66*. AB 19B. New Haven, CT: Yale University Press, 2003.

_____. "The Judaean Priesthood during the Neo-Babylonian and Achaemenid Periods: A Hypothetical Reconstruction." *CBQ* 60 (1998): 25–43.

Bloomhardt, Paul F. "The Poems of Haggai." *HUCA* 5 (1928): 153–95.

Boda, Mark J. "From Dystopia to Myopia: Utopian (Re)Visions in Haggai and Zechariah 1–8." Pages 210–48 in *Utopia and Dysopia in Prophetic Literature*. Edited by Ehud Ben Zvi. Helsinki: Finnish Exegetical Society; Göttingen: Vandenhoeck & Ruprecht, 2006.

_____. *Haggai and Zechariah Research: A Bibliographic Study*. Tools for Biblical Study 5. Leiden: Deo, 2003.

_____. "Haggai: Master Rhetorician." *TynBul* 51 (2000): 295–304.

_____. "Majoring on the Minors: Recent Research on Haggai and Zechariah." *CurBR* 2 (2003): 33–68.

Boda, Mark J., and Jamie Novotny, eds. *From the Foundations to the Crenellations*. AOAT 366. Münster: Ugarit-Verlag, 2010.

Böhme, Walter. "Zu Maleachi und Haggai." *ZAW* 7 (1887): 210–17.

Bonnard, Pierre. *Le second Isaïe, son disciple et leurs éditeurs: Isaïe 40–66*. Etudes bibliques. Paris: Gabalda, 1971.

Borowski, Oded. *Agriculture in Iron Age Israel*. Winona Lake, IN: Eisenbrauns, 1987.

Braun, Roddy L. "Cyrus in Second and Third Isaiah, Chronicles, Ezra and Nehemiah." Pages 146–64 in *The Chronicler as Theologian: Essays in Honor of Ralph W. Klein*. Edited by M. Patrick Graham, Steven L. McKenzie, and Gary N. Knoppers. New York, NY: T&T Clark, 2003.

_____. "Solomon, the Chosen Builder: The Significance of 1 Chronicles 22, 28, and 29 for the Theology of Chronicles." *JBL* 95 (1976): 581–90.

Briant, Pierre. *From Cyrus to Alexander: A History of the Persian Empire*. Translated by Peter T. Daniels. Winona Lake, IN: Eisenbrauns, 2002.

Briend, Jacques. "L'édit de Cyrus et sa valeur historique." *Transeu* 11 (1996): 33–44.

Briggs, Charles A. "The Use of רוח in the Old Testament." *JBL* 19 (1900): 132–45.

Brinton, Alan. "Situation in the Theory of Rhetoric." *Ph&Rh* 14 (1981): 234–48.

Brockington, L. H. *Ezra, Nehemiah and Esther*. NCB. London: Nelson, 1969.

Brockriede, Wayne, and Douglas Ehninger. "Toulmin on Argument: An Interpretation and Application." *QJS* 46 (1960): 44–53.

Brongers, Hendrik A. "Bemerkungen zum Gebrauch des adverbialen *we'attāh* im Alten Testament." *VT* 15 (1965): 289–99.

———. "Some Remarks on the Biblical Particle *halō'*." Pages 177–89 in *Remembering All the Way . . .: A Collection of Old Testament Studies Published on the Occasion of the Fortieth Anniversary of the Oudtestamentisch Werkgezelschap in Nederland.* OtSt 21. Leiden: Brill, 1981.

Brown, Michael L. "'Is It Not?' or 'Indeed!': *HL* in Northwest Semitic." *Maarav* 4 (1987): 201–19.

Bryant, Donald C. *Rhetorical Dimensions in Criticism.* Baton Rouge, LA: Louisiana State University Press, 1973.

Budd, Philip John. "Priestly Instruction in Pre-Exilic Israel." *VT* 23 (1973): 1–14.

Budde, Karl. "Zum Text der drei letzten kleinen Propheten." *ZAW* 26 (1906): 1–28.

Carr, David M. *Writing on the Tablet of the Heart: Origins of Scripture and Literature.* New York, NY: Oxford University Press, 2005.

Carter, Charles E. *The Emergence of Yehud in the Persian Period: A Social and Demographic Study.* JSOTSup 294. Sheffield: Sheffield Academic, 1999.

———. "The Province of Yehud in the Post-Exilic Period: Soundings in Site Distribution and Demography." Pages 106–45 in *Second Temple Studies II: Temple Community in the Persian Period.* Edited by Tamara C. Eskenazi and Kent H. Richards. JSOTSup 175. Sheffield: JSOT Press, 1994.

Chary, Théophane. *Aggée-Zacharie-Malachie.* SB. Paris: Gabalda, 1969.

Childs, Brevard S. "The Enemy from the North and the Chaos Tradition." *JBL* 78 (1959): 187–98.

———. *Introduction to the Old Testament as Scripture.* Philadelphia, PA: Fortress Press, 1979.

———. *Isaiah.* OTL. Louisville, KY: Westminster John Knox, 2001.

Clark, David J. "Discourse Structure in Haggai." *JOTT* 5.1 (1992): 13–24.

Clines, David J. A. *Ezra, Nehemiah, Esther.* NCB. Grand Rapids, MI: Eerdmans, 1984.

Cody, Aelred. "When Is the Chosen People Called a *gôy*?" *VT* 14 (1964): 1–6.

Cogan, Mordechai. *I Kings.* AB 10. New Haven, CT: Yale University Press, 2001.

Coggins, Richard J. "Haggai." Pages 135–49 in *Six Minor Prophets through the Centuries.* Edited by Richard Coggins and Jin H. Han. Blackwell Bible Commentaries. Malden, MA: Wiley-Blackwell, 2011.

Condit, Celeste Michelle. "The Functions of Epideictic: The Boston Massacre Orations as Exemplar." *CommQ* 33 (1985): 284–99.

_____. "Rhetorical Criticism and Audiences: The Extremes of McGee and Leff." *WJSC* 64 (1990): 330–45.

Conklin, Blane W. Review of *Handbuch des nordwestsemitischen Briefformulars: Ein Beitrag zur Echtheitsfrage der aramäischen Briefe des Esrabuches*, by Dirk Schwiderski. *JSS* 48 (2003): 137–40.

Consigny, Scott. "Rhetoric and Its Situations." *Ph&Rh* 7 (1974): 175–86.

Cooley, Jeffrey L. "The Story of Saul's Election (1 Samuel 9–10) in the Light of Mantic Practice in Ancient Iraq." *JBL* 130 (2011): 247–61.

Corbett, Edward P. J., and Robert J. Connors. *Classical Rhetoric for the Modern Student*. 4th ed. New York, NY: Oxford University Press, 1999.

Cowley, Arthur E. "The Meaning of מקום in Hebrew." *JTS* 17 (1916): 174–76.

Crenshaw, James L. "YHWH Ṣebaʾôt Šemô: A Form-Critical Analaysis." *ZAW* 81 (1969): 156–75.

Crevels, Mily. "Concessives on Different Semantic Levels: A Typological Perspective." Pages 313–39 in *Cause—Condition—Concession—Contrast: Cognitive and Discourse Perspectives*. Topics in English Linguistics 33. Edited by Elizabeth Couper-Kuhlen and Bernd Kortmann. Berlin: de Gruyter, 2000.

Cross, Frank Moore. *Canaanite Myth and Hebrew Epic: Essays in the History of the Religion of Israel*. Cambridge, MA: Harvard University Press, 1973.

Dalley, Stephanie. "Temple Building in the Ancient Near East: A Synthesis and Reflection." Pages 239–51 in *From the Foundations to the Crenellations: Essays on Temple Building in the Ancient Near East and Hebrew Bible*. Edited by Mark J. Boda and Jamie Novotny. AOAT 366. Münster: Ugarit-Verlag, 2010.

Dalman, Gustaf. *Arbeit und Sitte in Palästina*. 4 vols. Gütersloh: Bertelsmann, 1928.

Dandamaev, Muhammad A. "State and Temple in Babylonia in the First Millennium B.C." Pages 589–96 in vol. 2 of *State and Temple Economy in the Ancient Near East*. Edited by Edward Lipiński. Louvain: Department Oriëntalistiek, 1979.

Dandamaev, Muhammad A., and Vladimir G. Lukonin. *The Culture and Social Institutions of Ancient Iran*. Translated by Philip L. Kohl and D. J. Dadson. Cambridge: Cambridge University Press, 1989.

Dequeker, Luc. "Darius the Persian and the Reconstruction of the Jewish Temple in Jerusalem (Ezra 4,24)." Pages 67–92 in *Ritual and Sacrifice in the Ancient Near East: Proceedings of the International Conference Organized by the Katholieke*

Universiteit Leuven from the 17th to the 20th of April 1991. Edited by J. Quaegebeur. OLA 55. Leuven: Peeters, 1993.

Derousseaux, Louis. *La crainte de Dieu dans l'Ancien Testament*. LD 63. Paris: Cerf, 1970.

Dogniez, Cécile. "Aggée et ses supplements (TM et LXX) ou le développement littéraire d'un livre biblique." Pages 197–218 in *L'apport de la Septante aux études sur l'Antiquité*. Edited by Philippe Le Moigne and Jan Joosten. Paris: Cerf, 2005.

Driver, Godfrey R. "Affirmation by Exclamatory Negation." *JANESCU* 5 (1973): 107–14.

Driver, Samuel Rolles. *The Minor Prophets: Nahum, Habakkuk, Zephaniah, Haggai, Zechariah, Malachi*. Century Bible. New York, NY: Frowde, 1906.

Duguid, Iain M. *Ezekiel and the Leaders of Israel*. VTSup 56. Leiden: Brill, 1994.

Duhm, Bernhard. *Das Buch Jesaia*. 5th ed. Göttingen: Vandenhoeck & Ruprecht, 1968.

Dumbrell, William J. "Kingship and Temple in the Post-Exilic Period." *RTR* 37 (1978): 33–42.

Edelman, Diana V. *The Origins of the "Second" Temple: Persian Imperial Policy and the Rebuilding of Jerusalem*. Bible World. London: Equinox, 2005.

Edelman, Murray. *Constructing the Political Spectacle*. Chicago, IL: University of Chicago Press, 1988.

Eemeren, Frans H. van, Bert Meuffels, and Mariel Verburg. "The (Un)reasonableness of Ad Hominem Fallacies." *JLSP* 19 (2000): 416–35.

Eemeren, Frans H. van, and Rob Grootendorst. *Argumentation, Communication, and Fallacies: A Pragma-Dialectical Perspective*. Hillsdale, NJ: Lawrence Erlbaum Associates, 1992.

Eichrodt, Walther. *Ezekiel*. Translated by Cosslett Quin. OTL. Philadelphia, PA: Westminster, 1970.

Eissfeldt, Otto. *The Old Testament: An Introduction*. Translated by Peter R. Ackroyd. New York, NY: Harper & Row, 1965.

Elliger, Karl. *Das Buch der zwölf kleinen Propheten II: Die Propheten Nahum, Habakuk, Zephanja, Haggai, Sacharja, Maleachi*. ATD 25. Göttingen: Vandenhoeck & Ruprecht, 1967.

———. *Deuterojesaja in seinem Verhältnis zu Tritojesaja*. BWANT 4/11. Stuttgart: Kohlhammer, 1933.

Ellis, Richard S. *Foundation Deposits in Ancient Mesopotamia*. YNER 2. New Haven, CT: Yale University Press, 1968.

Exum, J. Cheryl. *Song of Songs*. OTL. Louisville, KY: Westminster John Knox, 2005.

Fahnstock, Jeanne R., and Marie J. Secor. "Grounds for Argument: Stasis Theory and Topoi." Pages 135–56 in *Argument in Transition: Proceedings of the Third Summer Conference on Argumentation*. Edited by D. Zarefsky. Annandale, VA: Speech Communication Association, 1983.

Faust, Avraham. "The Archaeology of the Israelite Cult: Questioning the Consensus." *BASOR* 360 (210): 23–35.

———. *Judah in the Neo-Babylonian Period: The Archaeology of Destruction*. ABS 18. Atlanta, GA: Society of Biblical Literature, 2012.

———. "Settlement Dynamics and Demographic Fluctuations in Judah from the Late Iron Age to the Hellenistic Period and the Archaeology of Persian-Period Yehud." Pages 23–51 in *A Time of Change: Judah and Its Neighbours in the Persian and Early Hellenistic Periods*. Edited by Yigdal Levin. LSTS 65. London: T&T Clark, 2007.

Fensham, F. Charles. *The Books of Ezra and Nehemiah*. NICOT. Grand Rapids, MI: Eerdmans, 1982.

Fernández, Andrés. "El profeta Ageo 2, 15–18 y la fundación del segundo tempel." *Biblica* 2 (1921): 206–15.

Fisher, Walter R. "A Motive View of Communication." *QJS* 56 (1970): 131–39.

Fitzgerald, Madeleine. "Temple Building in the Old Babylonian Period." Pages 35–48 in *From the Foundations to the Crenellations: Essays on Temple Building in the Ancient Near East and Hebrew Bible*. Edited by Mark J. Boda and Jamie Novotny. AOAT 366. Münster: Ugarit-Verlag, 2010.

Floyd, Michael H. *Minor Prophets, Part 2*. FOTL 22. Grand Rapids, MI: Eerdmans, 2000.

Fohrer, Georg. *Das Buch Jesaja, 3. Band: Kapitel 40–66*. ZBK. Zurich: Zwingli-Verlag, 1964.

Folmer, Margaretha L. *The Aramaic Language in the Achaemenid Period: A Study in Linguistic Variation*. OLA 68. Leuven: Peeters, 1995.

Foss, Sonja K. *Rhetorical Criticism: Exploration and Practice*. 4th ed. Long Grove, IL: Waveland, 2009.

Fox, Nili Sacher. *In the Service of the King: Officialdom in Ancient Israel and Judah*. HUCM 23. Cincinnati, OH: Hebrew Union College Press, 2000.

Fraine, Jean de. *L'Aspect religieux de la royauté israélite: L'Instutition monarchique dan l'Ancien Testament et dans les textes mésopotamiens*. AnBib 3. Rome: Pontifical Biblical Institute, 1954.

Frankfort, Henri. *Kingship and the Gods: A Study of Ancient Near Eastern Religion as the Integration of Society and Nature*. Oriental Institute Essays. Chicago, IL: University of Chicago Press, 1948.

Fried, Lisbeth S. "The Land Lay Desolate: Conquest and Restoration in the Ancient Near East." Pages 21–54 in *Judah and the Judeans in the Neo-Babylonian Period*. Edited by Oded Lipschits and Joseph Blenkinsopp. Winona Lake, IN: Eisenbrauns, 2003.

———. "Temple Building in Ezra 1–6." Pages 319–38 in *From the Foundations to the Crenellations: Essays on Temple Building in the Ancient Near East and Hebrew Bible*. Edited by Mark J. Boda and Jamie Novotny. AOAT 366. Münster: Ugarit-Verlag, 2010.

———, ed. *Was 1 Esdras First? An Investigation into the Priority and Nature of 1 Esdras*. AIL 7. Atlanta, GA: Society of Biblical Literature, 2011.

Fritz, Volkmar. *1 & 2 Kings*. Translated by Anselm Hagedorn. CC. Minneapolis, MN: Fortress Press, 2003.

Galling, Kurt. *Studien zur Geschichte Israels in persichen Zeitalter*. Tübingen: Mohr Siebeck, 1964.

Gardner, Anne E. "Isaiah 66:1–4: Condemnation of Temple and Sacrifice or Contrast between the Arrogant and the Humble?" *RB* 113 (2006): 506–28.

Garret, Mary, and Xiaosui Xiao. "The Rhetorical Situation Revisited." *RSQ* 23 (1993): 30–40.

Gelston, Anthony. "The Foundations of the Second Temple." *VT* 16 (1966): 232–35.

———. *The Twelve Minor Prophets* (תרי עשר). BHQ 13. Stuttgart: Deutsche Bibelgesellschaft, 2010.

Glazier-McDonald, Beth. *Malachi: The Divine Messenger*. SBLDS 98. Atlanta, GA: Scholars Press, 1987.

Gordis, Robert. "A Rhetorical Use of Interrogative Sentences in Biblical Hebrew." *AJSL* 49 (1933): 212–17.

Görg, Manfred. "Ṣb'wt: Ein Gottestitel." *BN* 30 (1985): 15–18.

Gorrell, Donna. "The Rhetorical Situation Again: Linked Components in a Venn Diagram." *Ph&Rh* 30 (1997): 395–412.

Grabbe, Lester L. *Ezra-Nehemiah*. OTR. London: Routledge, 1998.

———. "'Mind the Gaps': Ezra, Nehemiah and the Judean Restoration." Pages

83–104 in *Restoration: Old Testament, Jewish, and Christian Perspectives.* Edited by James M. Scott. JSJSup 72. Leiden: Brill, 2001.

_____. "The 'Persian Documents' in the Book of Ezra: Are They Authentic?" Pages 531–70 in *Judah and the Judeans in the Persian Period.* Edited by Oded Lipschitz and Manfred Oeming. Winona Lake, IN: Eisenbrauns, 2006.

_____. "'They Shall Come Rejoicing to Zion'—or Did They? The Settlement of Yehud in the Early Persian Period." Pages 116–27 in *Exile and Restoration Revisited: Essays on the Babylonian and Persian Periods in Memory of Peter R. Ackroyd.* Edited by Gary N. Knoppers, Lester L. Grabbe, and Deirdre N. Fulton. LSTS 73. London: T&T Clark, 2009.

Graffy, Adrian. *A Prophet Confronts His People: The Disputation Speech in the Prophets.* AnBib 104. Rome: Biblical Institute Press, 1984.

Grant-Davie, Keith. "Rhetorical Situations and Their Constituents." *RhetR* 15 (1997): 264–79.

Gunneweg, Antonius H. J. "עם הארץ: A Semantic Revolution." *ZAW* 95 (1983): 437–40.

_____. "Die aramäische und die hebräische Erzählung über die nachexilische Restauration: ein Vergleich." *ZAW* 94 (1982): 299–302.

_____. *Esra.* KAT 19/1. Gütersloh: Gütersloher, 1985.

Hallaschka, Martin. *Haggai und Sacharja 1–8: Eine redaktionsgeschictliche Untersuchung.* BZAW 411. Berlin: de Gruyter, 2011.

Halpern, Baruch. "A Historiographic Commentary on Ezra 1–6: A Chronological Narrative and Dual Chronology in Israelite Historiography." Pages 81–142 in *The Hebrew Bible and Its Interpreters.* Edited by William Henry Propp, Baruch Halpern, and David Noel Freedman. BJSUCSD 1. Winona Lake, IN: Eisenbrauns, 1990.

Hamerton-Kelly, Robert G. "The Temple and the Origins of Jewish Apocalyptic." *VT* 20 (1970): 1–15.

Hanson, Paul D. *The Dawn of Apocalyptic: The Historical and Sociological Roots of Jewish Apocalyptic Eschatology.* Rev. ed. Philadelphia, PA: Fortress Press, 1979.

Haran, Menahem. *Temples and Temple Service in Ancient Israel: An Inquiry into Biblical Cult Phenomena and the Historical Setting of the Priestly School.* Winona Lake, IN: Eisenbrauns, 1985.

Hart, Roderick P., and Suzanne Daughton. *Modern Rhetorical Criticism.* 3rd ed. Boston, MA: Pearson, 2005.

Hasel, Gerhard F. *The Remnant: The History and Theology of the Remnant Idea from*

Genesis to Isaiah. AUMSR 5. Berrien Springs, MI: Andrews University Press, 1972.

Hayes, John H. "Usage of Oracles against Foreign Nations in Ancient Israel." *JBL* 87 (1968): 81–92.

Heaton, Eric W. "The Root שאר and the Doctrine of the Remnant." *JTS* NS 3 (1952): 27–39.

Hildebrand, David R. "Temple Ritual: A Paradigm for Moral Holiness in Haggai ii 10–19." *VT* 39 (1989). 154–68.

Hill, Andrew E. "Dating Second Zechariah: A Linguistic Reexamination." *HAR* 6 (1982): 105–34.

———. *Malachi.* AB 25D. New Haven, CT: Yale University Press, 1998.

Hillers, Delbert R. *Treaty-Curses and the Old Testament Prophets.* BibOr 16. Rome: Pontifical Biblical Institute, 1964.

Hirsch, Emil G. "Book of Haggai." Pages 146, 148–49 in vol. 6 of *The Jewish Encyclopedia.* New York, NY: Funk & Wagnalls, 1916.

Holbrook, David J. "Narrowing Down Haggai: Examining Style in Light of Discourse and Content." *JOTT* 7.2 (1995): 1–12.

Holladay, William L. *Jeremiah 1: A Commentary on the Book of the Prophet Jeremiah Chapters 1–25.* Edited by Paul Hanson. Hermeneia. Philadelphia, PA: Fortress Press, 1986.

Holmstedt, Robert D. "The Relative Clause in Biblical Hebrew: A Linguistic Analysis." PhD diss., University of Wisconsin-Madison, 2002.

Horst, Friedrich. *Die zwölf kleinen Propheten.* 2nd ed. HAT 1/14. Tübingen: Mohr Siebeck, 1954.

Hultzén, Lee S. "Status in Deliberative Analysis." Pages 97–123 in *The Rhetorical Idiom: Essays in Rhetoric, Oratory, Language, and Drama.* Edited by Donald C. Bryant. Ithaca, NY: Cornell University Press, 1958.

Hurowitz, Victor A. *I Have Built You an Exalted House: Temple Building in the Bible in the Light of Mesopotamian and Northwest Semitic Writings.* JSOTSup 115. Sheffield: JSOT Press, 1992.

———. "The Priestly Account of Building the Tabernacle." *JAOS* 105 (1985): 21–30.

———. "'Solomon Built the Temple and Completed It': Building the First Temple according to the Book of Kings." Pages 281–302 in *From the Foundations to the Crenellations: Essays on Temple Building in the Ancient Near East and Hebrew Bible.*

Edited by Mark J. Boda and Jamie Novotny. AOAT 366. Münster: Ugarit- Verlag, 2010.

Hyatt, James P. "A Neo-Babylonian Parallel to Bethel-Sar-Eṣer, Zech 7:2." *JBL* 56 (1937): 87–94.

Ilie, Cornelia. *What Else Can I Tell You? A Pragmatic Study of English Rhetorical Questions as Discursive and Argumentative Acts.* SSE 82. Stockholm: Almqvist & Wiksell, 1994.

Jagersma, Henk. "The Tithes in the Old Testament." Pages 116–28 in *Remembering All the Way . . .: A Collection of Old Testament Studies Published on the Occasion of the Fortieth Anniversary of the Oudtestamentisch Werkgezelschap in Nederland.* OtSt 21. Leiden: Brill, 1981.

Japhet, Sara. "'History' and 'Literature' in the Persian Period: The Restoration of the Temple." Pages 174–88 in *Ah, Assyria . . .: Studies in Assyrian History and Ancient Near Eastern Historiography Presented to Hayim Tadmor.* Edited by Mordechai Cogan and Israel Eph'al. Jerusalem: Magnes, 1991.

———. "People and Land in the Restoration Period." Pages 103–25 in *Das Land Israel in biblischer Zeit: Jerusalem-Symposium 1981 der Hebräischen Universität und der Georg-August-Universität.* Edited by Georg Strecker. GTA 25. Göttingen: Vandenhoeck & Ruprecht, 1983.

———. "Sheshbazzar and Zerubbabel: Against the Background of the Historical and Religious Tendencies of Ezra-Nehemiah." *ZAW* 94 (1982): 66–98; 95 (1983): 218–29.

———. "The Temple in the Restoration Period: Reality and Ideology." *USQR* 44 (1991): 195–251.

Jasinski, James. *Sourcebook on Rhetoric: Key Concepts in Contemporary Rhetorical Studies.* Rhetoric and Society. Thousand Oaks, CA: SAGE, 2001.

Jones, Barry A. *The Formation of the Book of the Twelve: A Study in Text and Canon.* SBLDS 149. Atlanta, GA: Scholars Press, 1995.

Jones, Douglas. "The Cessation of Sacrifice after the Destruction of the Temple in 586 BC." *JTS* NS 14 (1963): 12–31.

Joyce, Paul M. "King and Messiah in Ezekiel." Pages 323–37 in *King and Messiah in Israel and the Ancient Near East: Proceedings of the Oxford Old Testament Seminar.* Edited by John Day. JSOTSup 270. Sheffield: Sheffield Academic, 1998.

Kapelrud, Arvid S. "Temple Building, a Task for Gods and Kings." *Or* 32 (1963): 56–62.

Karon, Louise A. "Presence in *The New Rhetoric.*" *Ph&Rh* 9 (1976): 96–111.

Kauffman, Charles, and Donna W. Parson. "Metaphor and Presence in Argument." Pages 91–102 in *Argumentation Theory and the Rhetoric of Assent*. Edited by David C. Williams and Michael D. Hazen. Studies in Rhetoric and Communication. Tuscaloosa, AL: University of Alabama Press, 1990.

Kelso, James Leon. *The Excavations of Bethel, 1934–1960*. Cambridge, MA: American Schools of Oriental Research, 1968.

Kessler, John. *The Book of Haggai: Prophecy and Society in Early Persian Yehud*. VTSup 91. Leiden: Brill, 2002.

———. "Building the Second Temple: Questions of Time, Text, and History in Haggai 1.1–15." *JSOT* 27 (2002): 243–56.

———. "The Shaking of the Nations: An Eschatological View." *JETS* 30 (1987): 159–66.

———. "'T (le temps) en Aggée 1 2–4: Conflit théologique ou 'sagesse mondaine'?" *VT* 48 (1998): 555–59.

King, Andrew A., and Floyd D. Anderson. "Nixon, Agnew, and the 'Silent Majority': A Case Study in the Rhetoric of Polarization." *Western Speech* 35 (1971): 243–55.

King, Philip J., and Lawrence E. Stager. *Life in Biblical Israel*. LAI. Louisville, KY: Westminster John Knox, 2001.

Klein, Ralph. "Were Joshua, Zerubbabel, and Nehemiah Contemporaries? A Response to Diana Edelman's Proposed Late Date for the Second Temple." *JBL* 127 (2008): 697–701.

Knauf, Ernst Axel. "Bethel: The Israelite Impact on Judean Language and Literature." Pages 291–349 in *Judah and the Judeans in the Persian Period*. Edited by Oded Lipschits and Manfred Oeming. Winona Lake, IN: Eisenbrauns, 2006.

Knowles, Melody D. *Centrality Practiced: Jerusalem in the Religious Practice of Yehud and the Diaspora in the Persian Period*. ABS 16. Atlanta, GA: Society of Biblical Literature, 2006.

Koch, Klaus. "Haggais unreines Volk." *ZAW* 79 (1967): 52–66.

Kochin, Michael S. *Five Chapters on Rhetoric: Character, Action, Things, Nothing, and Art*. University Park, PA: Pennsylvania State University Press, 2009.

Koenen, Klaus. *Ethik und Eschatologie im Tritojesajabuch: Eine literarkritische und redaktionsgeschichtliche Studie*. WMANT 62. Neukirchen-Vluyn: Neukirchener, 1990.

Koole, Jan L. *Isaiah 40–48*. Vol. 1 of *Isaiah III*. HCOT. Kampen: Pharos, 1997.

Kratz, Reinhard G. *Das Judentum im Zeitalter des Zweiten Tempels.* FAT 42. Tübingen: Mohr Siebeck, 2004.

Kugel, James L. *The Idea of Biblical Poetry: Parallelism and Its History.* Baltimore, MD: Johns Hopkins University Press, 1981.

Kuhrt, Amélie. *The Ancient Near East c. 3000–330 BC.* 2 vols. London: Routledge, 1995.

_____. "The Cyrus Cylinder and Achaemenid Imperial Policy." *JSOT* 25 (1983): 83–97.

Kutscher, Eduard Y. *A History of the Hebrew Language.* Jerusalem: Magnes, 1982.

Laato, Antti. *Josiah and David Redivivus: The Historical Josiah and the Messianic Expectations of Exilic and Postexilic Times.* Stockholm: Almqvist & Wiksell, 1992.

Lambdin, Thomas O. *Introduction to Biblical Hebrew.* Upper Saddle River, NJ: Prentice Hall, 1971.

Lanham, Richard A. *Analyzing Prose.* New York, NY: Scribner's, 1983.

Larson, Richard L. "Lloyd Bitzer's 'Rhetorical Situation' and the Classification of Discourse: Problems and Implications." *Ph&Rh* 3 (1970): 165–68.

Lau, Wolfgang. *Schriftgelehrte Prophetie in Jes 56–66.* BZAW 225. Berlin: de Gruyter, 1994.

Leene, Henk. "Universalism or Nationalism? Isaiah XLV 9–13 and Its Context." *Bijdr* 39 (1974): 309–34.

Leff, Michael. "Perelman, ad Hominem, and Rhetorical Ethos." *Argumentation* 23 (2009): 301–11.

Lemaire, André. "Zorobabel et la Judée à la lumière de l'épigraphie (fin du VIe s. av. J.-C." *RB* 103 (1996): 48–57.

Lemche, Niels Peter. "Did a Reform Like Josiah's Happen?" Pages 11–19 in *The Historian and the Bible: Essays in Honour of Lester L. Grabbe.* Edited by Diana V. Edelman and Philip R. Davies. LHBOTS 530. New York, NY: T&T Clark, 2010.

Leuenberger, Martin. "Gegenwart und Zukunft im Haggaibuch: Das dynamische Zeit-und Geschichtsverständnis von Hag 2,6–9.20–23." Pages 235–48 in *Gott in Bewegung: Religions- und theologiegeschichtliche Beiträge zu Gottesvorstellungen im alten Israel.* FAT 76. Tübingen: Mohr Siebeck, 2011.

Levenson, Jon D. "From Temple to Synagogue: 1 Kings 8." Pages 143–66 in *Traditions in Transformation: Turning Points in Biblical Faith.* Edited by Baruch Halpern and Jon D. Levenson. Winona Lake, IN: Eisenbrauns, 1981.

_____. "The Temple and the World." *JR* 64 (1984): 275–98.

Lindhagen, Curt. *The Servant Motif in the Old Testament: A Preliminary Study to the "Ebed-Yahweh Problem" in Deutero-Isaiah.* Uppsala: Almqvist & Wiksells, 1950.

Lipschits, Oded. "Achaemenid Imperial Policy, Settlement Processes in Palestine, and the Status of Jerusalem in the Middle of the Fifth Century B.C.E." Pages 19–52 in *Judah and the Judeans in the Persian Period.* Edited by Oded Lipschits and Manfred Oeming. Winona Lake, IN: Eisenbrauns, 2006.

_____. "Demographic Changes in Judah between the Seventh and the Fifth Centuries B.C.E." Pages 323–76 in *Judah and the Judeans in the Neo-Babylonian Period.* Edited by Oded Lipschits and Joseph Blenkinsopp. Winona Lake, IN: Eisenbrauns, 2003.

_____. *The Fall and Rise of Jerusalem: Judah under Babylonian Rule.* Winona Lake, IN: Eisenbrauns, 2009.

_____. "Judah, Jerusalem and the Temple 586–539 B.C." *Transeu* 22 (2001): 129–42.

_____. "Persian-Period Judah: A New Perspective." Pages 187–211 in *Texts, Contexts and Readings in Postexilic Literature.* Edited by Louis Jonker. FAT 2/53. Tübingen: Mohr Siebeck, 2011.

_____. "Persian Period Finds from Jerusalem: Facts and Interpretations." *JHebS* 9 (2009): article 20 available at http://purl.org/JHS and at http://www.JHSonline.org.

_____. "The Rural Settlement in Judah in the Sixth Century B.C.E.: A Rejoinder." *PEQ* 136 (2004): 99–107.

Lipschits, Oded, and David S. Vanderhooft. *The Yehud Stamp Impressions: A Corpus of Inscribed Impressions from the Persian and Hellenistic Periods in Judah.* Winona Lake, IN: Eisenbrauns, 2011.

_____. "Yehud Stamp Impressions in the Fourth Century B.C.E.: A Time of Administrative Consolidation?" Pages 75–94 in *Judah and the Judeans in the Fourth Century B.C.E.* Edited by Oded Lipschits, Gary N. Knoppers, and Rainer Albertz. Winona Lake, IN: Eisenbrauns, 2007.

Lohfink, Norbert. "Die deuteronomistische Darstellung des Übergangs der Führung Israels von Moses auf Josue: Ein Beitrag zur alttestamentliche Theologie des Amtes." *Scholastik* 37 (1962): 32–44.

Lund, Jerome A. "Aramaic Language." Pages 50–60 in *Dictionary of the Old Testament: Historical Books.* Edited by Bill T. Arnold and H. G. M. Williamson. Downers Grove, IL: InterVarsity Press, 2005.

Lundbom, Jack R. *Jeremiah 21–36.* AB 21B. New York, NY: Doubleday, 2004.

Lux, Rüdiger. "Das Zweiprophetenbuch: Beobachtungen zu Aufbau und Struktur von Haggai und Sacharja 1–8." Pages 191–217 in *"Word JHWHs, das Geschah…" (Hos 1,1): Studien zum Zwölfprophetenbuch*. Edited by Erich Zenger. Herders Biblische Studien 35. Freiburg: Herder, 2002.

Lys, Daniel. *"Rûach": Le souffle dans l'Ancien Testament*. EHPR 56. Paris: Presses Universitaire de France, 1962.

Mader, Thomas F. "On Presence in Rhetoric." *CCC* 24 (1973): 375–81.

Margain, Jean. "Observations sur *I Chroniques*, XXII à propos des anachronisms linguistiques dans la Bible." *Semitica* 24 (1974): 35–43.

Marti, Karl. *Das Dodekapropheton*. KHC 13. Tübingen: Mohr Siebeck, 1904.

Mason, Rex. "The Messiah in the Postexilic Old Testament Literature." Pages 338–64 in *King and Messiah in Israel and in the Ancient Near East: Proceedings of the Oxford Old Testament Seminar*. Edited by John Day. JSOTSup 270. Sheffield: Sheffield Academic, 1998.

_____. *Preaching the Tradition: Homily and Hermeneutics after the Exile*. Cambridge: Cambridge University Press, 1990.

_____. "The Purpose of the 'Editorial Framework' of the Book of Haggai." *VT* 27 (1977): 413–21.

Mays, James. *Hosea*. OTL. Philadelphia, PA: Westminster, 1969.

May, Herbert G. "'This People' and 'This Nation' in Haggai." *VT* 18 (1968): 190–97.

Mazzoleni, Marco. *Costrutti concessivi e costrutti avversativi in alcune lingue d'Europa*. Florence: Nuova Italia, 1990.

McCarthy, Dennis J. "An Installation Genre?" *JBL* 90 (1971): 31–41.

Mendelsohn, Isaac. "On Corvée Labor in Canaan and Ancient Israel." *BASOR* 167 (1962): 31–35.

Mettinger, Tryggve N. D. *The Dethronement of Sabaoth: Studies in the Shem and Kabod Theologies*. ConBOT 18. Lund: Gleerup, 1982.

_____. "YHWH SABAOTH—The Heavenly King on the Cherubim Throne." Pages 109–38 in *Studies in the Period of David and Solomon and Other Essays*. Edited by Tomoo Ishida. Winona Lake, IN: Eisenbrauns, 1982.

Metzger, Martin. "Himmlische und irdische Wohnstatt Jahwes." *UF* 2 (1970): 139–58.

Meyers, Carol L., and Eric M. Meyers. *Haggai, Zechariah 1–8*. AB 25B. Garden City, NY: Doubleday, 1987.

_____. *Zechariah 9–14*. AB 25C. New Haven, CT: Yale University Press, 1993.

Michaeli, Frank. *Les Livres des Chroniques, d'Esdras, et de Néhémie.* CAT 16. Neuchâtel: Delachaux & Niestle, 1967.

Middlemas, Jill. "Divine Reversal and the Role of the Temple in Trito-Isaiah." Pages 164–87 in *Temple and Worship in Biblical Israel.* LHBOTS 422. Edited by John Day. London: T&T Clark, 2005.

Milgrom, Jacob. *Leviticus 1-16.* AB 3. New York, NY: Doubleday, 1991.

Miller, Cynthia L. *The Representation of Speech in Biblical Hebrew Narrative: A Linguistic Analysis.* HSM 55. Atlanta, GA: Scholars Press, 1996.

Miller, J. Maxwell, and John H. Hayes. *A History of Ancient Israel and Judah.* 2nd ed. Louisville, KY: Westminster John Knox Press, 2006.

Miller, Patrick D., Jr. *The Divine Warrior in Early Israel.* Cambridge, MA: Harvard University Press, 1973.

Mitchell, Hinckley G., et al. *A Critical and Exegetical Commentary on Haggai, Zechariah, Malachi and Jonah.* ICC. New York, NY: Scribner, 1912.

Mowinckel, Sigmund. *He That Cometh: The Messiah Concept in the Old Testament and Later Judaism.* Translated by G. W. Anderson. Nashville, TN: Abingdon, 1954.

Muilenburg, James. "Form Criticism and Beyond." *JBL* 88 (1969): 1–18.

Müller, Werner E., and Horst Dietrich Preuß. *Die Vorstellung vom Rest im Alten Testament.* Neukirchen-Vluyn: Neukirchener, 1973.

Munch, Peter A. *The Expression* bajjôm hāhū': *Is It an Eschatological* terminus technicus? Oslo: Dybwad, 1936.

Muraoka, Takamitsu. *Emphatic Words and Structures in Biblical Hebrew.* Jerusalem: Magnes; Leiden: Brill, 1985.

———. "In Defence of the Unity of the Septuagint Minor Prophets." *AJBI* 15 (1989): 25–36.

———. "Introduction aux douze petits prophètes." Pages i–xxiii in *Les douze prophètes: Osée.* Edited by Eberhard Bons, Jan Jooster, and Stephen Kessler. BibAlex 23/1. Paris: Cerf, 2002.

Murray, D. F. "The Rhetoric of Disputation." *JSOT* 38 (1987): 95–121.

Myers, Jacob M. *Ezra, Nehemiah.* AB 14. Garden City, NY: Doubleday, 1965.

Na'aman, Nadav. "From Conscription of Forced Labor to a Symbol of Bondage: *mas* in the Biblical Literature." Pages 746–58 in *"An Experienced Scribe Who Neglects Nothing": Ancient Near Eastern Studies in Honor of Jacob Klein.* Edited by Yitschak Sefati et al. Bethesda, MD: CDL, 2005.

_____. "Royal Vassals or Governors? On the Status of Sheshbazzar and Zerubbabel in the Persian Empire." *Henoch* 22 (2000): 35–44.

Naidoff, Bruce D. "The Two-Fold Structure of Isaiah XLV 9–13." *VT* 31 (1981): 180–85.

Nicholson, Ernest W. "The Meaning of the Expression עם הארץ in the Old Testament." *JSS* 10 (1965): 59–66.

Nissinen, Martti. "How Prophecy Became Literature." *SJOT* 19 (2005): 153–72.

_____. *Prophets and Prophecy in the Ancient Near East.* Writings from the Ancient World 12. Atlanta, GA: Society of Biblical Literature, 2003.

_____. "The Socioreligious Role of the Neo-Assyrian Prophets." Pages 89–114 in *Prophecy in Its Ancient Near Eastern Context.* Edited by Martti Nissinen. SBLSymS 13. Atlanta, GA: Society of Biblical Literature, 2000.

Nogalski, James. *Literary Precursors to the Book of the Twelve.* BZAW 217. Berlin: de Gruyter, 1993.

Noll, K. L. "Was There Doctrinal Dissemination in Early Yahweh Religion?" *BibInt* 16 (2008): 395–427.

Novotny, Jamie. "Temple Building in Assyria: Evidence from Royal Inscriptions." Pages 109–39 in *From the Foundations to the Crenellations: Essays on Temple Building in the Ancient Near East and Hebrew Bible.* Edited by Mark J. Boda and Jamie Novotny. AOAT 366. Münster: Ugarit-Verlag, 2010.

Oesterley, W. O. E., and Theodore H. Robinson. *An Introduction to the Books of the Old Testament.* London: SPCK, 1961.

O'Kennedy, Daniel F. "The Use of the Epithet יהוה צבאות in Haggai, Zechariah and Malachi." *JNST* 33 (2007): 77–99.

Oswalt, John N. *The Book of Isaiah: Chapters 40-66.* NICOT. Grand Rapids, MI: Eerdmans, 1998.

Overholt, Thomas W. *Channels of Prophecy: The Social Dynamics of Prophetic Activity.* Eugene, OR: Wipf & Stock, 1989.

Pardee, Dennis. "The Judicial Plea from Meṣad Ḥashavyahu (Yavneh-Yam): A New Philological Study." *Maarav* 1 (1978): 33–66.

Parker, Richard A., and Waldo H. Dubberstein. *Babylonian Chronology 626 B.C.-A.D. 45.* BUS 19. Providence, RI: Brown University Press, 1956.

Paschen, Wilfried. *Rein und unrein: Untersuchung zur biblischen Wortgeschichte.* SANT 24. Munich: Kosel, 1970.

Patton, John H. "Causation and Creativity in Rhetorical Situations: Distinctions and Implications." *QJS* 65 (1979): 36–55.

Paul, Shalom M. *Isaiah 40-66*. ECC. Grand Rapids, MI: Eerdmans, 2012.

Pauritsch, Karl. *Die neue Gemeinde: Gott sammelt Ausgestossene und Arme (Jesaja 56-66)*. AnBib 47. Rome: Biblical Institute Press, 1971.

Perelman, Chaim, and L. Olbrechts-Tyteca. *The New Rhetoric: A Treatise on Argumentation*. Translated by J. Wilkinson and P. Weaver. Notre Dame, IN: University of Notre Dame Press, 1969.

Peter, Friedrich. "Zu Haggai 1,9." *TZ* 7 (1951): 150–51.

Petersen, David L. *Haggai and Zechariah 1-8. A Commentary*. OTL. Philadelphia, PA: Westminster, 1984.

_____. "The Temple in Persian Period Prophetic Texts." Pages 125–44 in *Second Temple Studies I: Persian Period*. Edited by Philip R. Davies. JSOTSup 117. Sheffield: JSOT Press, 1991.

_____. *Zechariah 9-14 and Malachi*. OTL. Louisville, KY: Westminster John Knox, 1995.

_____. "Zerubbabel and Jerusalem Temple Reconstruction." *CBQ* 36 (1974): 366–72.

Petty, Richard E., John T. Cacioppo, and Martin Heesacker. "Effects of Rhetorical Questions on Persuasion: A Cognitive Response Analysis." *Journal of Personality and Social Psychology* 40 (1981): 401–32.

Pfeil, Rüdiger. "When Is a *Gôy* a 'Goy'? An Interpretation of Haggai 2:10-19." Pages 261–78 in *A Tribute to Gleason Archer*. Edited by Walter C. Kaiser, Jr. and Ronald F. Youngblood. Chicago, IL: Moody, 1986.

Polak, Frank H. "Sociolinguistics and the Judean Speech Community in the Achaemenid Empire." Pages 589–628 in *Judah and the Judeans in the Persian Period*. Edited by Oded Lipschitz and Manfred Oeming. Winona Lake, IN: Eisenbrauns, 2006.

Porten, Bezalel. "Elephantine and the Bible." Pages 51–84 in *Semitic Papyrology in Context: A Climate of Creativity: Papers from a New York University Conference Marking the Retirement of Baruch A. Levine*. Edited by Lawrence H. Schiffman. CHANE. Leiden: Brill, 2003.

Postgate, J. N. "The Role of the Temple in the Mesopotamian Secular Community." Pages 811–25 in *Man, Settlement and Urbanism: Proceedings of a Meeting of the Research Seminar in Archaeology and Related Subjects, Held at the Institute of Archaeology, London University*. Edited by Peter J. Ucko, Ruth Tringham, and G. W. Dimbleby. London: Duckworth, 1972.

Preuss, Horst D. "... ich will mit dir sein!" *ZAW* 80 (1968): 139–73.

Prince, Gerald. "Introduction to the Study of the Narratee." Pages 213–33 in *Essentials of the Theory of Fiction*. 2nd ed. Edited by Michael J. Hoffman and Patrick D. Murphy. Durham, NC: Duke University Press, 1996.

Raabe, Paul R. "Why Prophetic Oracles against the Nations?" Pages 236–57 in *Fortunate the Eyes That See: Essays in Honor of David Noel Freedman in Celebration of His Seventieth Birthday*. Edited by Astrid B. Beck et al. Grand Rapids, MI: Eerdmans, 1995.

Rabinowitz, Peter J. "Truth in Fiction: A Reexamination of Audiences." *CritInq* 4 (1977): 121–41.

Rad, Gerhard von. "Die Anrechnung des Glaubens zur Gerechtigkeit." *TLZ* 76 (1951): 129–32.

Rainey, Anson F. "Compulsory Labour Gangs in Ancient Israel." *IEJ* 20 (1970): 191–202.

Rendsburg, Gary A. "Late Biblical Hebrew in the Book of Haggai." Forthcoming.

Rendtorff, Rolf. *Die Gesetze in der Priesterschrift: Eine gattungsgeschichtliche Untersuchung*. Göttingen: Vandenhoeck & Ruprecht, 1954.

―――. "Zum Gebrauch der Formel *ne'um jahwe* im Jeremiabuch." *ZAW* 66 (1954): 27–37.

Reuss, Eduard. *Die Propheten*. Vol. 2 of *Das Alte Testament: Übersetzt, eingeleitet und erläutert*. Braunschweig: Schwetschke, 1892.

Reventlow, Henning G. *Die Propheten Haggai, Sacharja und Maleachi*. Göttingen: Vandenhoeck & Ruprecht, 1993.

Robert, A., and R. Tourney. *Le Cantique des cantiques: Traduction et commentaire*. Études bibliques. Paris: Gabalda, 1963.

Robinson, Theodore H. *Prophecy and the Prophets in Ancient Israel*. London: Duckworth, 1923.

Rofé, Alexander. "Isaiah 66:1–4: Judean Sects in the Persian Period as Viewed by Trito-Isaiah." Pages 205–17 in *Biblical and Related Studies Presented to Samuel Iwry*. Edited by Ann Kort and Scott Morschauser. Winona Lake, IN: Eisenbrauns, 1985.

Rollston, Christopher A. *Writing and Literacy in the World of Ancient Israel: Epigraphic Evidence from the Iron Age*. Archaeology and Bible Series 11. Atlanta, GA: Society of Biblical Literature, 2010.

Rose, Wolter H. "Messianic Expectations in the Early Postexilic Period." Pages 168–85 in *Yahwism after the Exile: Perspectives on Israelite Religion in the Persian*

Era. Edited by Rainer Albertz and Bob Becking. STR 5. Assen: Van Gorcum, 2003.

_____. *Zemah and Zerubbabel: Messianic Expectations in the Early Postexilic Period*. JSOTSup 304. Sheffield: Sheffield Academic Press, 2000.

Rosenthal, F. *Die aramaistische Forschung seit Th. Nöldekes Veröffentlichungen*. Leiden: Brill, 1939.

Roskos-Ewoldsen, David R., et al. "What is the Role of Rhetorical Questions in Persuasion?" Pages 297–321 in *Communication & Emotion: Essays in Honor of Dolf Zillmann*. Edited by Jennings Bryant, David Roskos-Ewoldsen, Joanne Cantor. LEA Communication Series. Mahwah, NJ: Lawrence Erlbaum Associates, 2003.

Rothstein, Johann W. *Juden und Samaritaner: Die grundlegende Scheidung von Judentum und Heidentum: Eine kritische Studie zum Buche Haggai und zur jüdischen Geschichte im ersten nachexilischen Jahrhundert*. BZAW 3. Leipzig: Hinrichs, 1908.

Rudolph, Elisabeth. *Contrast: Adversative and Concessive Expressions on Sentence and Text Level*. Research in Text Theory. Berlin: de Gruyter, 1996.

Rudolph, Wilhelm. *Esra und Nehemia samt 3. Esra*. KAT 20. Tübingen: Mohr Siebeck, 1949.

_____. *Jeremia*. KAT 12. Tübingen: Mohr Siebeck, 1968.

_____. *Haggai, Sacharja 1–8, Sacharja 9–14, Maleachi*. KAT 13/4. Gütersloh: Gütersloher, 1976.

Sasson, Jack M. "Oracle Inquiries in Judges." Pages 149–68 in *Birkat Shalom: Studies in the Bible, Ancient Near Eastern Literature, and Postbiblical Judaism Presented to Shalom M. Paul on the Occasion of His Seventieth Birthday*. Edited by Chaim Cohen et al. Winona Lake, IN: Eisenbrauns, 2008.

Schaper, Joachim. "The Jerusalem Temple as an Instrument of Achaemenid Fiscal Administration." *VT* (1995): 528–39.

_____. "The Temple Treasury Committee in the Times of Ezra and Nehemiah." *VT* 47 (1997): 200–206.

Schaudig, Hanspeter. "The Restoration of Temples in the Neo- and Late Babylonian Periods: A Royal Prerogative as the Setting for Political Argument." Pages 141–64 in *From the Foundations to the Crenellations: Essays on Temple Building in the Ancient Near East and Hebrew Bible*. Edited by Mark J. Boda and Jamie Novotny. AOAT 366. Münster: Ugarit-Verlag, 2010.

Schlimm, Matthew R. "Biblical Studies and Rhetorical Criticism: Bridging the

Divide between the Hebrew Bible and Communication." *RComm* 7 (2007): 244–75.

Schmid, Konrad. *Literaturgeschichte des Alten Testaments: Eine Einführung.* Darmstadt: Wissenschaftliche Buchgesellschaft, 2008.

Schmidt-Radefeldt, Jürgen. "On So-Called 'Rhetorical' Questions." *JPragmat* 1 (1977): 375–92.

Schneider, Heinrich. *Die Bücher Esra und Nehemia.* HSAT 4/2. Bonn: Hanstein, 1959.

Schramm, Brooks. *The Opponents of Third Isaiah: Reconstructing the Cultic History of the Restoration.* JSOTSup 193. Sheffield: Sheffield Academic, 1995.

Schwiderski, Dirk. *Handbuch des nordwestsemitischen Briefformulars: Ein Beitrag zur Echtheitsfrage der aramäischen Briefe des Esrabuches.* BZAW 295. Berlin: de Gruyter, 2000.

Sebök (Schönberger), Mark. *Die syrische Übersetzung der zwölf kleinen Propheten und ihr Verhältniss zu dem massoretischen Text und zu den älteren Übersetzungen namentlich den LXX und dem Targum.* Breslau: Preuss & Jünger, 1887.

Sellin, Ernst. *Einleitung in das Alte Testament.* Revised and rewritten by Georg Fohrer. Heidelberg: Quelle & Meyer, 1969.

_____. *Die Restauration der jüdischen Gemeinde in der Jahren 538-516: Das Schicksal Serubbabels.* SEJGBE 2. Leipzig: Deichert, 1905.

_____. *Das Zwölfprophetenbuch.* KAT 12. Leipzig: Erlangen, 1922.

Smart, James D. *History and Theology in Second Isaiah: A Commentary on Isaiah 35, 40-66.* Philadelphia, PA: Westminster, 1965.

_____. "A New Interpretation of Isaiah lxvi 1–6." *ExpTim* 46 (1934/1935): 420–24.

Smith, Craig R., and Scott Lybarger. "Bitzer's Model Reconstructed." *CommQ* 44 (1996): 197–213.

Smith, Morton. *Palestinian Parties and Politics That Shaped the Old Testament.* New York, NY: Columbia University Press, 1971.

Smith, Paul A. *Rhetoric and Redaction in Trito-Isaiah: The Structure, Growth and Authorship of Isaiah 56-66.* VTSup 62. Leiden: Brill, 1995.

Smith, Ralph L. *Micah-Malachi.* WBC 32. Waco, TX: Word, 1984.

Snaith, Norman H. "Isaiah 40–66: A Study of the Teaching of the Second Isaiah and Its Consequences." Pages 135–264 in *Studies on the Second Part of the Book of Isaiah.* VTSup 14. Leiden: Brill, 1967.

Soggin, J. Alberto. "Compulsory Labor under David and Solomon." Pages 259–67 in *Studies in the Period of David and Solomon and Other Essays: Papers Read at the*

International Symposium for Biblical Studies, Tokyo, 5-7 December, 1979. Edited by Tomoo Ishida. Winona Lake, IN: Eisenbrauns, 1982.

_____. *Introduction to the Old Testament: From Its Origins to the Closing of the Alexandrian Canon.* 3rd ed. Translated by John Bowden. OTL. Louisville, KY: Westminster John Knox, 1989.

Sommer, Benjamin. "Dating Pentateuchal Texts and the Perils of Pseudo-Historicism." Pages 85–108 in *The Pentateuch: International Perspectives on Current Research.* Edited by Thomas B. Dozeman, Konrad Schmid, and Baruch J. Schwartz. FAT 78. Tübingen: Mohr Siebeck, 2011.

_____. "Did Prophecy Cease? Evaluating a Reevaluation." *JBL* 115 (1996): 31–47.

Speiser, Ephraim A. "'People' and 'Nation' of Israel." *JBL* 79 (1960): 157–63.

Steck, Odil H. *Der Abschluß der Prophetie im Alten Testament: Ein Versuch zur Frage der Vorgeschichte des Kanons.* BTSt 17. Neukirchen-Vluyn: Neukirchener, 1991.

_____. *Studien zu Tritojesaja.* BZAW 203. Berlin: de Gruyter, 1991.

_____. "Zu Haggai 1:2–11." *ZAW* 83 (1971): 355–79.

Steiner, Richard C. "Bishlam's Archival Search Report in Nehemiah's Archive: Multiple Introductions and Reverse Chronological Order as Clues to the Origin of the Aramaic Letters in Ezra 4–6." *JBL* 125 (2006): 641–85.

Steinmann, Andrew E. "Letters of Kings about Votive Offerings, the God of Israel, and the Aramaic Document in Ezra 4:8–6:18." *JHebS* 8 (2008): article 23, available at http://purl.org/JHS and at http://www.JHSonline.org.

Stern, Ephraim. *The Assyrian, Babylonian, and Persian Periods (732-332 BCE).* Vol. 2 of *Archaeology of the Land of the Bible.* ABRL. New York, NY: Doubleday, 2001.

Stevens, Marty E. *Temples, Tithes, and Taxes: The Temple and the Economic Life of Ancient Israel.* Peabody, MA: Hendrickson, 2006.

Stiff, James B., and Paul A. Mongeau. *Persuasive Communication.* 2nd ed. New York, NY: Guilford, 2003.

Strong, John T. "Grounding Ezekiel's Heavenly Ascent: A Defense of Ezek 40–48 as a Program for Restoration." *SJOT* 26 (2012): 192–211.

Swinburnson, Benjamin W. "The Glory of the Latter Temple: A Structural and Biblical-Theological Analysis of Haggai 2:1–9." *Kerux* 23 (2008): 28–46.

Tadmor, Hayim. "'The Appointed Time Has Not Yet Arrived': The Historical Background of Haggai 1:2." Pages 401–8 in *Ki Baruch Hu: Ancient Near Eastern, Biblical and Judaic Studies in Honor of Baruch A. Levine.* Edited by Robert Chazon, William W. Hallo, and Lawrence H. Schiffman. Winona Lake, IN: Eisenbrauns, 1999.

Thackeray, Henry. "The Greek Translators of the Prophetical Books." *JTS* 4 (1903): 578–85.

Thiel, Winfried. *Die deuteronomistische Redaktion von Jeremia 26–45*. WMANT 52. Neukirchen-Vluyn: Neukirchener Verlag, 1981.

Tiemeyer, Lena-Sofia. Review of *Haggai und Sacharja 1–8*, by Martin Hallaschka. *RBL* (2012): 1–9.

Tollington, Janet E. *Tradition and Innovation in Haggai and Zechariah 1–8*. JSOTSup 150. Sheffield: JSOT Press, 1993.

Torrey, Charles C. *Ezra Studies*. Chicago, IL: University of Chicago Press, 1910. Repr., New York, NY: Ktav, 1970.

——. "The Foundry of the Second Temple at Jerusalem." *JBL* 55 (1936): 247–60.

Tov, Emanuel. *The Septuagint Translation of Jeremiah and Baruch: A Discussion of an Early Revision of the LXX of Jeremiah 29–52 and Baruch 1:1–3:8*. HSM 8. Missoula, MT: Scholars Press, 1976.

——. *The Text-Critical Use of the Septuagint in Biblical Research*. 2nd ed. JBS 8. Jerusalem: Simor, 1997.

——. *Textual Criticism of the Hebrew Bible*. 3rd ed. Minneapolis, MN: Fortress Press, 2012.

——. "The Writing of Early Scrolls: Implications for the Literary Analysis of Hebrew Scripture." Pages 206–20 in *Hebrew Bible, Greek Bible, and Qumran: Collected Essays*. TSAJ 121. Tübingen: Mohr Siebeck, 2008.

Townsend, T. N. "Additional Comments on Haggai 2:10–19." *VT* 18 (1968): 559–60.

Trible, Phyllis. *Rhetorical Criticism: Context, Method, and the Book of Jonah*. OTG. Minneapolis, MN: Fortress Press, 1994.

Trotter, James M. "Was the Second Jerusalem Temple a Primarily Persian Project?" *SJOT* 15 (2001): 276–93.

Tucker, Robert E. "Figure, Ground and Presence: A Phenomenology of Meaning in Rhetoric." *QJS* 87 (2001): 396–414.

Tuell, Steven S. "Divine Presence and Absence in Ezekiel's Prophecy." Pages 97–116 in *The Book of Ezekiel: Theological and Anthropological Perspectives*. Edited by Margaret S. Odell and John T. Strong. SBLSymS 9. Atlanta, GA: Society of Biblical Literature, 2000.

——. "Ezekiel 40–42 as Verbal Icon." *CBQ* 58 (1996): 649–64.

Uehlinger, Christoph. "Was There a Cult Reform under King Josiah? The Case for a Well-Grounded Minimum." Pages 279–316 in *Good Kings and Bad Kings*. Edited by Lester L. Grabbe. LHBOTS 393. European Seminar in Historical Methodology 5. New York, NY: T&T Clark, 2005.

Van der Toorn, Karel. *Scribal Culture and the Making of the Hebrew Bible*. Cambridge, MA: Harvard University Press, 2007.

Vanderford, Marsha L. "Vilification and Social Movements: A Case Study of Pro Life and Pro Choice Rhetoric." *QJS* 75 (1989): 166–82.

Vanderhooft, David S. "Babylonian Strategies of Imperial Control in the West: Royal Practice and Rhetoric." Pages 235–62 in *Judah and the Judeans in the Neo-Babylonian Period*. Edited by Oded Lipschits and Joseph Blenkinsopp. Winona Lake, IN: Eisenbrauns, 2003.

_____. "Dwelling Beneath the Sacred Place: A Proposal for Reading 2 Samuel 7:10." *JBL* 118 (1999): 625–33.

_____. *The Neo-Babylonian Empire and Babylon in the Latter Prophets*. HSM 59. Atlanta, GA: Scholars Press, 1999.

VanderKam, James C. *From Joshua to Caiaphas: High Priests after the Exile*. Minneapolis, MN: Fortress Press, 2004.

Vatz, Richard E. "The Myth of the Rhetorical Situation." *Ph&Rh* 6 (1973): 154–61.

Vaux, Roland de. "The Decrees of Cyrus and Darius on the Rebuilding of the Temple." Pages 63–96 in *The Bible and the Ancient Near East*. Translated by Damian McHugh. Garden City, NY: Doubleday, 1971.

_____. "Le 'reste d'Israël' d'après les prophètes." *RB* 44 (1933): 526–39.

Verhoef, Pieter A. *The Books of Haggai and Malachi*. NICOT. Grand Rapids, MI: Eerdmans, 1987.

Volz, Paul. *Jesaia II: Kapitel 40–66*. KAT 9/2. Leipzig: Scholl, 1932. Repr. Hildesheim: Olms, 1974.

Walton, Douglas. *Ad Hominem Arguments*. Tuscaloosa, AL: University of Alabama Press, 1998.

_____. "Argumentation Schemes and Historical Origins of the Circumstantial Ad Hominem Argument." *Argumentation* 18 (2004): 359–68.

Wambacq, B. N. *L'Épithète divine Jahvé Seba'ôt: Étude philologique, historique et éxégétique*. Paris: Desclée de Brouwer, 1947.

Waterman, Leroy. "The Camouflaged Purge of Three Messianic Conspirators." *JNES* 13 (1954): 73–78.

Watson, Duane F., and Alan J. Hauser, eds. *Rhetorical Criticism of the Bible: A Com-*

prehensive Bibliography with Notes on History and Method. BibInt 4. Leiden: Brill, 1994.

Watts, John D. W. *Isaiah 34–66.* WBC 25. Waco, TX: Word, 1987.

Weinberg, Joel. *The Citizen-Temple Community.* Translated by D. L. Smith-Christopher. JSOTSup 151. Sheffield: JSOT Press, 1992.

Weinfeld, Moshe. *Deuteronomy and the Deuteronomic School.* Oxford: Clarendon, 1972.

Weiser, Artur. *The Old Testament: Its Formation and Development.* Translated by Dorothea M. Barton. New York, NY: Association Press, 1961.

Wellhausen, Julius. *Die kleinen Propheten übersetzt und erklärt.* Berlin: Reimer, 1898.

———. *Prologemena to the History of Israel.* Translated by J. Sutherland Black and Allan Menzies. New York, NY: Meridian Books, 1957.

Wendland, Ernst R. "The Structure, Style, Sense, and Significance of Haggai's Prophecy Concerning the 'House of the LORD': With Special Reference to Bible Interpretation and Translation in Africa." *OTE* 18 (2005): 907–26; 19 (2006): 281–306.

Westermann, Claus. *Basic Forms of Prophetic Speech.* Translated by Hugh Clayton White. Louisville, KY: Westminster John Knox, 1991.

———. *Isaiah 40–66: A Commentary.* Translated by David M. G. Stalker. OTL. Philadelphia, PA: Westminster, 1969.

Whately, Richard. *Elements of Rhetoric.* 7th ed. New York, NY: International Debate Education Society, 2009.

Whybray, Roger N. *Isaiah 40–66.* NCB. London: Oliphants, 1975.

Williamson, H. G. M. "The Aramaic Documents in Ezra Revisited." *JTS* NS 59 (2008): 41–62.

———. "The Composition of Ezra i–vi." *JTS* NS 34 (1983): 1–30.

———. *Ezra, Nehemiah.* WBC 16. Waco, TX: Word Books, 1985.

Wilson, Robert R. *Prophecy and Society in Ancient Israel.* Philadelphia: Fortress Press, 1980. Wöhrle, Jakob. *Der Abschluss des Zwölfprophetenbuches: Buchübergreifende Redaktionsprozesse in den späten Sammlungen.* BZAW 389. Berlin: de Gruyter, 2008.

———. *Die frühen Sammlungen des Zwölfprophetenbuches: Entstehung und Komposition.* BZAW 360. Berlin: de Gruyter, 2006.

Wolff, Hans W. *Dodekapropheton 6: Haggai.* BKAT 14/6. Neukirchen-Vluyn: Neukirchener, 1986.

_____. *Haggai: A Commentary.* Translated by M. Kohl. CC. Minneapolis, MN: Augsburg, 1988.

_____. "Haggai literarhistorisch untersucht." Pages 129–42 in *Studien zur Prophetie—Probleme und Erträge.* TB 76. Munich: Kaiser, 1987.

Yap, Audrey. "Ad Hominem Fallacies, Bias, and Testimony." *Argumentation* 27 (2013): 97–109.

Ziegelmueller, George W., and Jack Kay. *Argumentation: Inquiry and Advocacy.* 3rd ed. Boston, MA: Allyn & Bacon, 1997.

Ziegelmueller, George W., Jack Kay, and Charles A. Dause. *Argumentation: Inquiry and Advocacy.* Englewood Cliffs, NJ: Prentice Hall, 1990.

Ziegler, Joseph. *Duodecim prophetae.* Septuaginta 13. Göttingen: Vandenhoeck & Ruprecht, 1984.

_____. "Die Einheit der Septuaginta zum Zwölfprophetenbuch." Pages 29–42 in *Sylloge: Gesammelte Aufsätze zur Septuaginta.* MSU 10. Göttingen: Vandenhoeck & Ruprecht, 1971.

Zillmann, Dolf. "Rhetorical Elicitation of Agreement in Persuasion." *JPSP* 21 (1972): 159–65.

Zillmann, Dolf, and Joanne R. Cantor, "Rhetorical Elicitation of Concession in Persuasion." *JSP* 94 (1974): 223–36.

Zimmerli, Walther. "Planungen für den Wiederaufbau nach der Katastrophe von 587." *VT* 18 (1968): 229–55.

Zorn, Jeffrey R. "Tell en-Naṣbeh and the Problem of the Material Culture of the Sixth Century." Pages 413–47 in *Judah and the Judeans in the Neo-Babylonian Period.* Edited by Oded Lipschits and Joseph Blenkinsopp. Winona Lake, IN: Eisenbrauns, 2003.

Index of Scriptures

Exodus
6:7 245
25:1–31:11 99
31:3 211
35:30–31 211

Numbers
3:12 245

Deuteronomy
4:20 245
18:21–22 184
31:7 213
31:23 213

Joshua
1:6 213
1:7–9 213
6:24 129

Judges
19:30 164

2 Samuel
7:5–7 99

7:8 244
7:13 99
20:24 135

1 Kings
4:6 135
5:17 119
5:18–19 99
5:27 134
5:28 135
8:16 119
8:20 119
9:22 134
11:37 244
12:18 135
17:24 184
22:5–28 184

2 Kings
14:21 245
23:30 245
25:18–21 151

1 Chronicles
3:17 149

3:19 149
5:37–41 151
22:11–13 212
22:16 213
28:10 213
28:20 213

2 Chronicles
5:26 198
19:11 212
36:15–16 197
36:21 112
36:22–23 75
36:22 198

Ezra
1–6 . . . . . . 71, 72, 75, 120, 206
1:1 87
1:1, 5 198
1:2–4 72
1:7–11 120
2:2 149
3:2, 8 149
3:7 120
3:12 206
4:1–5 222
4:11 81
4:7–6:18 80
4:8–9 85
4:17 81
5:1–2 80
5:1 183
5:2 149
5:3–6:12 75
5:3–5 80
5:7 81

5:14 85
6:1–5 76
6:3–5 . . . . . . 72, 78, 87
6:8–9 120
6:14 183
6:15 80
10:4 212

Nehemiah
3:15, 19 128
7:7 149
10:33–40 137
12:1 149
13:10–11 137

Job
1:8 164
2:3 164

Proverbs
1:28 167

Song of Songs
8:6 245

Isaiah
44:24–45:7 120
44:26 197
44:28 119
45:1–6 120
45:1 120
45:4 120
45:9–13 121
45:11 121
66:1–2 . . . . . . 100, 102–10
66:2–4 108–10

66:21 245

Jeremiah

22:23 135
22:24 245
23:1–8 191
25:11–12 112
27:7 112
29:10 112
31:7–14 191
41:4–5 128–29
41:5 128
44:15–19 127
50:20 191
52:12 145
52:24–27 151

Ezekiel

8:5–18 127
30:9 197

Daniel

9:2 112
9:24–27 112

Hosea

8:1 129
9:4 . . . . . . 129n184

Amos

4:9 . . . . . . 35, 44, 45

Zephaniah

3:12–13 191

Haggai

1:1–4 152–63
1:1 . . . . . . 24, 152–53
1:2 . . . . . . 24–25, 63n184, 153–58
1:3 158
1:4 . . . . . . 26, 63n185, 158–63
1:5–7 163–70
1:5 . . . . . . 63n185, 163–64
1:6 . . . . . . 26, 64nn187–88, 164–70
1:7 . . . . . . 27, 170
1:8 . . . . . . 27, 64n189, 171–74
1:9–11 174–78
1:9 . . . . . . 27–28, 64n190, 174–77
1:10 . . . . . . 28–29, 64n191, 177–78
1:11 . . . . . . 30, 64n192, 177–78
1:12–13 194–97
1:12 . . . . . . 30–31, 65nn194–96,
     189–97
1:13 . . . . . . 31, 43–44, 65nn197–98
1:14–15 198–99
1:14 198
1:15–2:2 203–4
1:15 . . . . . . 46–50, 66n199, 198–99,
     203–4
2:1 . . . . . . 31, 46–50, 203–4
2:2 203–4
2:3 . . . . . . 66n200, 204–9
2:4 . . . . . . 66n201, 209–13
2:5 . . . . . . 31, 40–43, 211–13
2:6–9 . . . . . . 51–60, 214–19
2:6 . . . . . . 32, 66n202, 203, 214–16
2:7 . . . . . . 32, 214–16
2:8 216–17
2:9 . . . . . . 33, 66n204, 205, 217–18
2:10–14 . . . . . . 60–62, 220–31
2:11 220

2:12–14 220–21

2:13 . . . . . . 67n206, 220–21

2:14 . . . . . . 67n207, 220–31

2:15–19 . . . . . . 46–50, 231–38

2:15 . . . . . . 67n208, 231–33

2:16 . . . . . . 33–34, 67n209, 210,
233–34, 237–38

2:17 . . . . . . 34–37, 44–46, 46n211,
233–34

2:18 . . . . . . 46–50, 234–36

2:19 . . . . . . 37–38, 67n212, 68n213,
236–37

2:20–23 . . . . . . 51–60, 238–47

2:20–22 239–42

2:20 239

2:22 . . . . . . 38–39, 240–42

2:23 242–47

Zechariah

1–8 . . . . . . 71, 79, 80, 97, 100, 123,
143n12, 145, 146, 152, 254

1:12 . . . . . . 112, 113

2:13 100

2:14 100–101

2:15 100–101

3:1–10 152

4:6–10 . . . . . . 123, 150n38

4:9–10 100–101

5:1 148

6:13 148

6:15 100

7:1–6 128

7:1–4 129–30

7:5 113

8:6–12 190–91

9–14 (Deutero-Zechariah) . . . . . .
114, 115

Malachi

1:1 . . . . . . 42n105, 153n49, 197

3:8 138

Index of Name and Subjects

antithesis, 165, 165n182, 165n184, 175, 196

Aristotle, 17, 165, 180n125, 182–83, 201

authority, prophetic: *ethos* or authority, 101–2, 148, 182–86. *See also* Haggai

Bedford, Peter R., 72–73, 75, 83, 89, 113–14, 125, 132, 156–57, 182

Blenkinsopp, Joseph, 91–92, 109–10, 128–30, 185

calendar, in Haggai, 143n12, 144

concession, 204–8

cultic worship in Yehud, 126–31; Bethel, 128–30; Mizpah (Tell en-Naṣbeh), 128–30

curses, futility 166–67, 189n141

Cyrus (of Persia), 70–78, 87–95, 119–22, 198

Cyrus Cylinder, 72, 76, 91–95, 118n153

Darius I (of Persia), 55, 59, 95n86, 120, 120n158, 143–45

David (king), 99, 119, 120, 122, 123, 212–13, 242–49. *See also* Davidic monarchy

Davidic monarchy, 54, 59, 114, 119, 120, 122, 123, 150, 242–49

Ebbabar (temple in Larsa), 98

Elephantine, 73–74, 88, 90n70

epideictic, 201–2

epithets, divine, 146–47

Esarhaddon (of Assyria), 111

Ezra (book), 75–95; Aramaic memorandum (6:3–5), 77–95; Hebrew edict (1:2–4), 76–77

fear (of YHWH), 65n196, 188, 194–97, 211–12

Floyd, Michael H., 192–93, 210n20

Gudea (of Sumer), 97–98, 134, 196

Haggai (prophet), 1–7, 147–48; *ethos* or authority, 148, 174, 182–86

Hallaschka, Martin, 50–62

Jerusalem and Yehud in early Persian period: economic conditions, 114–17, 164–66, 207–8, 217–18; population, 115–17

Joshua (ben Jehozadak), 151–52, 153–54, 189–90, 198, 204, 210, 256
judgment, divine: indications of, 113–17; period of seventy years, 111–13, 155–56

Kalû ritual, 123, 235
Kessler, John, 2, 9–10, 41, 148, 156–57, 171, 192–93, 215
Kuhrt, Amélie, 71n3, 93–94

labor, forced (corvée), 133–36
Leuenberger, Martin, 51, 55–59

Marduk (god), 91–93, 98, 111
Meyers, Carol L., and Eric M., 5, 26, 29, 61, 130, 156, 191

Nebuchadnezzar II (of Babylon), 98, 102, 149, 244
Ningirsu (god), 97–98, 196

permission to build temples, divine: in ANE, 97–98; in Bible, 98–100; doubts about in Yehud, 100–108
Persian Empire: and Jerusalem temple, 71–95; interest in cultic matters, 71–74

Petersen, David L., 123, 166, 205–6
polarization, 220, 229–30, 238
presence, divine. *See* YHWH, presence of
presence (rhetorical concept), 141, 169–70, 210–11

remnant (שארית), 189–93, 195, 198–99, 201–2, 256–57
rhetorical criticism: of book of Haggai, 7–13; method, 13–18. *See also* antithesis; concession; epideictic; Haggai (prophet), ethos or authority; presence; polarization; situation, rhetorical; stock issues in policy debates; vilification
Rothstein, Johann W., 47–48, 222

Schwiderski, Dirk, 81–83
situation, rhetorical, 9, 15–17
Solomon (king), 99–100, 118–19, 134–35, 208n16, 212–13, 244
stock issues in policy debates: cause or blame, 17–18, 141–42; cost or consequences, 17–18, 142–43; definition, 17–18, 139–40; ill or harm, 17–18, 141; remedy, 17–18, 142

Temple, Jerusalem: condition, 158–63, 175–7, 204–8; and divine blessing, 234–38; "glory," 172–73, 214–15; rededication, 234–35; as YHWH's house, 102–7, 158–63, 175–77 temple building, royal prerogative, 117–24

temples, economic aspects; cost of building, 131–36, 207–8, 214–17; taxes, tithes, offerings, 136–38

Torrey, Charles C., 78–82, 83–84, 87–88

vilification, 227–29, 238

Williamson, H. G. M., 77n20, 79–82, 84–86, 89

Wöhrle, Jakob, 50–62

YHWH: of hosts, 146–47; presence of, 74–75, 103–6, 146, 173, 209–13, 234, 248; sovereignty of, 239–42; spirit of, 211–12

Zerubbabel (ben Shealtiel): Davidic identity, 149–50, 242–47; as royal builder, 242–47